# Lonely Planet

# Parenthood Around the World

40 PARENTS ON HOW WHERE WE LIVE SHAPES WHO WE ARE

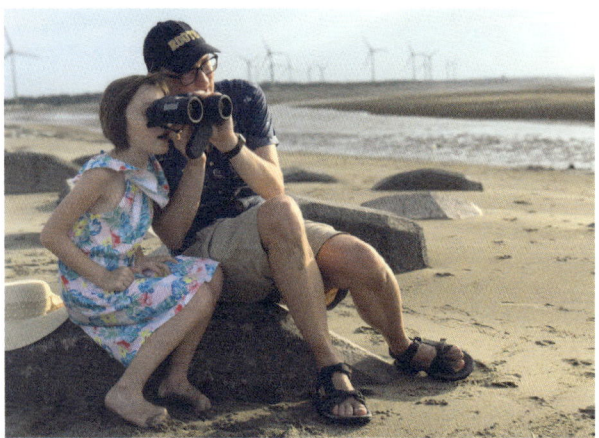
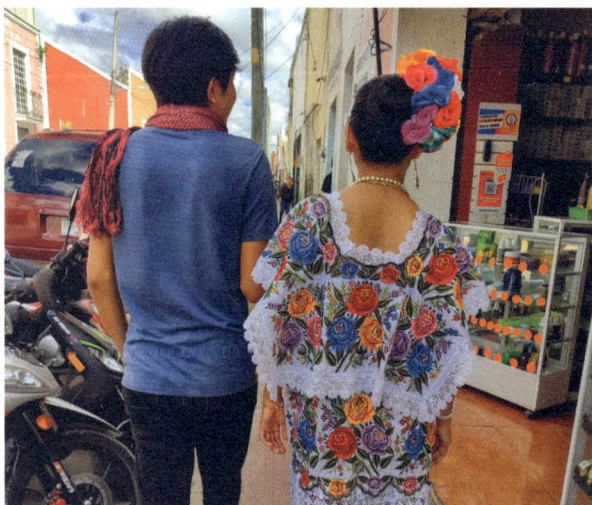
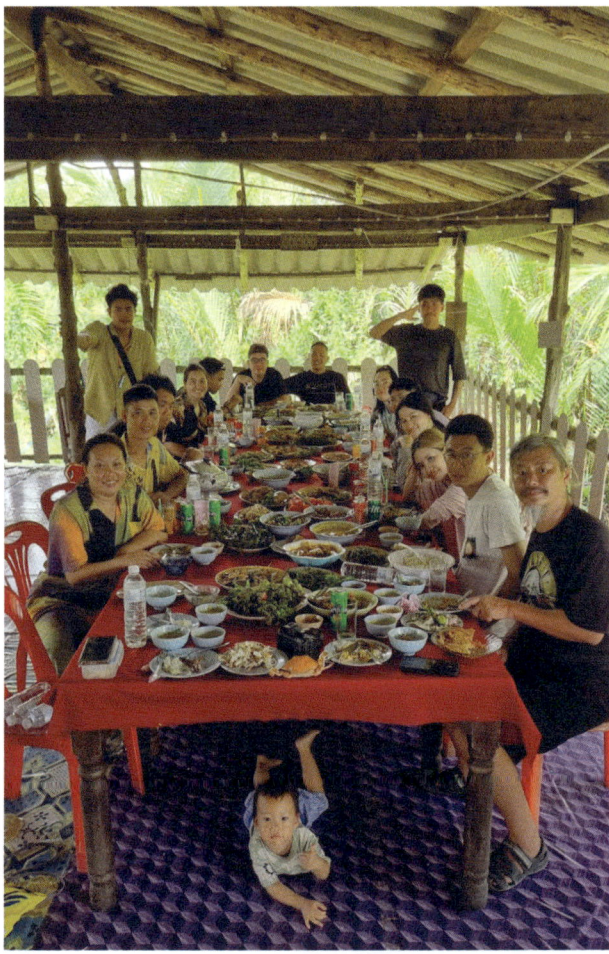
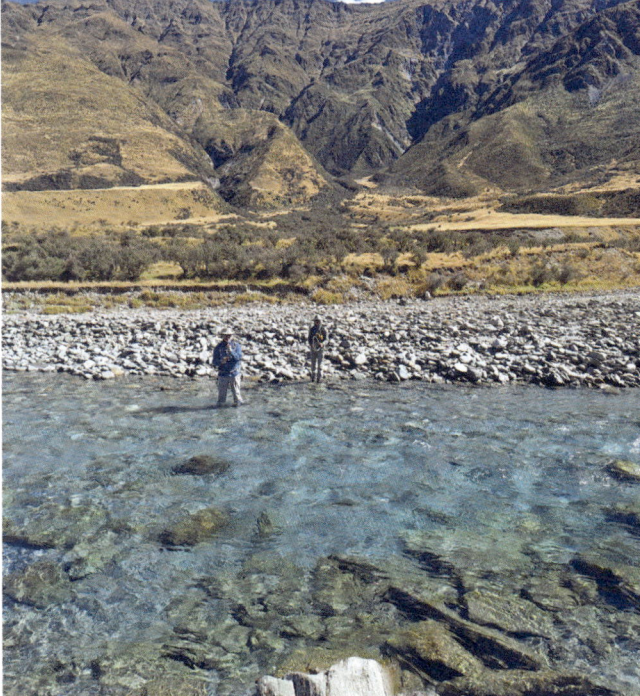
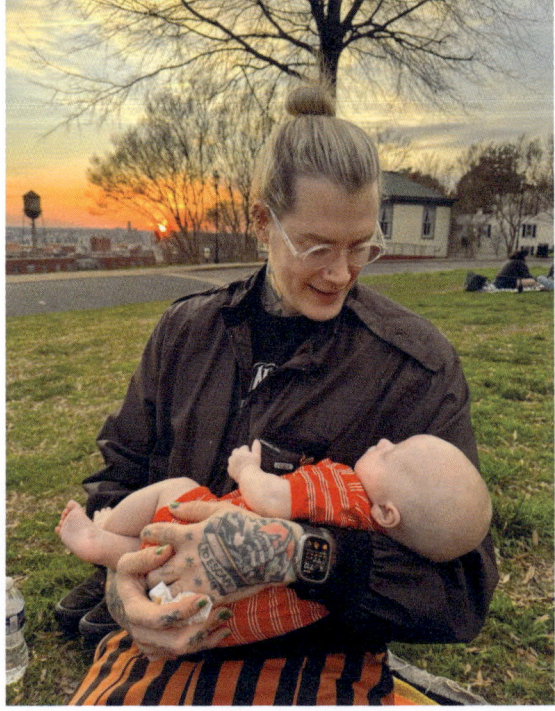

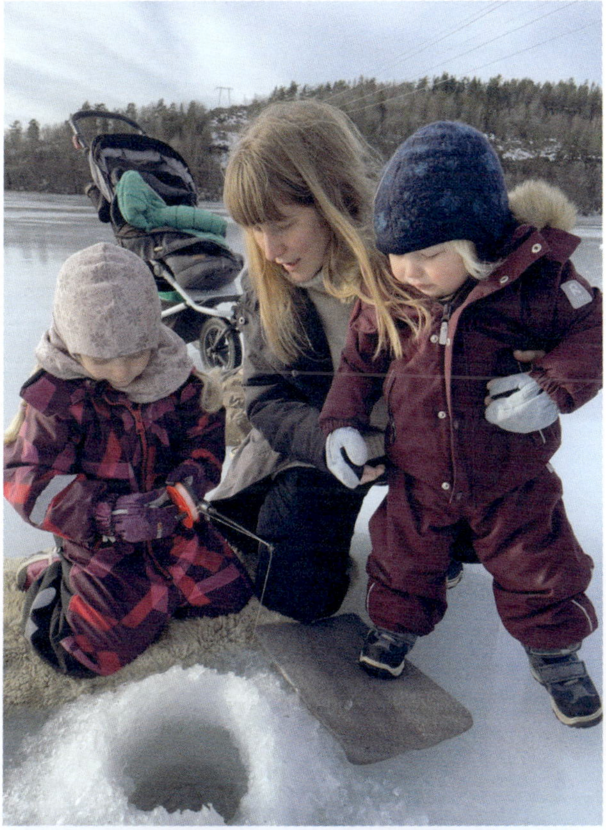

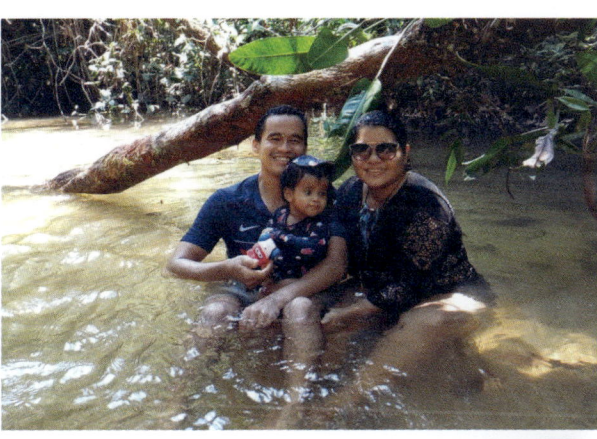
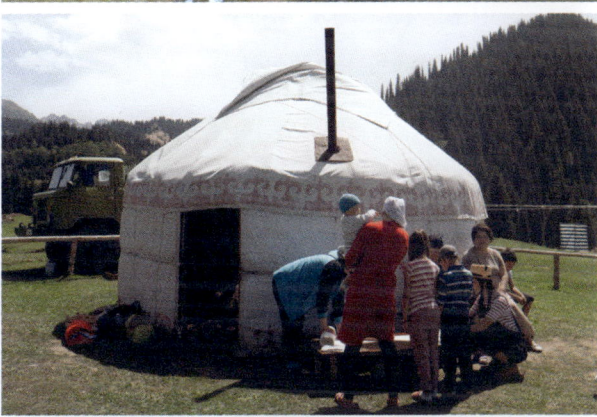
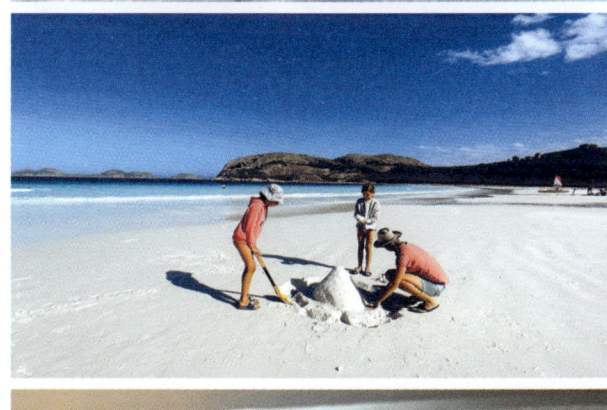
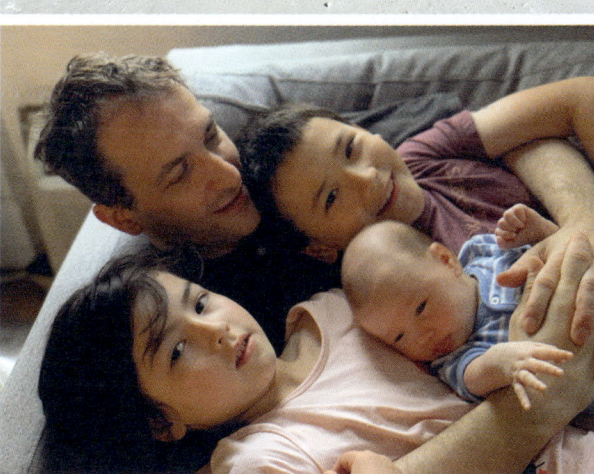
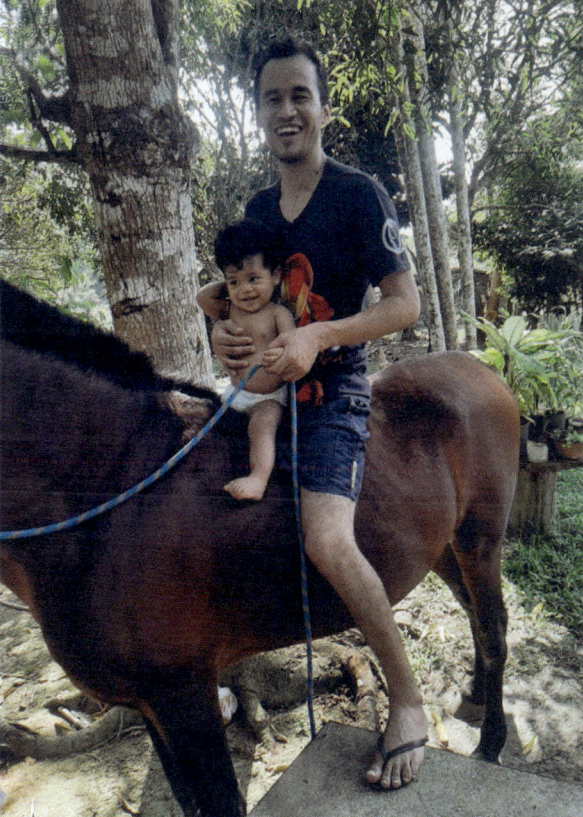

# Contents

## OCEANIA

Jen Whitfield
LINDEN, AUSTRALIA .................... 9

Elia & Nicole Petzierides
MELBOURNE, AUSTRALIA ................ 13

Henare & Ikuko Dewes
QUEENSTOWN,
NEW ZEALAND/AOTEAROA ............. 17

## AFRICA

Anna Songhurst &
Graham McCulloch
MAUN, BOTSWANA ...................... 21

Evita Dunee
TAMALE, GHANA ........................ 25

Christine Sefein
CAIRO, EGYPT .......................... 29

Kaouther & Mounir Bokchari
SOUSSE, TUNISIA ....................... 33

Ciru Kaigwa
NAIROBI, KENYA ........................ 37

## ASIA

Mint Jarukittikun &
Prin Polsuk
BANGKOK, THAILAND .................. 41

Asha Devi
KISHAN NAGAR VILLAGE, INDIA ........ 45

Jessica Wang Simula
TAIPEI, TAIWAN ........................ 49

Yvonne Chu
HONG KONG, CHINA .................... 53

Dharini Bhaskar
BENGALURU, INDIA ..................... 57

Aizada Kalybekova &
Dastan Chekirov
ICHKE BULUN, KYRGYZSTAN ........... 61

## MIDDLE EAST

Dina Tabbaa
AMMAN, JORDAN ....................... 65

Nadia
ABU DHABI, UNITED ARAB EMIRATES ... 69

Sevim Artar
ALTINÜZÜM, TÜRKIYE .................. 73

Zeina Mansour
ANTELIAS, LEBANON ................... 77

## EUROPE

Valentina Fragalà
CATANIA, ITALY ........................ 81

Alexandra Rehberger
BAVARIA, GERMANY .................... 85

Piers Benatar
**MOFFAT, SCOTLAND** .................... 89

Chris Battye
**BERKSHIRE, ENGLAND** .................. 93

Maria Woodward
**PONTARDAWE, WALES** .................. 97

Kaja Andersen
**HORTEN, NORWAY** ...................... 101

Céline Leclerc & Caleb House
**PRAGUE, CZECHIA** ...................... 105

Nicola Marić
**MOSTAR, BOSNIA & HERCEGOVINA** ... 109

Lilli & Iiro Kulta
**TAMPERE, FINLAND** .................... 113

## LATIN AMERICA & THE CARIBBEAN

Gonzalo Bascuñán & Gisela Posavac
**PUERTO VARAS, CHILE** .................. 117

Marcos & Daniela
**BUENOS AIRES, ARGENTINA** ............ 121

Eduardo Hernández & Estela Rodríguez
**COLIMA & AHUIRÁN, MEXICO** .......... 125

Jenny Cauich
**VALLADOLID, MEXICO** .................. 129

Raïssa & Emmanuel Kern
**DESHAIES, GUADELOUPE** ................ 133

Fernanda Andrade & Jaime Acosta
**QUITO, ECUADOR** ...................... 137

Mari Duque & Jeferson Rocha
**MANAUS, BRAZIL** ...................... 141

## NORTH AMERICA

David Lefer & Yvonne Lui
**NEW YORK CITY, USA** .................. 145

Katy Chandler-Isacksen
**RENO, USA** ............................ 149

Karimah Henry
**TAMPA, USA** .......................... 153

Harrison & Carly Moenich
**RICHMOND, USA** ...................... 157

Cristina Navoa
**TORONTO, CANADA** .................... 161

Tina Moore
**LAXGALTS'AP, NISGA'A NATION, CANADA** ................................ 165

**INDEX** .................................. 168
**PHOTO CREDITS** ........................ 172

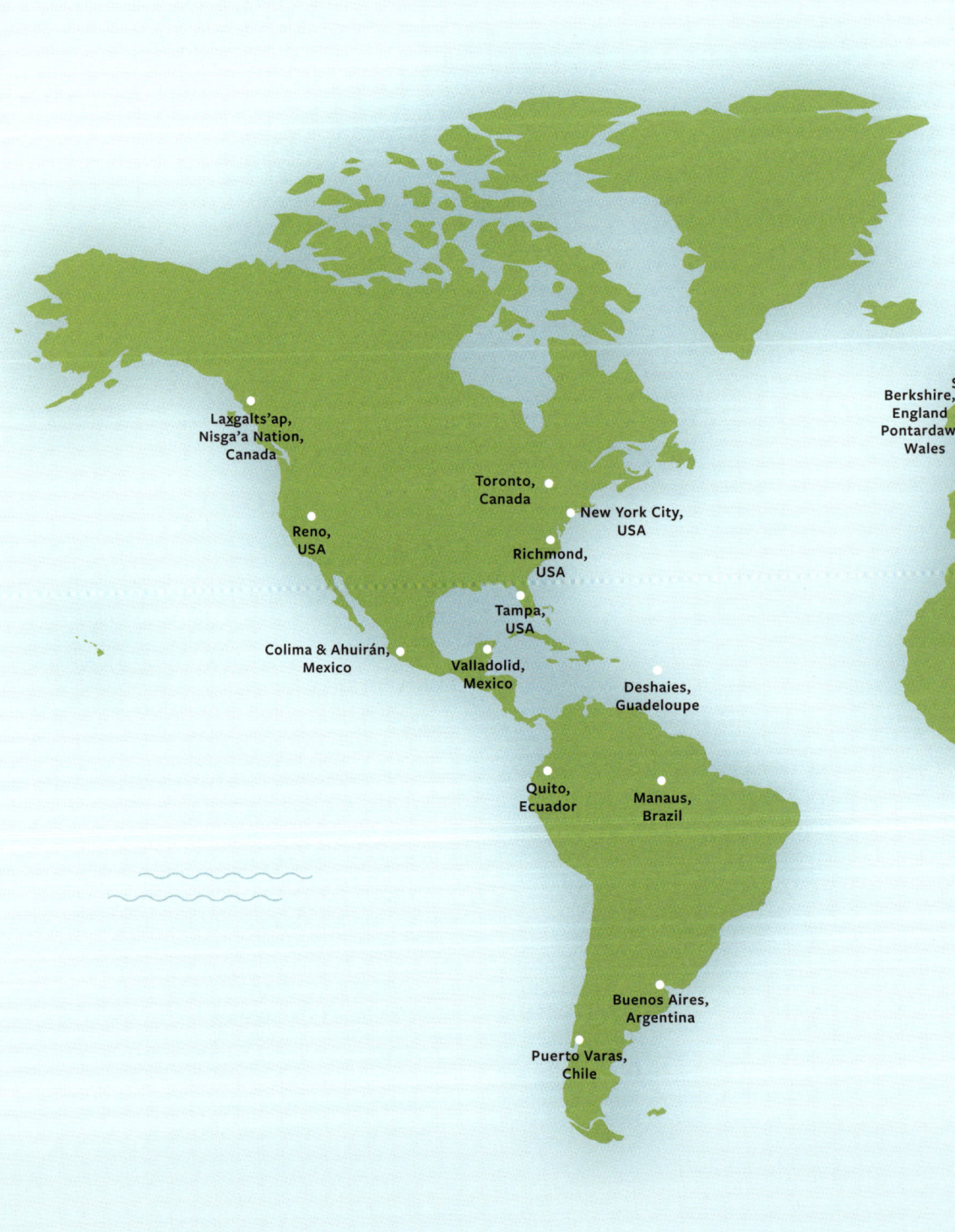

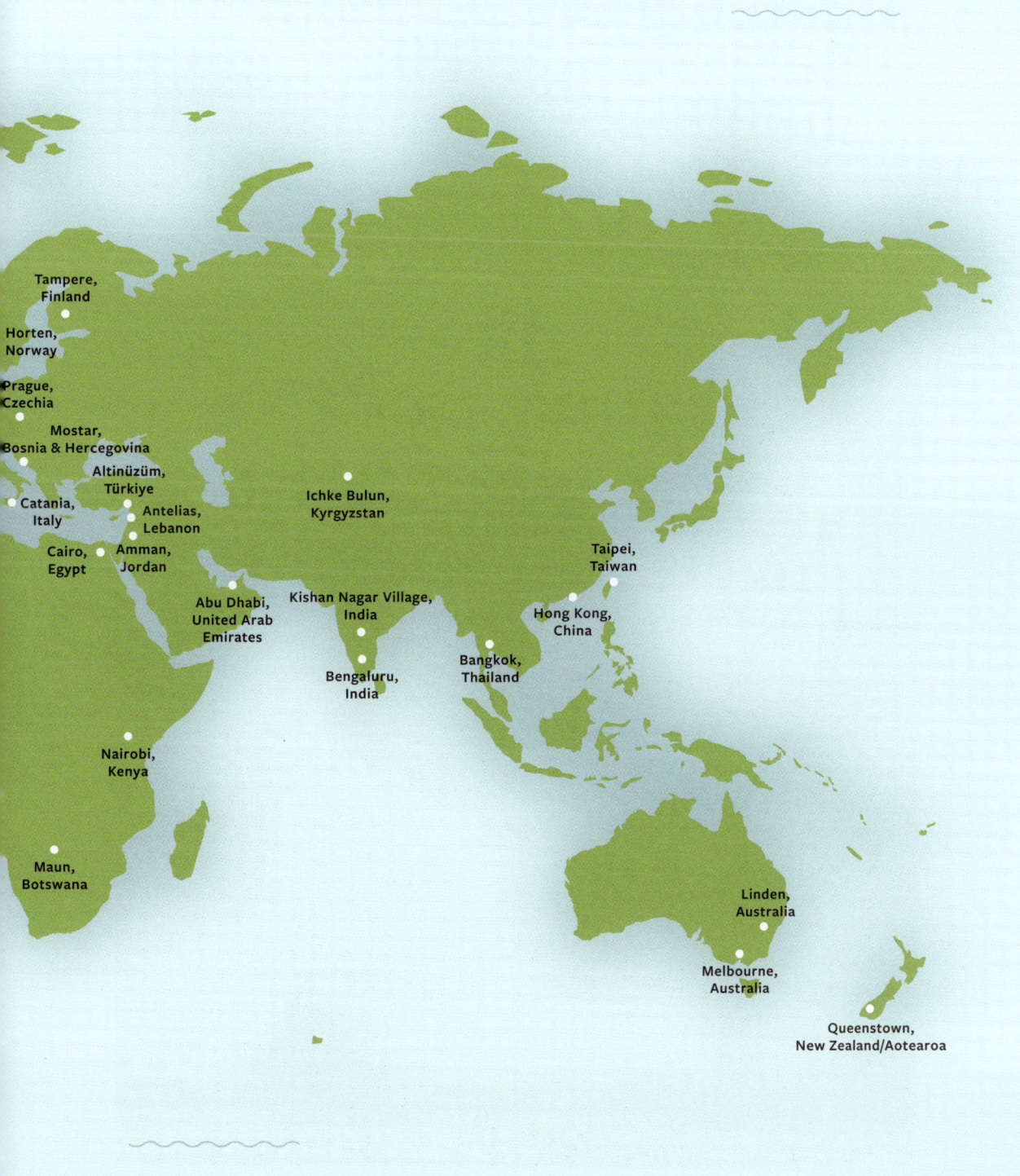

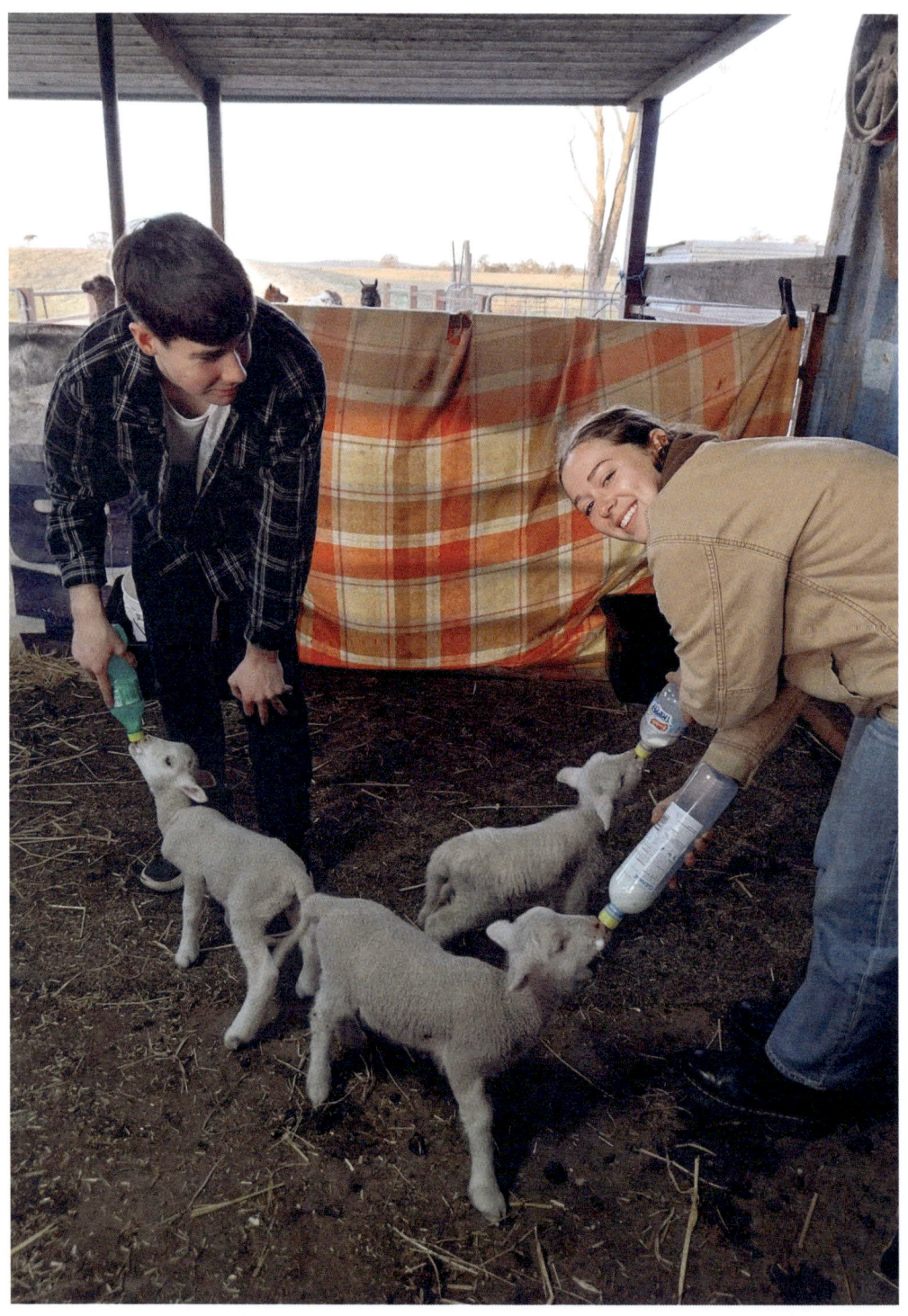

# Australia

## JEN WHITFIELD

**WHERE JEN LIVES:**
Linden, Australia

**WHERE JEN IS FROM:**
Sydney, Australia

Jen and Matt Whitfield are raising their three children, Sarah (23), Ally (21) and Jack (16) in the Blue Mountains. Jen flips the camera on her phone so I can see their property better. 'We're on the edge of the bushland here, so if you head out that way, it's just all bush, no houses out there, and over that way, over the hill is the highway that goes into Sydney, which is an hour-and-a-half away.' When the family isn't home in Linden (population 471), they're often at Matt's parents' alpaca farm, a 40.4-hectare (100-acre) property in Goulburn. Jen is a teacher, Matt is a mechanic by training, and the original outdoorsman. Jen, self-proclaimed 'more princess-y' of the family, has learned the ways of the bush.

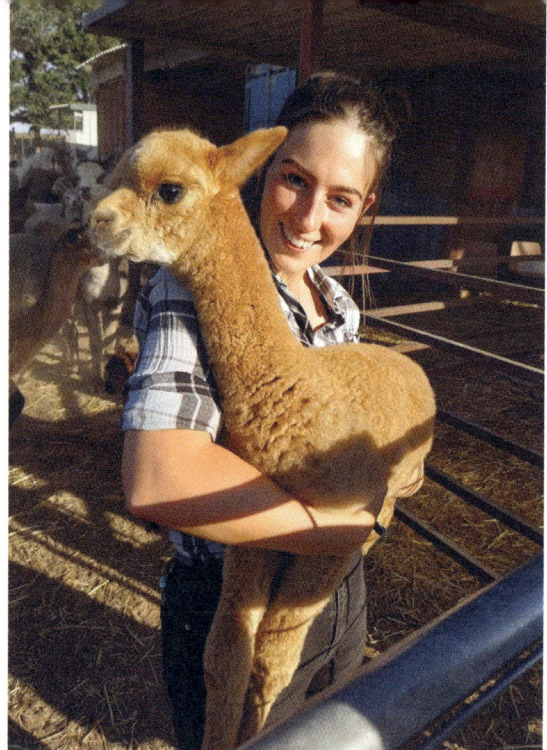

**INDEPENDENCE, INGENUITY:** Being further out, Jack's quite happy in his own company. He's rebuilding a ute - a pick-up - with Matt! He's learnt to entertain himself. Sarah's really into her nature artworks. She's obsessed with nature and just finished her environmental science degree.

**MORE PADDOCK, LESS TIKTOK:** Last night, the kids were all out playing soccer in the paddock, they didn't ask to go into town. They're just happy with one another's company, playing outdoors, and hanging out. Jack's gone with Cooper to build a fort, that was their aim this morning. They're quite content bushwalking and being outside.

**SNAKY SECRETS:** The kids are off in the paddock. I said 'take snake bandages, it's a snaky kind of a day!' The tiger snakes are deadly. You get, maybe, 20 minutes and you're dead. Actually, Ally trod on a tiger snake once, and they never told me for years; the kids were sworn to secrecy. There are quite a few accidents I'm not told about till years later!

**NATURE AS A SALVE:** We've had our blows health-wise. They've made us consider how we live and connect to nature, and the need for peace. It's restoration for the soul when you're out in the bush. When life is tough you can turn to the birds and the animals and the trees, and then go back to doing what you need to do.

**FINDING COMMUNITY:** There's usually a volunteer bush-fire brigade for wildfires. That's where we met the first couple who were living nearby. We ended up having babies at a similar time.

**THE CYCLE OF LIFE:** With animals around, you're not shielded from birth, life and death. We got guinea pigs for the kids so they could learn about caring for others, and to teach them that contentment is not about getting things for yourself, really.

There were about 30 guinea pigs free-ranging around our water tanks. You'd pass a window and one would run by – it was joyful! One day something peeled back the wire in our coop. Turns out it was a spotted quoll, this crazy-looking possum-crossed Tasmanian devil. We gathered the survivors, but the children were forever traumatised by the guinea-pig massacre!

They've grown up seeing birds, possums, and kangaroos injured on the roads. They're pretty good with it now, this morning Sarah's out dealing with fly-blown sheep (where parasitic flies lay eggs in a sheep's wounds). It's hands-on gross stuff, for sure.

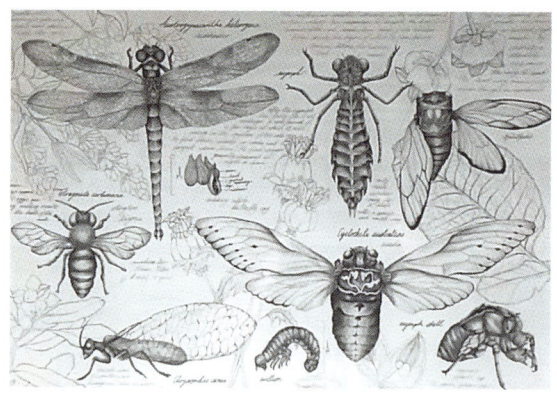

# "It's restoration for your soul when you're out in the bush."

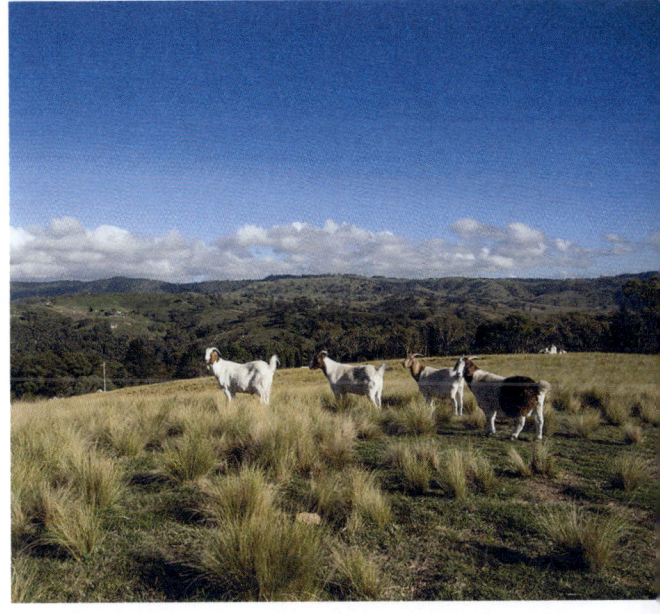

**NO WEATHER APP REQUIRED:** You know the weather's bad the moment you've walked outside. You traipse through mud to get to your car. You gotta get out and open the gate in pouring rain. You're dressed and snag yourself on a fence, tread on chicken poo, and think: 'God, this is just so hard!'

If you're stuck there's no one around to help you – you have to solve your own problems. The kids learnt to be quite adaptable, to understand a loss of control over their environment. Out here, you certainly know you're alive.

**NO UBER EATS HERE:** None of us are huge on takeaway. Mountain kids often aren't – it's just not around. We've the hamburger shop, a chicken shop, and a few restaurants. We only just got sushi a couple of years ago. Everyone was like, 'Oh my God, amazing!' But with the drive, it's usually: 'nah, let's just have eggs!'

**BEST OF ALL WORLDS:** We go into the city occasionally (Matt under sufferance). There's a sense of security – it's there if we want it – and not seven hours away to see a ballet or be part of greater society.

We can stand on the mountain and see Sydney; it's massive – always a bit smoggy – just a mass of buildings. There's a feeling that humanity is not far, but you've a sense that, maybe, you're not one of the crowd. You feel a bit more unique being away from it.

*NICOLE HAGG*

## Our favourite traditions

*Campfires:* We often have a couple of logs around and a big pot of hearty stew on – chorizo and other sausages, tomatoes – cowboy food!

*Play:* We've a big tub of outdoor equipment – lots of volleyball nets, soccer goals, and such. The same with dress-ups – including half of Matt's wardrobe. The kids dressed up all the time; playing together, creating imaginary worlds. During COVID-19 we had great dress-up times every day.

*BBQs:* We have a big silver barbeque on our veranda, which we'll cook on twice a week, at least, and all through summer. The barbeque is Matt's responsibility and I do the sides. All summer we usually eat on the back deck. That's very Aussie, isn't it?

*Farm life:* When the kids were growing up, they would spend most holidays at Matt's parents' farm. They were good at showing the kids farm life: a few sheep, goats, 120 chickens, guinea fowl and geese. There is a herd of about 170 alpacas. They're cute, but the adults kick and spit!

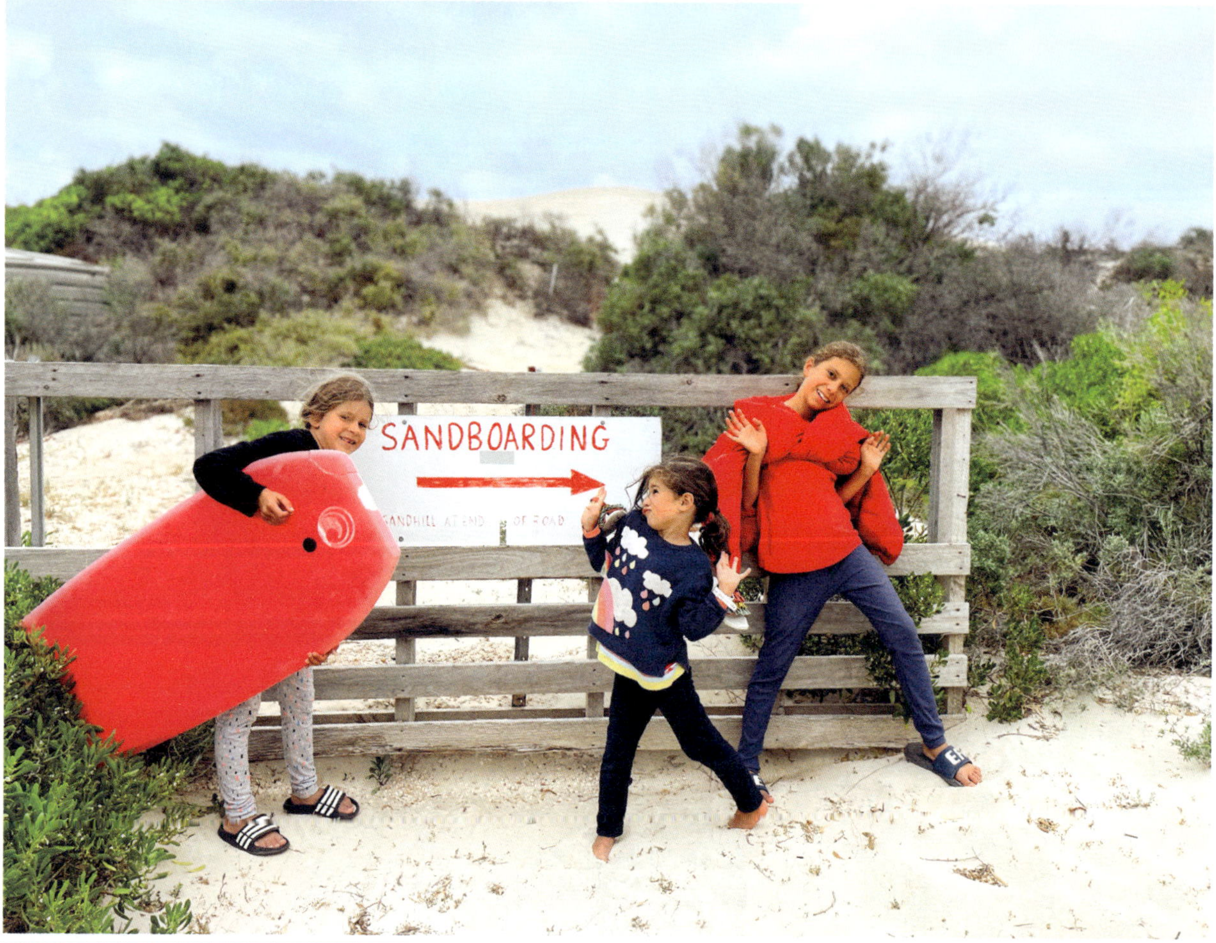

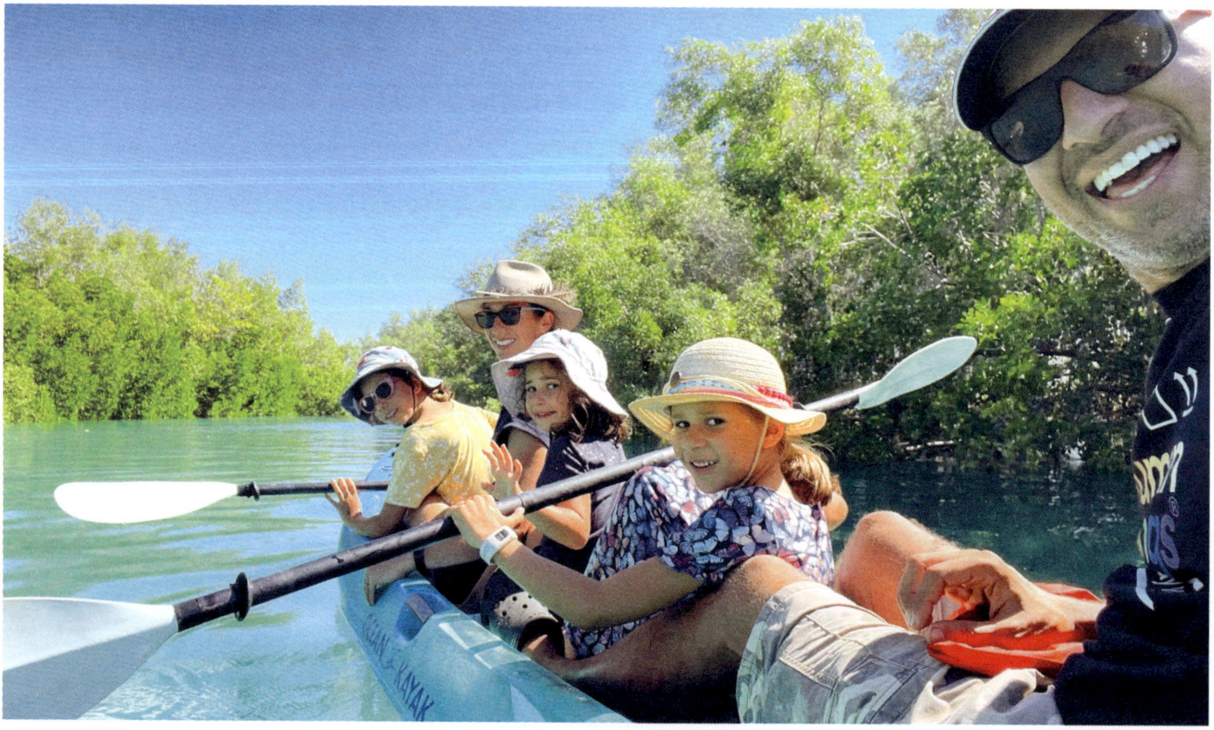

# Australia

## ELIA & NICOLE PETZIERIDES

**WHERE ELIA & NICOLE LIVE:**
Melbourne, Australia

**WHERE ELIA & NICOLE ARE FROM:**
Melbourne, Australia

Paramedics Elia and Nicole met by chance when their shifts overlapped at the same ambulance branch. Brought together by a biking mishap, they bonded over their love of the outdoors and were soon heading out on camping escapes. They'd already travelled around Australia before they married, so they spent their honeymoon campervanning across Europe. 'It blew our minds. It changed travel from something we enjoyed to something that was necessary for us', says Nicole. As their young family grew, they wanted to instil in their three daughters the same curiosity that drove them to travel. When the COVID-19 pandemic was declared in 2020, they hit the road with the kids to complete Australia's famous Big Lap – a 15,000km (9320-mile) road trip circumnavigating the country – not once, but twice.

**'PERFECT' TIMING:** We spent a lot of time mapping out the kids' milestone years, like starting prep or secondary school, trying to find the perfect window to travel around the country; 2020 was the ideal year, but we didn't plan for COVID-19! We had intense lockdowns in Australia, and when state borders temporarily reopened, we realised there would never be one 'perfect' moment to travel. We just loaded the van and went for it. (*Nicole*)

**THE LONG AND DUSTY ROAD:** Over 16 weeks, we drove up the interior of eastern Australia, through Victoria, New South Wales and Queensland, then turned west into the Northern Territory and Western Australia. Often, we were staying in the middle of nowhere in basic caravan parks filled up with other like-minded campervanning families. Sometimes we'd discover spots near the beach where we could do our own thing, or bump into families we'd made friends with a few weeks earlier. We came back home via the Great Australian Bight, which runs along the south of the country. (*Elia*)

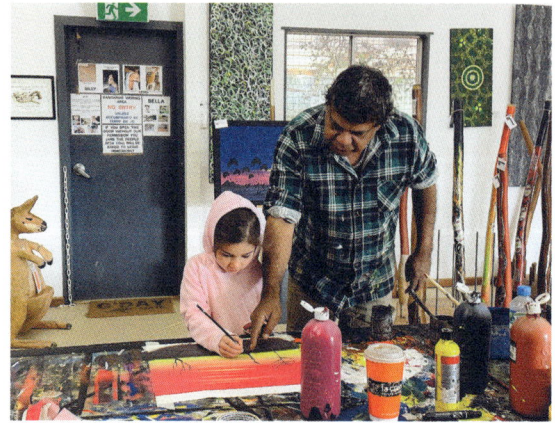

**VAN SCHOOLING:** We were lucky the girls' teachers shared their lesson plans with us, which meant we could have structured learning on the road. (*Nicole*) We had a rule that driving days were school days, no matter what day of the week they fell on. Nicole would pass worksheets to the kids in the back seat, and every morning we'd practise spelling or handwriting. Even though we weren't in a classroom, there was still a lot of whingeing. (*Elia*)

**THE WORLD IS A CLASSROOM:** Australia is a massive place, and distances between A and B are greater than they appear on a map. This was a great way to teach the girls how to calculate distance and time. In Karijini National Park in Western Australia, we collected iron-ore fragments out of the red dirt using magnets. In Coober Pedy, we foraged discarded opal from the remains of old mine sites. They also loved looking out for animals by the campsite or while snorkelling along the Ningaloo Coast. (*Elia*)

**LIVE REPORTING:** We organised livestreamed video calls to the girls' classrooms, showing where we were and what they'd learned. It was rubbing it in, as most kids were being homeschooled during lockdowns that followed after we left, but it was nice that we could brighten their days a bit. We also sent regular postcards to the school. (*Elia*)

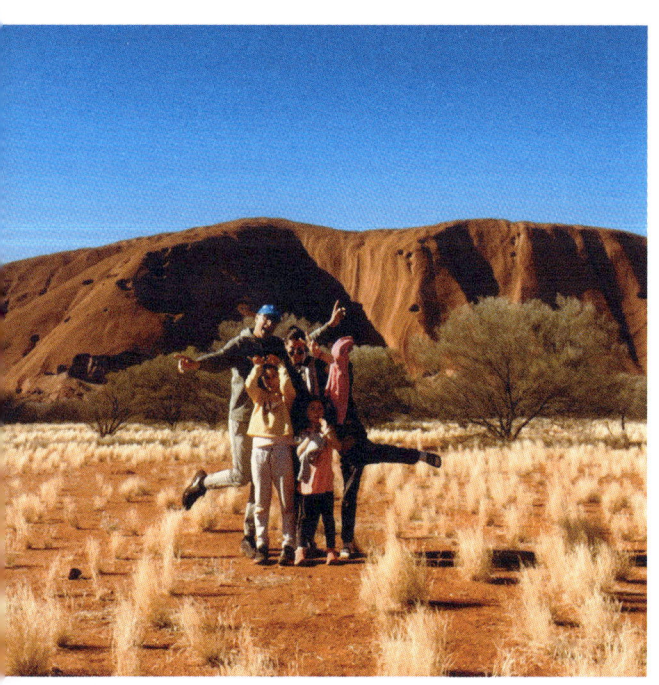

**OUT OF SIGNAL:** We realised very quickly internet access and livestreaming wasn't always possible. We had to be proactive and download maps or school resources in advance. (*Elia*) We'd get very sketchy internet in smaller towns, and once you're a few kilometres out of those places it feels like you've dropped off the face of the planet. (*Nicole*) In the Kimberley, we had no phone or internet connection for weeks. The kids were fine. They didn't feel it at all. They were just loving living life and being outdoors. It was us who were addicted! (*Elia*)

**CONSISTENCY:** Caravanning was ideal because we could be like a snail and take our house with us on the road. Sleeping in the same bed with the same pillow every night – that's what hotels can't beat. And if something goes wrong, you have everything with you. Kids need consistency, and they don't get that when you move from hotel to hotel with new environments each time. (*Elia*)

**TREE RINGS:** We talk a lot about tree rings, those periods of time that define your life, much like the bands of a tree. That's what the two Big Laps were. (*Elia*) Our daughters are always saying: 'remember before the first trip this...' or 'after we did the second trip that...'. Those trips were pivotal to them and have created a reference point for the rest of their lives. As parents, all we can do is create tree rings for our kids. They might not remember the dates or finer details, but they'll never forget the memories. (*Nicole*)

JUSTIN MENEGUZZI

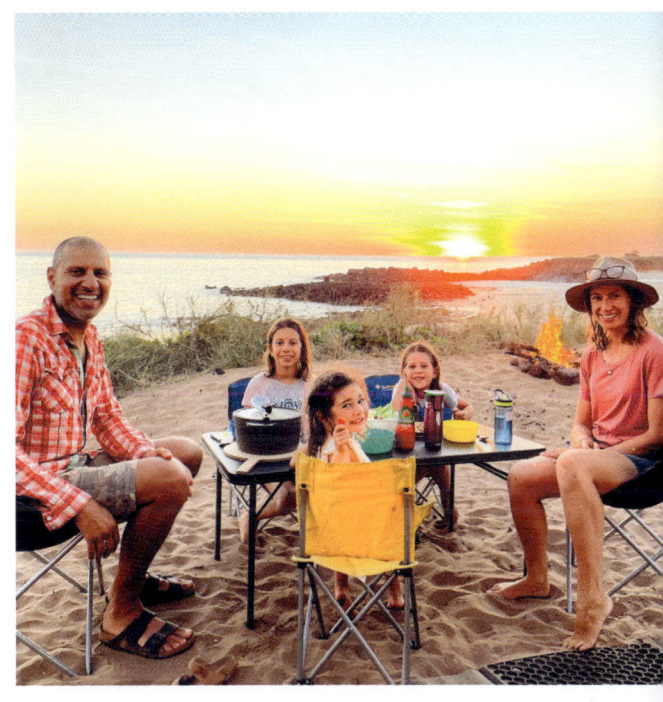

## Our favourite traditions

***Selfies:*** Elia would take a selfie every night at dinner and the girls would roll their eyes. (*Nicole*)

***Journals:*** As part of their school day in the car, the kids would spend 10–15 minutes writing in their journals about where we were leaving. We know from our own travels, before kids, that journals make great time capsules. (*Elia*)

***Walks:*** When we arrived at a new place, there would inevitably be a walk to a waterfall or lookout to do. The kids would begrudgingly come with us, but now that is the stuff they remember most. One time we had to swim across a shallow river that had crocodiles in it. (*Elia*)

***Making camp:*** Everyone had a role to play in setting up camp that they were responsible for. This was things like laying out the mats, getting stuff out of the car, unhitching the van. There was one job we could never get them to do, which was empty the septic tank. That was always Nicole's job. (*Elia*)

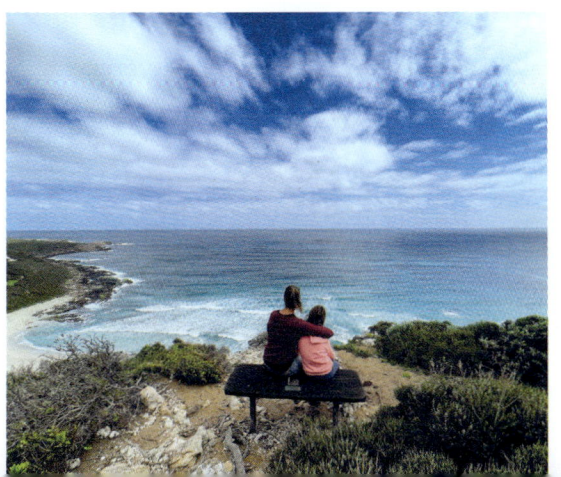

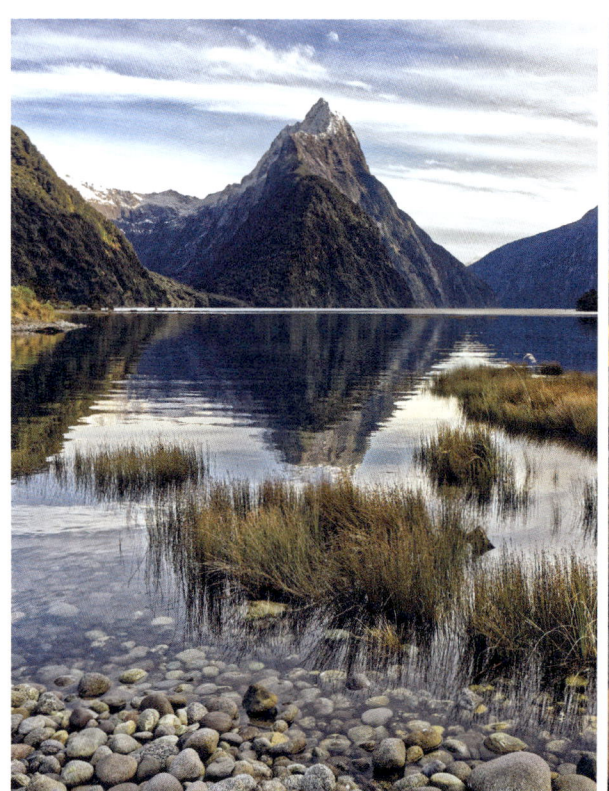
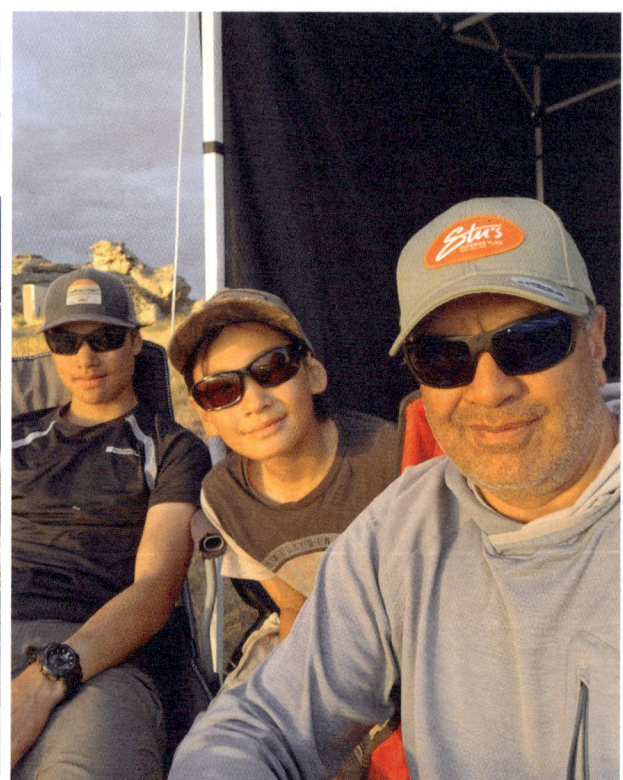

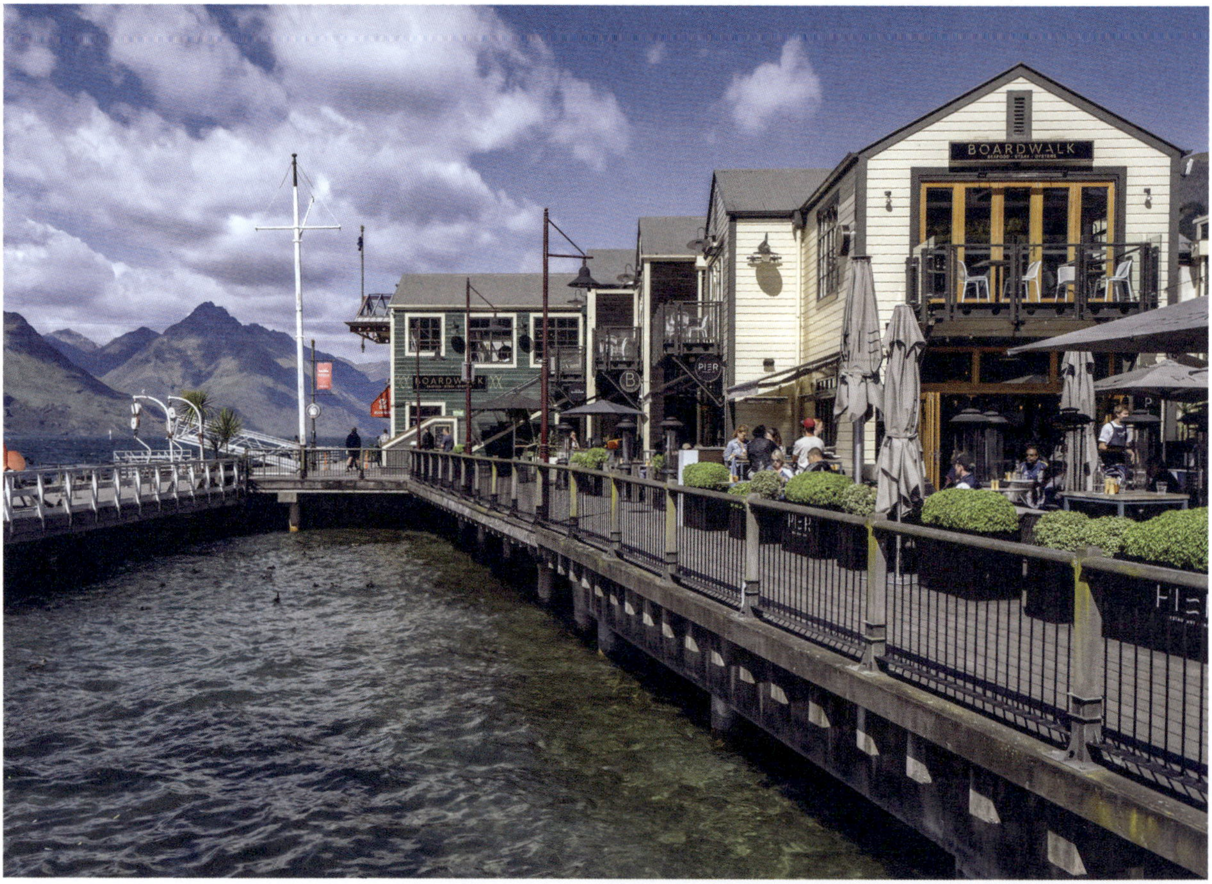

# New Zealand/Aotearoa

## HENARE & IKUKO DEWES

**WHERE HENARE & IKUKO LIVE:**
Queenstown, New Zealand

**WHERE HENARE & IKUKO ARE FROM:**
New Zealand and Japan

Henare is Māori, descended from the North Island *iwi* (tribe), Ngati Porou. He moved to Queenstown in 1996 to work in tourism and is now a heli-ski guide in winter and heli-fishing guide the rest of the year. Ikuko, from Kōbe, Japan, came to Queenstown in 2004 on a working holiday, met Henare and has never left. Before she departed Japan, she saw a television programme on New Zealand that featured Henare guiding, then when she arrived in Queenstown, she bumped into and instantly recognised him in a Japanese restaurant. The rest is history. With Queenstown a major wedding destination, Ikuko runs her own business as a make-up and hair artist. The Dewes family, with sons Jazz (15) and Lani (10), live a short drive from downtown Queenstown.

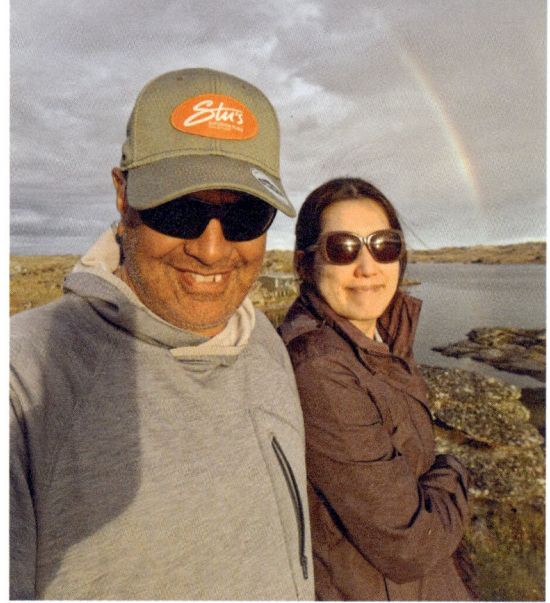

> "They understand that food doesn't just come from the supermarket."

**HAVING TIME IS KEY:** I've worked with a lot of really wealthy and successful people when out guiding, and most of them say the same thing – they wish they'd spent more time with their children when they were young. As a family, we've really taken that to heart. We spend a lot of time together with our boys. The most important thing you can give your kids is your time. (*Henare*)

**HOME IS IKUKO'S TERRITORY:** It's really important to me that we bring our kids up to be multilingual. They're going to speak English, anyway. But our boys are half Japanese. At home, they have to speak Japanese. They're not allowed to speak English to me. It's how they show respect for their mother. Once a week, on Sundays, we video chat in Japanese with my parents in Japan, and when we get the chance, we visit my family. Both boys have spent time in Japanese-language classes here, run by the local Japanese community. The boys know and understand their mixed heritage. (*Ikuko*)

**LIMITED TIME ON DEVICES:** Jazz got a mobile phone when he started high school at age 13, but that was at our suggestion, not his. Lani is 10 and still doesn't have one. That can be a bit of a hassle when we can't find him. Most of his friends already have a smartphone. The boys have access to a laptop, but don't really spend much time on social media; except that now Jazz is marketing himself as a fishing guide on Instagram. He's figuring out how to use it as a tool for what he wants to do. We're really happy to see that. (*Henare & Ikuko*)

**THEY'LL NEVER GO HUNGRY:** Our boys are really into the outdoors. They love hunting and fishing and know how to look after themselves. Queenstown is a paradise, with amazing mountains, lakes and rivers just outside our door. Plus, Fiordland and Mt Aspiring National Parks aren't far away. Both boys know how to hunt a deer, clean it, bone it and cook it – and catch a trout, gut it and cook it. Jazz loves smoking trout. They understand that food doesn't just come from the supermarket. (*Henare*)

**BREEDING CONFIDENCE:** Jazz comes out on my fish-guiding trips with me sometimes. My clients love him. He's only 15, but he could work as a fishing guide now. I tried to get him registered with the NZ Professional Fishing Guides Association, but they said he's too young. He'd need a full driver's licence; kind of ironic since he only guides on heli-fishing trips and doesn't fly the helicopter... yet! One of my best clients, who comes back year after year, says that we're 'breeding confidence' in our boys. I felt really proud when he said that. (*Henare*)

**STREET SMART:** It's important for the boys to be smart with people. Of course, we want them to do well academically as well. Jazz doesn't like school so much, but he's intelligent and gets along well with people. As the younger brother, Lani tags along and does whatever his big brother does. They're both pretty street smart. *(Henare & Ikuko)*

**LEARNING RESPECT:** Both boys are into kickboxing. They train hard at the local gym, mostly with young adults, and that's also helped them gain confidence and to learn respect. Queenstown is a special place. It's a multicultural, multiethnic community, with people from all over the planet. It's a tolerant, inclusive place, but it's always good to know how to look after yourself, especially if you feel 'different' – and there aren't many half-Japanese half-Māori kids around. This place might be really inclusive, but it's a big world out there and who knows where they might head off to in the future. We're happy that we're setting our kids up for their future lives. *(Henare & Ikuko)*

CRAIG McLACHLAN

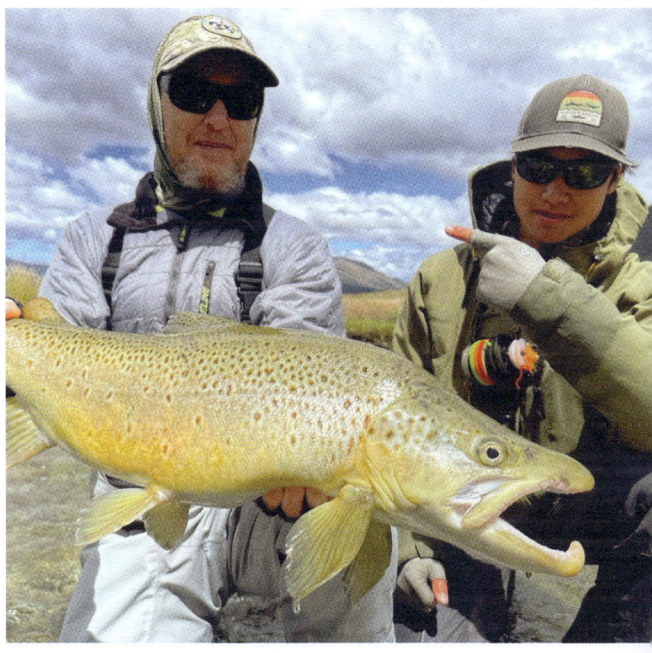

## Our favourite traditions

***A 'boil up':*** Everyone's favourite meal in our family and a popular Māori way of eating. Put pork, potatoes and kumara (sweet potatoes) in a big pot and boil it up. Really good served with watercress. Then Ikuko takes the leftover soup, adds miso and we use it as a broth for ramen for the next few days. *(Henare)*

***Summer camping trip:*** We like to get away camping as a family in summer, over the Christmas and New Year period if we can. The boys are off school then, but our work can be busy, as everything in Queenstown is connected to the tourism industry and the town is packed in midsummer. *(Henare)*

***Toshi-koshi noodles:*** In Japan, we eat *toshi-koshi* soba on New Year's Eve. *Toshi-koshi* means 'changing over to the new year'. Our boys like udon better than soba noodles though, so we make it with udon in our family. New Year is the middle of summer in New Zealand, so it feels a lot different than it does in Japan. *(Ikuko)*

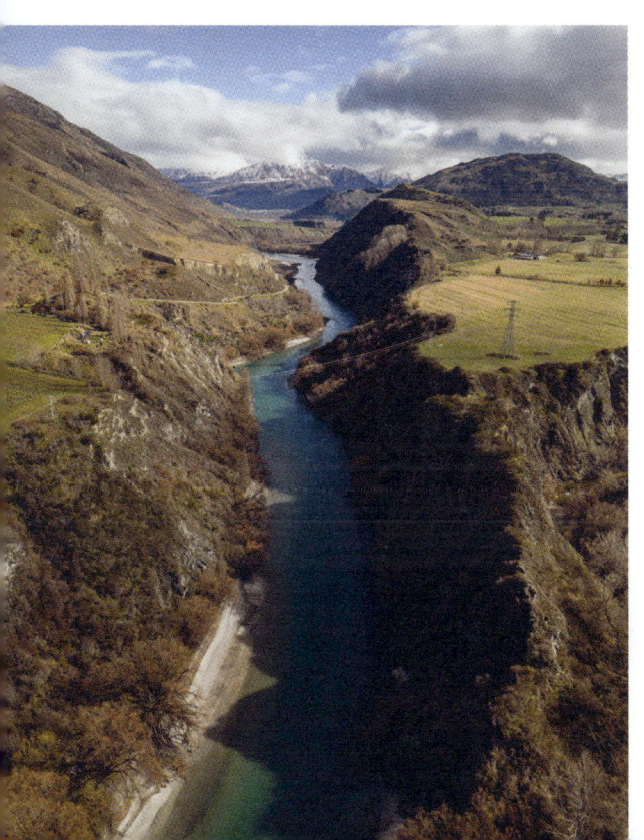

OCEANIA

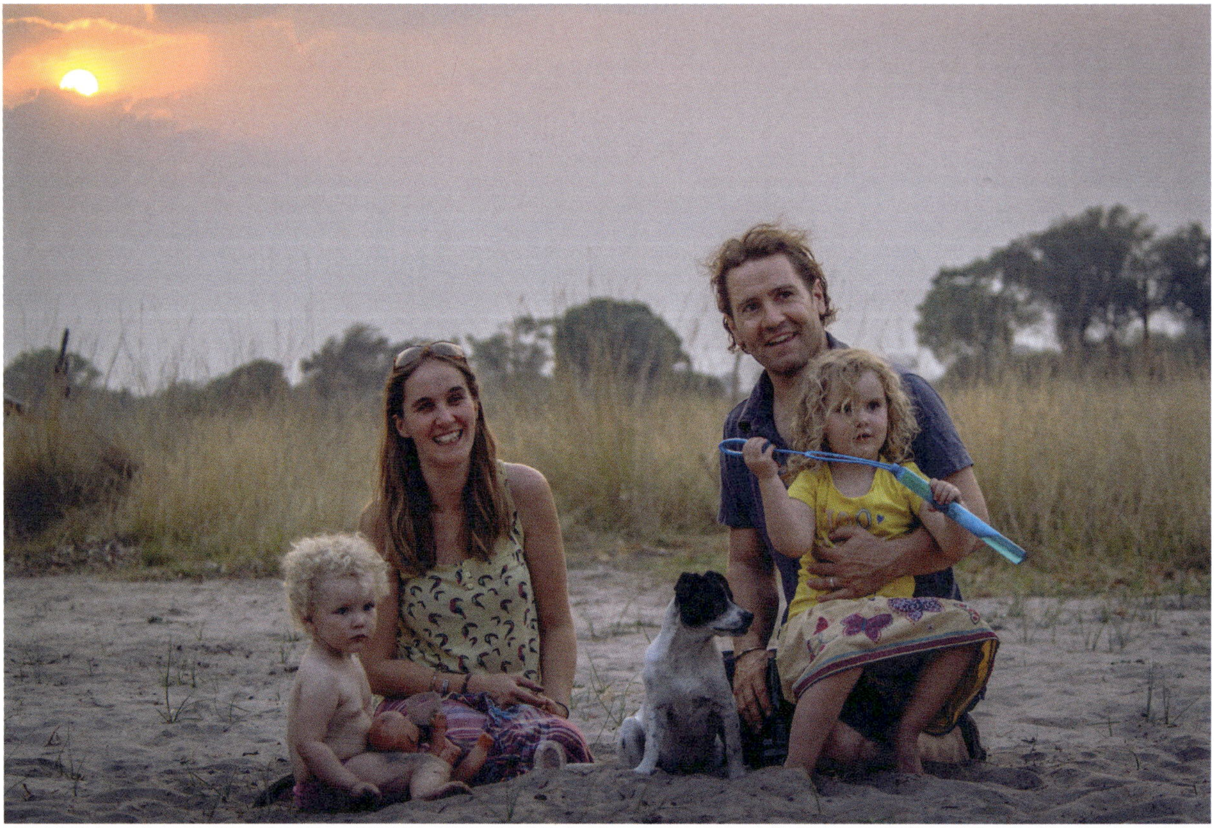

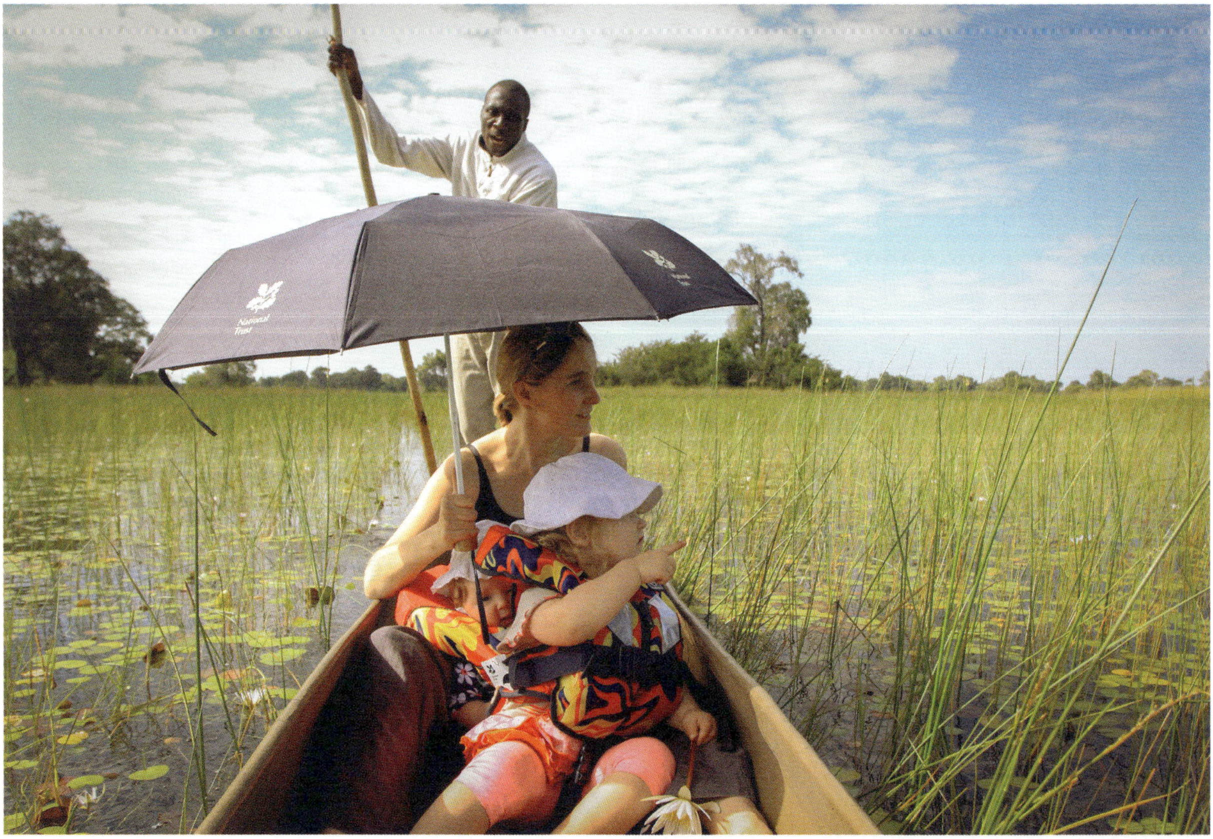

# Botswana

## ANNA SONGHURST & GRAHAM MCCULLOCH

**WHERE ANNA & GRAHAM LIVE:**
Maun, Botswana

**WHERE ANNA & GRAHAM ARE FROM:**
UK and Ireland

Fresh from a degree in zoology, Graham headed to Botswana for a year to continue his research. While writing up his PhD in Ireland, he met fellow zoologist Anna at a faculty Christmas party. Anna had wanted to study elephants since the tender age of four, and meeting Graham made all the pieces fall into place. He was based in northern Botswana, home of the largest elephant population in the world. Anna's groundbreaking PhD on elephant behaviour led to them setting up Ecoexist, an NGO that focuses on the coexistence between elephants and people, specifically in the Okavango Delta. Their daughters, Ebany (11) and Aria (nine), were born in the UK but grew up in a safari tent in the far north of Botswana, surrounded by the African bush.

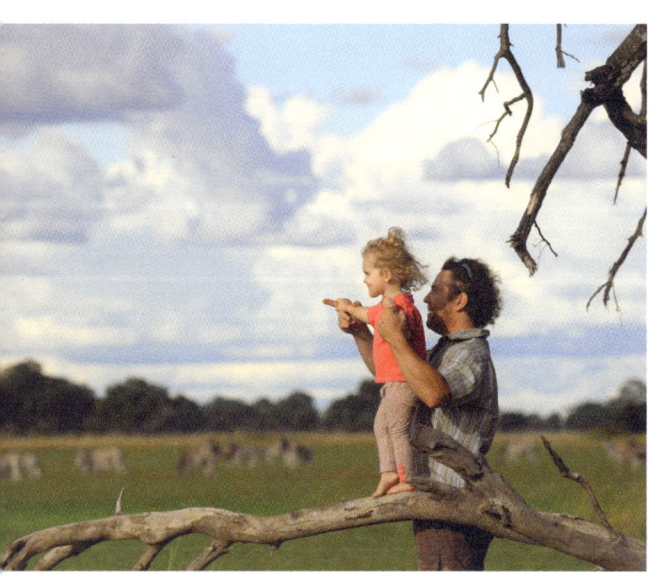

**BABIES IN THE BUSH:** When we brought Ebany back to the Delta she was two months old. A lot of people were asking how we were going to cope with raising a baby in the bush; we were basically living in a tent. We got home to our camp and to get to our tent you had to take a *mokoro* (dugout canoe) across a channel. We had to unpack everything from the car to load onto the *mokoro*. Anna put a blanket on the ground and laid Ebany down while we loaded up. I remember our codirector of Ecoexist at the time was freaking out that there was a baby on the ground in the reeds, and it hit us that a lot of other people were more anxious about how we were going to raise children in the bush than we were. We had of course seen hundreds of women raising their children on the edge of the Delta, so for us it wasn't a massive deal. *(Graham)*

**KEEPING IT SIMPLE:** You realise that you don't need all the stuff that people say you do. A baby is the most natural thing to bring into the world and as long as you've got somewhere safe for them to sleep, you don't need much else. We had a cot with a zip-up mozzie (mosquito) net to also keep out snakes and spiders. I breastfed, so we didn't have to deal with sterilising bottles, and we used reusable nappies so we didn't have to bother with disposables, although that of course came with its own challenges. We didn't have a washing machine, so we had to boil them in big pans! *(Anna)*

**SAFETY CHECKS:** Aria is fascinated by snakes – I guess because we brought so much attention to the fact that they are around and to be vigilant. Checking the beds, to make sure there are no spiders, no scorpions, no snakes, is a nightly ritual.

There are hippos and crocodiles nearby and, of course, elephants. Lions do come through the camp, as well as hyenas. Sometimes the lions would come right up by the tent and we'd see footprints in the morning, particularly when the girls were babies – I think it was perhaps from hearing them crying. The girls have never encountered a lion in camp, but they would know what to do if they did. *(Anna)*

**IT TAKES A VILLAGE:** The whole community just embraced that there were two new children in their midst. When Ebany first arrived, the ladies from the nearby village came to welcome her to the area. It was quite magical – they came to sing and to have a cuddle with the new baby, and the same thing happened for Aria. They were very special moments. The community have always been there for us and it wasn't hard to get help if we needed it. *(Anna)*

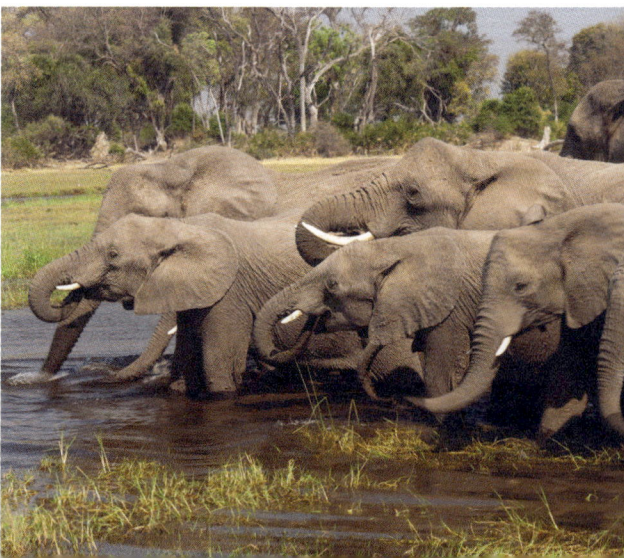

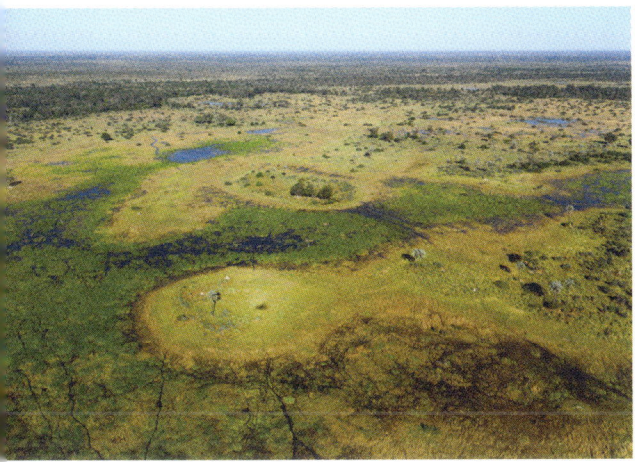

**ALL CHANGE:** We homeschooled the girls for a few years, then Ebany asked us if she could start school. The one thing they found most difficult living in the bush was that they wanted some friends, so we relocated closer to Maun and then travelled up and down to the Delta – a 10-hour drive. It was harder for us because of the travelling, but it was the right decision. (*Anna*)

**RESPECT FOR NATURE:** We are definitely growing budding conservationists. The girls have travelled all over with us since they were tiny babies, to meetings and elephant collarings and all sorts. They're the real experts now. Ebany wants to be a pangolin conservationist, although she also wants to be a dancer or perhaps a politician. Aria has been talking about giraffe conservation and both of them have done conservation talks at school. (*Anna*)

They've built up a heightened awareness of the bush, and would certainly be able to navigate the bush more than a city in the UK. I think as they get older they're going to miss the sounds of the bush and when they hear them again it will really bring them back to their home in the Panhandle – whether it's bird calls, a lion roaring, zebras barking or elephants trumpeting. (*Graham*)

LUCY CORNE

## Our favourite traditions

***Family sundowners:*** Going somewhere to watch the sunset is a big tradition across Africa. Sometimes we wait for elephants on the corridors they follow through the bush. Sometimes we leave the map behind and drive into the Delta on an adventure. The girls have their favourite spots, like the 'termite mound stage' where they like to do a song-and-dance show. (*Anna*)

***Briefing the guests:*** When people come to visit, we give them an induction to the bush – animals that are around, what to be careful of. Now the girls do it and it's really funny because all of the stories of snake encounters come out. I worry that they'll scare the guests but for them it's all just a part of life. (*Anna*)

***Dancing together:*** Every time we get together with the community there's traditional dancing, so the girls got their own reed skirts made. They're both mad into dancing. Now they're learning hip-hop and modern and tap, and when we go back to the camp they share what they've learned with the community women. (*Anna*)

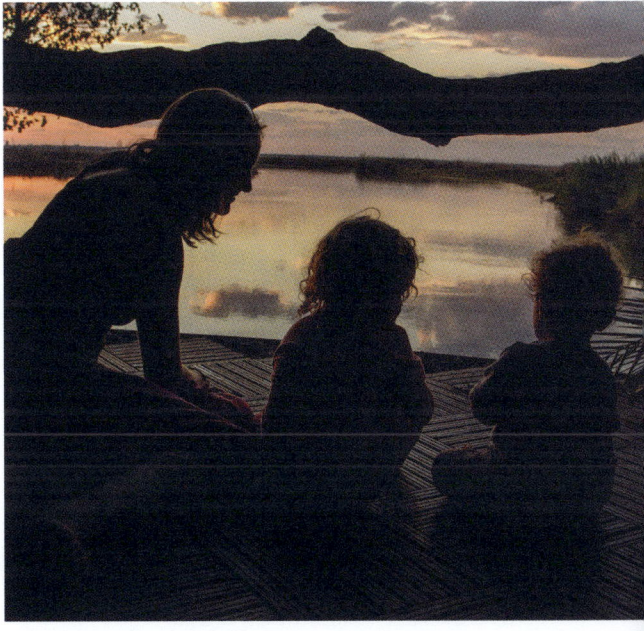

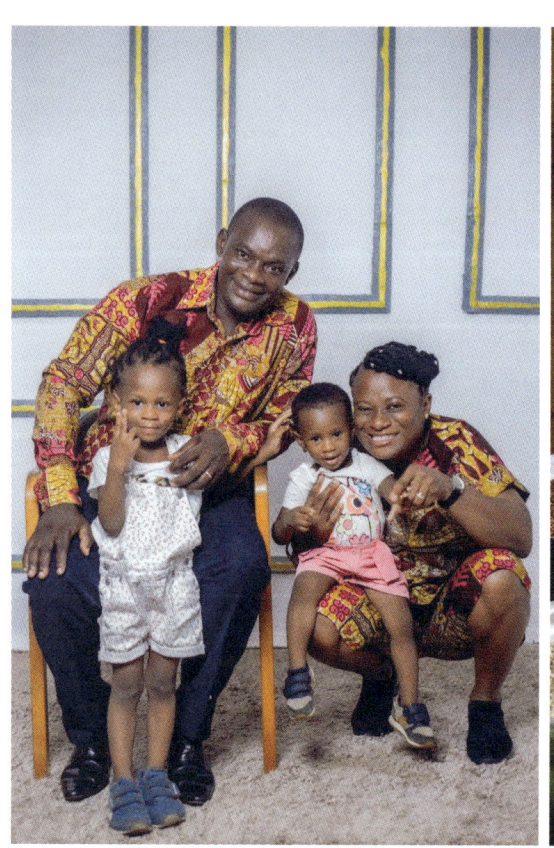
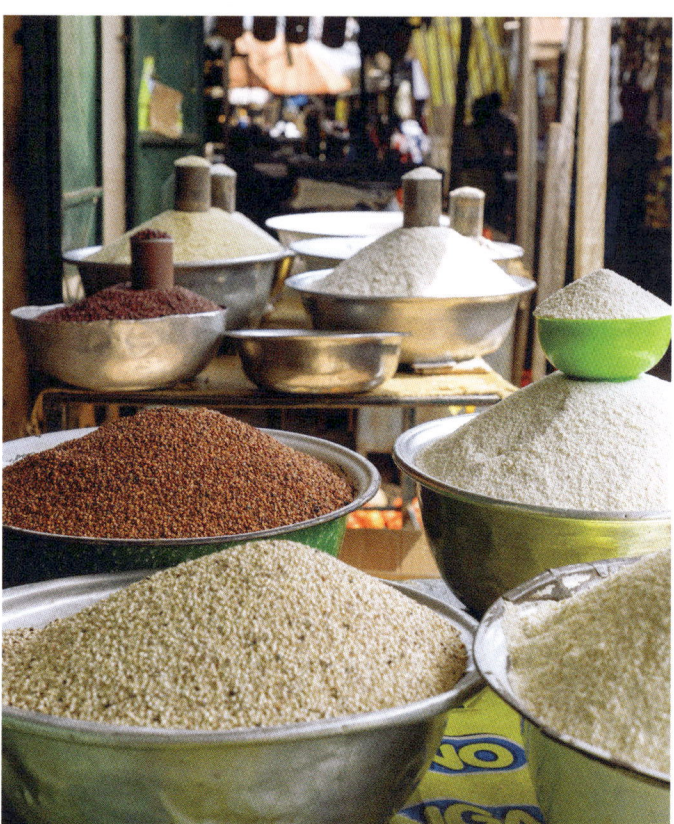

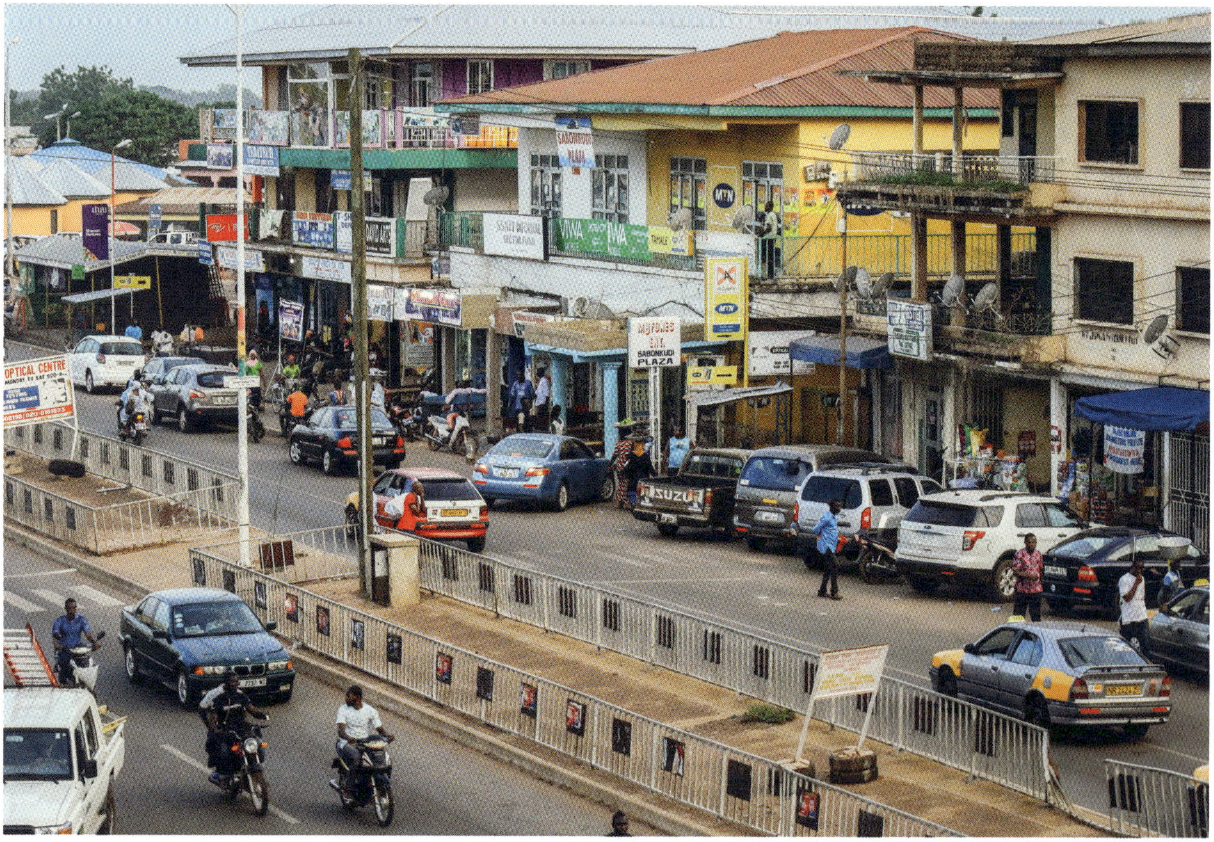

# Ghana

## EVITA DUNEE

**WHERE EVITA LIVES:**
Tamale, Ghana

**WHERE EVITA IS FROM:**
Rural northern Ghana

When Evita felt ready to settle down and start a family, she looked no further than her childhood best friend, Isaac. They both grew up in a small village in rural northern Ghana, met at the only school, and dreamt of going to university one day. 'Your children cannot choose their father, but you can choose your husband', Evita says. 'I knew he was the one because we were looking in the same direction in terms of family values.' Today Isaac works as a doctor in Tamale, northern Ghana's main city, and Evita goes back to the rural areas to help empower women through economic development projects. Their mission is to raise two independent and educated daughters, while respecting their ancestors' traditions.

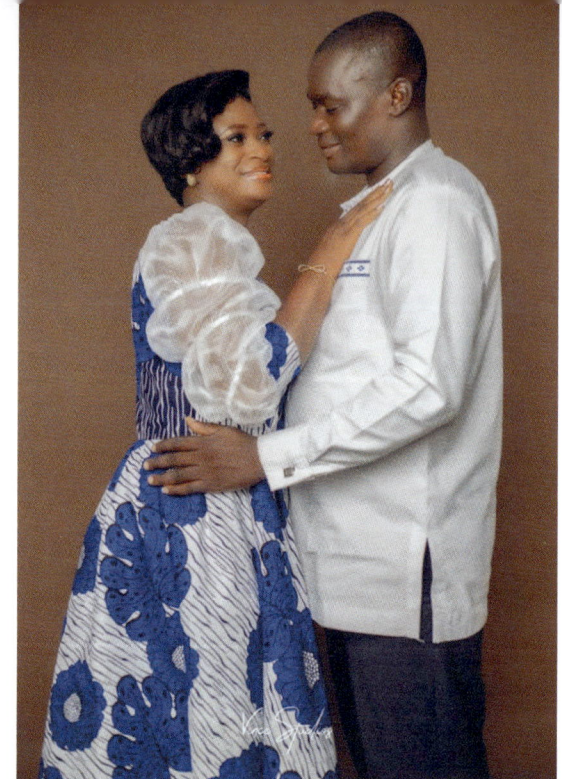

**ATYPICAL FAMILY:** Ghanaian families are traditionally quite big, with more than three children and several generations living in the same house or compound. But ours is an exception: we only have two daughters, Mireya (five) and Mirella (three), and all our relatives live elsewhere, in bigger cities. Anytime there's a holiday we gather to celebrate, but that's just for special occasions. Families with fewer children are becoming the norm nowadays, and our family is a reflection of changing times.

**FESTIVALS:** There are 52 ethnic groups in our country, making Ghana's culture extremely varied. This means there are dozens of traditional festivals and ceremonies every year, each with its own specific colours, sounds and smells. We try to attend most of them; I think it's important for our daughters to learn and appreciate the diversity of our country.

**EDUCATION:** Both Isaac and I agree that education is crucial to our daughters' upbringing. What I noticed during my own upbringing, and at my current job, is that an educated woman is free, and doesn't have to depend on marriage to succeed in life. As parents of two young girls, it's important for us to see them grow independent and strong. Just because we come from a rural area in Africa doesn't mean we cannot aim for higher education levels to improve our conditions.

**RELIGION:** We think that education can only be sustained by a strong faith. We are a Christian family, we pray every night before going to bed and attend church every Sunday. We teach our daughters to be respectful and God-fearing, and to love thy neighbour as thyself.

**COURTYARDS:** In a Ghanaian household, it is considered rude to spend a lot of time by yourself. We like to do everything together as a family, and our courtyard is the main space where we cook, socialise with our neighbours or enjoy soaking up some sunshine. Learning to enjoy courtyard time is a core part of our culture, and it's necessary to pass this tradition on to younger generations who are becoming too dependent on their phones.

**RESPECT FOR THE ELDERLY:** Despite modernity, we still keep our strong sense of community, especially in our family. That means respecting the elderly; we show that by teaching our daughters to always refer to adults as 'auntie' or 'uncle', as a sign of respect, instead of calling them by their first name. We find that rude.

**NO BIRTHDAYS:** Ageing here is not the same concept as in the West. In rural communities like those of northern Ghana, where we live, birthdays are rarely registered and most elderly people we know can only guess their actual age. So for us it's not so common to celebrate birthdays, including our daughters'. We did celebrate their first birthdays, but since then we live it more like a normal day – there are no candles on a cake.

> "Despite modernity, we still keep our strong sense of community, especially in our family."

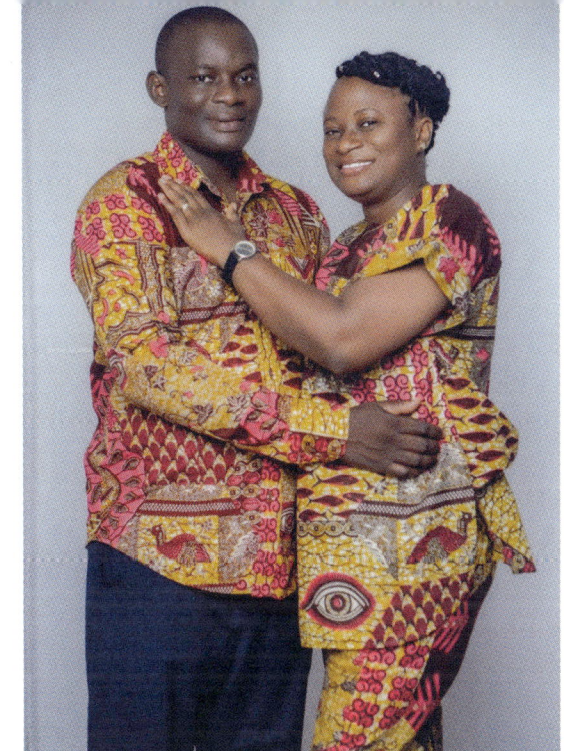

**FUFU:** We take food very seriously in Ghana, and learning to share and eat it as a community is a part of growing up. Our favourite meal to share is *fufu*: a starchy root-vegetable dish common in many western African countries that originated in northern Ghana. We make it at least once a week and enjoy it as a family meal, usually for dinner, on a day when we know we are not coming home late from work.

**TIME MANAGEMENT:** In Ghana, we always go with the flow. Maybe a bit too much! So when we meet friends, or even at work, the time we agree on is never the actual time you show up. That reflects our relaxed approach to life, but I realise it can be very frustrating in certain circumstances. So, although we want our daughters to have a calm lifestyle, especially as kids, we are also trying to make sure they don't pick this up as a bad habit, as it could be considered rude behavior elsewhere.

STEFANIA D'IGNOTI

## Our favourite traditions

***New Year:*** Renamed 'Cross Over', it's become an even more religious holiday than Christmas for us. We like to spend it watching billboards of famous local pastors (erected especially for the occasion) that light up the city of Tamale. Then we go to Our Lady of Annunciation Cathedral to attend the first mass of the year, to make sure we all 'cross over' with a good dose of luck.

***Ramadan:*** Although we are Christians, we love this time of year. We celebrate it with our Muslim neighbours and get invited at least once a week to break the evening fast with them. Then, for the last day of the month, we dress in colourful clothes and head over to the villages to distribute food or gifts.

***Farmers day:*** Every first Friday of December, we take a moment to recognise the farmers and fishermen of our land through this holiday. I like to spend the day teaching my daughters the importance of labour in rural areas; the backbone of our country.

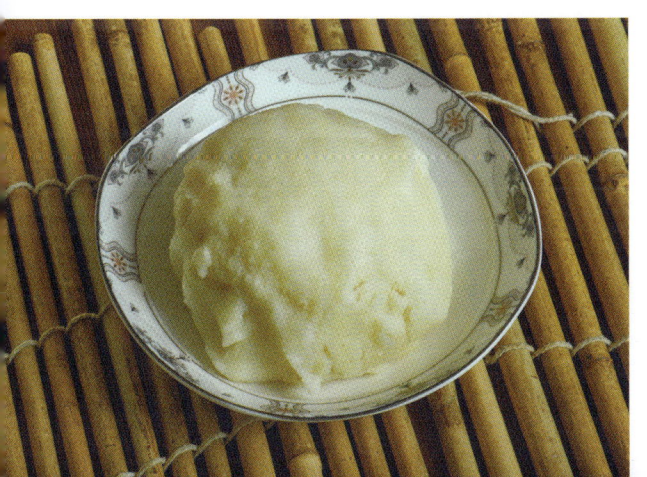

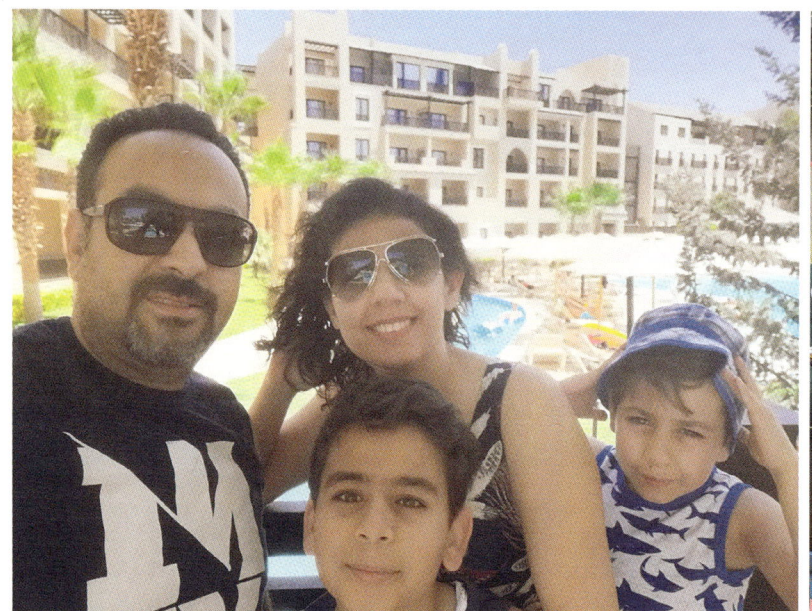
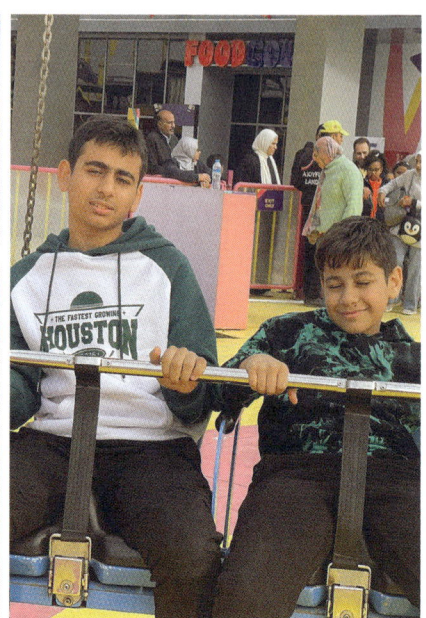
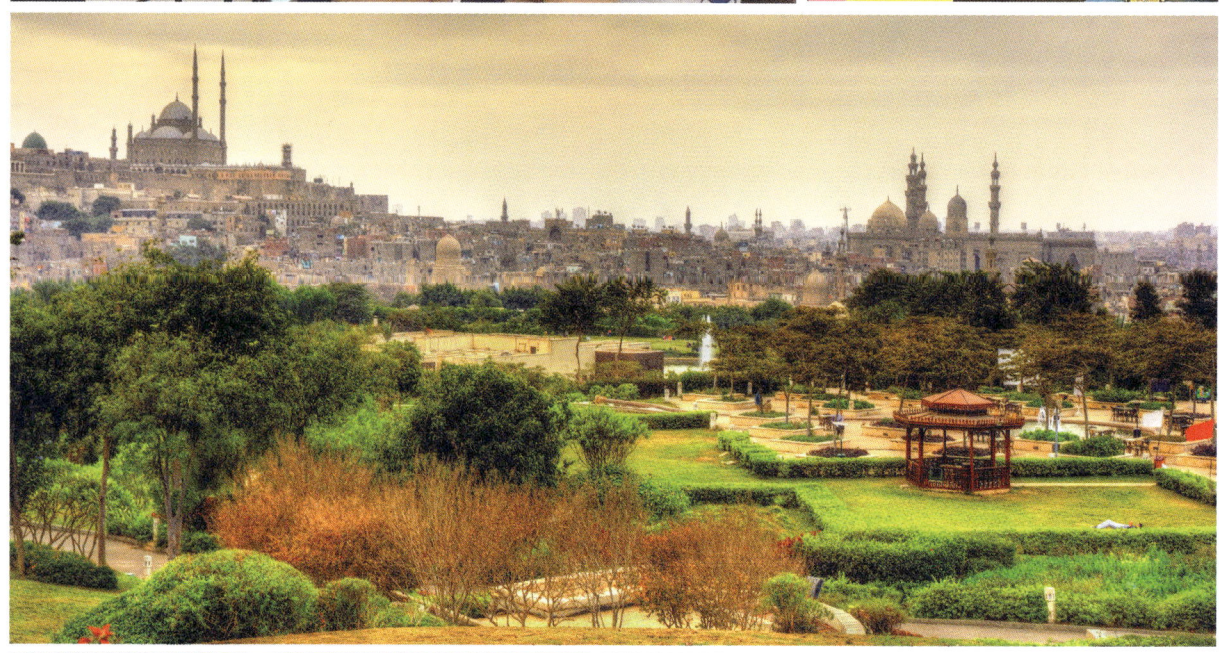
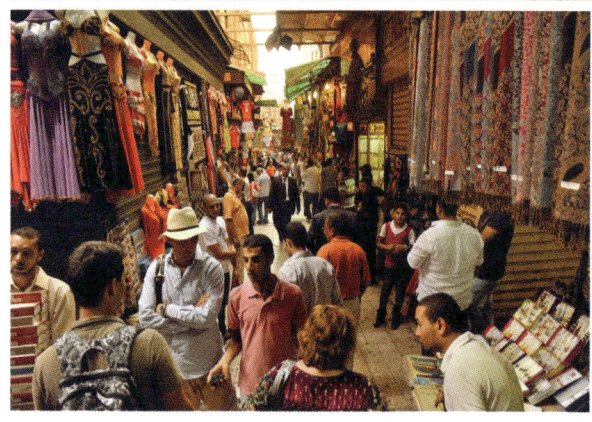
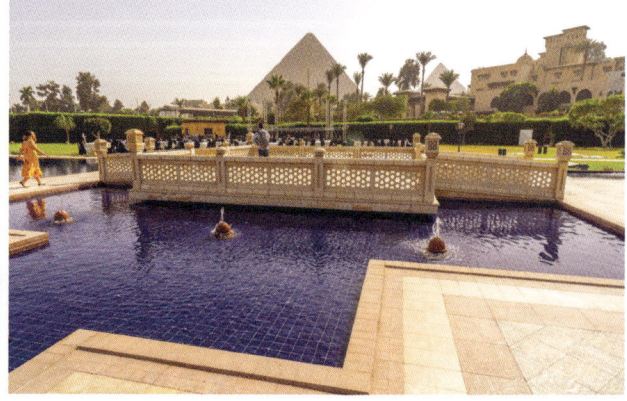

# Egypt

## CHRISTINE SEFEIN

**WHERE CHRISTINE LIVES:**
Cairo, Egypt

**WHERE CHRISTINE IS FROM:**
Cairo, Egypt

Christine Sefein and Sameh Ramzy's life together started in 2008 through a marriage arranged by her mother and his sister. They dated for six months to get to know each other, then got officially engaged and tied the knot eight months later. They live in a compound in New Cairo, 'which is like a mini town, complete with shops, schools, a church and mosque, alongside parks – a prime spot for a growing family', Christine says. They have two boys, Daniel (15) and Jonathan (13). Christine, who pursued pharmaceutical sciences at Cairo University, has balanced her career with motherhood. Sameh studied veterinary medicine, later shifting his focus to medical-supply sales and, in recent years, serving as a priest in the Orthodox Church.

**GRANDPARENTS' SUPPORT:** For us, family ties are profoundly deep, and having my parents just around the corner has been nothing short of a blessing. Normally, after school, our sons used to spend their afternoons with their father, awaiting my return from work to eat together whenever possible. However, on days when work commitments kept us away, my mom prepared their favourite meals like chicken cordon bleu, kofta or Scotch eggs, turning any day spent with her into a festive feast. As a former teacher, she also used to help them with their homework. Currently, whenever their studies permit, they visit for some cherished time after school.

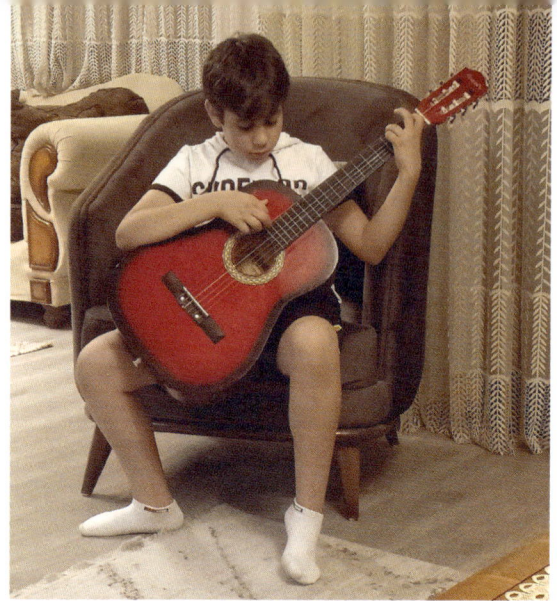

**SUPPORTING TEENS:** As our sons entered their teenage years, we recognised the importance of fostering their independence. We transitioned them to a school better-suited to their growing needs, complete with a direct bus service. They've begun taking on more responsibilities, such as heating their own lunches and tackling their homework immediately upon returning home – common practice for children over 12 in our area. If they finish their homework early, they are allowed some leisure time playing PlayStation games or watching TV.

Synchronising our schedules remains crucial, and we make every effort to share lunch together. It is the highlight of our day, where we each discuss the daily happenings, and the children open up about their school life, friends, study plans and activities. This quality time is essential, offering a nurturing environment where we can reinforce our family values and provide advice as they go through adolescence.

**EVENING ROUTINE:** As a tranquil conclusion to our day, we gather each night after dinner – served flexibly between 9pm and 11pm – for around 30 minutes of prayer. This practice is not just a reflection of our faith, it serves as a valuable time to reflect on the events of the day, express gratitude, seek guidance for overcoming any challenges, and to strengthen our family bond.

**YOUNG ATHLETES:** In Cairo, sports transcend mere activities; they're a vital part of the cultural landscape for every keen youngster. I introduced my boys to swimming at the age of four, fostering a dedication to sessions three times a week that they're committed to to this day. Football? It's the glue of our community. My boys live for the thrill of the game, organising mini World Cup tournaments at a playground near our home or at the club – a secure setting for their weekend and summer activities. They also manage to fit a weekly training session into their busy schedules.

**SOCIAL ACTIVITIES:** The vibrant club culture has been a cornerstone of our children's social and personal development. We, as parents, value the diverse range of activities these clubs offer, providing a rich and safe environment where our children engage in swimming, football and music lessons, mastering instruments like the organ and guitar. They also participate in the church choir and thrive in the Scouts group. We encourage the latter, as it builds discipline and a sense of responsibility.

As our children have grown into teenagers, we've allowed them to broaden their horizons by exploring more of what our city has to offer. They relish outings to malls with friends, where they watch movies, dine and play billiards.

**THE OUTDOORS:** As a family, our favourite outdoor spot is the nearby Family Park, a perfect blend of education and recreation. Here, we spend an entire day engaging with our children in open spaces. The park also offers a historical zone, with a cinema that delves into the country's past events and profiles notable leaders, enriching our children's understanding of Egypt's history. Beyond this, the park offers dining options, a thrilling amusement park, and a small zoo where the kids can interact with animals. These outings nurture a deep family connection while educating our children, too.

NIDAL MAJDALANI

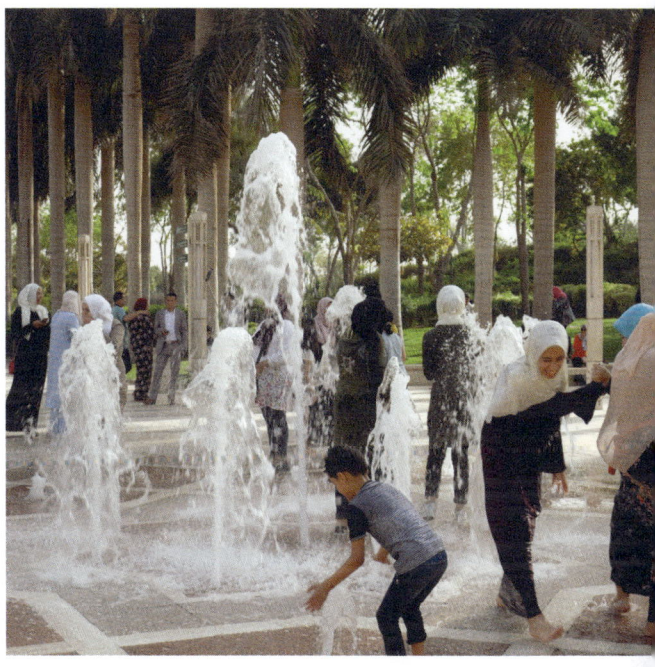

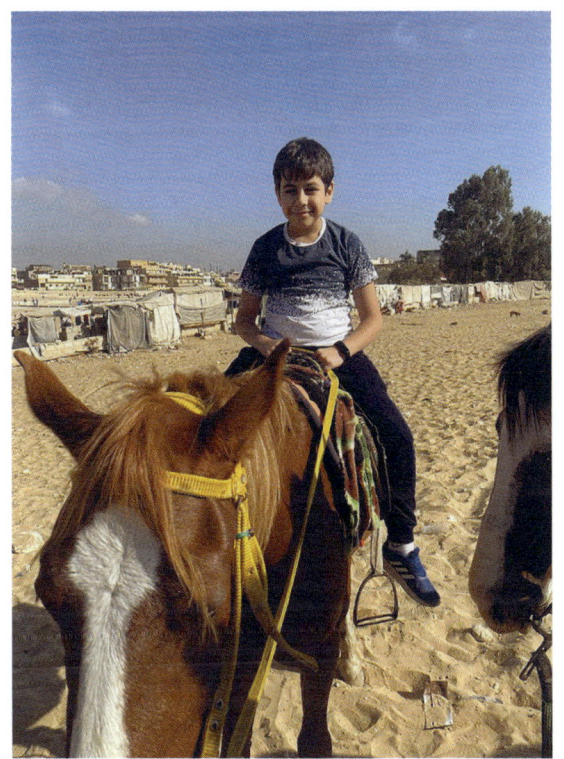

## Our favourite traditions

**Weekend rituals:** Our weekend routine stays the same year-round. We attend Mass every Friday, followed by lunch at one grandparents' house, then the church's school in the evening. On Saturdays, we have lunch at the other grandparents' house; it's when aunts, uncles and cousins from both sides gather, and the grandmother happily takes on the role of chef.

**Sham el-Nessim:** This Egyptian holiday, marking the arrival of spring the day after Easter Sunday, is eagerly anticipated by our family. While we previously celebrated with picnics and egg hunts, now we spend the morning at my parents', followed by a traditional lunch of salted fish.

**Festive days:** We fast before Christmas and Easter Eves for 43 and 55 days respectively, and the boys eagerly await breaking their fast at midnight after Mass; my mother prepares a feast of everyone's favourite dishes. The next day, we continue the festivities with lunch at my in-laws', where the cousins play games.

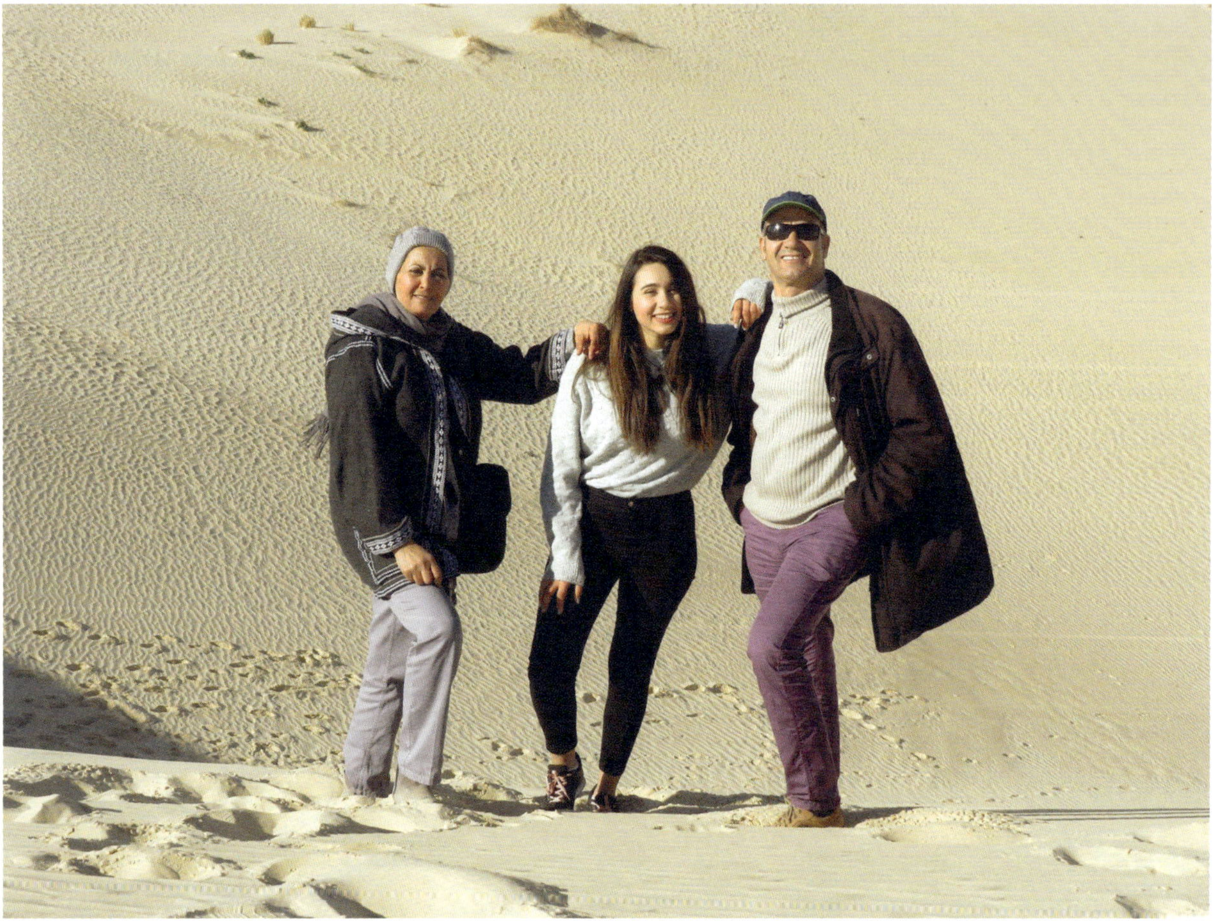

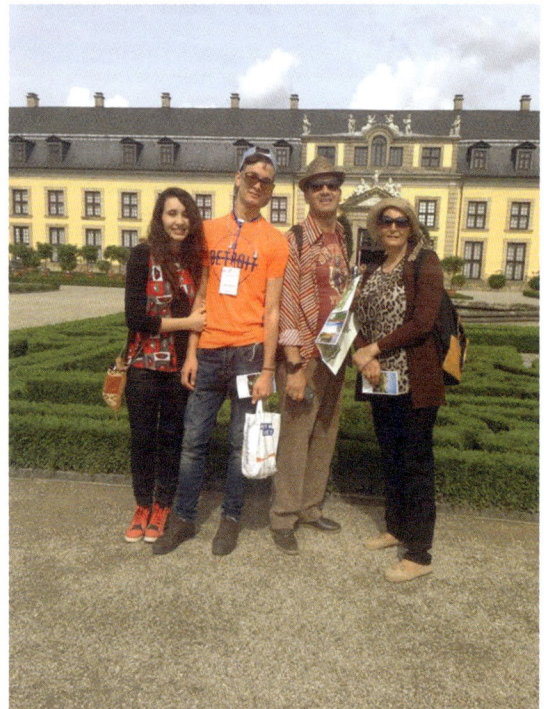
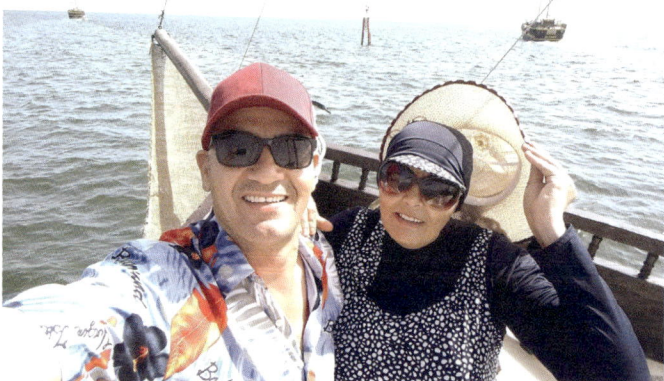
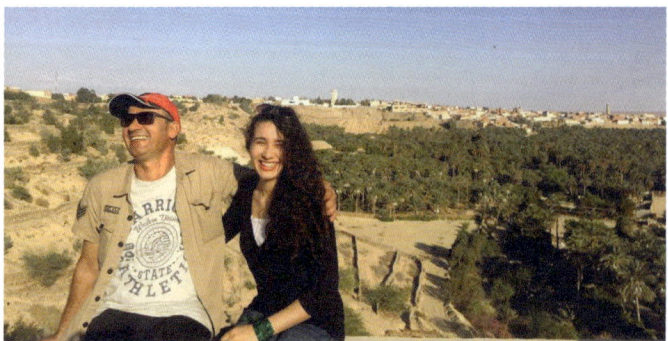

# Tunisia

## KAOUTHER & MOUNIR BOKCHARI

**WHERE KAOUTHER & MOUNIR LIVE:**
Sousse, Tunisia

**WHERE KAOUTHER & MOUNIR ARE FROM:**
Sousse, Tunisia

As a child, Kaouther didn't know she was growing up next to her future husband. She remembers running around her garden searching for the most beautiful flowers, and sometimes peeking over the fence to check if the neighbours had more colourful ones. "Your father used to help me collect them into nice bouquets," she tells her 29-year-old daughter Oumeyma while they peruse a florist shop in their home city of Sousse. Kaouther and Mounir's innocent childhood friendship naturally evolved into romantic love as they grew older, with their families' blessing. "It's a joy when family friends – your chosen family – become actual family," Kouther adds with a smile. Thirty years after their marriage, old memories resurface as they help their eldest daughter prepare for her wedding day.

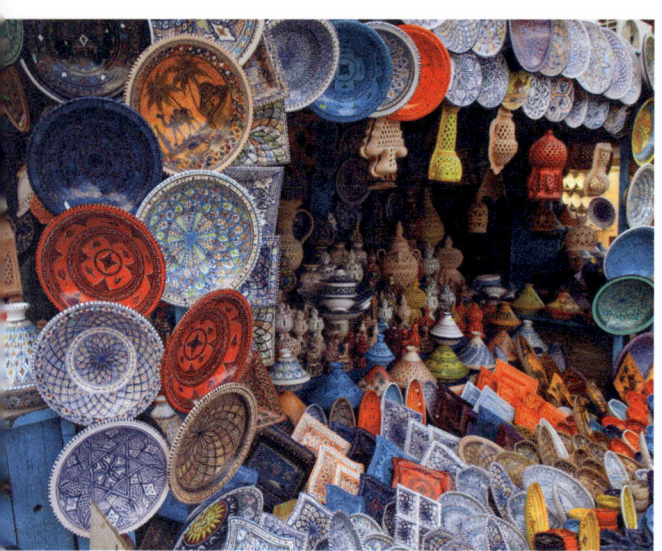

**BREAKING THE CYCLE:** Although we come from very traditional families – our fathers are imams (Muslim religious leaders) – we agreed on not raising Oumeyma (29) and Amine (26) in a very traditional way, or pressure them to be strictly religious. That's because we wanted to challenge the stereotype of Tunisia being portrayed solely as a traditionally Muslim country, and raise them as free and open-minded as possible. That's why we never opposed Oumeyma's choice of not wearing the veil, or Amine's decision to live abroad.

**CUISINE:** In recent years, take-out sandwiches are becoming more and more the average meal of Tunisian families, because they're cheaper and faster. But learning how to cook a proper meal at home is a tradition we proudly pass on from mother to daughter (and son!), even in our family. While some dishes – think of couscous, for example – are a given, we also taught Oumeyma and Amine lesser-known recipes, such as *brik* (a type of fried pastry), or *lablabi* (a chickpea stew), which showcase Tunisia's culinary diversity.

**WEDDINGS:** Tunisian weddings are vibrant communal events with specific customs, such as the *khotba* (engagement ceremony), the 'henna night' (pre-wedding celebration, where henna is applied to the bride), and the *merweh* (wedding procession with music and dancing). Attending the preparation, even as children, is an important moment of social inclusion. Now that we are planning Oumeyma's wedding, all those years of wedding observation are coming in handy! We are letting her choose which traditions and cultural practices to follow, but we are not forcing her to conform to what older generations expect her wedding to look like. So, her ceremony will be a mix of Western and Arab features.

**ARCHITECTURE:** We raised our kids as fine connoisseurs of their country's rich urban architecture. During their childhood, and up to today, when our youngest son comes back for vacation from Germany, where he now resides, we've always spent time visiting our country from north to south. From troglodyte houses, offering natural insulation and reflecting a unique adaptation to Tunisia's harsh climate in the desert, to observing the old blue doors of our city's medina, teaching the cultural heritage of our country was a fundamental step in our children's upbringing.

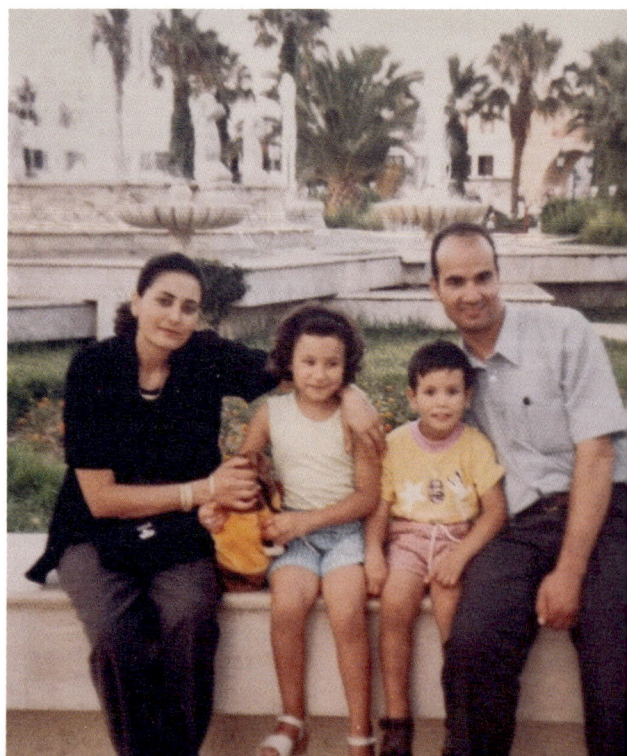

**CULTURAL EXCHANGE:** For us it was so important to cherish our beautiful country's rich culture, that we decided to expand our goal and share our knowledge with the entire world. Fifteen years ago we founded an association in Sousse called ASED, which promotes Tunisian cultural heritage and hosts volunteers from around the world. We also promote international youth exchanges, and have always encouraged our kids to be adventurous, and embark on exchange programmes abroad, to disseminate our culture, but also learn about others to enrich our own knowledge.

**HANDICRAFTS AND TEXTILES:** Tunisian artisans are known for their intricate weaving, pottery and embroidery. Traditional textiles like the *fouta* (hammam towel) and *jebba* (light caftan) reflect the country's cultural heritage and are often hand-crafted with elaborate designs. These traditions are a testament to Tunisia's rich cultural tapestry and offer a glimpse into the country's history and identity. That's why we had our kids learn about them: even though they'll never use those handicraft skills in their lives, it's important to learn about them, to help preserve our heritage.

**TEATIME:** Morning or afternoon tea is an essential feature of our Tunisian tradition, and our household. *Shaï* (Tunisian tea) is different [here] from the rest of North Africa because we add peeled almonds to it. It's a way to pause time for at least an hour in the day, relax and chat. It's also a communal moment, as we bring in neighbours or visitors and exchange personal news, achievements or simply vent about something, or unwind while enjoying the patio views.

**DESERT OUTINGS:** At least twice a year, we head to the Sahara for some camel riding and sandboarding, and take new photos at the *Star Wars* shooting locations. It's not just for foreign tourists!

STEFANIA D'IGNOTI

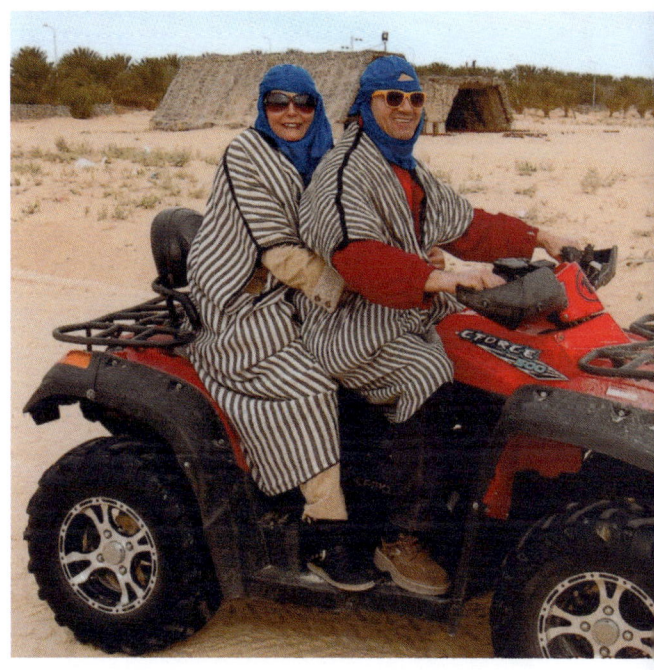

## Our favourite traditions

***Eid el-Fitr breakfast:*** The end of Ramadan marks the end of a month of fasting, so we get overexcited to have our coffee and tea in the morning again. It's a special time when all the family gathers together, and we enjoy a variety of delicious sweets after such a long wait.

***Bougainvillea hunt:*** We are a family of flower lovers, and we are lucky to live in a country that has a great variety of them. Our favourites are the purple bougainvillea, and every year in May we indulge ourselves with a scavenger hunt in Hergla – a seaside village near Sousse, famous for its white-and-blue houses overlooking the Mediterranean Sea – to find the best photo spots and add memories to our family album.

***The Festival of Carthage:*** Every summer, we head to the capital to attend this festival, held in the suggestive location of an ancient Roman amphitheatre. We love to celebrate Tunisia's rich history and enjoy a variety of performances, including music, theatre and dance.

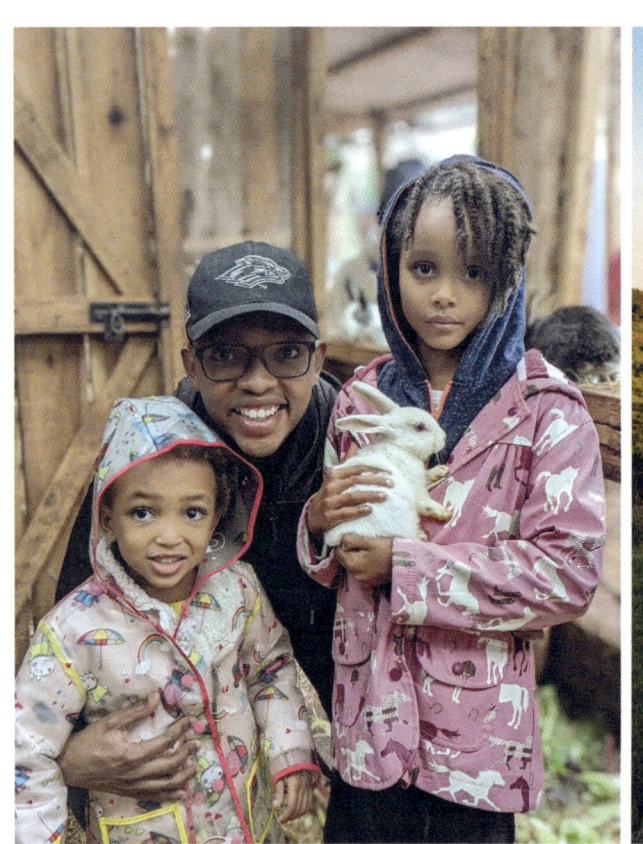
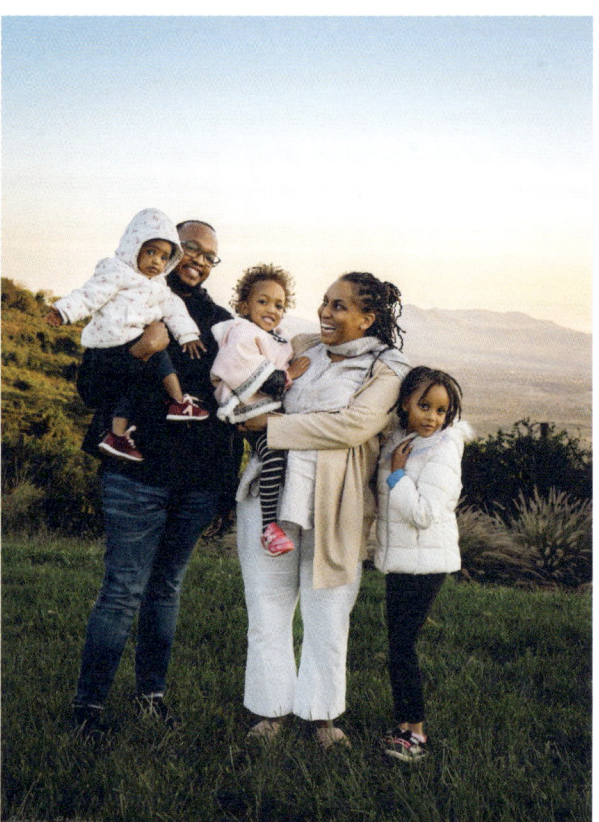

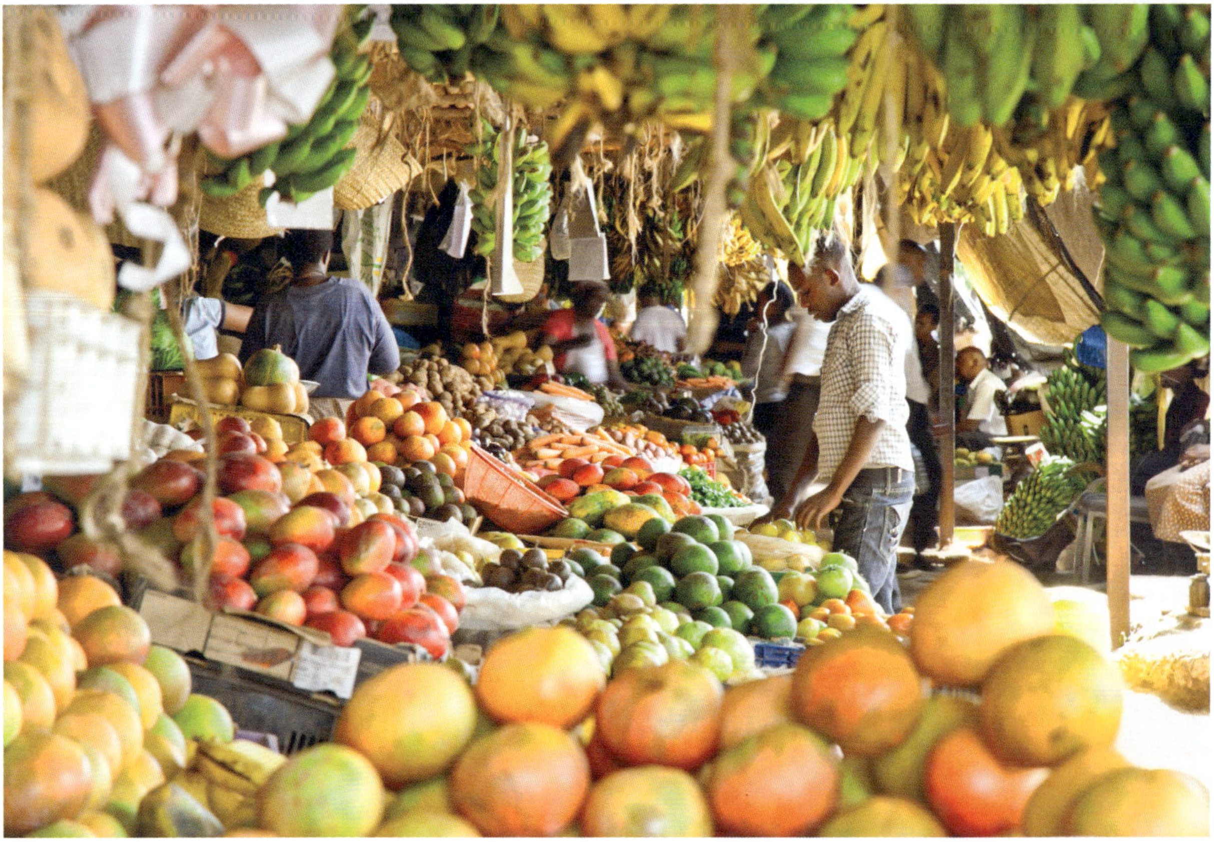

# Kenya

## CIRU KAIGWA

**WHERE CIRU LIVES:**
Nairobi, Kenya

**WHERE CIRU IS FROM:**
Nairobi, Kenya

Ciru was born in Nairobi to a Kenyan mother and half-Scottish father, and works as a physician. Her husband, Mark, was also born in Nairobi and works as a public speaker and entrepreneur in the technology space. The two met on a hike with a group of friends and then reconnected a few months later in Mark's research homeland, Twitter (now X). Ciru and Mark raise their children – Bella (8), Maya (5) and Wamuyu (3) – in a supportive web of extended family, which includes Mark's mother, Bella, and his grandmother, Nancy. The three generations live close to one another; their neighbourhoods are the epitome of the best parts of Nairobi – wide open spaces, lush greenery, and close-knit community.

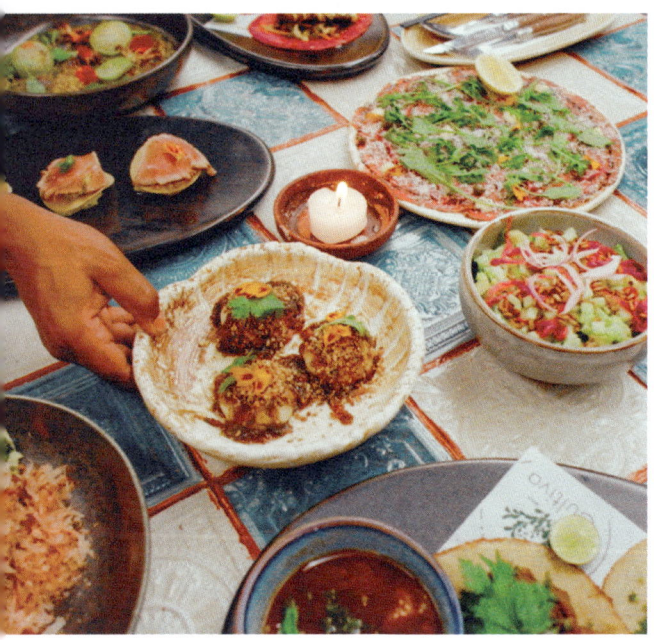

**CITY-VILLAGE:** A lot of people in Nairobi don't get to spend much time with their extended family. Many kids don't see their grandparents and great-grandparents that often compared to how it used to be, so maintaining those relationships comes down to our initiative as parents in making elders an active part of the family. We're lucky because *Cũcũ* Bella ('grandma' in Kikuyu) and *Maitũ* Nancy ('great-grandma' in Kikuyu) live close to us. I really do consider them as our co-parents.

**MATRIARCHS:** Our culture realises that women carry the bulk of the parenting responsibility, especially the day-to-day nurturing and the day-to-day planning that comes along with it. A lot of this parenting stuff is really not obvious. Sometimes it feels like there aren't enough hours in the day to balance taking care of myself with taking care of the kids, but I have been supported by women in the family since the beginning. From helping with meal prep to getting the girls to their extracurricular activities, their support has made all the difference.

**CEREMONY:** The way that women in the family welcomed me into motherhood made the transition much easier. When I was pregnant with my firstborn, *Cũcũ* Bella and her friends came together to formally welcome me in a ceremony called *itara*. It was somewhat of a baby shower but more so a rite of passage. Bella ended up being born on the same day as her *Cũcũ* Bella, which – considering the ceremony – was culturally meaningful. After baby Bella came, my mum also held a ceremony for me called *cugia mwana* (and this happened after each of my births) to bless me and bless the baby.

**BIRTH AFTERCARE:** We stayed with *Cũcũ* Bella for two weeks after I gave birth. I was plied with porridge and meals and people came to visit – it was a lot of love all around. Being surrounded by this deep understanding that my body had just gone through something genuinely massive and, honestly, traumatising, and to be given the space to heal – to not have to do that alone – was invaluable. I needed that more than I realised.

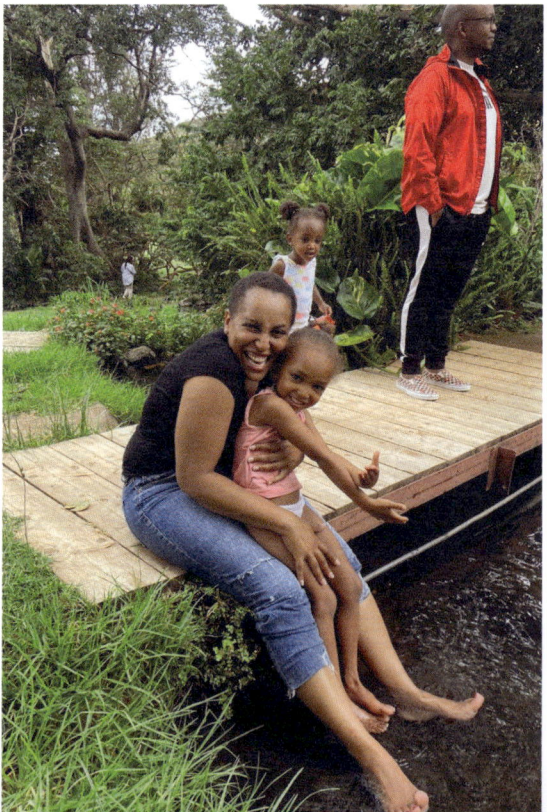

**GENTLE PARENTING:** Every child has their own personality, and each is a rebel in their own way. Spanking is a big trend here in Kenya, but I've chosen to embrace gentle parenting, which is a deviation from what is considered 'traditional'. We do still hold firm boundaries – these create a sense of security and bring structure to our little ones' lives – but that can play out while still foregrounding gentleness. We talk to our children a lot.

**ATTENTION SHIFTS:** At the beginning of our parenting journey, the support we received was oriented towards Mark and me as new parents, but now it's focused on the children. Cũcũ and Maitũ are actively involved in passing down lessons, teaching our girls cultural bits of wisdom, and helping to discipline them when needed. Our girls get the best of everything and everyone because we are each different parental figures, with different styles of engaging the kids.

**LANGUAGE:** Language is the deepest gateway to culture, and I want my girls to be empowered in their Kikuyu heritage. I've been conscientious about speaking Kikuyu (our tribal language) at home, and teaching the girls specific words and ways to express themselves. Some things don't have an English or even Kiswahili (one of Kenya's official languages) word for them – and these kinds of words and phrases are the ones I am intentional about passing down to our daughters.

**PROUDLY KENYAN:** On the way to school each morning, we play local radio stations – even ones that are in languages that are not our own. We want the kids to get used to hearing different indigenous languages, so that they can grow up being exposed to other tribes in order to truly understand and take pride in how diverse our country is.

NEEMA GITHERE

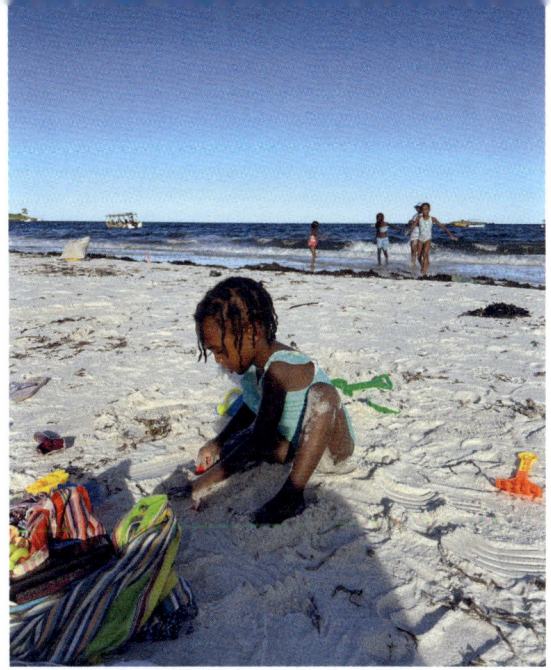

## Our favourite traditions

*Movie night:* The girls do a movie night with Cũcũ Bella on Fridays, and they always end up begging to sleep over. They love being at her house because she lives on a big compound with lots of fruit trees, and they have all the space to run around. She spoils them in the most wholesome way.

*Bible study:* Faith has been something that bonds us intergenerationally. The girls do Bible study on Thursdays together with Maitũ, and then go somewhere afterwards to eat. They spend the whole car ride singing hymns Maitũ teaches them. We say a prayer together before we part ways, and recently Maya's been leaping at the opportunity to lead it.

*Christmas lunch:* Our extended family is all so spread out – even as far as in Japan – so Christmas is our equivalent of a family reunion. It's helped us maintain strong connections, despite living on different continents. We recently started hosting a Christmas lunch at our house, and it warms my heart to see how much fun the girls have jumping on the trampoline in our backyard with all their cousins.

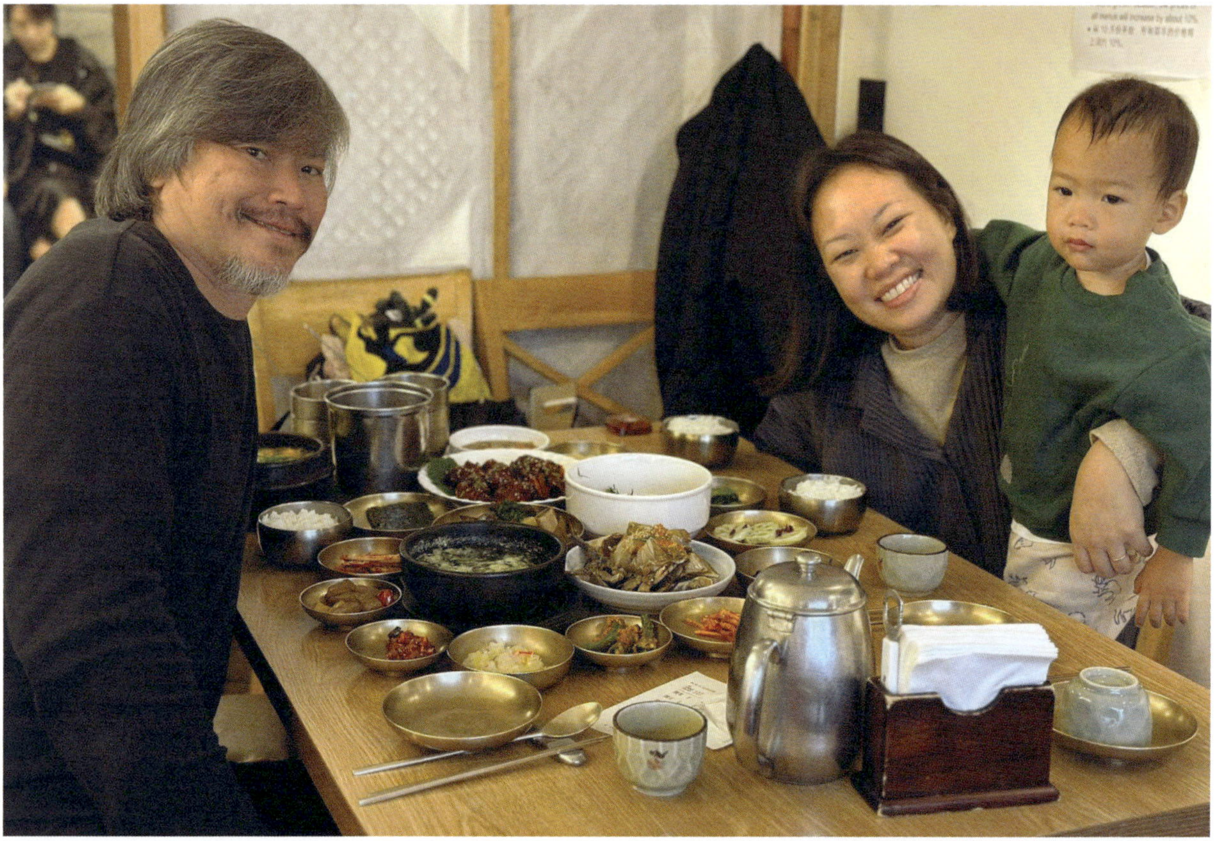

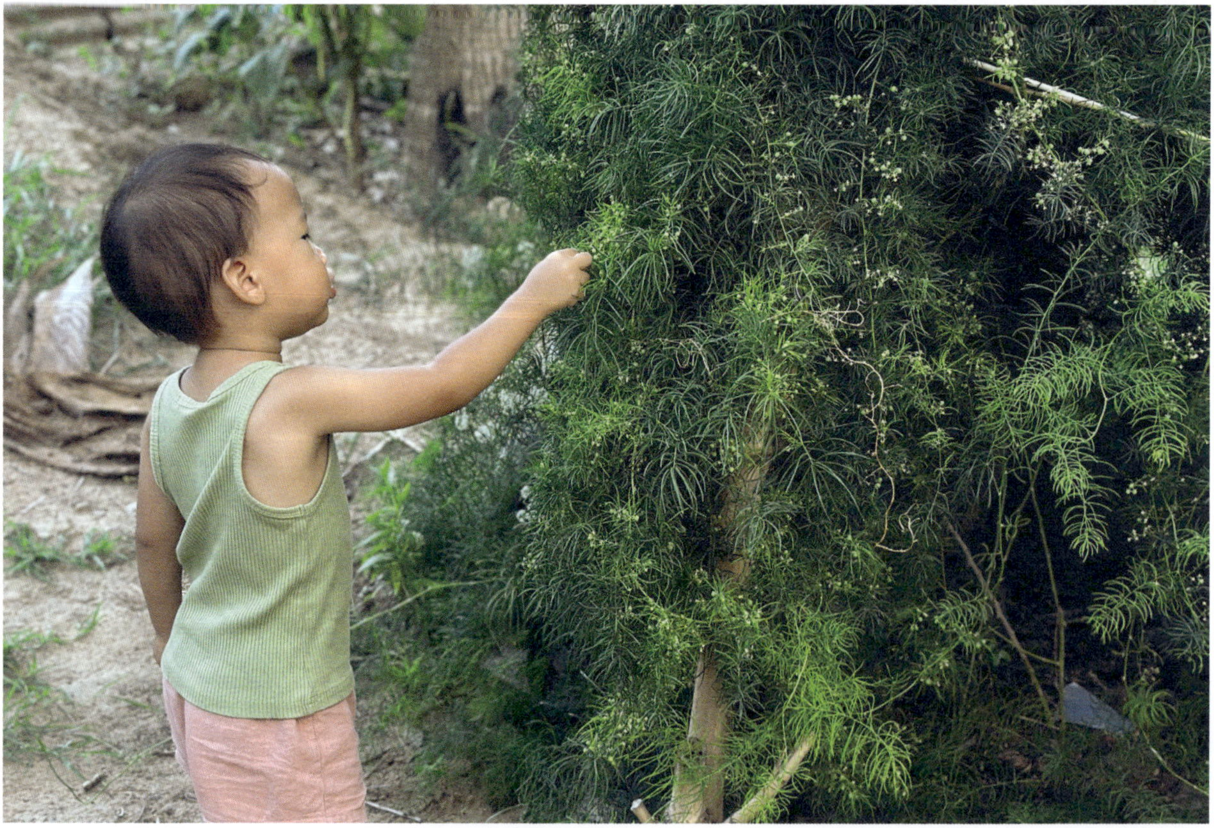

# Thailand

## MINT JARUKITTIKUN & PRIN POLSUK

**WHERE MINT & PRIN LIVE:**
Bangkok, Thailand

**WHERE MINT & PRIN ARE FROM:**
Bangkok and Chiang Mai, Thailand

Prin and Mint are the husband-and-wife team behind Samrub Samrub Thai. What started in 2016 as a clandestine chef's table – where in-the-know foodies would savour modern Thai comfort food – is now an internationally lauded restaurant. With a small team (kitchen and service run by Prin and Mint respectively), Samrub Samrub Thai once travelled around Bangkok as a pop-up. Since 2022, it's in a new dining space: the house where Mint grew up (her parents still live upstairs). The pair are now also parents to two-year-old Saam. Saam's name means 'three' in Thai (signifying the third component of their family), but Mint and Prin also joke that it's inspired by the restaurant too – *samrub* is a traditional Thai meal of rice paired with complementary dishes, like curry and stir-fry.

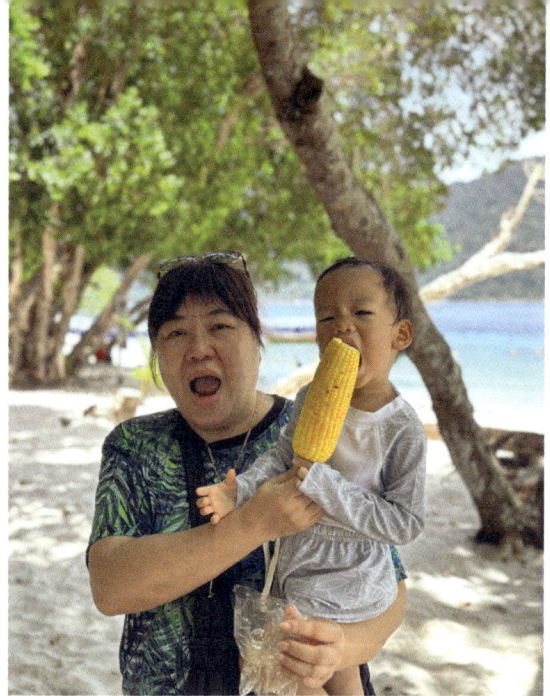

**GENERATIONS CARING FOR EACH OTHER:** When I was young, I tried to separate myself from my family to find freedom and independence. After becoming a parent, I started to think more about Saam's relationship to his grandparents. Running a busy restaurant, it was sometimes difficult to find time to see each other – especially Prin's family, who are in Chiang Mai. Respect and loyalty for one's family is an important part of Thai culture. So, to be closer to my parents, we asked them if we could renovate the ground floor of their four-storey house and convert it into a restaurant. We take care of them (by paying rent, a passive income for their retirement); and every day they support our busy lifestyles by taking care of Saam. (*Mint*)

**DAILY ROUTINE:** Running a restaurant, open five nights a week, our lives have to be very structured. Work days start walking with Prin and Saam from our home just a couple minutes away. My parents take care of Saam, cook him breakfast or sometimes take him to a nearby mall. Of course, Prin and I visit throughout the day as we're in between working. (*Mint*)

Saam spends at least a little time in the restaurant every day. Sometimes, he eats dinner together with us and the staff. We put him to bed upstairs before service starts and, when we're closed for the evening, take him home for a good night's rest. (*Prin*)

**COOKING AS A LOVE LANGUAGE:** I cooked a lot with my *yaai* (grandmother) growing up. We would go to the market every week and buy ingredients together. She taught me how to cook and, as I got older, I loved to cook a lot for her. Many of her recipes, like radish cake, I still make often today. Showing someone you love them by making food for them is very special. Today, Saam cooks a lot with his *yaai*. When they make radish cake, it reminds me of my grandmother. One day, I hope he can cook for them and experience that joy, too. (*Mint*)

**SHARING ETHNICITY THROUGH FOOD:** I am a quarter Chinese through my grandparents, who emigrated to Thailand from China, and I want Saam to know and value this heritage. We often go to Chinatown so he can see Bangkok's important Thai-Chinese legacy, and spend time walking around the bazaar on Sampeng Lane or eating traditional street food. (*Mint*)

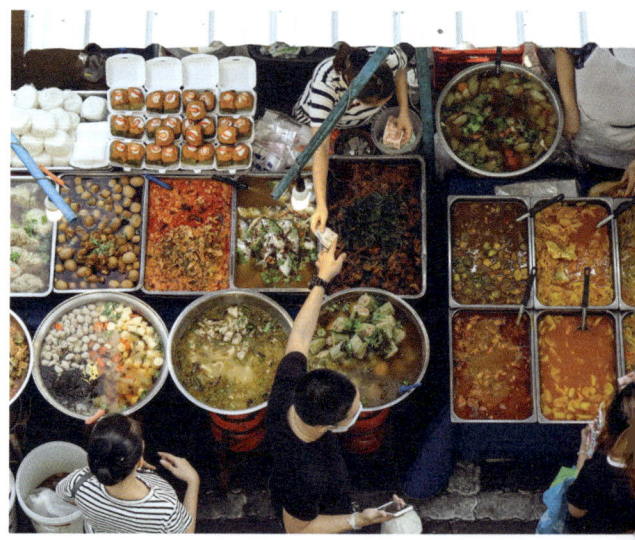

# "Sharing dishes celebrates togetherness."

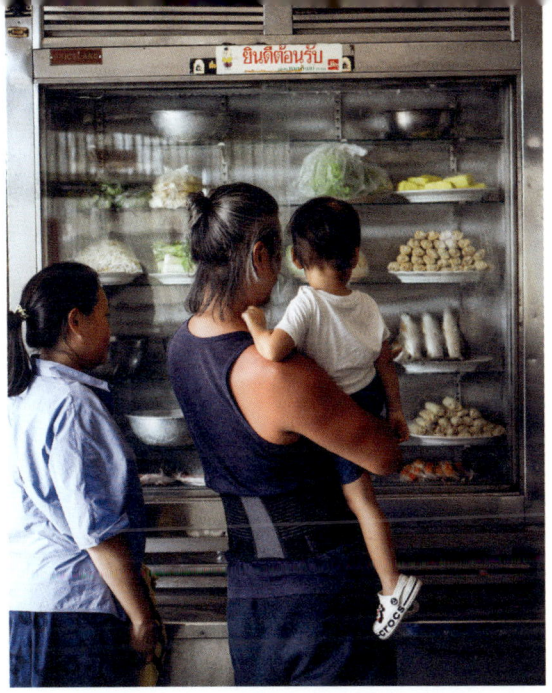

**LEARNING BY EXAMPLE:** When Saam comes down to the restaurant, he sees us tasting and trialling recipes and wants to 'explore' the ingredients too. Sitting on the counter, he picks a little of this and that – bitter beans, rice noodles, whatever's around. He'll watch us add seasoning to something, and he'll want some. Even when it's chilli, he might tear up, but soon, he's right back to being curious! (*Mint*)

**BUILDING MATURITY:** Saam spends a lot of time with adults. He is exposed to an atmosphere that is not only very creative and open-minded, but also very multicultural and community oriented. (*Mint*)

This means he's constantly around new people and trying new things, thanks to our 'extended family' in gastronomy. He often eats 'staff dinner' (a shared nightly meal before service) with our team which includes a revolving door of 'stages' (restaurant interns) from all over the world – India, Switzerland, Bali and beyond. So, one night he'll have Thai street food, the next night, steak, Indonesian seafood, whatever! (*Prin*)

By raising a mature child, this allows our family to travel together to conferences or Prin's spots as a guest chef in other countries; for example, recently in Germany and Denmark. Saam joins us at fine-dining restaurants, eating at tables alongside Michelin-starred chefs. We often joke that he's a little adult, and a friend to us. (*Mint*)

BARBARA WOOLSEY

## Our favourite traditions

***Going out for dinner:*** Bangkok is chaotic, but we always find peaceful family time dining out. We go out for everything: street food, Japanese, Korean, Italian. Our approach to eating together is thoughtful, like meditation. (*Prin*)

***Market-hopping:*** As chefs, we want to teach Saam that food doesn't come from supermarkets; it's grown and harvested. On days off, we visit fresh markets and farms, walking around tomato fields and saying hi to buffaloes. (*Mint*)

***Sunday family dinners:*** Once a week, our extended family meets at my aunt's house. The kids play together, grandma makes curry paste, and the house smells like garlic and chilli. We sit down family-style or *gap kao* (literally 'with rice' or 'Let's eat!' in Thai); sharing dishes celebrates togetherness. (*Mint*)

***Cooking family recipes:*** Since Prin's away from where he grew up in northern Thailand, he cooks a lot of northern dishes for Saam: jackfruit curry, Burmese pork curry, tomato soup with rice noodles. Prin's mother sends us veggies from her organic garden in Chiang Mai, too. (*Mint*)

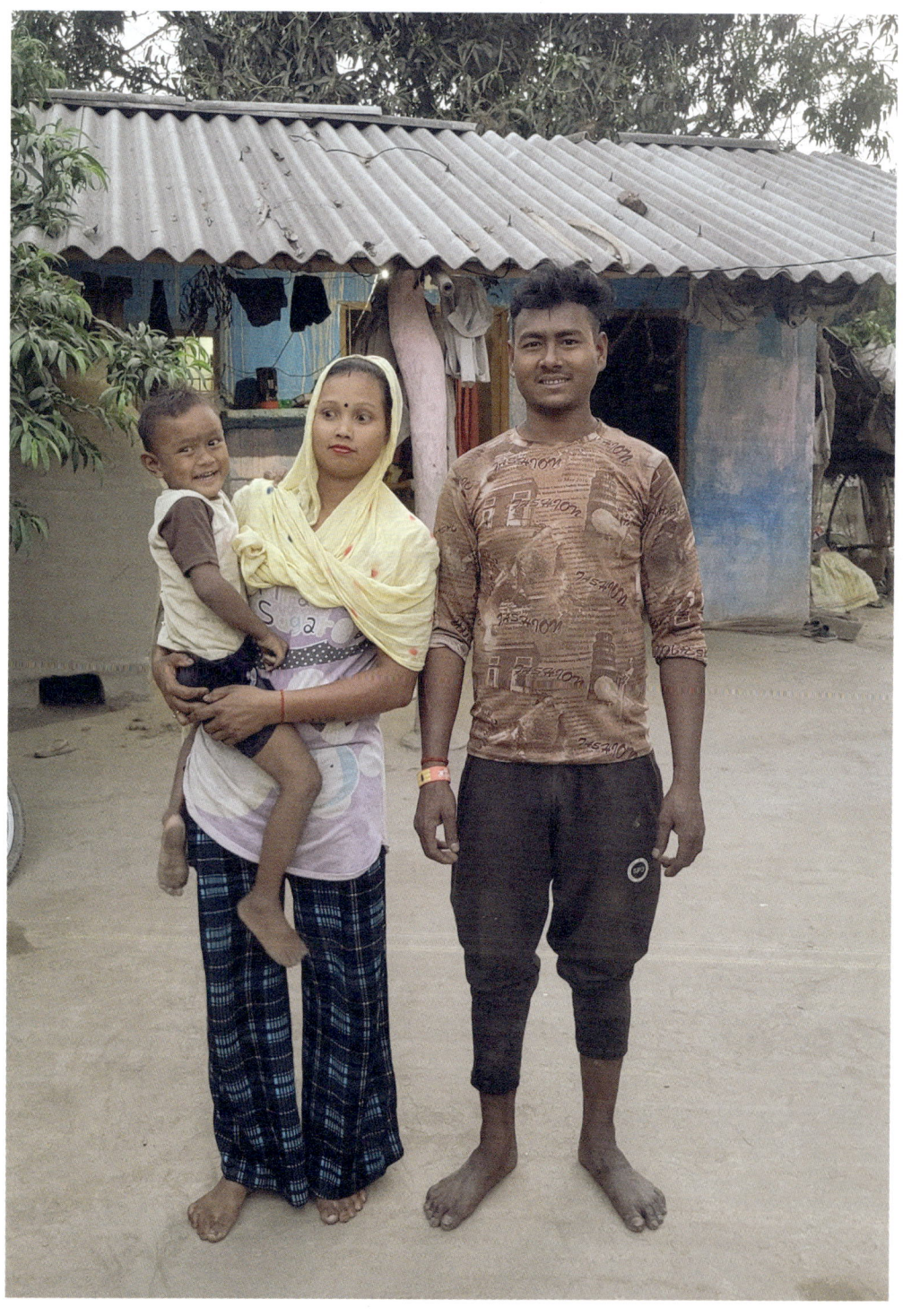

# India

## ASHA DEVI

**WHERE ASHA LIVES:**
Kishan Nagar Village, India

**WHERE ASHA IS FROM:**
Kishan Nagar Village, India

Asha was born in a farming village near the Indo–Nepal border. She belongs to a Tharu tribe that migrated from Nepal to work on nearby farms in India. As a young girl, Asha spent her days gathering firewood and tending to grazing goats with the other children in her village; she didn't have a chance to go to school. She met her husband Shiva when they were teenagers and they courted for two years, often meeting in the same sugar-cane field, where Asha gathered fodder for animals, and Shiva serendipitously came to cut cane. Asha takes care of their two young sons, Aryan (eight) and Parveen (four) – and a large flock of sheep – while Shiva works as a builder in another part of India.

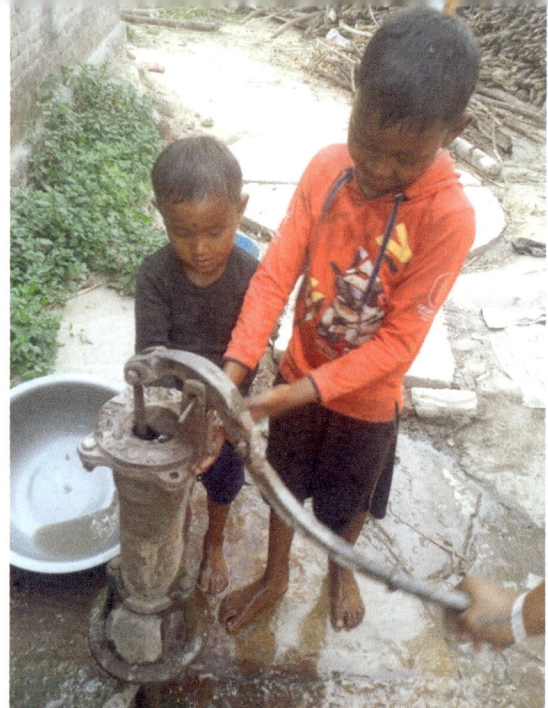

**EARLY TO RISE:** We all wake up at 5am and go outside to the tap to wash. Sometimes the boys collect firewood or fetch water and help me sweep the house; otherwise, they look at my mobile phone. I make the fire and by 6am we all have chai (spiced black tea). After preparing food and eating breakfast, I take the boys to school and go to work at the sheep shed.

**FOOD AND WATER MANAGEMENT:** The water in our tap is usually yellow, so I collect drinking water from our neighbour's tap instead. I usually cook rice and vegetables for breakfast and also make lentils and rotis (flatbreads) for dinner. I always store breakfast leftovers for lunch, but need to put everything in a basket in the kitchen cupboard to keep it safe from the monkeys, cats and birds.

**MONDAY PRAYER TIME:** Monday mornings I pray with my sons at Lord Shiva's statue in my room and make a clay Shiva lingam (symbol) outside. I have always prayed for our family like this: that my husband, my children, and all of us will be free of trouble and sickness.

**RESPECTING (AND IGNORING!) PARENTS:** My four-year-old son always touches my feet in respect before he goes to school. If he forgets even one day, he says 'Mummy, I'm sorry I forgot!' But not my eight-year-old; he doesn't pay so much attention to his parents. The moment he gets my mobile phone to watch YouTube, he forgets his mummy and papa!

**FAMILY MEALS AND DISPUTES:** We used to eat our meals with my in-laws in the family compound: grandparents, parents, uncles, aunties and children together. But then my father-in-law became angry with my husband about money issues. The village leaders told us to separate our finances and our kitchens. We still live in the same compound, but now I cook in my own kitchen and eat separately with my sons in our room. My in-laws still play a lot with my sons (and my older son often sleeps with grandma), but they don't speak to me or my husband.

**SCHOOLING:** I never had a chance to go to school, so the most important thing for me is that my children are educated. Our older son used to go to school every day, but now he doesn't want to learn. The local school doesn't have enough

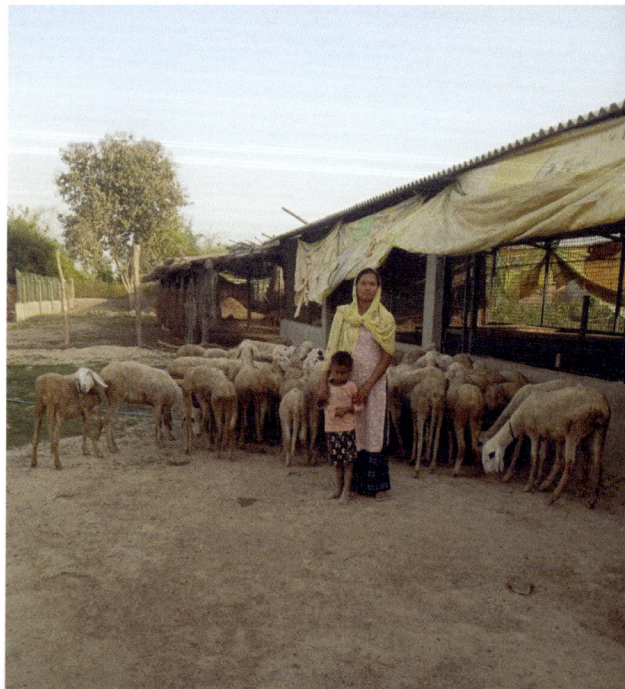

teachers, and they don't care about the kids. So now my son just goes to play by the river with his friends. Maybe if he can get through Grade 5, I can get him admission to a better school.

**FAMILY SUPPORT:** I am happy I live in the place where I was born and got married. I can always see my parents, brothers and sisters, and I have their support. When the kids are sick, my family helps get medicine, consults the shaman and takes us to the hospital. And if I am sick, the whole family helps take care of me. And since my husband is away, my family comes to help maintain the house.

**MONSOON PARENTING:** It is very difficult in the rainy season: we all have to help each other. We have to keep the firewood dry, otherwise we can't cook. And if the goats can't graze, we have to collect leaves for them to eat inside. The recent earthquake damaged our roof. We had to put so many bowls out to collect the water leaking in our bedroom! But now it is fixed.

**BEDTIME:** We all sleep in the same room, on two beds which are pushed together. Before we sleep, we watch recent episodes of the latest TV series on YouTube on my mobile phone. Then my younger son tells me about his day. This is one of my favourite times: no matter how tired I am, I feel happy when my children tell me stories about their days.

AMBIKA ANAND PROKOP

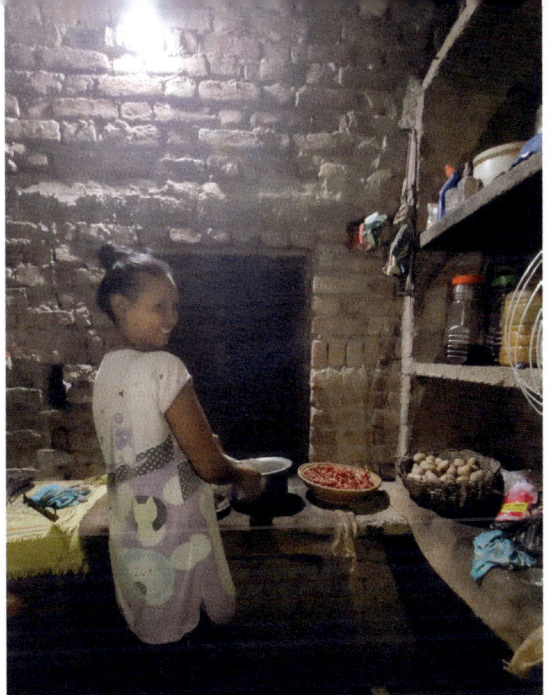

> "We all sleep in the same room, on two beds which are pushed together."

## Our favourite traditions

***Newborn celebration:*** On the sixth day after birth, the whole village comes to bless the baby. The women of the family cook food and set the table with flowers, oil lamps and a platter to collect gifts. Both times [after the birth of each child] I sat there for two hours with my baby, but people stayed into the night, dancing to the music till 3am!

***Dussehra Festival of the Mother Goddess:*** Every household gathers at the river with straw idols of the Mother Goddess which we light and set afloat. Then the whole village feasts together by the water. If a baby boy was born that year, we sacrifice a male goat and make goat curry for the village to share. I love celebrating with everyone. It's a time of happiness.

***Annual village outing:*** Once a year, the whole village goes to Poonagiri Temple together. We walk or bike together to the river, cross by boat and hire a bus to the mountains. Then we all climb to the temple and pray to Durga Maa (Mother Goddess) to bless our home and family for the year.

ASIA

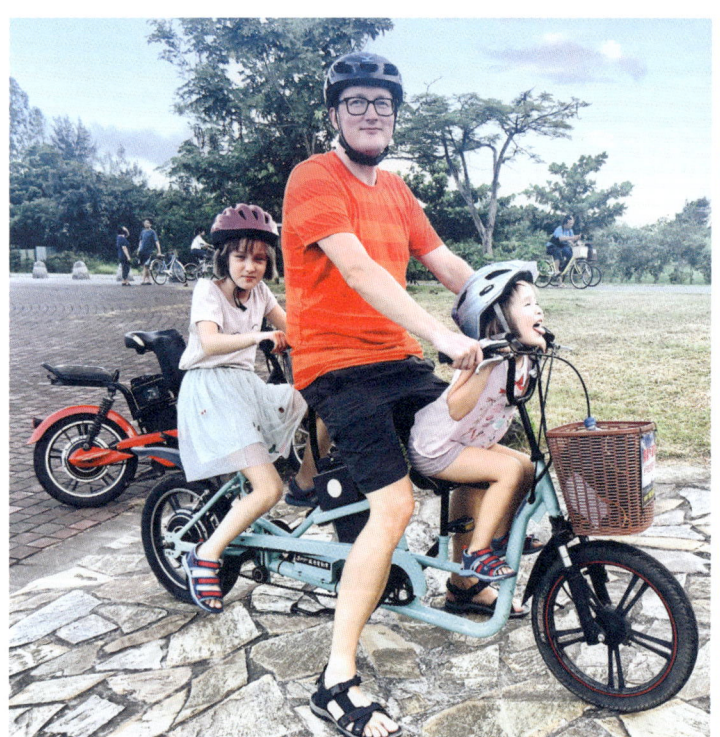
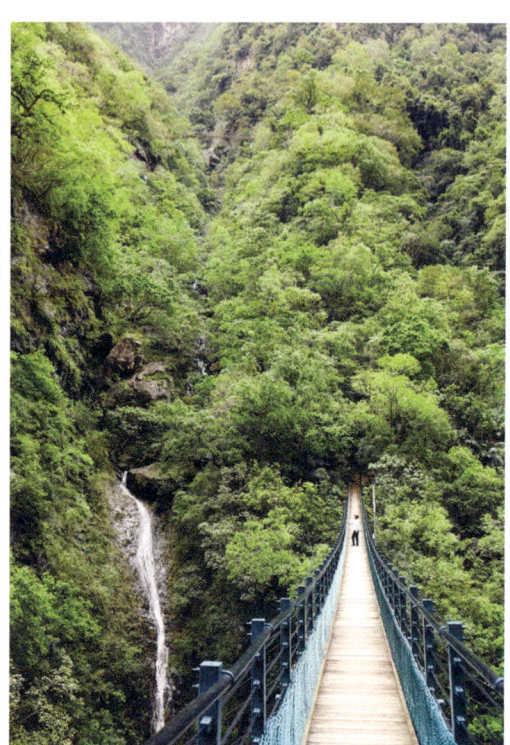
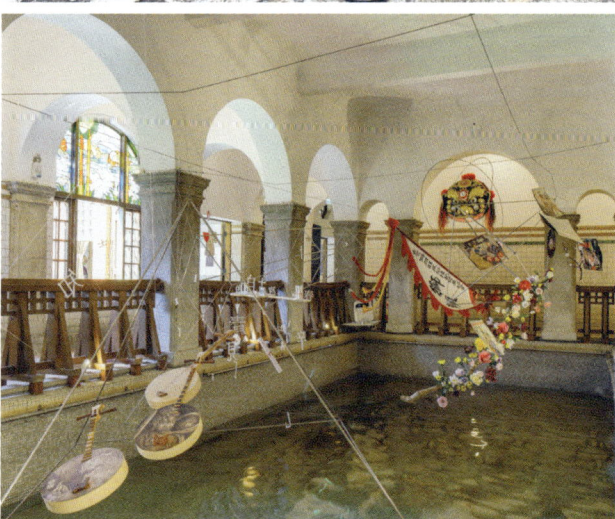
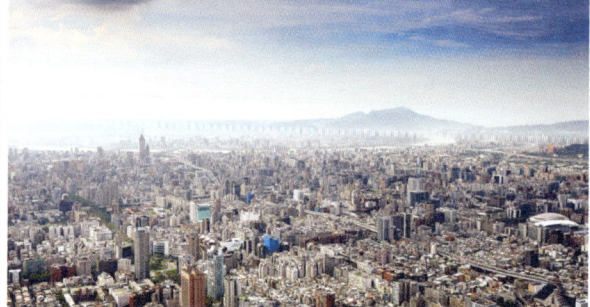
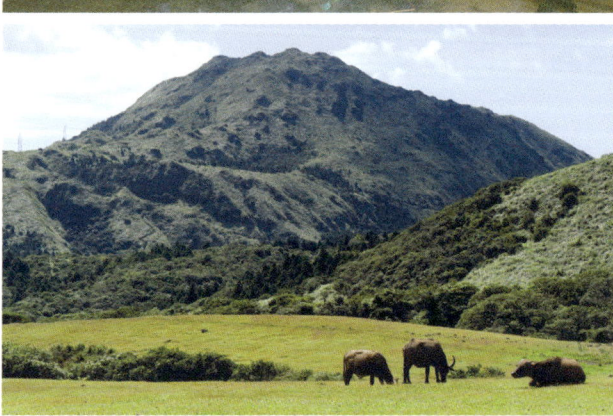
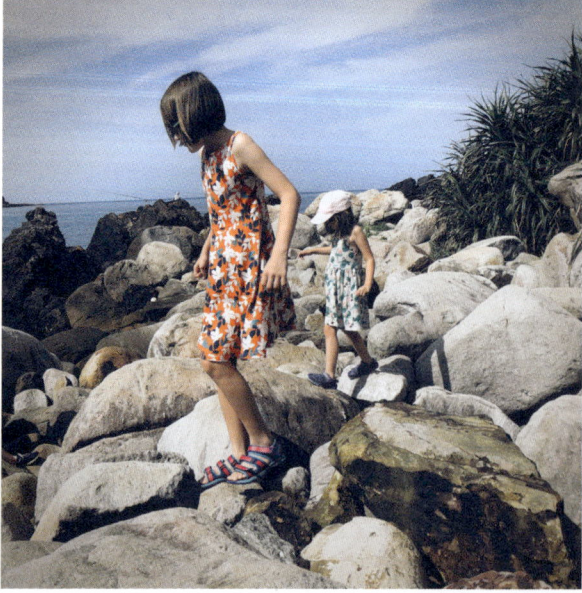

# Taiwan

## JESSICA WANG SIMULA

**WHERE JESSICA LIVES:**
Taipei, Taiwan

**WHERE JESSICA IS FROM:**
Taipei, Taiwan

Jessica and her family moved back to Taipei, her birthplace, five years ago. Before that, she had been 'all over the place'. She emigrated to Auckland at age 13; studied in Auckland, Brisbane, Sydney and London; worked in London and Shanghai; and it was in Sydney that she met her Finnish husband Mikko, while both were doing their master's degrees. Suvi (12) and Nora (nine), were born in England during the family's decade there before relocating to Taipei. Jessica, an only child, wants to spend more time with her parents. Mikko, who works in renewables, says, 'Taiwan started tapping into offshore wind about seven years ago. Jessica was keen to come here, so I actively looked for a job. It's worked out very well for us.'

**FAVOURITE HOLIDAY SPOT:** Xiaoliuqiu Island is so relaxed. You can swim and snorkel with green turtles. There are no cars. You can just get an electric bike and go round the island. Mikko got a tandem so he carried the kids. I had my own bike. And we just cycled from one place to another, for ice-cream, food, bubble tea… I also like Dong He, a tiny village on the east coast between Taichung and Hualian. The beaches there are not for swimming, but they're very, very pretty.

**SCHOOL WORK:** I'd say Finnish culture has influenced the way I see education. I grew up in Taiwan, so it was more academic for me. But now I find myself quite relaxed compared to many Asian parents. I'm not too worried about grades. Well, maybe a little. But in general, I'm fine as long as the kids finish their homework. I like them to have hobbies that have nothing to do with extra academic work. The girls, especially Suvi, like drawing and painting. But I don't believe in art lessons. It's more important for them to see rather than learn.

**MUSEUMS:** I studied literature and art history, and worked for a museum and an arts charity. In the UK, I started taking the children to museums when they were very young. I can't say they love visual arts but they're used to museums, they can manage. We've been to the majority of museums in Taipei. Suvi and Nora like the National Taiwan Museum, including its exhibition hall, [which is housed in an old bank just across the road], because there's a lot on Taiwan's flora and fauna, including huge dinosaur models – my kids love animals. We also like exploring smaller, lesser-known museums, such as the Hot Spring Museum in Beitou. We take the metro to Beitou station. There's a park and a thermal steam, and there are two Japanese-era houses with a museum inside. It's one of our favourites, I'd say.

**STRUGGLES:** [One] thing I find a bit difficult is 'aunties' telling the kids what to do. Strangers coming up to me and asking: 'Are your kids not cold wearing so little?' Or my mum's sisters telling them to greet people, and why don't you do this or that. I find 'Why don't you' questions irritating. That said, I do like that the kids realise how safe Taiwan really is. We've just been to America and you can see them physically relax when they're back in Taiwan. Also, the first thing they want after a long trip is bubble tea and beef noodles.

**THE OUTDOORS:** Nature is wonderful in Taiwan, even in Taipei. The girls may not like the hard work of going up a mountain, but they enjoy flat, grassy areas, such as Qingtiangang Grassland with the buffaloes. We go for family bike rides along the river. We have six bikes at home, one for each of us and two for Mikko, and a trolley for the dog. We've also done three road trips around the island – clockwise, anticlockwise, then a zigzag down the middle. Taiwan is quite a small place so it's not hours and hours of driving like in the US or Australia. The trips took about nine days each, including two weekends. The only difficult part was the mountains down the middle. It's beautiful but the kids got car sick.

**CULTURAL IDENTITY:** I struggled with my own identity – I did not like being Asian as a teen in New Zealand, but I feel my daughters are very comfortable with their multiple identities. I think it's cool. Nora will list everything – 'Oh my grandfather's from there, my dad's from Finland, my mum's from…' She's proud of that diversity in her. Suvi may feel more Taiwanese, not Taiwanese-Taiwanese, but she doesn't want to leave Taiwan – that I know.

*PIERA CHEN*

## Our favourite traditions

**Stories:** On road trips, the children listen to audiobooks and tell stories to each other in the car. No iPads because it's bad for the eyes and they get car sick.

**Crafty Christmas:** I decorate the house full-on at Christmas. The kids do the tree and wreath with me. We use dry flowers, recycle old baubles and decorations that are falling apart. We take turns choosing a theme. Last year Nora decided it was going to be colourful, this year I get to choose.

**Gratitude:** Every night, we ask the children what they are grateful for that day. It doesn't matter what they say. It could be 'I ate this' or, for the older one, 'The exam's not as hard as I thought.'

**Porridge:** I make *kaurapuuro* (Finnish oatmeal porridge) for breakfast every weekend. The girls don't like it but I think they'll miss it when they're in their 30s. Our first weekend in Taiwan, I cooked porridge and they were shocked. 'What? In Taiwan too?' I said, 'Yes, it's something we take with us wherever we go.'

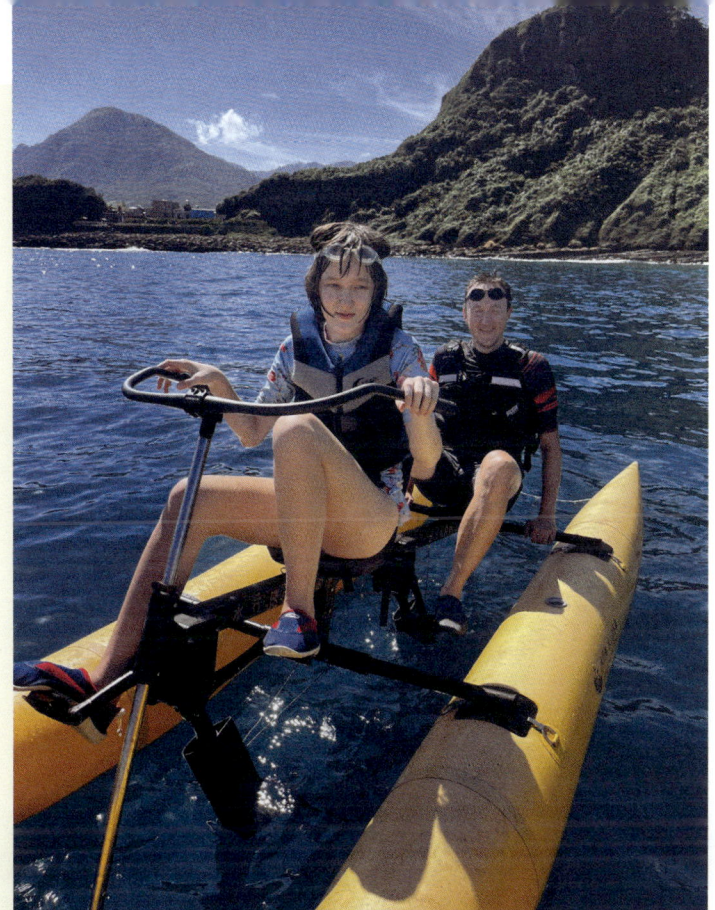

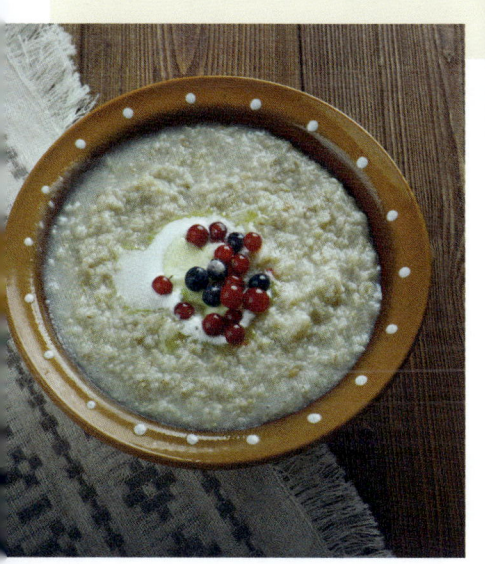

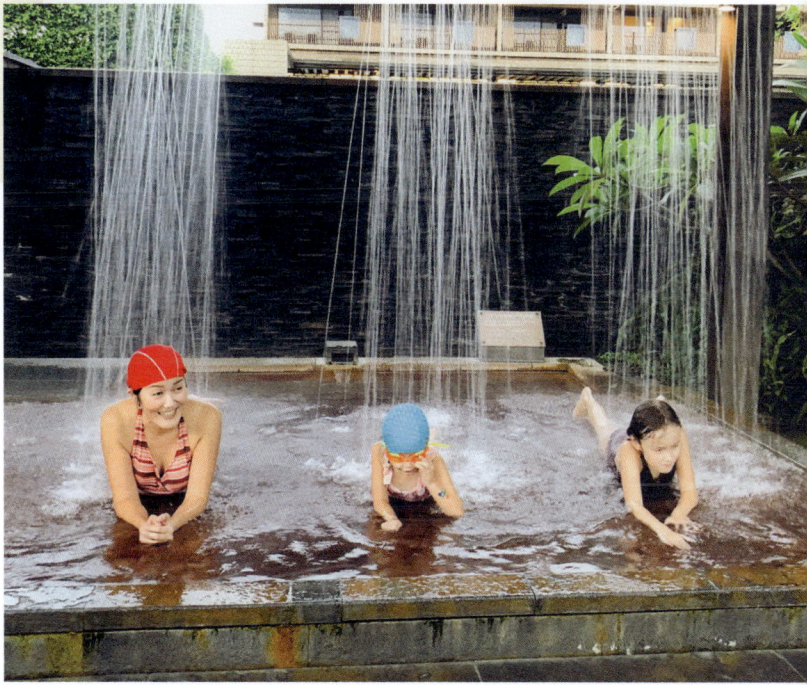

ASIA

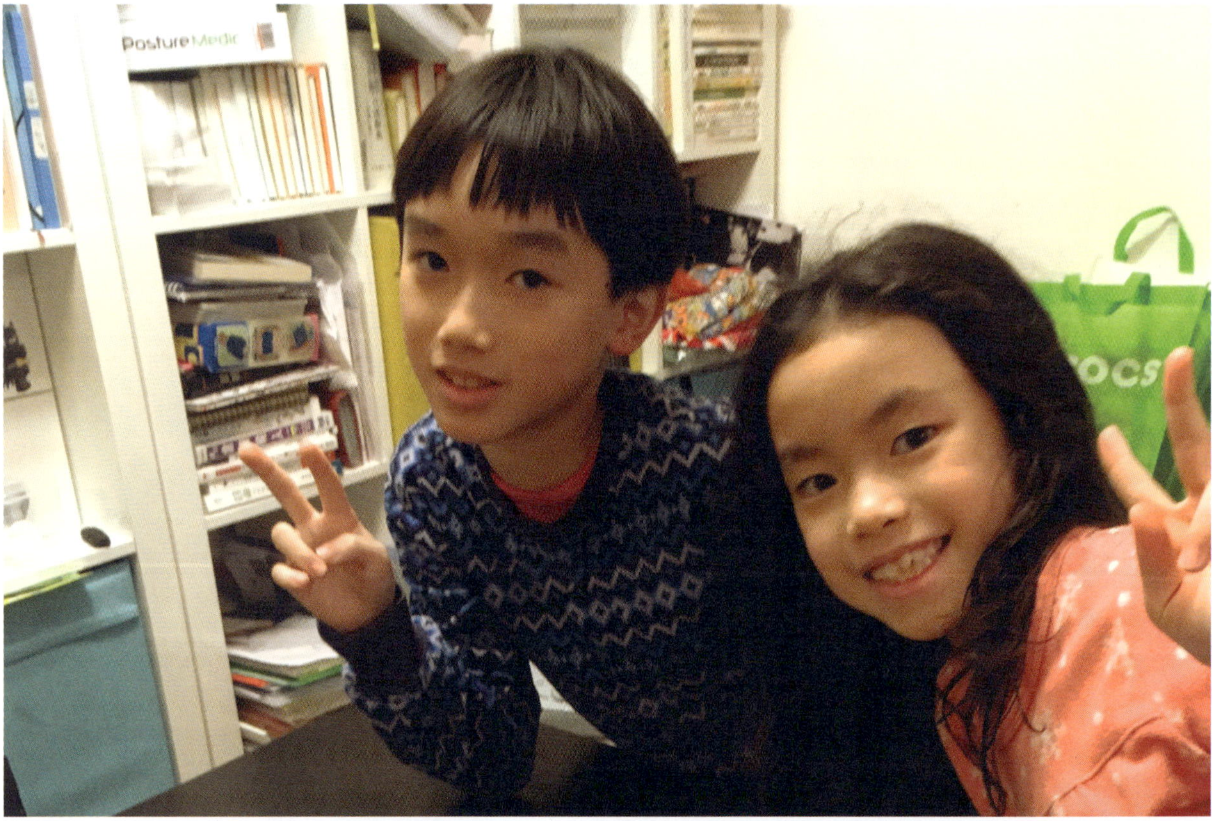

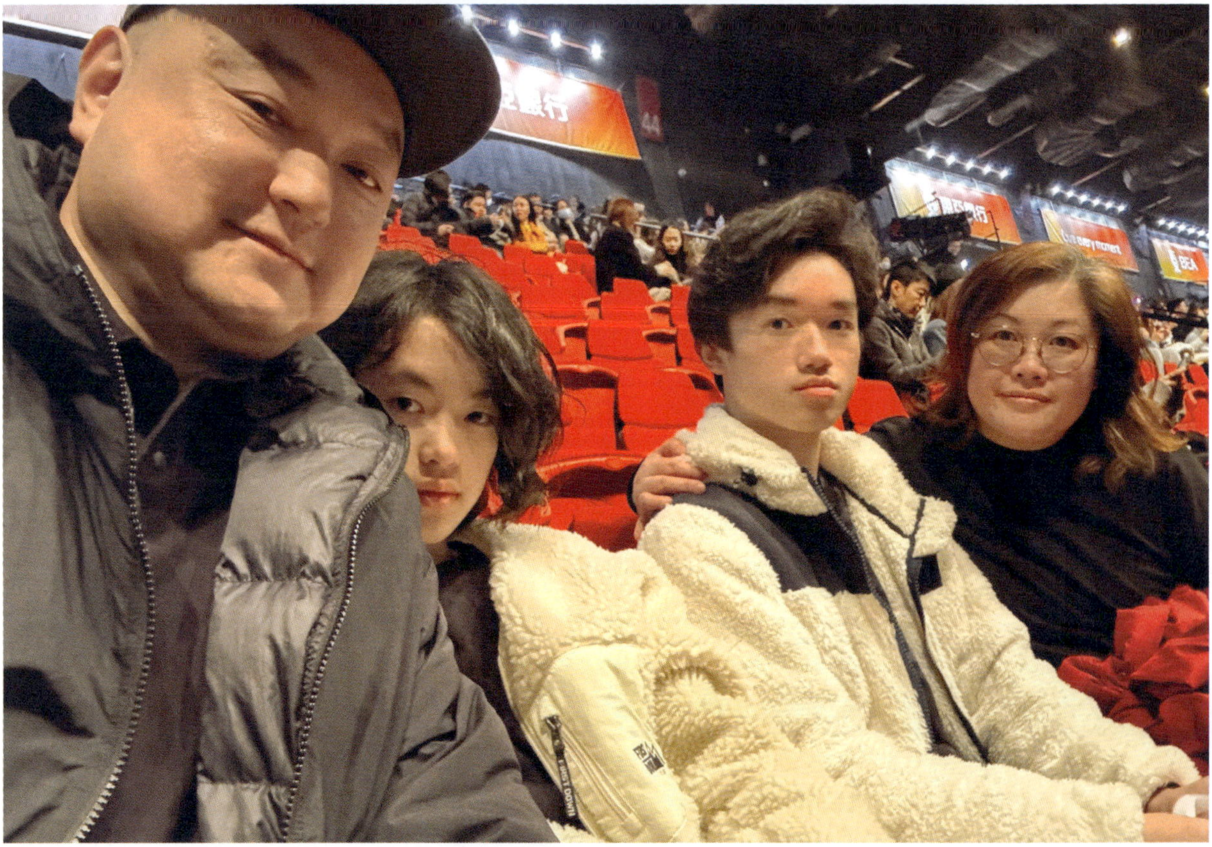

# China

## YVONNE CHU

**WHERE YVONNE LIVES:**
Hong Kong, China

**WHERE YVONNE IS FROM:**
Hong Kong, China

Yvonne was born in Hong Kong to an Indigenous Hakka family dating back to the 18th century, and lived in the ancestral village home until she was 20. She met her husband Terry at university, but it was a decade after graduation, when she was an editor for parenting publications, and he, a creative director at an ad agency, that they began dating. During both her pregnancies, Yvonne was told her babies might have Down's syndrome. Both times, she decided to have the child. Fuji, now 17, and Bella, 15, were born without Down's syndrome. But weeks of waiting for test results left their mark. 'It dawned on me and Terry that our children's lives are not within our control. This has deeply affected our parenting style', she says.

**RADISH RITUAL:** When the kids were little, we wanted to give them a taste they'll associate with their childhood, no matter where they are. Back in the village, my dad used to make the most delicious radish cake during the Lunar New Year. I wanted to replicate the taste and the ritual of making it. So, radish cake it was. We let them help with washing radishes when they were just shy of two. Then we gave them a small chunk to shred. Later we showed them how to mix the radish with the meat and the mushrooms. Then how to stir-fry and steam. We let go a little each year – it was a mess at first – until finally, this year, they made several cakes by themselves. We give away dozens to friends every Lunar New Year.

**STARGAZING:** One of my friends is a night-sky photographer who takes stunning photos. Two years ago, I brought the kids on a stargazing trip with him to East Dam along the MacLehose Trail. On the way there, Bella was texting her friend: 'What the heck is Mum doing dragging us to the boonies at this hour?' We didn't see many stars that night because of the clouds and the sky was too bright – from the moon, not city lights. But it was so quiet and beautiful, even Bella agreed the trip was worth it. Some time later, we went to Shek O on a clear night and finally saw a sky full of stars.

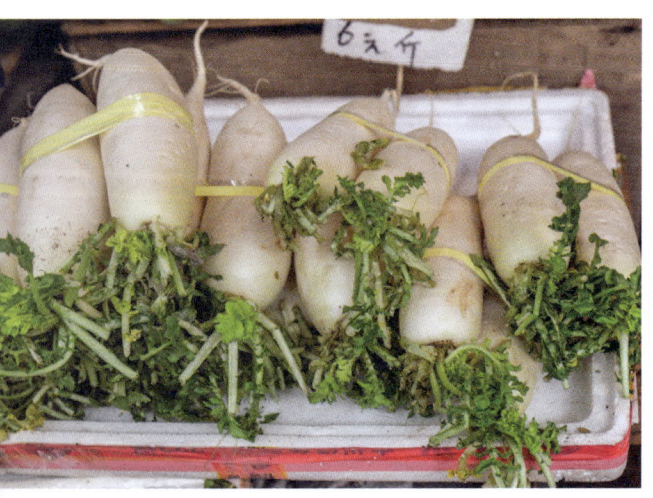

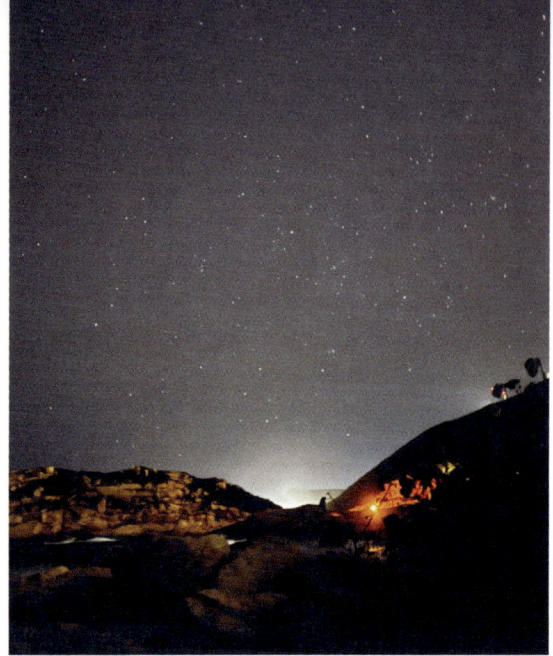

**ROPE SKIPPING:** Fuji and Bella are on the official Hong Kong Rope Skipping Team. Last year they went to Iowa for a contest, then to New York for the Double-Dutch championships. But back when they first started, I had no idea they were going to be serious. One day after school in Primary One, Bella said she saw classmates skipping and that it's 'Super cool'. A year later she made the school team and eventually Fuji joined as well. I treated it as a nice-to-have activity and would tell them before contests: 'Don't worry, just do your best.' One time, Bella retorted: 'Mum, do you think any contestant actually wants to lose?' Now I try to calm her nerves by doing breathing exercises with her and analysing her jumbled up emotions so she is not overpowered by imaginary fears.

**SOPHISTICATED TASTES:** They never really watched children's cartoons because we don't like them ourselves. We shoved them right into Hayao Miyazaki [award-winning Japanese animator and filmmaker] from the get-go. In school, they realised their classmates were brought up with different cartoons. As they got older, we introduced them to movies. Fuji loves historical films, like *Dunkirk* and *Churchill*.

**FARMING AND FISHING:** When the kids were younger, we would go with other families to Yi O on Lantau Island, where a cooperative is bringing abandoned rice paddies back to life. [One time] Bella and Fuji went wild; running around, chasing frogs. We all got in the mud to plant rice seedlings. On another visit, we weeded the fields – different things to do in different seasons. Another time, we joined a shrimp-boat tour of Yi O to learn about fishing practices in Hong Kong and see how shrimp are harvested. Afterwards the fishers boiled some water and blanched the shrimp right there on the deck. What a feast it was.

**WET MARKET:** We take the kids to wet markets, such as Tai Po Hui Market, so they know what food actually looks like – steamed chicken had feathers and fried fish used to swim. Some kids are scared of livestock because they're so used to seeing animals dead. We want them to know what goes into a meal, from picking ingredients, to prep, to cooking. Things they wouldn't have known if we only ate out or shopped at supermarkets.

PIERA CHEN

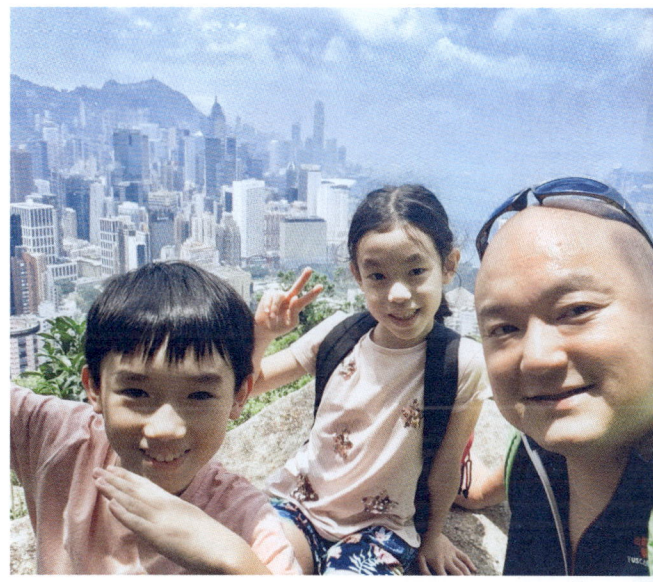

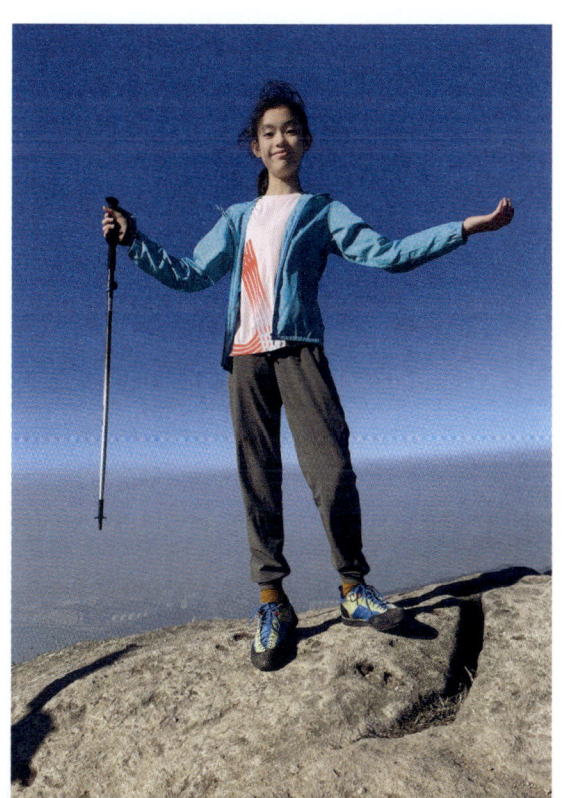

## Our favourite traditions

**Household chores:** We started the kids on housework early because we wanted them to see chores in a positive light, as a contribution to the house. Fuji washed his first bowl at six. Now when we're busy, the kids cook. Fuji can make Hong Kong dishes, like chicken wings and potatoes, but also steak and spaghetti bolognese. Bella's signature is cakes and crepes.

**Books:** We always left books lying around the house when they were younger. I read with them too, of course. And every summer, they were with me in the publisher's booth at the Book Fair.

**Eating out:** We rarely eat out but when we do, we pick a nice place. One time, we asked Fuji where he wanted to go for his birthday. He said, 'A restaurant where I'll need to wear a suit.' So, we went to a fancy Mediterranean place. His verdict was: 'Dad cooks better!'

**Crafts:** We make gifts by upcycling newspaper, old tissue boxes and bottles. Bella once made a lovely clay tableau for her brother's birthday. It had a pond, birds and trees, like a quaint ornamental garden.

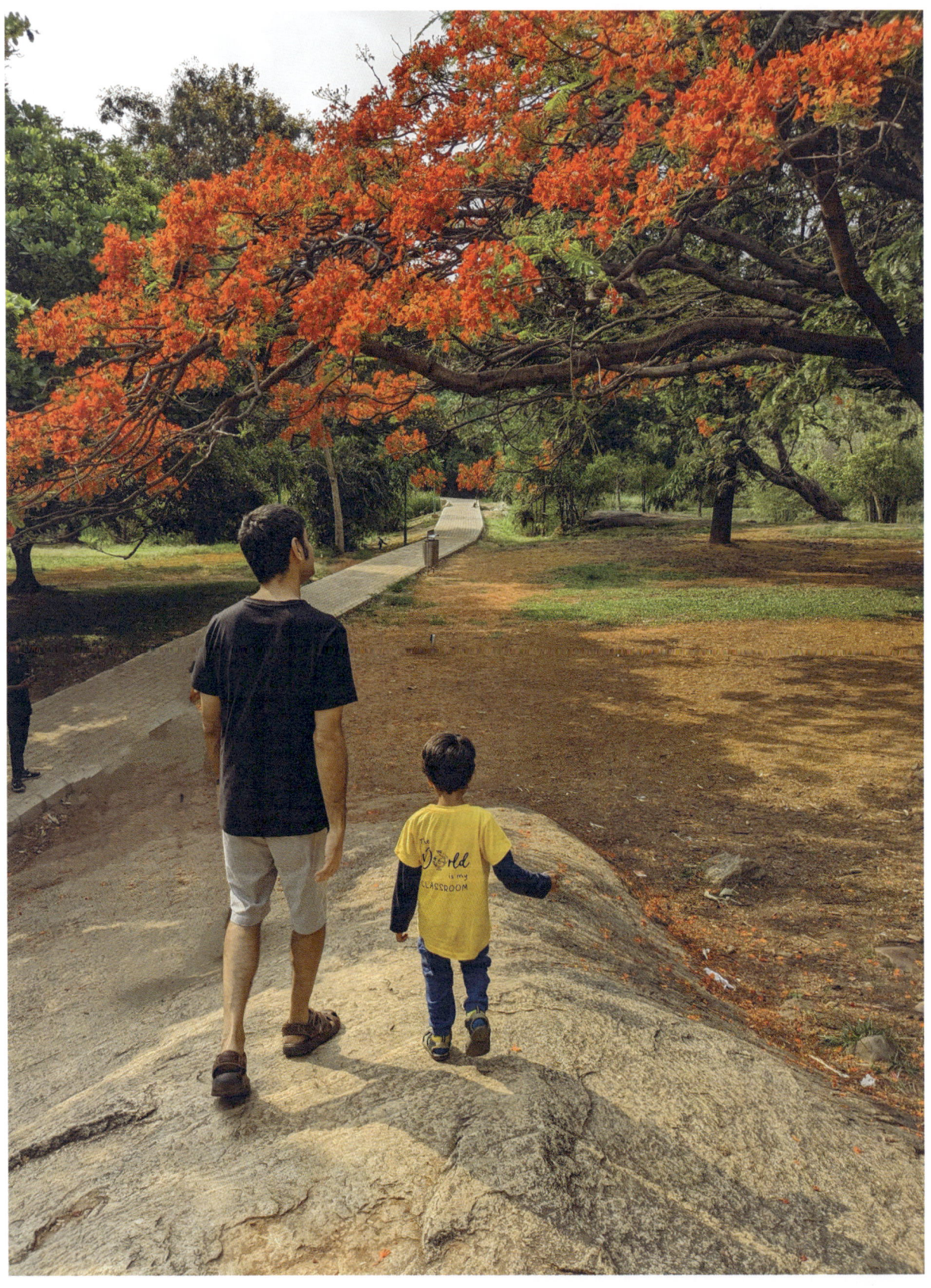

# India

## DHARINI BHASKAR

**WHERE DHARINI LIVES:**
Bengaluru, India

**WHERE DHARINI IS FROM:**
Mumbai, India

Dharini grew up in Mumbai, lived for several years in the UK and Greece, and worked for over a decade in publishing in New Delhi. As a model student herself, Dharini did not expect she would make the parenting choices she did – and yet, living in different cities across the world fed into the family's decision to unschool their 5-year-old son. 'Learning happens through play, on his terms. We don't follow a curriculum', says Dharini. In 2020, her husband's work in fintech took them to Bengaluru. Studded with lakes and expanses of green, and alive with a melding of cultures and a laid-back vibe, the city has become their classroom, as they explore a different part of it every day.

**SLOW BEGINNINGS:** My son really likes his mornings slow. We don't go anywhere before noon. He likes to make his own breakfast. Then we cycle around the neighbourhood together for a few hours. We take cues from him on how the day should unfold, and we trust his choices.

**OUT IN THE CITY:** We usually head out after lunch. Some days, he wants to ride a toy train in the park. On other days, he asks to visit a construction site or a science centre. Sometimes, we ride the metro or take a bus ride. People here are generally warm and welcoming, even in spaces not designed for children – like a car showroom – except on occasion when we are in the bus and are expected to know the local language, Kannada, which we don't.

**CITY THROUGH A LENS:** My son recently decided that he wanted a camera. It has given us a chance to view the city afresh, noticing the little things through the lens, like observing the season of flowers, with *gulmohar* [royal poinciana] and jacaranda trees blossoming everywhere. On these outings, I realised it's important for him to have some part of nature in his photographs. Bengaluru allows for that easily – it is a city of gardens after all, with rolling green spaces like Cubbon Park and Lalbagh Botanical Garden. We photograph flowers, feathers, trees… And we take turns – he takes a photograph first and then I take a photograph, so we can witness the world through each other's eyes.

**UNSTRUCTURED DAYS:** When I lived in Greece, I would go on weekly hikes. My photography teacher encouraged me to chase sunsets. That informed so much of my parenting – I wanted my son to be able to have space to move, connect with the city, be in touch with nature. There is so much in Bengaluru in terms of greenery, alternative play areas, and artistic spaces that we explore every day. We often spend our days at farms like Red Soil and Hamsah, and animal rescue centres such as Prani, that are in close proximity. He gets to play in the soil, dig, plant seeds, and observe and interact with animals.

**FINDING OUR VILLAGE:** Bengaluru is an easier city to make lifestyle choices that are not entirely conventional, compared to Mumbai and Delhi, which are more competitive. It is also easier to get around, plan outings with other parents, with shorter distances to cover. We are part of a vibrant homeschooling/unschooling network in Bengaluru, so we go for weekly meet-ups at times – it could be a session of art in the park or a book reading followed by a related craft activity in a library.

**DATES:** Some afternoons, my son and I go on what we call 'dates'. One of our favourite places to visit is Champaca, a coffee shop attached to a lovely bookstore, so we read together while we eat, and if we like the book, we buy it. We also really like to go to Bistro Claytopia, where we can pick a clay item to paint while our meal is being prepared.

**READING CORNERS:** I love that Bengaluru has an active reading community and spaces devoted to literature that have existed for a long time – like Blossoms, Lightroom – which are almost like institutions, with a great awareness of books and the meaning they hold for people. One of the first things we did when we came to this city was to bookshop-hop. We still go on one every week. Independent and secondhand bookshops thrive here. There are also libraries in almost every neighbourhood, including community libraries for the less privileged sections of society who don't have easy access to books.

NEHA BHATT

## Our favourite traditions

***Making breakfast:*** My son has been cooking his own breakfast for a long time now. So, a 45-minute process can take 2½ hours, but he hasn't given up on it!

***Riding bikes:*** After he started pedalling away to glory, I got myself a bike as well. So now it is a ritual – both of us take a long bike ride after breakfast, usually within the gated community we live in.

***Solar photography:*** The first thing he does every morning is work on a cyanotype image. He primes the paper the previous night. He presses the dried leaves and flowers he picked up on his bike ride the previous day and exposes it to the sun and waits for the photograph to develop.

***Crafty creations:*** Every day we spend some time quilling, painting or doing something crafty. We go to a crafts shop called Itsy Bitsy every week and come back with something we can do together. Before bedtime, my son loves working on science experiments with his father, or building a sports-related kit with him.

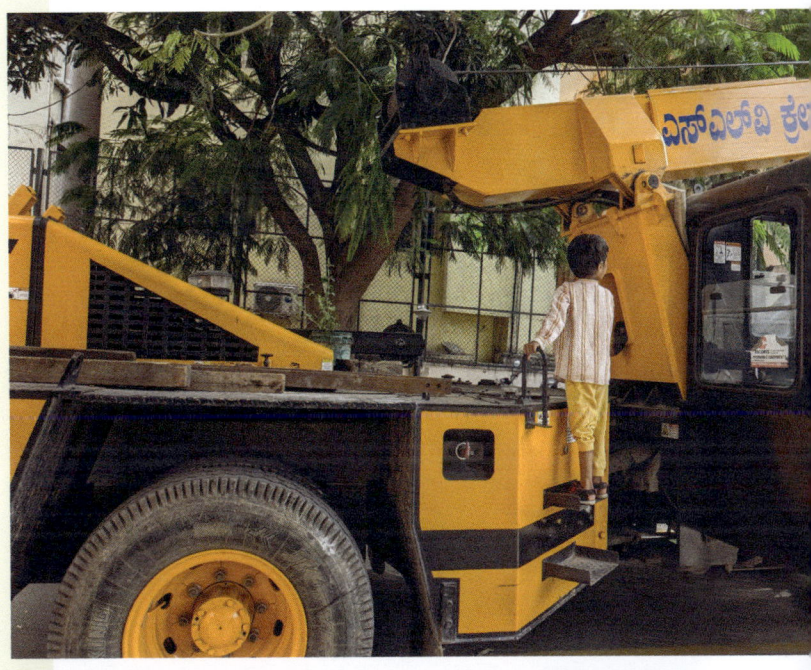

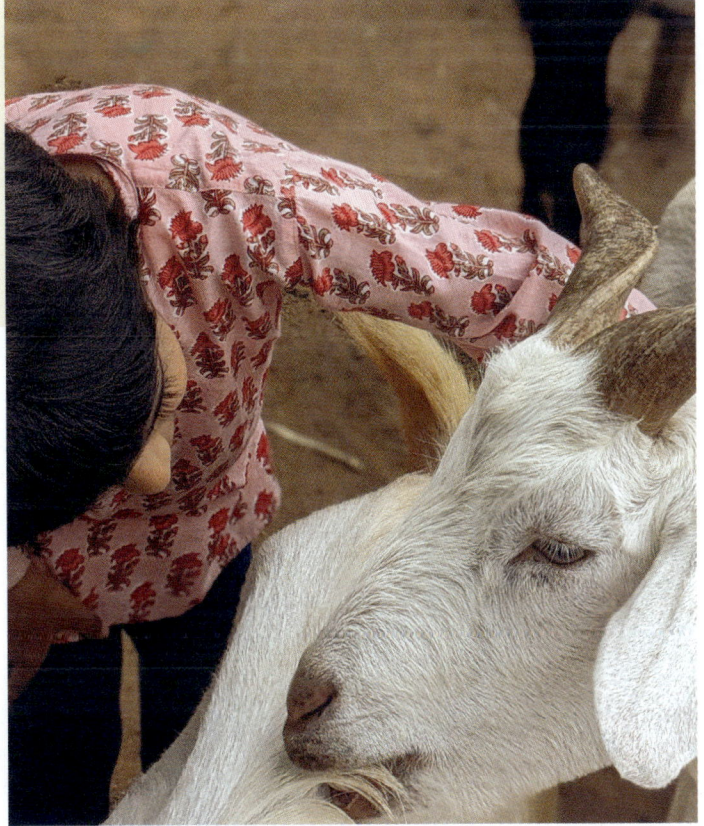

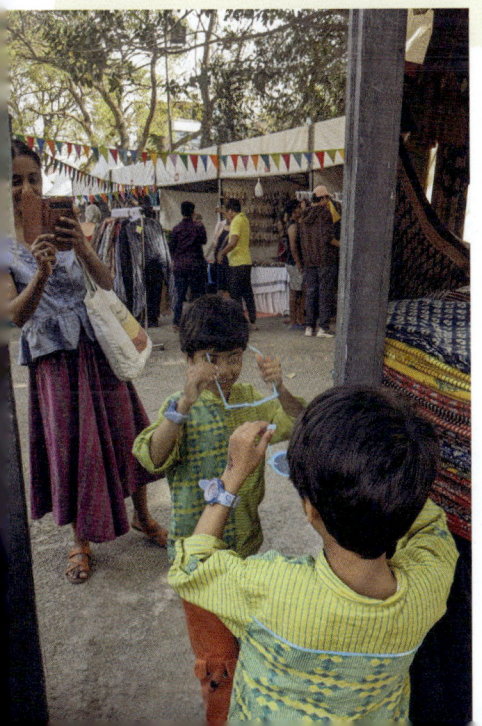

ASIA 59

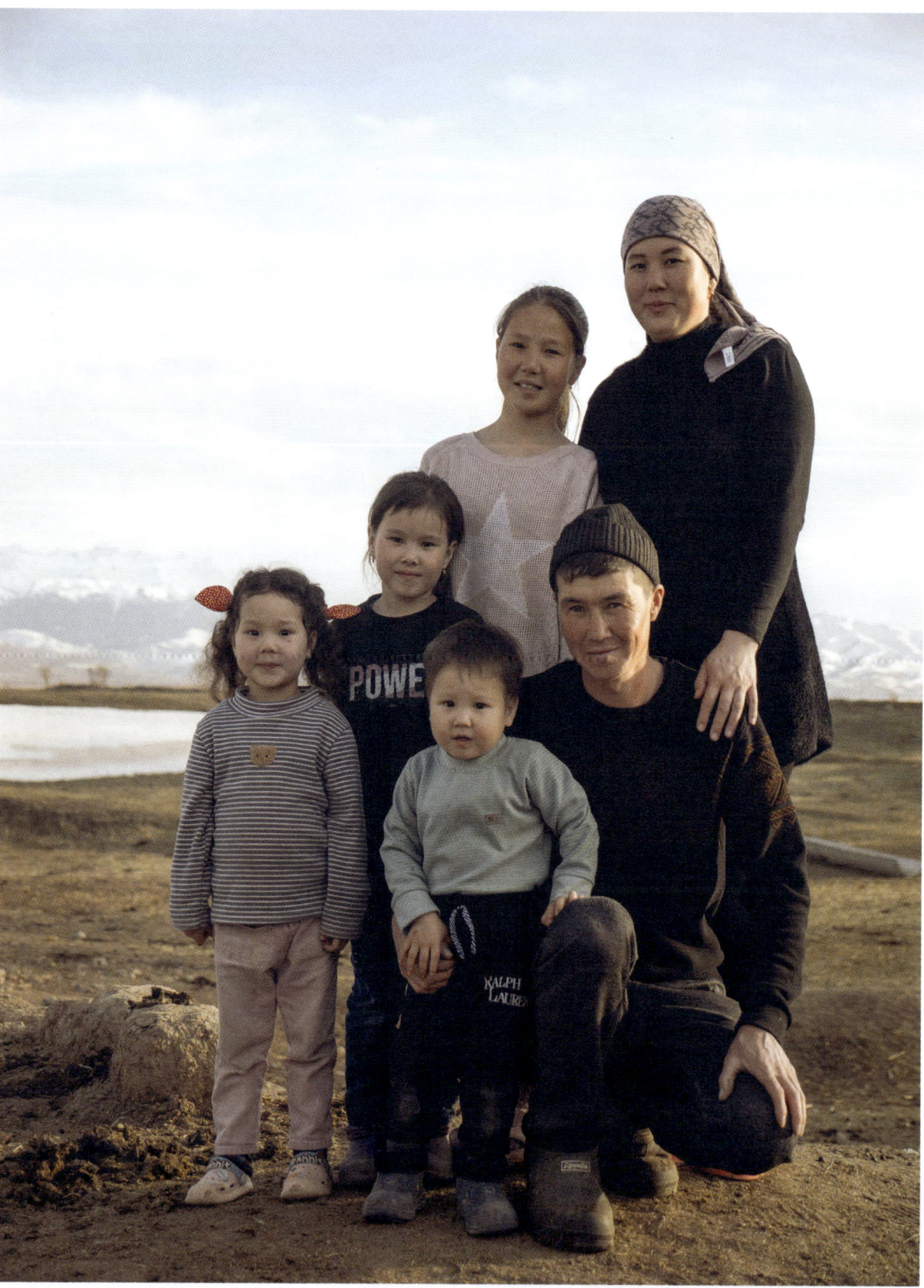

# Kyrgyzstan

## AIZADA KALYBEKOVA & DASTAN CHEKIROV

**WHERE AIZADA & DASTAN LIVE:**
Ichke Bulun, Kyrgyzstan

**WHERE AIZADA & DASTAN ARE FROM:**
Issyk-Köl region, Kyrgyzstan

Aizada and Dastan are seminomadic Kyrgyz farmers, both born in northern Kyrgyzstan. Their families approved of their match more than a decade ago. Since then, their own family has grown to include four children: Yıldız (10), Aelina (six), Uuljan (three), and their youngest, the only boy, Mirza (two). During the school year, they live in a small village on the shores of Issyk-Köl, the world's second-largest mountain lake. When the snows of the frigid winter melt, they move their flocks and set up their yurt in the highlands of the Tian Shan mountains. Upholding centuries of traditions while carving a path for their children to succeed in the modern world is the line they walk with skill. It's also a challenge they accept with pride and celebration every chance they get.

**ROUTINES:** During the school year, Dastan drives the girls to school after checking on the livestock – around a hundred sheep, a dozen cows and a few horses. The kids have different lessons and classes that don't end at the same time each day. Sometime after lunch, I get a call from the teacher and go pick them up. Once they get home, I prepare tea. Dastan does most of the farmwork: feeding the animals, cleaning out the stables. ('It's a lot of maintenance to keep caring for the animals, and keeping the machines working', Dastan adds.) But he comes in for tea too, without fail. (*Aizada*)

**AFTER-SCHOOL SNACK:** Chai, or tea, is a staple in our whole family's routine. Tea sweetened with rock sugar or homemade jams is the base, but there's much more to this after-school snack. The kids usually eat a meal, like *kurduk* (succulent mutton and potatoes), some fruits, bread, jam and sweets. If we have any visitors, this break might last more than an hour, but if Dastan has work to do, or Yıldız has homework, they might not stay as long at the table. The other children play in and around the house until evening. During winter, it's a moment of respite from Dastan's cold farmwork, and a chance for me to catch up on the day with the kids. (*Aizada*)

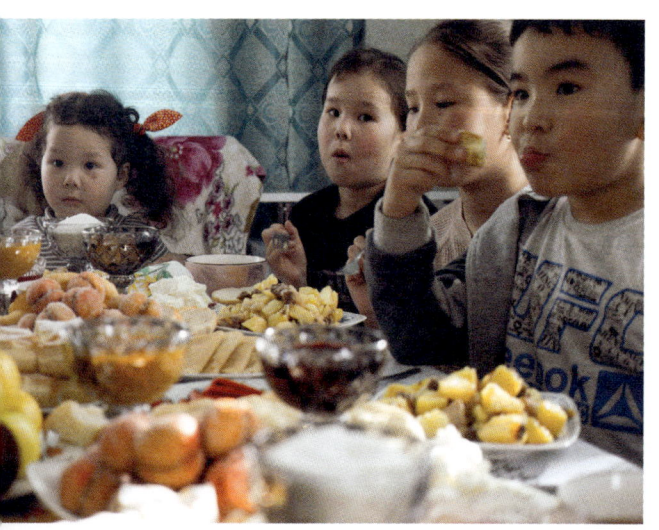

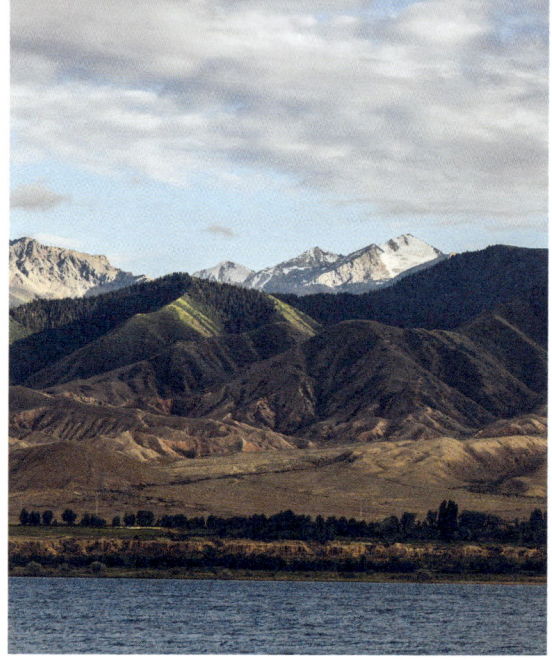

**PARENTAL OBLIGATIONS:** In Kyrgyz culture, as parents, we have three important obligations: the first is choosing a good name; the second, for the boys, is circumcision; and the third is helping organise their marriage, boy or girl. (*Dastan*)

**REMEMBERING THE PAST:** The old Turkic root 'Kyrgyz' means 'we are forty', and references the original 40 clans of our land. Every Kyrgyz child learns this and is taught seven generations of their ancestors to help make sure that the families are different when it's time to get married. (*Aizada*)

**LARGE FAMILIES:** Having a large family is important in our culture, and there are always many celebrations to prepare for. For us, family and community are like the same thing. The kids see their 11 cousins and other family often. It's important that we teach them the value of family bonds, and maintaining good support systems in a big family. (*Aizada*)

**THINKING OF THE FUTURE:** In everything we do, we are thinking about our children's future. The girls must get a good education, because they're going to be teaching the next generation of the family. Yıldız, our oldest, is taking English lessons with a programme run by the US Embassy in Karakol. Last week she brought home a book with one side of the page in English, the other side in Russian: *Where the Wild Things Are*. And Mirza, we'll see what he likes learning, if he wants to be a shepherd too or if he wants to do something else. (*Aizada*)

**JAILOO LIFE:** In April, I take part in the transhumance to the *jailoo* (the highlands). Once school is finished in May, Aizada comes with the kids. The *jailoo* we go to is accessible by car, which makes it perfect for hosting celebrations. On weekends, relatives from the valley come up for fresh air. (*Dastan*)

Being in the *jailoo* is a great time for the children because they are outside all the time, eating healthy, drinking mare's milk and growing strong. During the day, the kids collect gum from the trees or wild onions. And I am teaching the girls to make all the traditional drinks: *kumiss*, *ayran*, *maksym*, *chalap*, and creams like *kaymak* and butter. If we don't know where the children are, it's sure they've gone to the big hill. There is one hill that takes a few hours to reach. They'll go together and there they get telephone reception. Once they have the news from the village, they come back. (*Aizada*)

ASHLEY PARSONS

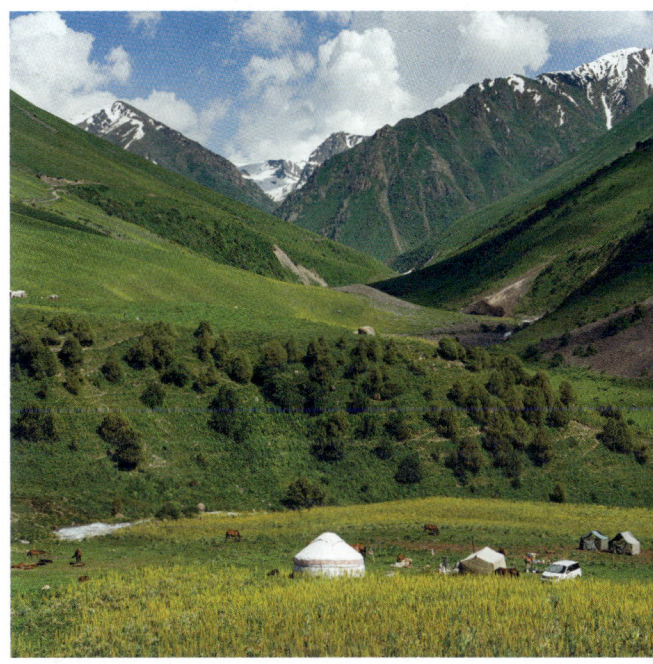

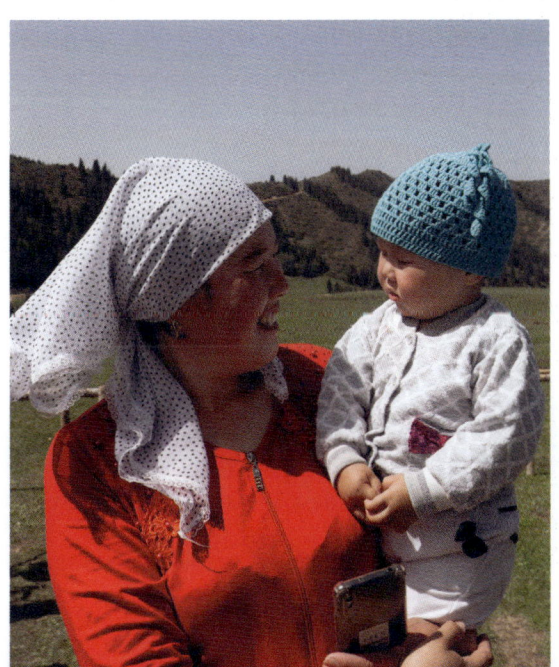

## Our favourite traditions

**Chai with guests:** Chai is really central in our culture – it's around a table of tea overflowing with sweets and snacks that we socialise. Any occasion, like a social visit, after school, [or] a family party is a good reason to serve chai. If I know ahead of time, I'll make *borsooks* (fried balls of dough). (*Aizada*)

**Beshik toi:** After a child's birth, they shouldn't be visited for the first 40 days, to keep them from getting ill. The *beshik toi* is the ceremony of placing the baby in the cradle for the first time, by an older woman. (*Dastan*)

**Tushoo toi:** Once the baby takes their first steps, we host a *tushoo toi*. The baby's feet are tied together with black and white yarn to represent good and bad days in life. The older children race toward the child, cut the yarn, and then walk forward together as a group. All the children receive some gifts and we have a feast, like *beshbarmak*, which is mutton or horsemeat eaten with the hands. (*Aizada*)

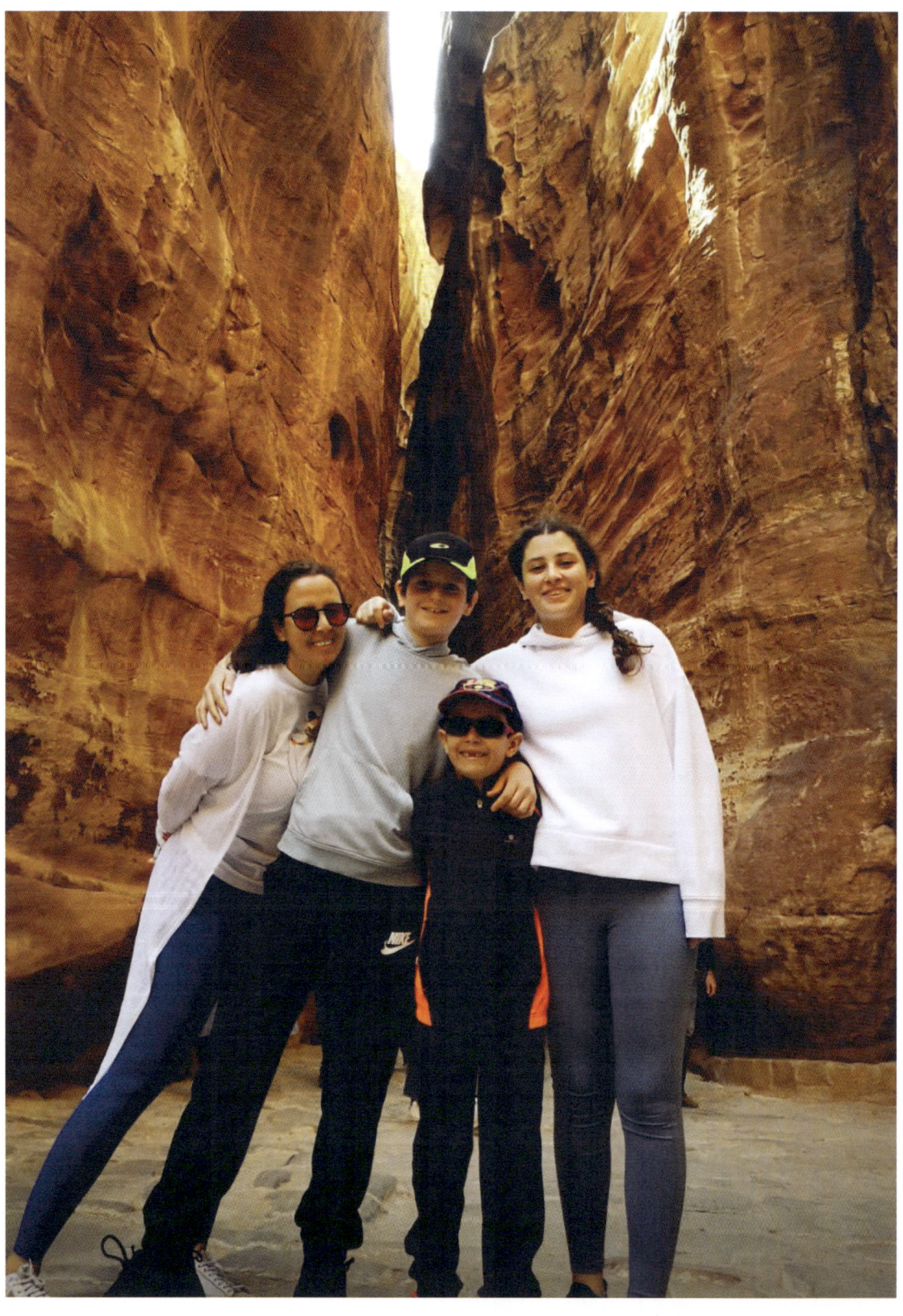

# Jordan

## DINA TABBAA

**WHERE DINA LIVES:**
Amman, Jordan

**WHERE DINA IS FROM:**
Amman, Jordan

Born and raised in Amman, Dina started dating her future husband, Omar, in ninth grade. They were originally together before university. 'Omar was supposed to go to college in America but he saw me filling out my UCAS (the UK's portal for applying to universities) and asked me to fill one out for him. When I asked which schools he said, "Just put yours." We broke up for the summer and I thought he was in Miami or something, then I saw him in town, on the university orientation day!' More than 20 years later they have three kids, Layla (14), Hussein (13) and Bader (five), and live in their home town of Amman, where Dina runs a translation agency and a small charity, Masarrah, while teaching part-time.

**FAMILY MEALTIMES:** It's really important to me that we eat together, so I've made it a point to make lunch an event as often as possible. We eat as an extended family at my mum's three times a week. She always makes way too much food, but the kids love the variety of *meze* (appetisers) and mains on the table. While there's something for everyone it seems like we all tend to hover over the chicken escalope whenever she makes it!

**TRADITIONAL VALUES:** It can be really tough to balance traditions here, because on one hand there are things that are beautiful – hospitality, family, community – but on the other hand there are some things that are limiting. Hussein and Layla can't date, but how is that fair? We started in grade nine and now my eldest is that age but somehow she's not allowed? It definitely takes time, patience, and a lot of deep discussion. Although these conversations are never easy, Omar is a good friend as well as a good husband, and we have a lot of practice understanding each other.

**KEEPING UP THE LANGUAGE:** Omar's side of the family is big on speaking only Arabic at home and mine isn't really. As a compromise we have the kids read and memorise some Quran with a tutor every Friday morning. The Quran is the basis of the modern Arabic language and it provides a really strong foundation. I try to let the kids interpret the text on their own and I've specifically asked the tutor to just focus on the language, and to avoid the topic of religion. Now, after four years, it's really paying off. Layla doesn't memorise much, but her two younger brothers have got quite a lot down. Their Arabic is also way better!

**TRANQUIL TIMES:** I'm really strict about sleep and everyone is asleep at 10pm max, so now we're all early risers. Besides, by 9.30pm I deserve to have my quiet time! Omar and I like to sit quietly with each other, and we live on the outskirts of the city so there's no shortage of quiet. We get up around 7am, even on our days off.

**BREAKING OUT OF THE BUBBLE:** My kids are fortunate to go to a private school, the same one I teach at, but that comes with its own set of issues. The kids pick up some really yucky values at school, like cliquey behaviour and thinking that money is something really special. It's been a constant struggle breaking them out of this bubble, but exposure is really the only way to do it. We try to travel abroad to somewhere different once a year just so the kids are exposed to new places and ways of thinking, and now I'm really pushing them to intern and see how everyone else lives. The charity, Masarrah, is also really good for that. We fulfill 'wishes' for kids with incurable illnesses, whether they're terminal or disabled, through donations. I make it a point to bring the kids along. I think they benefit a lot from being able to see that their lifestyles really are blessed.

**THE OUTDOORS:** Amman is close to a lot of great green spaces, like the city of Salt and town of Fuheis, which have tons of olive groves, as well as the Ghamadan and Scandinavian pine forests. I make an effort to take the kids out for some backwoods hiking with my brother as often as we can. They're picking up a lot about the local edible greens, native flowers, and the different types of trees in the region. It also helps them connect more with their dad, who works in agriculture.

*SANAD TABBAA*

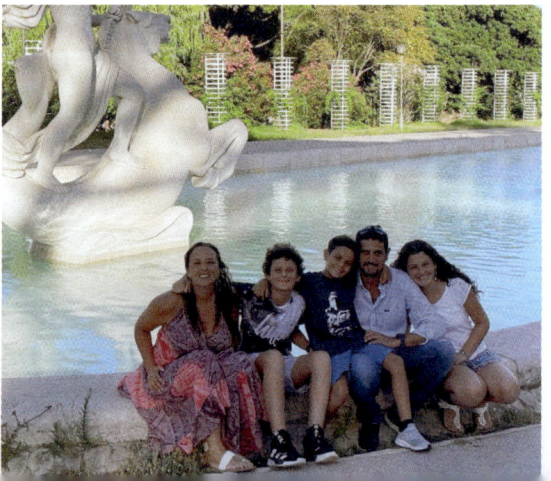

## Our favourite traditions

**Family Fridays:** Every Friday we used to have pancakes but now the kids prefer crepes – they find their own recipes and everything! Afterwards, there's Quran study and Omar takes the boys out for Friday prayer, then we visit his grandma. In the afternoon he takes the kids out to the family farm and by sunset they're always totally pooped.

**Dolphin Dolphin:** When the kids were young, we used to fill up half the tub for the kids to pretend that they were dolphins and trick them into bathing. Unexpectedly, they still want to do it and as they got bigger it seemed irresponsible, since Jordan's the second-most water-poor country on Earth. Whenever we travel, though, we still save time for 'Dolphin Dolphin'.

**Taekwondo time:** Jordan has some kind of obsession with Taekwondo, and we're no exception. Three times a week we have an hour-and-a-half of Taekwondo class as a family. I'll admit that it was a strange choice, but it's nice to have routine time dedicated to the family unit.

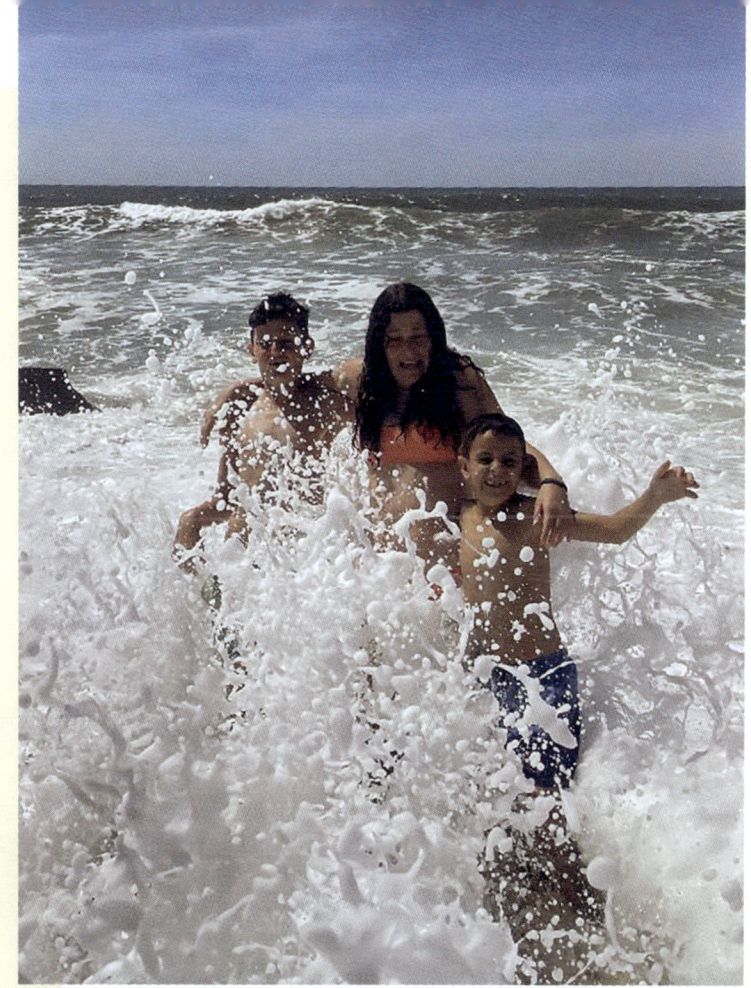

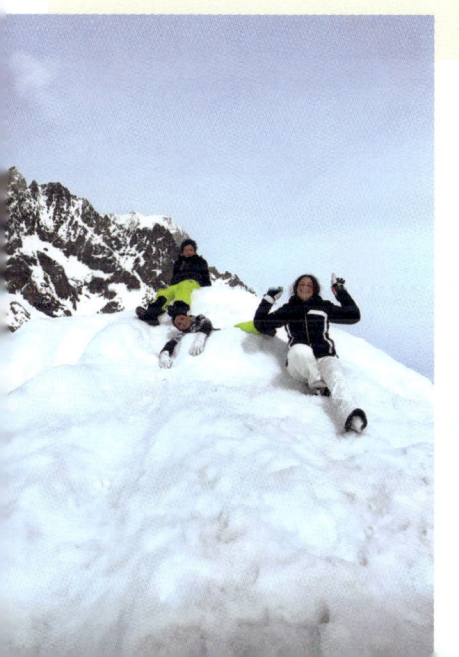

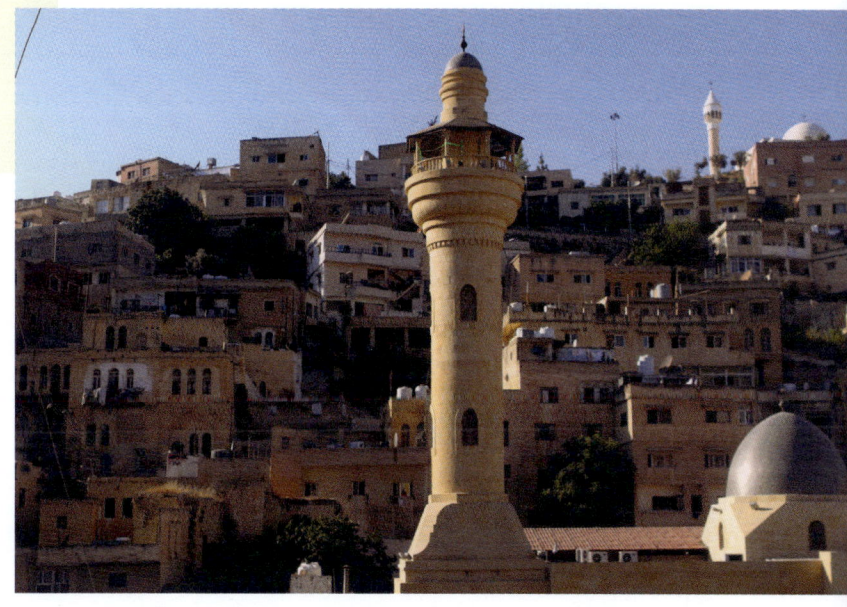

MIDDLE EAST

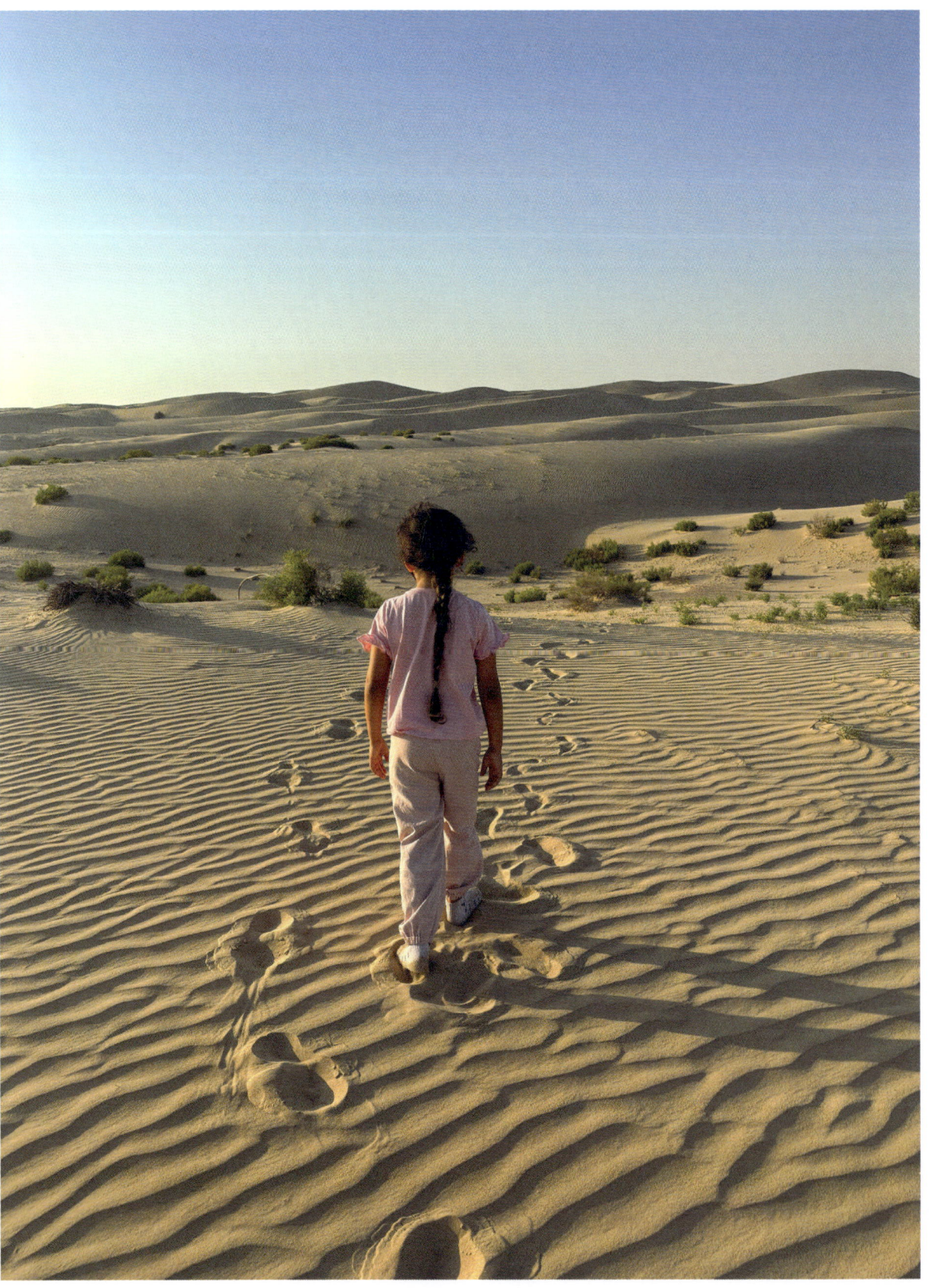

# United Arab Emirates

## NADIA

**WHERE NADIA LIVES:**
Abu Dhabi, United Arab Emirates

**WHERE NADIA IS FROM:**
Bacchus Marsh, Australia

Nadia was born in Australia and moved to the oasis town of Al Ain in the United Arab Emirates (UAE) with her family aged 10. Her husband, Saeed, was born in Al Ain. They met at school when she was 16, but their families were against the teenage romance. 'Both sets of parents were worried about us getting together so young', Nadia says. 'It wasn't so much about the different cultures but because they thought we needed to find ourselves a bit more first.' Nadia returned to Australia to finish school and Saeed moved to the USA for college. They met again a few years later when she was holidaying in Al Ain and their love blossomed. 'We've been married for 17 years now.' They have four children.

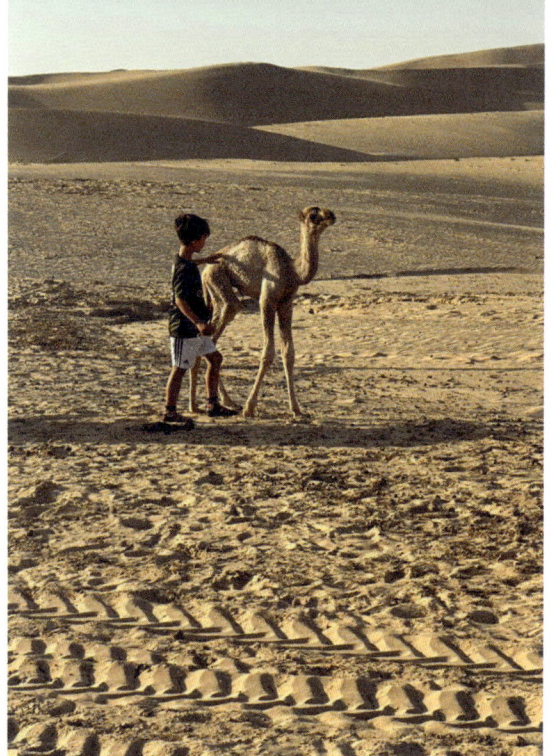

**CULTURAL MIX:** I tell my kids it's special to be from two different backgrounds. It's not a hindrance at all. They go to an American school where everyone speaks English. They have Arabic lessons every day. I want them to love both their backgrounds. Saeed and I are very much on the same page, raising our children to be well-rounded and open-minded people. I'm really proud of them and how they navigate the differences.

**RELIGION:** As a Western woman marrying an Emirati man, I didn't have to convert to Islam. (A Western man marrying an Emirati woman would have to convert.) Growing up, my family didn't celebrate Christmas or Easter as religious holidays. It was more about enjoying time together. Saeed and the kids are Muslim. The kids study Islam at school and they follow the Muslim way of life. Mansour (14) has just gone on his first pilgrimage to Mecca with his aunt and grandmother. We always find a way to compromise and make it work for us. At the end of the day, like most mums and dads, we just want our kids to be happy.

**HOSPITALITY:** We love having the kids' friends over. The Emirati way is that everybody's children are your children. Saeed comes from a large family. When we visit his mother, Hessa, she's always bringing out food and coffee. Hospitality is a big thing in this culture. A lot of my Western friends haven't experienced an Emirati household, so I like to have them over to enjoy this hospitality with my family.

**BUSY LIFE:** The kids have lots of activities after school, so my afternoons are busy driving them around. For the past few months Jamila (11) has spent four afternoons a week rehearsing for a school play. Mansour and Sultan (both eight) and Ameena (six) have football training during the week and matches on weekends. I try to go to all their competitions, school shows and events. I have a housemaid helping me, which makes my role as a mum more relaxed so I can really focus on the kids and my family. Saeed works in Dubai and because everybody has such different schedules it's often hard to have dinner together. But we always spend time with each other on the weekends – we go to the beach or the pool, take the boat out, visit my dad in Dubai or spend the day at Hessa's.

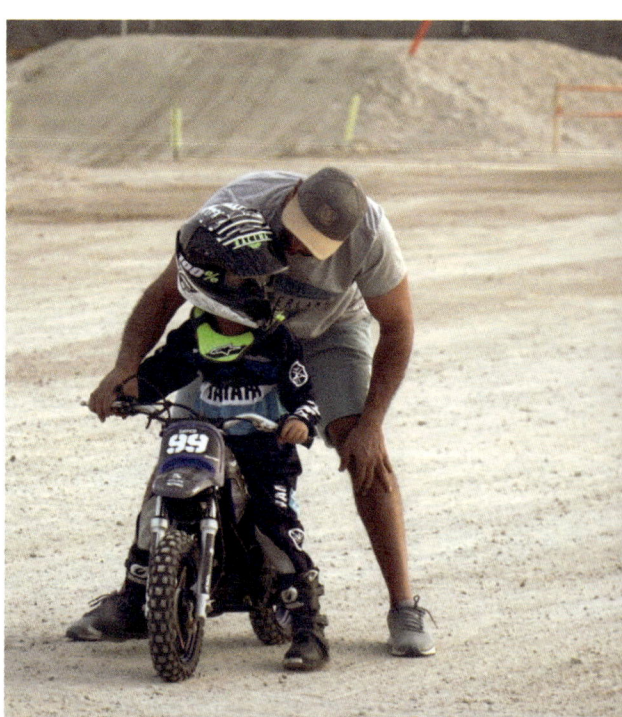

# "We love having the kids' friends over. The Emirati way is that everybody's children are your children."

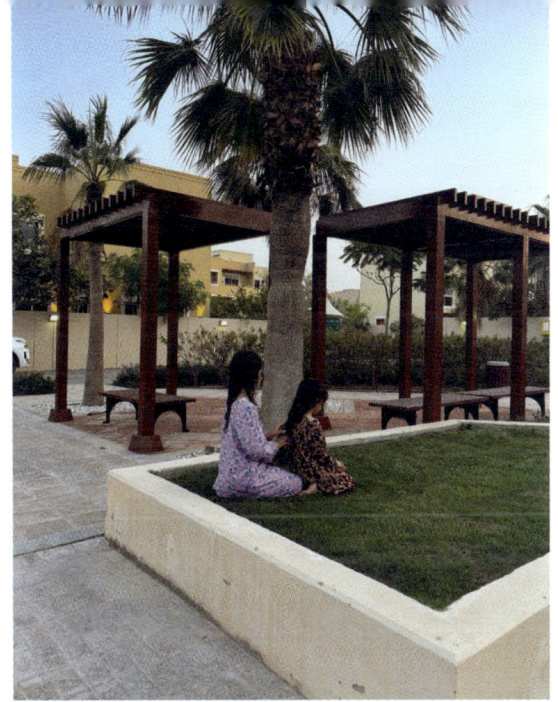

**CALMER PACE:** Saeed and I lived in Dubai before we had kids but I wouldn't like to return. Dubai is all glitzy and glamorous, the traffic is crazy and it's so fast-paced. Abu Dhabi has a traditional family feel to it; at the beach or the pool you see more families than the younger crowd you'd find in Dubai. I think the kids have a quieter upbringing in Abu Dhabi. It has a nice balance with plenty to do – good restaurants, beaches and theme parks. It's perfect for raising a family.

**DESERT RIDES:** Saeed likes to ride motorbikes on the weekends and has taught the boys how to ride safely at the motocross track. I go horse-riding at 4.30am every morning – later in winter. It's quiet, like gazelles running in the desert. Horse-riding is a link to my childhood. Al Ain was a small, safe town and I had a lot of freedom. It was a lovely childhood. I had two white stallions, which is like a dream for a little girl who loves horses. Ameena sometimes rides with me and I hope she will share my joy in horses.

**CHANGES:** I've seen many changes in the UAE. There are more opportunities and choices that weren't here before. Girls play more sports. Everyone speaks English. There are more mixed marriages, which was very rare in my day. I love living in the UAE. We have such a great life.

OLIVIA POZZAN

## Our favourite traditions

**Ramadan boxes:** Ramadan is the holy month when Muslims fast from dawn to sunset. It's also a time for generosity and giving. We make up food boxes for workers and low-income earners. The kids form a line and pack the boxes with yoghurt and noodles and other foodstuffs. The kids from the neighbourhood will often come by and help. Then we go around and hand them out.

**New clothes for Eid:** After Ramadan, Eid is a celebration. Saeed takes the boys to the tailor to be fitted for new *khandouras* (traditional white ankle-length tunics worn by Emirati men). The local barber trims their hair. I take the girls to buy new dresses and shoes. They have their nails painted and their hair freshly washed and blow-dried. And at Eid, the kids are given *eidya* (pocket money), with the youngest getting the most.

**Celebrations:** Any excuse to celebrate is our motto. We celebrate holidays and festivals from both cultures and from other cultures as well. Christmas, Easter, Eid, the Tooth Fairy, Halloween, Diwali...everything!

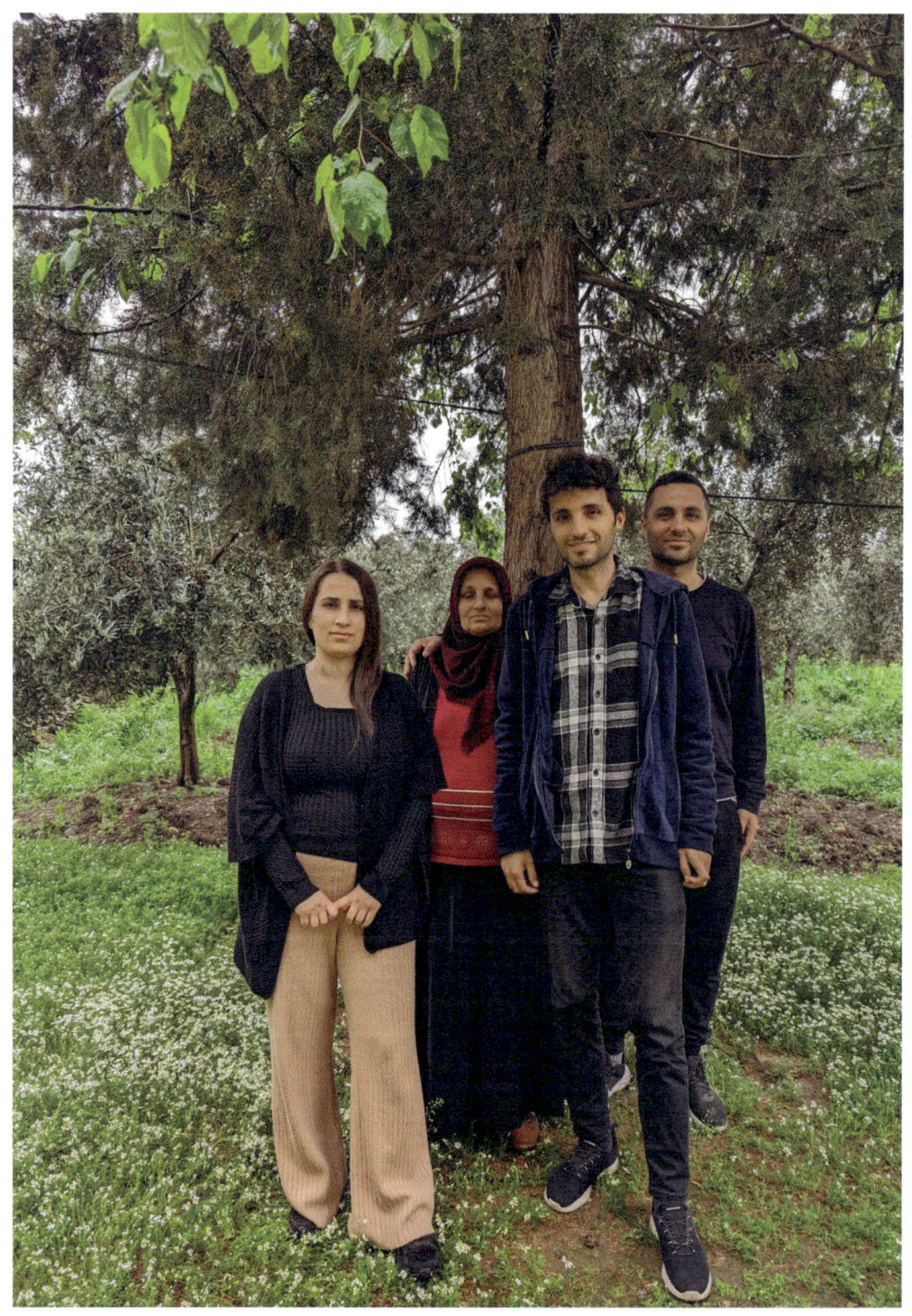

# Türkiye

## SEVIM ARTAR

**WHERE SEVIM LIVES:**
Altınüzüm, Türkiye

**WHERE SEVIM IS FROM:**
Nurdağı, Türkiye

In October 2022, Sevim lost her beloved husband, Ali, to brain cancer. They had been married for 37 years, and as farmers in a remote Anatolian village, together they raised four children on solid principles of hard work and love for nature. Today she lives alone with her 17-year old son Yusuf. She initially felt lost, having to take care of the house, the animals and a teenage son all by herself. 'Then I rolled up my sleeves and continued to live, honouring Ali's family values.' Little did Sevim know that she would be confronted with an even bigger challenge just a few months later: an earthquake that destroyed her whole village. 'I could only start over thanks to the support of my children.'

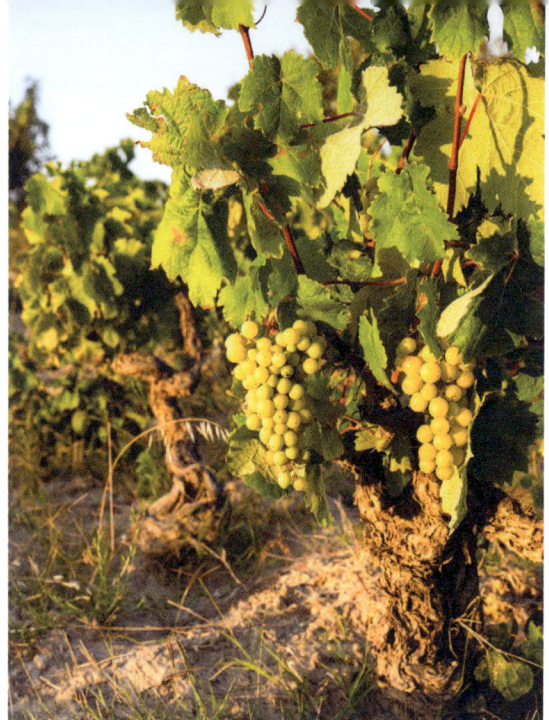

**TAKING CARE OF THE LAND:** The southern Turkish countryside is mainly inhabited by Kurds, like my family. We are an ethnic group with a strong connection to land and nature. Ali and I have always wanted to transfer that spirit to our children. For us, taking care of the land is like taking care of our home and family. Yusuf and I wake up early, around 6am, then we have a nutritious breakfast. We need to eat well in order to be able to work in the field. Before going to school, Yusuf helps me tend our livestock, mainly chickens and goats. It teaches him responsibility, hard work, but also reinforces his connection to the land.

**SEASONS:** Since we live off our agricultural fields, our lives revolve around seasons. In our culture, spring is the most important of all four. For us it means rebirth, and we celebrate it with our families and as a community on the night between 20 and 21 March, lighting some fires and dancing in circles.

**EARTH'S PRODUCTS:** My children learnt to associate certain months of the year to specific vegetables or grass. They know that, for instance, May is grape-pruning time. We collect grape leaves, brine them with salt, and put them in boxes to make *sarma* (rolls filled with rice). During October and November we collect olives to make olive oil. It's important to know the lifecycle of our Earth's products. And it helps us be economically independent: we villagers mostly don't need to buy anything from supermarkets, we produce almost everything ourselves.

**SCHOOL EDUCATION:** Although the common stereotype depicts southeastern Türkiye as a land of uneducated farmers, school has been a priority in my children's upbringing. I wanted to change the narrative, at least for my kids, because when I was little I didn't have a chance to study. I wanted them to be able to stand on their own feet, especially my daughter. Today my proudest achievement is that my daughter Fatoş became a PE Teacher, Ömer works for the government, and Ayhan works in an international NGO, speaks English fluently and has travelled to the US, Europe and other countries that I don't even know. I didn't want my kids to think that, just because they were raised as farmers, they couldn't choose to become anything else they wanted.

**THE 2023 EARTHQUAKE:** Poor Yusuf was so traumatised when a 7.8-magnitude earthquake hit our village in February 2023. Our village lies in a

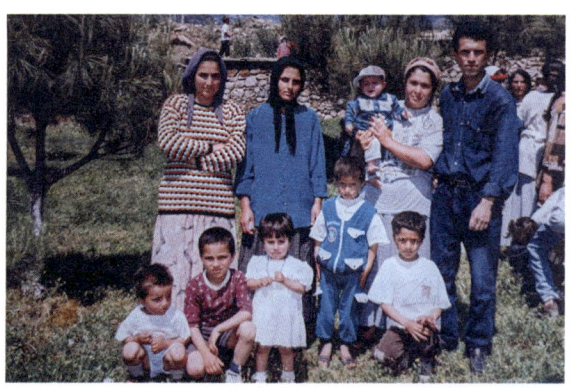

highly seismic area. Because of the high risks of earthquakes, it was forbidden to build homes with more than three floors. My husband knew well how the land is our biggest ally, but it can also turn into an enemy at times. So we made sure to build a solid home, both with construction materials and valuable life lessons. It was traumatic to see the roads crack open, and we almost lost our house. Schools were shut for a whole semester, and Yusuf had time to help me manage our farm.

**NO TV, BETTER SUCCESS:** For years I refused to have a TV at home, to not allow any distractions for my children while doing their homework. It worked, and they've always succeeded in their exams. Now we do have a TV, but Yusuf prefers reading books under our olive trees. I believe that raising kids as far away as possible from technology gives them a healthier childhood. And in our village, far from urban life, that's easier to achieve.

**ELDERS:** It is important to honour the wisdom of elderly people. We value their practical knowledge and want our kids to not forget their preachings. Even my older children, who live elsewhere with their own families, come back to the village monthly to meet with the heads of our community and listen to them over a cup of tea.

STEFANIA D'IGNOTI

> "Since we live off our agricultural fields, our lives revolve around seasons."

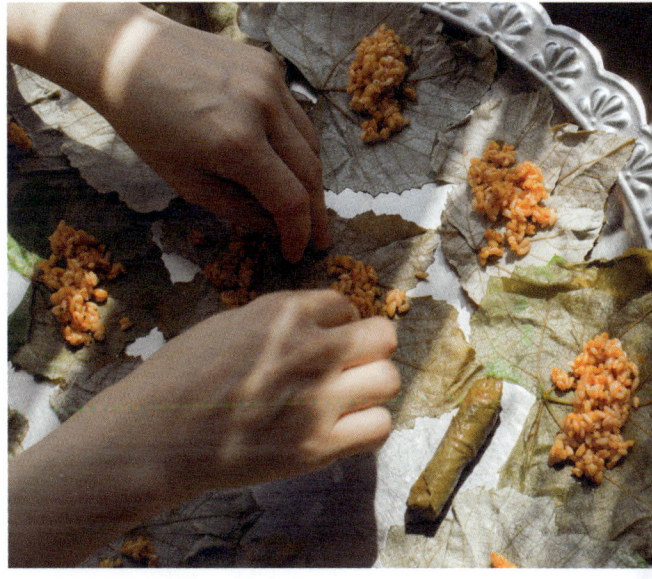

## Our favourite traditions

**Bayram:** For the holy Islamic month, we invite each other for dinner. We are generally four to five families and we do dinners on rotation in our houses. Then for Bayram – what we call the end of Ramadan in Türkiye – we celebrate it at our house, with all my children and grandkids. It strengthens the bond between families in our community.

**Evacuation safety measures:** We practise weekly how to hide under a desk and protect our head when an earthquake happens, and run towards open-air fields rather than staying near buildings. It may sound sad, but it's become a practical and useful habit.

**Çay talks:** Tea is a vital part of Turkish culture. Every afternoon at 4pm we have outside guests, either family members or neighbours, and we sit and drink tea we make from dried cherry stalks.

**Terrace dining:** Every summer we open a blanket, sit on the floor with our legs crossed and eat with our hands, watching the sunset from our terrace. Sometimes, if it's too warm, we even fall asleep there!

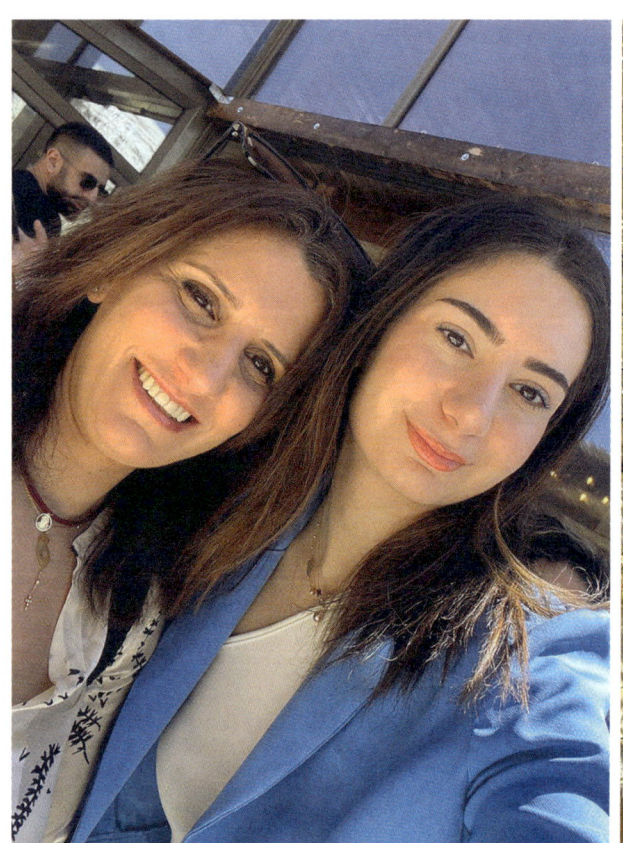
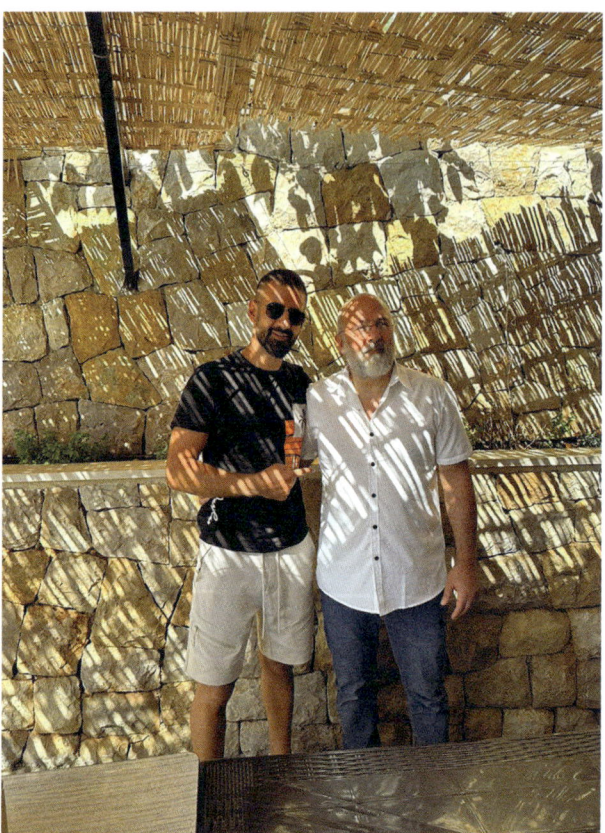

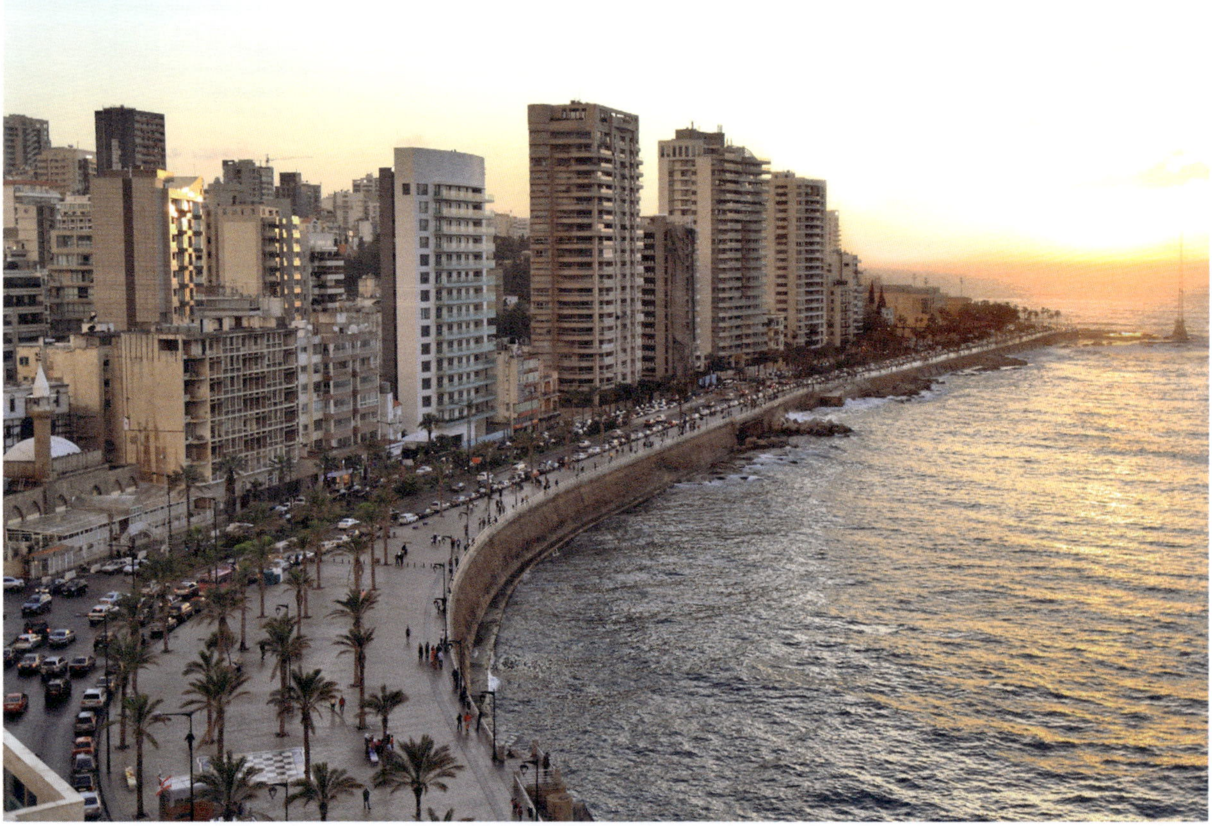

# Lebanon

## ZEINA MANSOUR

**WHERE ZEINA LIVES:**
Antelias, Lebanon

**WHERE ZEINA IS FROM:**
Ashrafiyeh, Lebanon

'George and I were neighbours in Ashrafiyeh, a suburb of Beirut. We fell in love and overcame many challenges to build our life together', says Zeina. After their engagement, they bought an apartment in Antelias, just outside Beirut, paying in instalments as it was being built. 'We moved in five years later when we got married', she adds, noting the timing with a smile. 'George, then 29, worked two jobs to cover our daily expenses, and I pitched in too', she says. Eventually George, with the help of bank loans, delved into entrepreneurship, becoming the proud owner of a press and printing company: 'Starting his own business was a leap of faith.' Today, they still reside in that same apartment with their children, Vanessa (21) and Kevin (23).

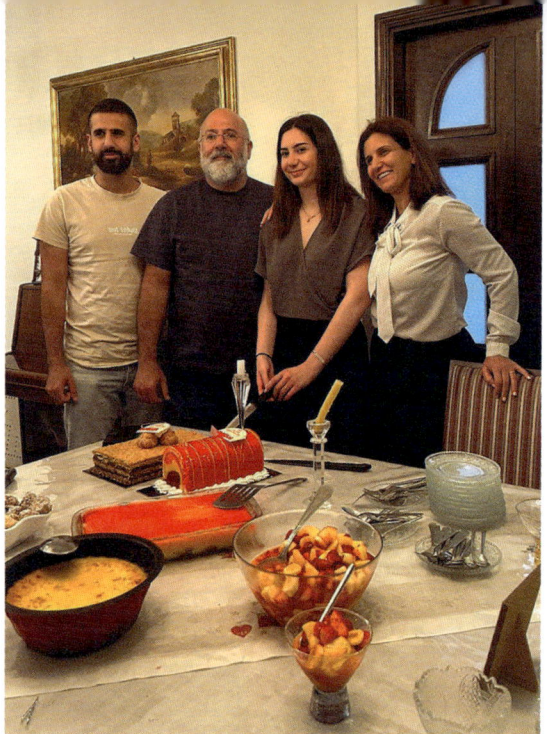

**MARRIAGE AND HAVING BABIES:** Back in the day, getting officially engaged was my golden ticket to dating before marriage, which wasn't just about saying 'I do' – it was all about laying the foundations of a future family. Even now, while dating is widely accepted in the community, and we're totally fine with it, we do run a quick 'background check' on the person and their family first.

**EVOLVING FAMILY ROLES:** In our family and throughout the community, children stick around the nest until marriage, unless they're off chasing dreams abroad. Living solo? Not exactly the norm here! But life changes. Our kids grew more independent – they now drive their own cars and help around the house with chores like fixing things, washing dishes, and even cooking. Kevin supports his father by helping out at the business during busy times, balancing this with his university commitments. While they've grown more autonomous, we still maintain a level of authority, preferring open discussions over imposing rules. We'll continue to cover their expenses, even when they start full-time employment.

**FAMILY PRIORITIES:** In Lebanon, grandparents play a vital role in childcare while parents manage work commitments. In my experience, my mother – a dedicated teacher – wasn't always available to help. Many babies, including my son Kevin, end up in daycare, where they often battle bouts of illness. With the arrival of my daughter Vanessa, I chose to temporarily leave my job, prioritising the children's care while I pursued a teaching diploma. A year later, I returned to teaching, which allowed me to commute to and from school with my kids. Meanwhile, George was investing long hours in starting his business, a legacy he intends to pass on to our children, fostering roots for them here.

**NEIGHBOURS LIKE FAMILY:** We cherish our neighbours here; we're an extended support system for each other as we go about the daily challenges of raising kids. This includes small favours like cooking or sharing meals – particularly lunch when someone's busy. We also care for each other's young kids at night when parents are away. Beyond this, we offer rides to activities, birthdays, and other events. As the kids have grown, the nature of our neighbours' support has evolved into lending a hand with car troubles and helping with university projects.

For our children, neighbours are playmates and confidantes, sharing lifelong memories and friendships. They have gone through all the stages of life together, from after-school play dates to applying for colleges together.

**THE OUTDOORS:** While we're big fans of spending time in nature parks and the great outdoors, public gardens are scarce around here, and reaching nature reserves can feel like a major expedition! We compensate through leisurely strolls along the Marina Dbayeh seafront, or Beirut's 'corniche'. During summer, we're regulars at sea resorts like Sawary and Portemilio, while children with working parents often participate in weekday summer camps. Our ultimate joy is escaping to our mountain retreat in Kfardebian for some vital immersion in nature.

**PRIORITY EDUCATION:** Like most in Lebanon, we prioritise our children's education, and saved up to send them to private schools and universities renowned for high standards. As parents, we've chosen private institutions with robust curricula and well-equipped facilities, unlike the underfunded public schools, to enhance our children's prospects for higher education.

**MEAL RITUALS:** Dinner is the highlight of our family life as we gather around the table. Everyone sets the table and preps sides while I mostly handle the cooking: labneh, cheese, pastries, fried eggs, salad or tabbouleh.

**DAILY HURDLES:** Parenting in Lebanon presents its own set of challenges for our family, like managing the weak internet and electricity outages that often hinder the children's online coursework and research. To overcome these disruptions, we rely on a 24/7 motor generator, ensuring our daily routines remain uninterrupted.

NIDAL MAJDALANI

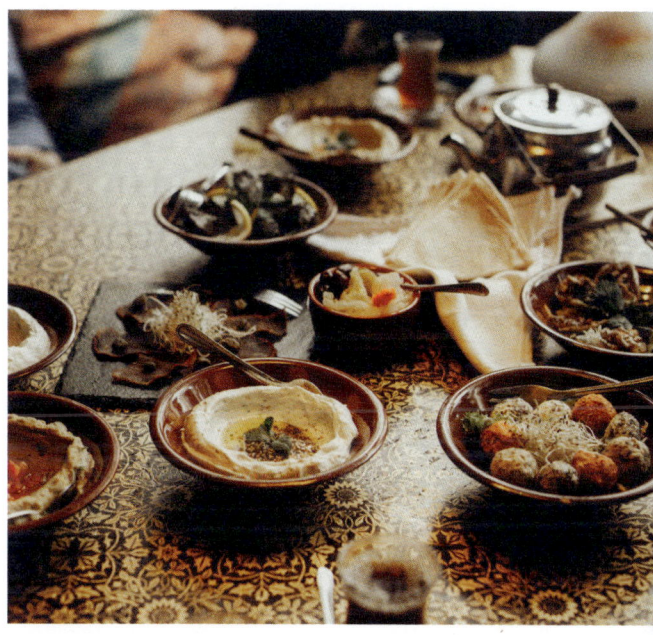

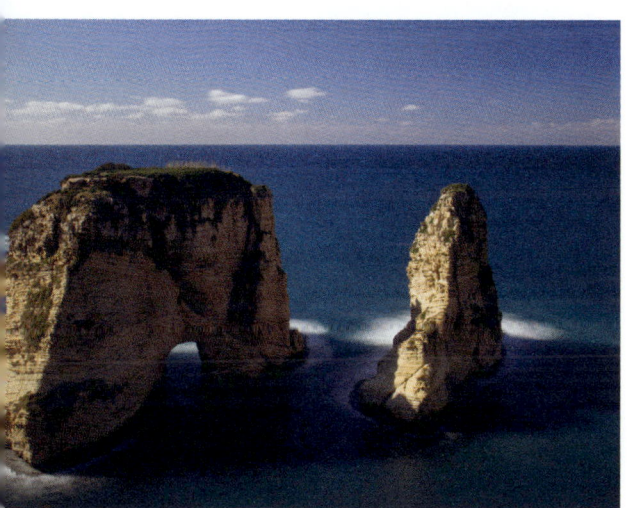

## Our favourite traditions

***Birthdays and milestones:*** In our family, as in many others, birthdays and milestones aren't just marked on the calendar – they're celebrated with flair! For a baby's first tooth, we serve a rainbow of sugar-coated chocolates, and tiny jars of cooked wheat jazzed up with rosewater, marshmallows, nuts and raisins to our nearest and dearest.

***Weekend rituals:*** Our family attends church Mass every Sunday, followed by a leisurely lunch out. Think *meze* (a variety of small appetisers) galore, sizzling barbecue, and a splash of ice-cold *arak* (an anise-flavoured alcoholic spirit). As for our Friday and Saturday nights, we host highly competitive family game nights, playing board games and traditional card games.

***St Barbara's Day:*** Our kiddos' favourite holiday was on 3 December. All decked out in costumes, they used to dash through the neighbourhood, sweet-talking our neighbours into handing over treats and coins; a tradition rooted in the story of St Barbara.

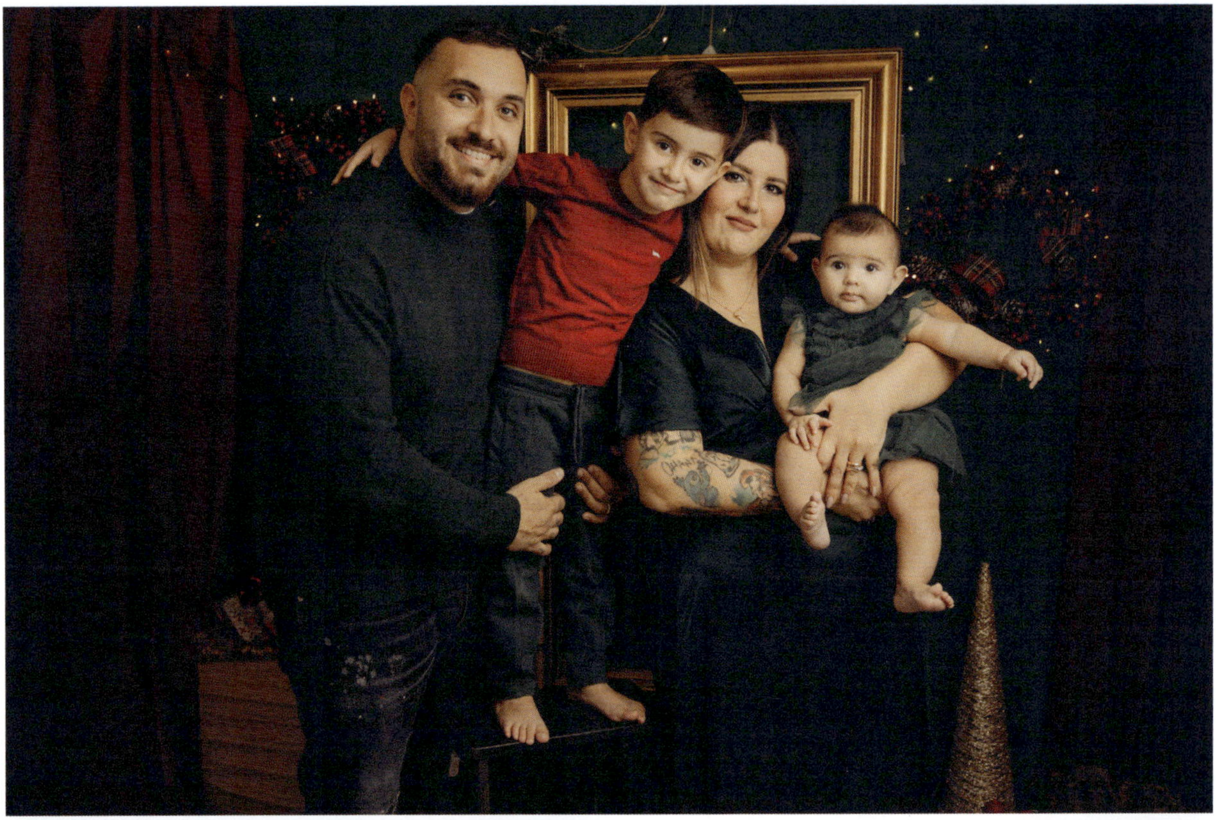

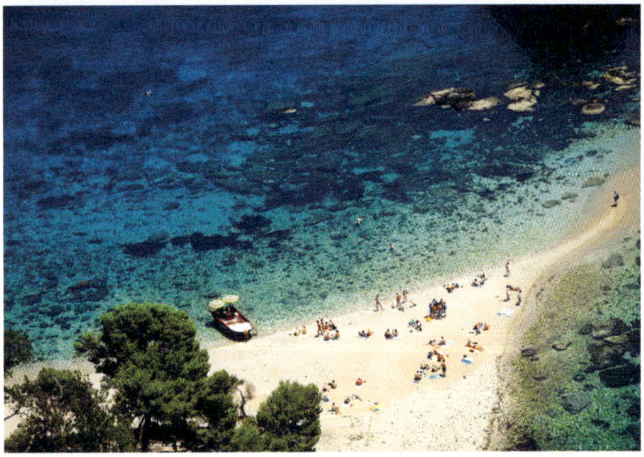

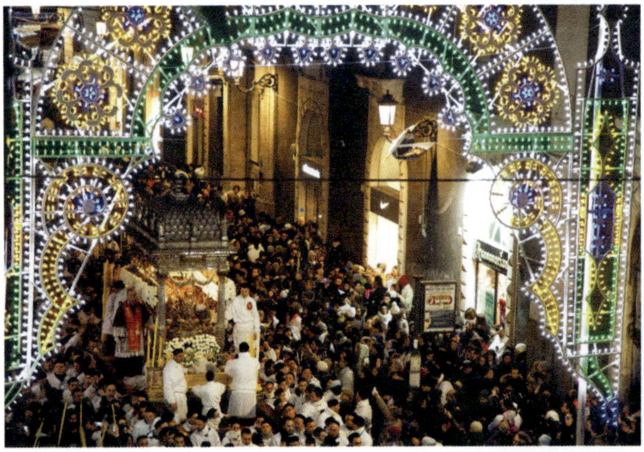

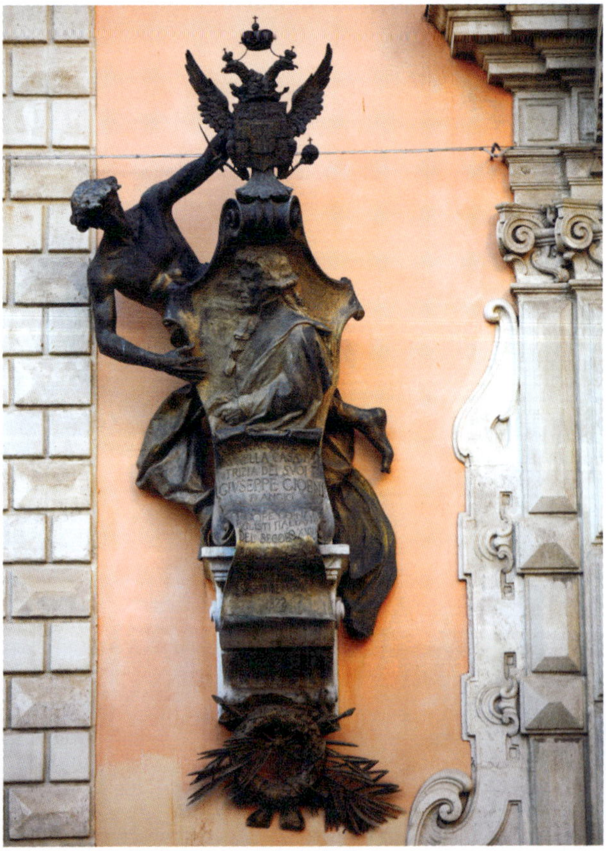

# Italy

## VALENTINA FRAGALÀ

**WHERE VALENTINA LIVES:**
Catania, Italy

**WHERE VALENTINA IS FROM:**
Catania, Italy

At first look, Valentina may not seem like the classical Italian mum. She's tall, with arms covered in tattoos. Many might not guess she's the mother of a five-year-old boy and one-year-old. Shortly after a heartbreak, Valentina met Salvo. Five months into their relationship, they found out Valentina was pregnant. Although living on a conservative island where having children before marriage is not well received, the two went against the odds and successfully raised their first-born, Rosario. 'Not many would have gambled on us staying together after an unplanned pregnancy', Valentina says. 'Perhaps it was impulsive to start a family after knowing each other for less than six months. But here we are, stronger than ever.'

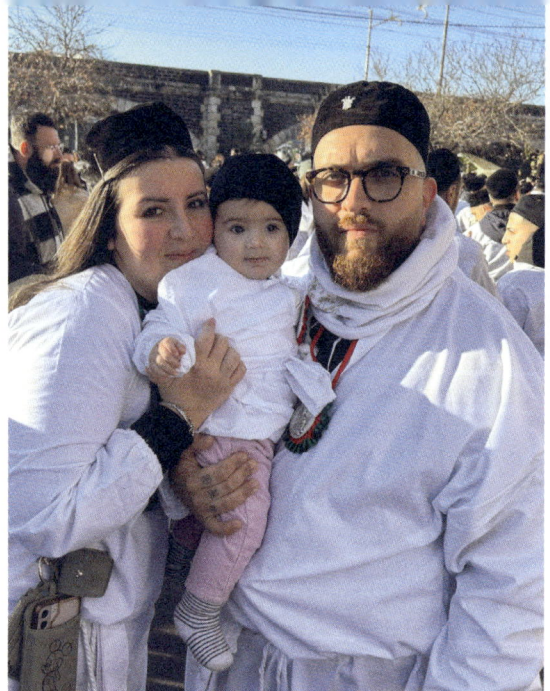

**FAMILY IS LIFE:** If it's true everywhere that it takes a village to raise a child, in Italy it takes at least six people: the parents, and also the grandparents. That's why it's a tradition in the south to name our first-born after one of them (usually the paternal grandfather). It's hard to be working parents in a country that doesn't offer great options for maternity leave or childcare benefits. We didn't qualify for government assistance to attend a public preschool, so we relied on our parents to take care of our babies while we worked. Italians don't have a babysitting culture because we take our family's help – from parents and siblings to aunts and cousins – for granted, and I think it's much better for our kids to be raised by familiar faces they can rely on while growing up, rather than outsiders.

**SANT'AGATA:** In Italy we have a deep connection with religion. Every city has its own patron saint, a Catholic tradition identifying a specific saint as protector of a city and its inhabitants, who worship the saint in return. When you have troubles in life, you can do a *voto* – a sort of pact between you and the saint. That's what I did when Bianca was born: she had respiratory problems, and was immediately put in the intensive care unit. For her first 10 days of life, I couldn't see her face, covered by an incubator mask. I prayed to St Agatha, the patron saint of Catania, to save her life. After she was safe, we promised our devotion to the saint. Every year in February, the city celebrates St Agatha with the third-biggest Catholic procession in the world. We take part as worshippers, wearing a white robe and a black hat to symbolise that we made a *voto* to the saint. I want to raise my kids with solid religious values, and this yearly procession has become an opportunity to help me connect them with God and spirituality.

**THE 'MAMMONE':** In Italy there's this myth that boys who are particularly attached to their mothers grow up to be highly dependent men who find themselves single and still pampered by their mothers until their 40s. I've always received unsolicited advice about my overly affectionate relationship with Rosario, and although I'm aware that I'll have to give him more space and independence soon, for now I want to enjoy our closeness as much as possible.

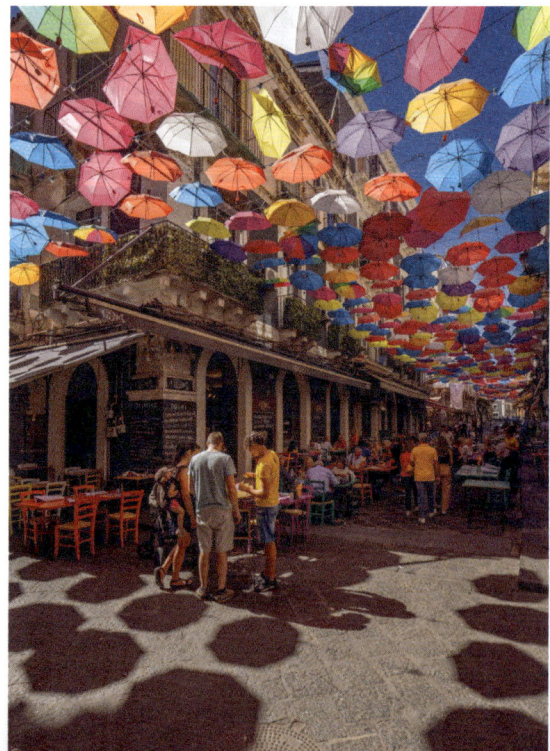

82   PARENTHOOD AROUND THE WORLD

# "In Italy we have a deep connection with religion."

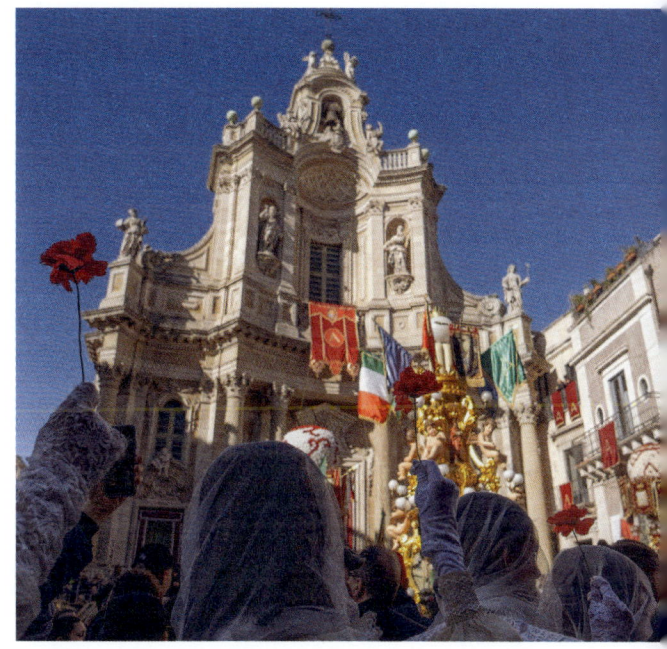

**WEDDING WITH KIDS:** We were supposed to finally get married in the summer of 2020 – we wanted Rosario to be old enough to be our ring-bearer. But since we really wanted a big party – impossible under post-COVID-19 lockdown rules – we decided to wait until summer 2022. Only a couple of weeks before the event, I found out I was expecting Bianca. I've always thought that including your kids in your wedding is a different type of blessing than following social rules that expect marriage first, kids after. I was so lucky to have both my children next to me on our special day. It's equally special for a child to witness the happily-ever-after of his parents.

**MUSIC AND EXERCISE:** Salvo and I bonded over music, so it was natural that it would play an important part in our children's upbringing. We also believe in taking care of our health and we wanted to pass this on to our kids, so we found a way to combine music and exercise by signing up Rosario to a biweekly hip-hop dance class. Most of his classmates do classic Italian sports like football or swim classes, but we thought that dance was a great way to keep fit in a fun way, and it also teaches a lot about coordination and gender equality. He loves it and I enjoy dressing him up in streetwear style!

STEFANIA D'IGNOTI

## Our favourite traditions

*Photo sessions:* Once a month we take a day for a photo session and file away these memories in a photo album. Time flies so fast and it's hard to keep track of their growth, but photos help me reflect on how they're changing.

*Sundays:* Every Sunday morning we attend Mass at the church of Santa Maria del Carmelo, followed by a family lunch with the grandparents at our house – or a restaurant, for special occasions.

*Sushi outings:* Italian families rarely have takeaways; we always cook because it's healthier. But twice a month, we indulge in eating out. One might think we'd go for pizza, but it's actually sushi! I have a really hard time getting Rosario to eat fish, but when we go to an all-you-can-eat sushi restaurant, he eats plenty.

*Nap time:* Like Spain, in Southern Italy we have our siesta after lunchtime, for a couple of hours. The four of us cuddle each other to sleep in the same bed. It's an intimate moment that strengthens our bond.

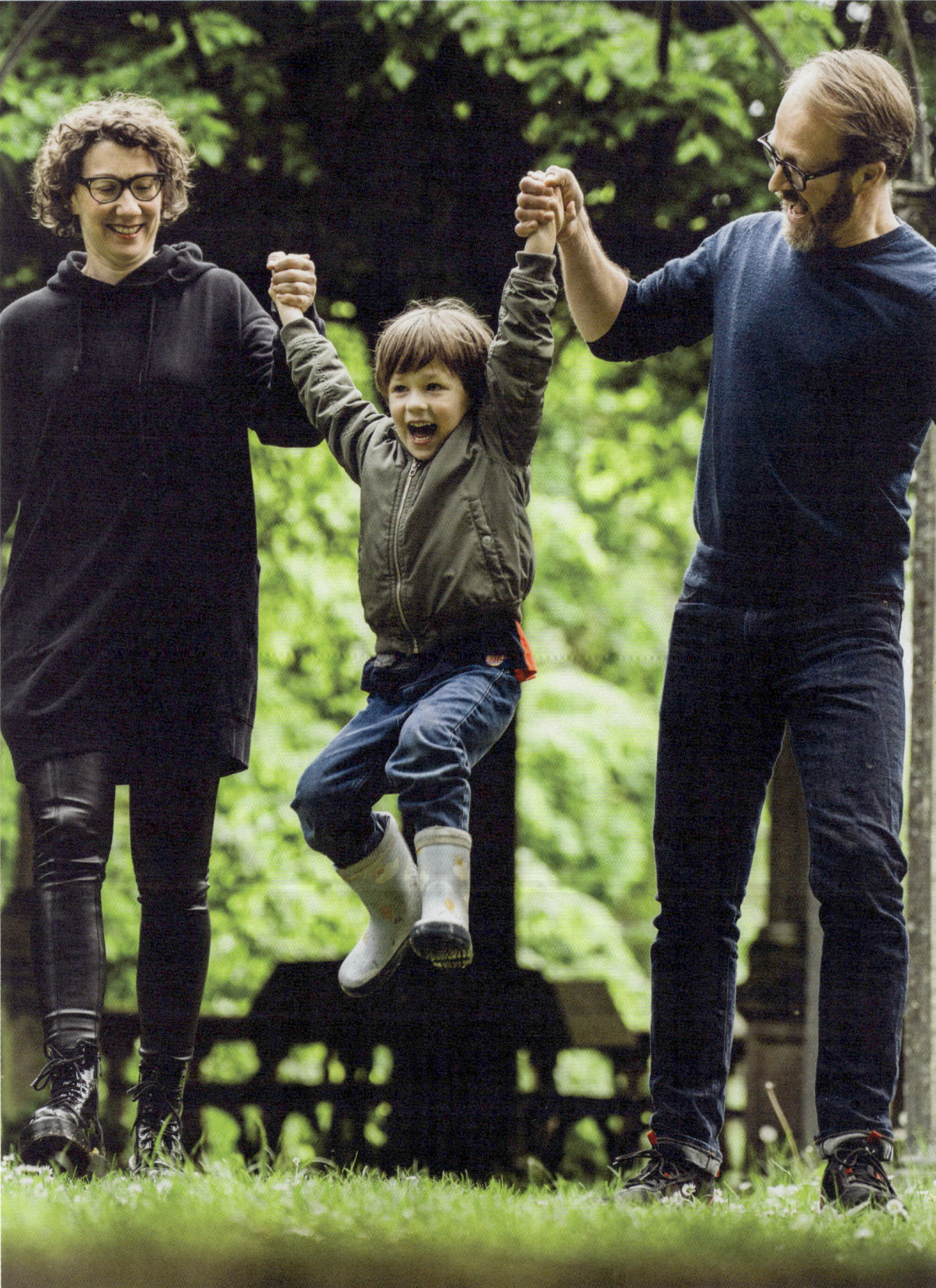

# Germany

## ALEXANDRA REHBERGER

**WHERE ALEXANDRA LIVES:**
Bavaria, Germany

**WHERE ALEXANDRA IS FROM:**
Schärding, Austria

Alexandra and Andreas met two decades ago as colleagues at a Michelin-awarded restaurant in their native Austria. They have since moved from France to Spain to Switzerland, following their passion for working in haute cuisine and are often employed at the same establishments – Alexandra as a sommelier, Andreas as a chef. In 2012, they settled in Berlin, where Andreas became a Michelin-starred head chef and Alexandra a natural-wine merchant. During the COVID-19 pandemic they had a son, Leopold (four), and decided to leave Germany's capital for the countryside. They're now on a new, exciting adventure as the management behind a boutique hotel and restaurant, set in a castle (dating back to 1306) in rural Upper Franconia, a part of Bavaria around 160km (100 miles) from the Czechia border.

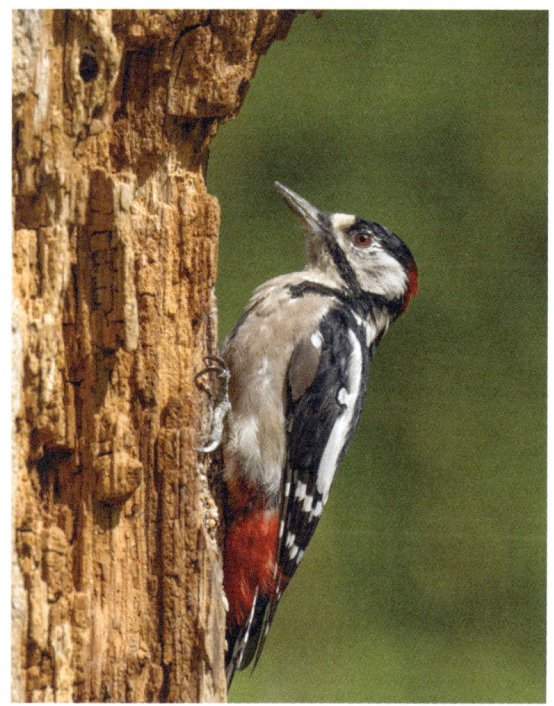

**BACK TO THE ROOTS:** We both grew up in the countryside and have always loved spending time in nature. We visited Coburg, a place in Bavaria neither of us had ever heard of, and instantly fell in love. We live in the middle of Hohenstein Forest with the most beautiful meadows and tall, ancient woodland. We love that Leopold can play outdoors and let his imagination run wild with all this open space – just like we did as kids.

**BAVARIAN TOWN LIFE:** Each German state has different childcare and school regulations. Bavaria especially provides excellent infrastructure for working parents like us. We drive him every day to an all-day school five minutes away. Most German schools are only half-day, and this gives us great flexibility.

There are also great after-school activities and there's always a spot for everybody. Leopold takes swimming lessons, and plays with a soccer club. When we pick him up before dinnertime, he always has so much to tell us from his full, happy days.

**MORE FREE TIME:** We don't spend two hours a day commuting to daycare and work any more like we did in Berlin. Being self-employed, and living where we work, lets us take time off when we need it, like if Leopold is sick or we just feel we need a little time to relax.

We have quality time together as a family every day, and that's not limited to the evenings only. For me, quality time means unplanned time – snuggling together on the couch or playing Legos because it's raining. Right now, all three of us are sitting on the terrace. It's a nice, warm summer day, the sun is slowly setting, the birds are chirping. These little moments are what life is all about.

**UNDERSTANDING NATURE'S POWER:** Nature, simply because it is often unforeseeable, teaches a lot about humility. Exploring the forest, Leopold experiences the seasonal rhythms much more precisely and differently than when we lived in the city. For example, the negative impact of a storm or strong rain on the flowers and trees, but also the beauty of when everything blooms and spring awakens. This year, 90% of the harvest in Franconian vineyards will fail due to frost, and Leopold will see that and understand the importance of protecting nature and never taking it for granted.

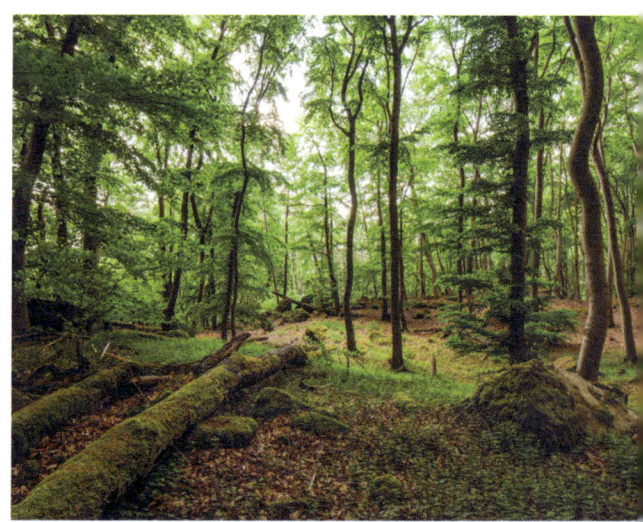

*"Nature, simply because it is often unforeseeable, teaches a lot about humility"*

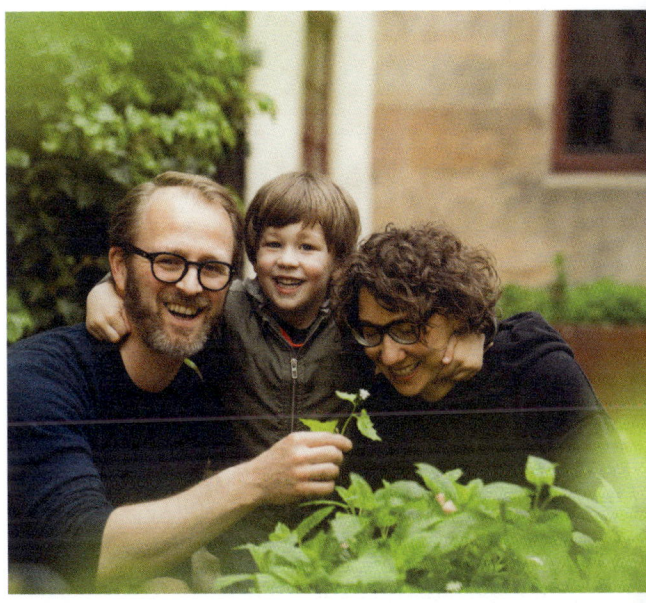

**NATURE AND CURIOSITY:** I always say it's impossible for a kid to ever get bored in the countryside. Being able to play outdoors so much has made Leopold very independent, and we hope all these moments of discovery and exploring also make him a freethinking, creative adult one day. He goes around the nearby forest, either alone or with his au pair, and then comes back inside for five minutes, to dad in the kitchen or me at the reception desk or wherever, and he can't wait to tell us all about it: a cool snail shell to show us, or that there were fireflies, dormice, ladybugs.

**SUSTAINABLE NOURISHMENT:** As gastronomers, our life's passion is raising awareness about the importance of food sustainability and the health benefits of organic, biodynamic food. Living between Nuremberg and Bamberg – the largest vegetable-growing area in Germany! – is a fantastic opportunity to nourish our family with some of the best produce Europe has to offer.

It is important for us that Leopold understands that food doesn't just show up in supermarkets, but that a lot of effort goes into its production, and to never take for granted the roles of dedicated people and nature in these supply chains. So, we go to markets and buy fresh farm milk, artisan sausage and cheese directly from the people who make it. Sometimes Andreas goes hunting in the forest and catches deer, which we eat together; the meat tastes natural and delicious.

*BARBARA WOOLSEY*

## Our favourite traditions

***Collecting herbs:*** We have a small family garden where we grow herbs like knotweed and garlic, and some vegetables. It's so wonderful to go out together and see what's ready to harvest. Leopold also waters the garden himself, and he's learned so much about how to tell if a plant is thirsty or needs more sun.

***Forest walks:*** We go for many walks through Hohenstein Forest. There are many short trails; they're not paved but generally smooth enough for Leopold to ride his bike, while Andreas and I go on foot. Sometimes on the weekends, we'll pack a picnic and eat it on a bench. The scenery is so beautiful and pure, with lots of tall beech and oak trees, and interesting rocky outcrops. This time together fills our family up with so much energy and calms the spirit. It's like meditation in movement.

***Make-believe outdoors:*** In the forest, Leopold loves to make up fantasies, so we'll run around on 'knight adventures', pretending the trees are invisible dragons and fighting with sticks. We invent the wildest worlds together!

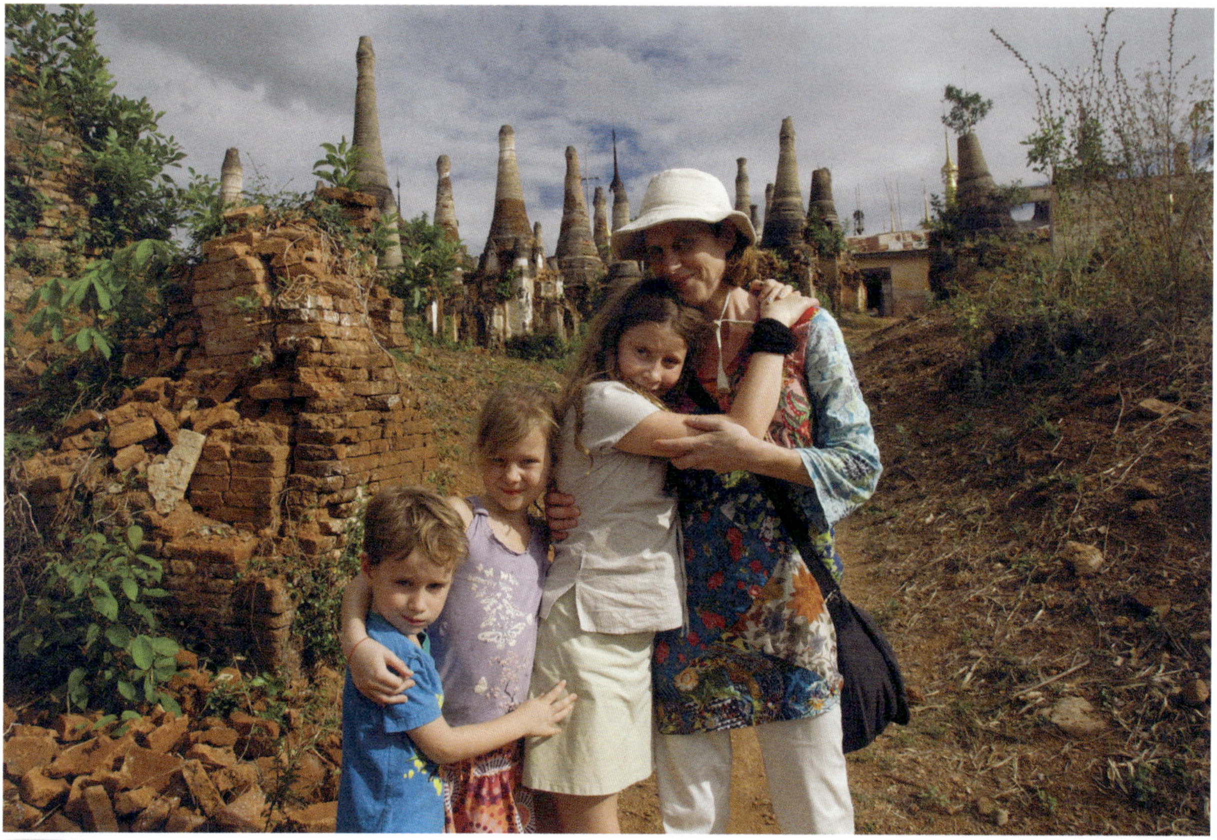

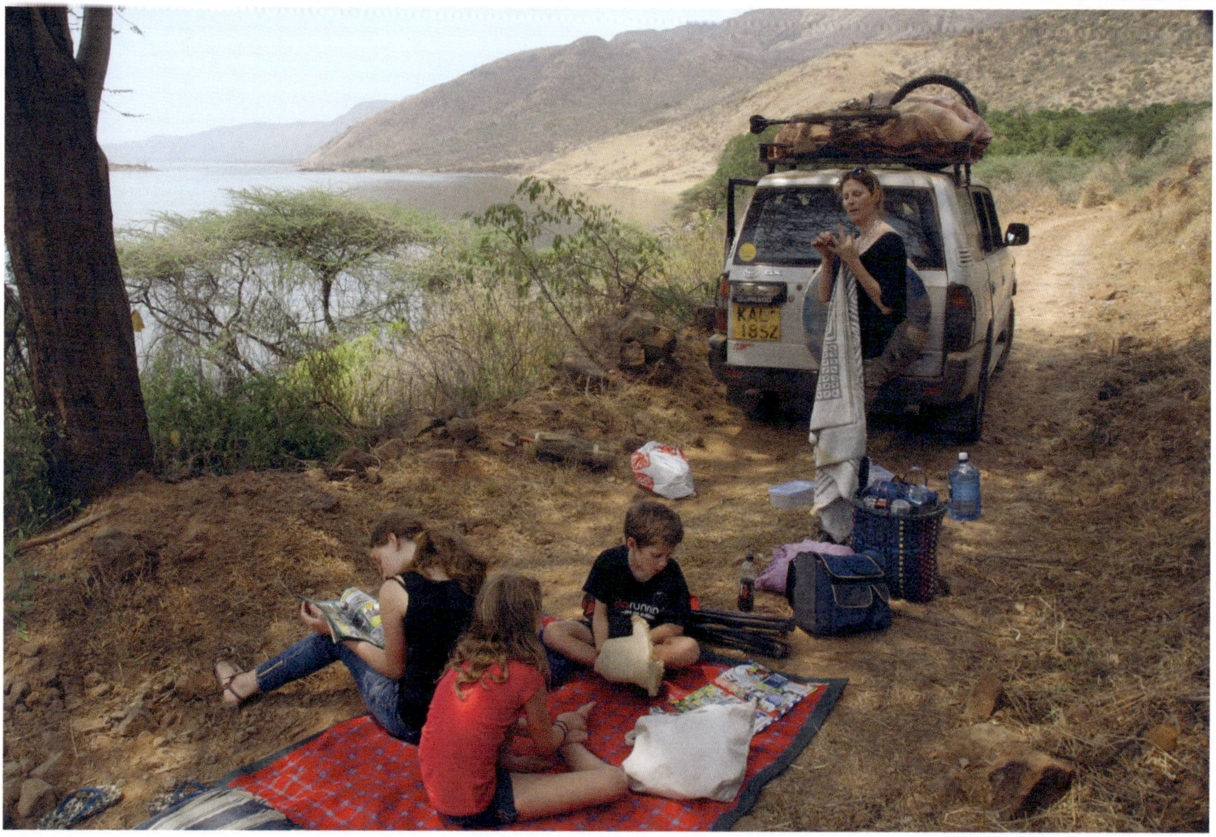

# Scotland

## PIERS BENATAR

**WHERE PIERS LIVES:**
Moffat, Scotland

**WHERE PIERS IS FROM:**
Bromley, England

Piers and Nikki met at Durham University and started a family while Piers was studying photojournalism in London and Nikki was working for an international women's health organisation. Shortly afterwards, they began a peripatetic life of three- to seven-year postings overseas, with stints in Pakistan, Nepal, Myanmar and Kenya, during which time the family grew to three. 'Beatrice (26) was two when we moved to Pakistan, Stella (22) was born while we were living in Islamabad, and Bart (20) was born while we were in Kathmandu. The children have grown up with travel in their veins!' After childhoods spent overseas, the family returned to the UK, starting a new life in the hills of Dumfriesshire as the children headed off to university.

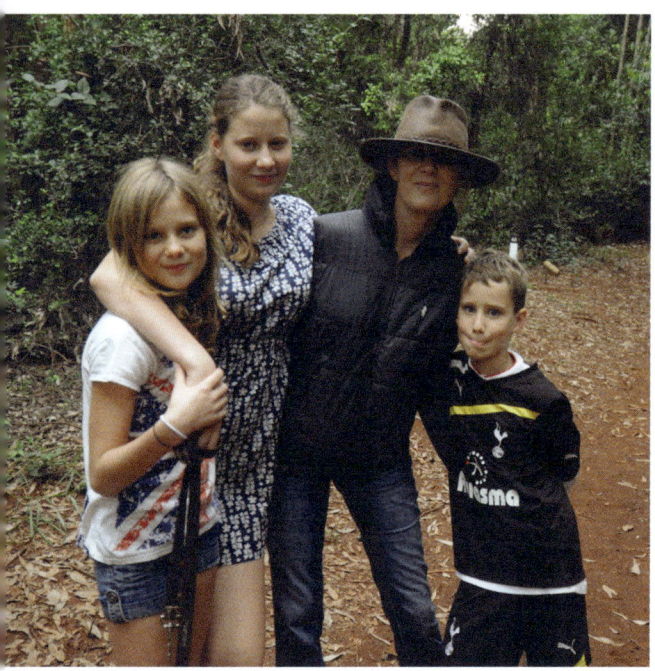

**A LUCKY LIFE:** Being an expat isn't like being a traveller. Through Nikki's work, we got a brilliant package of health insurance and top-quality education for the children at British and American international schools. We got to live in nice houses with big gardens and hire staff, drivers and nannies – it was a very comfortable life. And we were able to move in rarefied circles; the kids went to school with the children of ambassadors, politicians and pop stars. In Pakistan, we took tea with Imran and Jemima Khan, whose children were at the same school as Beatrice.

**LINKING THE GENERATIONS:** While we were living in Asia and Africa, Nikki's parents were living in Oman and Cyprus, so they were able to visit regularly. It helped keep the connection between the generations. The kids probably saw more of their grandparents growing up than many children living in the UK. Nikki's mum made eight trips to see us in one year in Islamabad! It was also a great opportunity for my mum, who hadn't travelled much, to see more of the world.

**MEALS TOGETHER:** One perk of having staff was us all being able to sit down together for almost every meal. It made us very close as a family. We made a routine of having regular roast dinners to keep a connection to home, but the kids had an adventurous diet. In many places, English food wasn't an option – in Kenya, the main choices were Indian, Korean and Japanese food, or local dishes such as *nyama choma* (roasted meat) and *ugali* (corn meal).

**HEALTH CONSIDERATIONS:** Healthcare was probably our biggest worry as parents. Dengue fever was a risk in several places we lived (I ended up very ill with it) and we couldn't keep taking anti-tablets forever, so we had to be extra careful about keeping the kids from being bitten by mosquitoes. It was scary at times not having quick access to medical care – on one occasion in Myanmar, our son had breathing difficulties in the night and our only option was to rush him to the house of some French doctors we knew who were living in Yangon.

**A BROAD EDUCATION:** Living in all these different countries and going to school with people from all over the world made the children very tolerant and positive about life. They're comfortable mixing with all kinds of people from all types of

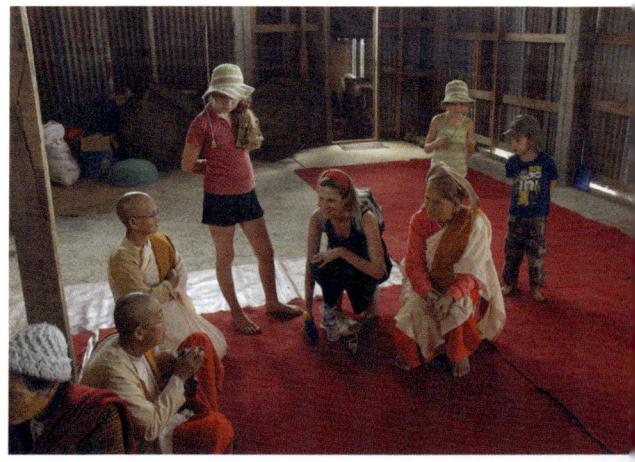

backgrounds. When we moved from one country to the next, it was tough for them to leave their school friends, but we made a point of arranging regular trips back and forth so they could stay in touch – Bart took his first solo flight aged 14 to stay with his best friend in Kenya!

**PERKS OF RETURNING:** It might sound surprising, but moving from Nairobi to Scotland was an adventure for the kids – it was very different to what they were used to. They instantly had loads more freedom. They could walk to the shops and meet up with friends without needing us to take them everywhere. They even enjoyed moving into the Scottish education system – it was the first time they'd ever had to wear school uniforms!

**REINTEGRATING:** Part of the reason we decided to move back to the UK was to give the children more experience of doing things for themselves, without always being able to rely on staff. It's easy to get used to having everything done for you as an expat – we've visited people's houses and been told off for pouring ourselves a glass of water!

We also wanted the children to see us doing 'normal' things like making dinner and cleaning the house, to set them up with the skills they need to be independent. And we wanted them to see the system working – people paying taxes and getting functioning services – after seeing so much corruption in the developing world.

JOE BINDLOSS

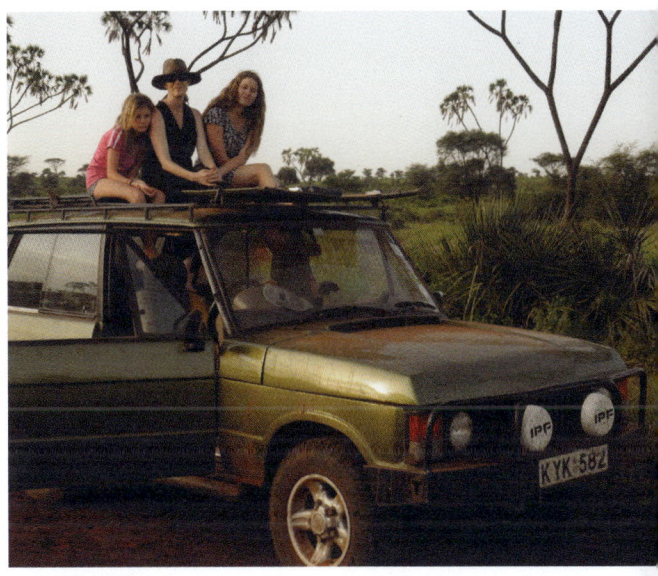

## Our favourite traditions

**Plugging into the destination:** On weekends, we'd always try to visit historical and religious sights and other points of interest – to remind us how lucky we were to be there and stay linked to the local culture. The children grew up visiting temples, stupas and pagodas – once, on holiday in Scotland, my young son saw a bronze bust of Eisenhower and shouted out 'Buddha! Buddha!', to the great surprise of other visitors!

**Hanging out at the club:** During our time in Asia, we became members of the international clubs, including the British and American clubs, to give the children a sense of Western culture and home. The clubs were always interesting microcosms of their native countries.

**Making a feature of Christmas:** We always made a point of hosting large Christmas parties at our home, inviting local expats, friends, colleagues and the children's grandparents. Festivities such as Christmas held extra symbolic importance when so many friends and family were either far away in England or on postings in other countries. This tradition continued even when we moved to Scotland.

> "We made a routine of having regular roast dinners to keep a connection to home."

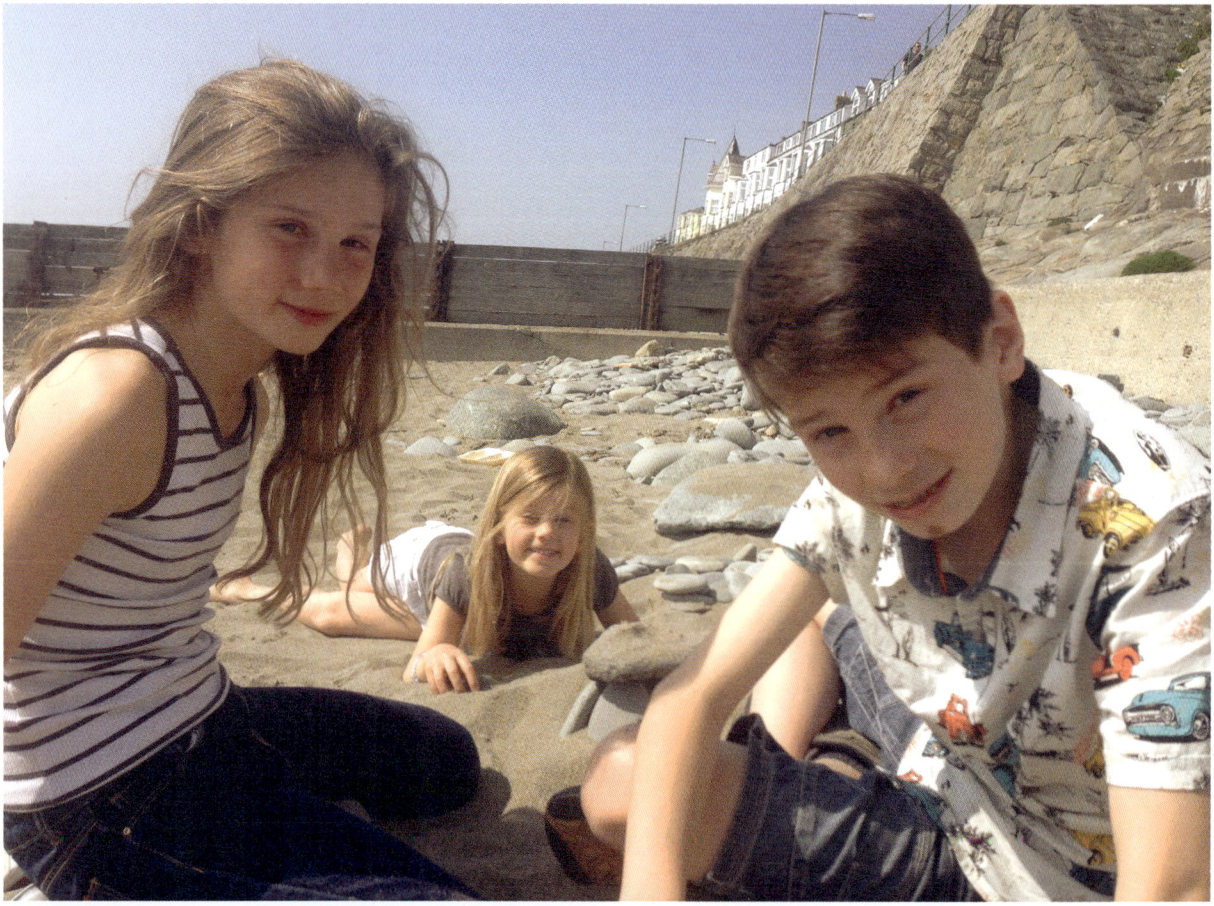

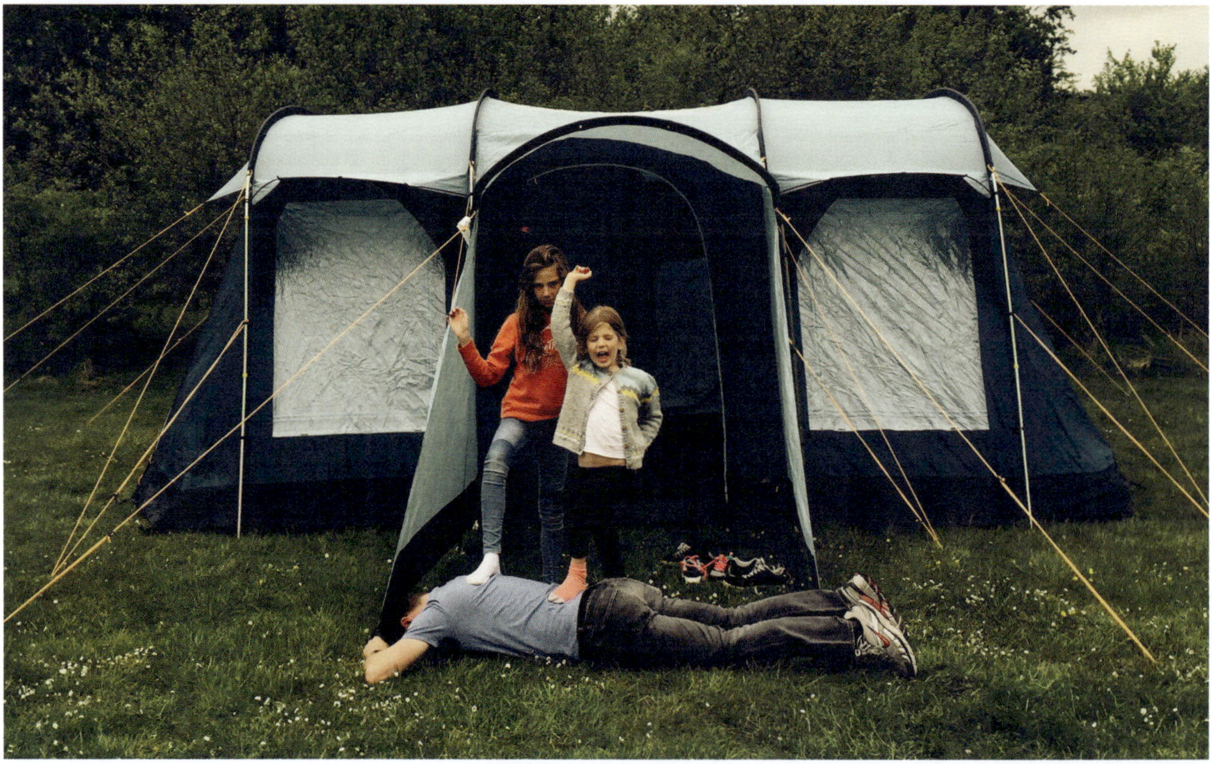

# England

## CHRIS BATTYE

**WHERE CHRIS LIVES:**
Berkshire, England

**WHERE CHRIS IS FROM:**
Leeds, England

Chris is one of those Englishmen who was born and raised in the north but migrated to England's south. After taking a gap year to travel the world and then studying at university in Newcastle, he moved to London where he and his wife (from Manchester) had two children. They later relocated to a village in Berkshire to bring up their three kids – now aged 20, 19 and 14. 'Living in London was fun when we were young, but when you have children it can get pretty challenging. People aren't very kid-friendly in my experience: you can feel the public disdain if your toddler has a tantrum on the bus. Plus, we wanted more room and a garden.'

**NUCLEAR VS EXTENDED FAMILY:** We don't live very close to our kids' grandparents. Typically, grandparents are called on in an emergency, such as school-holiday childcare cover, and they'll visit for birthdays and Christmas. One of our overarching values in the UK is to not be a bother, which means grandparents will take off as soon as they see an opportunity.

**CHRISTMAS:** We take family Christmases very seriously…it's the one day of the year when the entire extended family gets together to feast on a traditional roast dinner and watch TV all afternoon. Our little nuclear family will usually go to church in the lead-up to Christmas, even though we don't go any other time of the year. The entire village crams into an old Norman church for carols, followed by mulled wine and mince pies.

**SUMMER CAMPING HOLIDAYS:** The summer camping trip is a rite of passage. Brits scatter all around the coastline where the beaches are gorgeous, but the weather is not. We usually head to the wilds of North Wales to then be corralled into a crowded campsite. One year it'll be rainy and windy, the next it's baking hot and you'll wake in your tent at 5am in a sweat, sleep-deprived and wondering if you should go home early.

**SKIING IN EUROPE:** We do the annual – very middle-class – ski trip to Europe. It's wildly expensive, and to save costs you have to book just ahead of the official February half-term dates then come up with faux illnesses to take your kids off school for a few days before, or after, the break. We love the French Alps but for the last few years we've been skiing in Andorra.

**TEENS AND FREEDOM:** We try to give our kids a fair bit of freedom and autonomy, but technology has changed everything. We let our teens go off to house parties knowing they will make mistakes like drink too much alcohol and regret it. We're not very strict. I think most parents of my generation have the same attitude. I'd rather they did stupid stuff, but they know they *can* talk to us about it.

**SCHOOL LIFE:** While I do want my kids to do well at school, academic achievement is not the most important thing to me. Parents we socialise with tend to care more about whether their kids have good friends than their grades. Government schools are generally good but parents are kept at arm's length. You're invited in for parents' evening once a year, that's it.

**WEEKEND SPORTS:** Schools in our area don't have much in the way of sports facilities (there are no indoor courts or large playing fields except at the private schools – land is just too expensive). I have spent the good part of many weekends ferrying kids to netball and football, usually in a larger town nearby. You need to be pretty organised: the parents all share the drop-offs and pick-ups so you also get to know your kids' friends (and of course embarrass them with your dad jokes).

**ACADEMIC COMPETITION:** Education is very stratified in England. Some parents aspire to get their kids into a 'red-brick university' – even secretly getting their kid tutored for the 11+ exam which decides if they get into selective grammar school, which increases your chance of going to Oxbridge. But I preferred that my kids focused on their passions rather than prestige.

**HONEST TALK:** I'm open and honest with my kids about my feelings and worries. I've felt like I should set an example to them. Things have changed a lot since I was growing up, parents were remote, and if you told them a problem, they pretty much told you to 'get over it'. It can be hard to admit if you're struggling sometimes, but I have found my kids are more emotionally intelligent than me.

*TASMIN WABY*

## Our favourite traditions

**One-on-one time:** I make sure I get some one-on-one time doing something my kids want to do, whether it's fishing on a river near our house with my eldest, watching the local football team with my youngest, or going skiing with Amelie, the 'middlest' one.

**The weekend fry-up:** This is a sort of rallying cry on a Sunday morning. You've had a busy Saturday, but someone will say: 'Kids, we're having a fry-up tomorrow.' A fry-up is a British breakfast: we're talking fried egg, bacon, sausage, black pudding, beans, mushrooms, tomatoes and toast.

**Bonfire Night:** Every village around the country will have a winter Bonfire Night on 5 November. It's all a bit anarchic: kids run around in the dark with sparklers, the parents get a bit tipsy, fireworks are set off, and a giant effigy of Guy Fawkes is thrown on a huge bonfire to celebrate the overthrowing of a 17th-century terrorist plot.

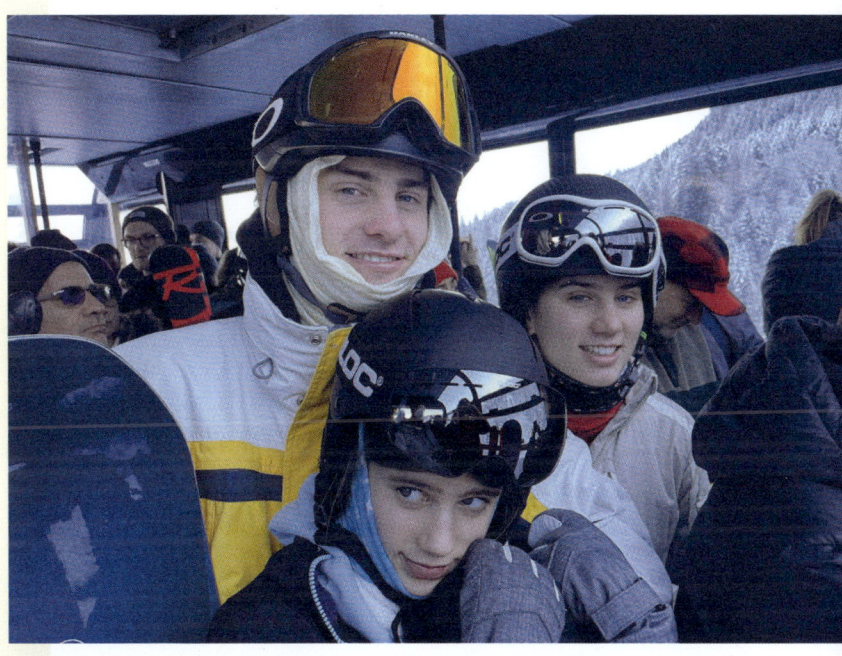

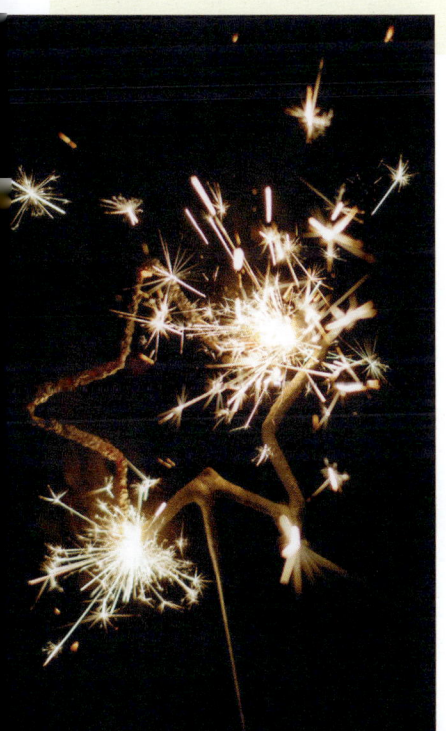

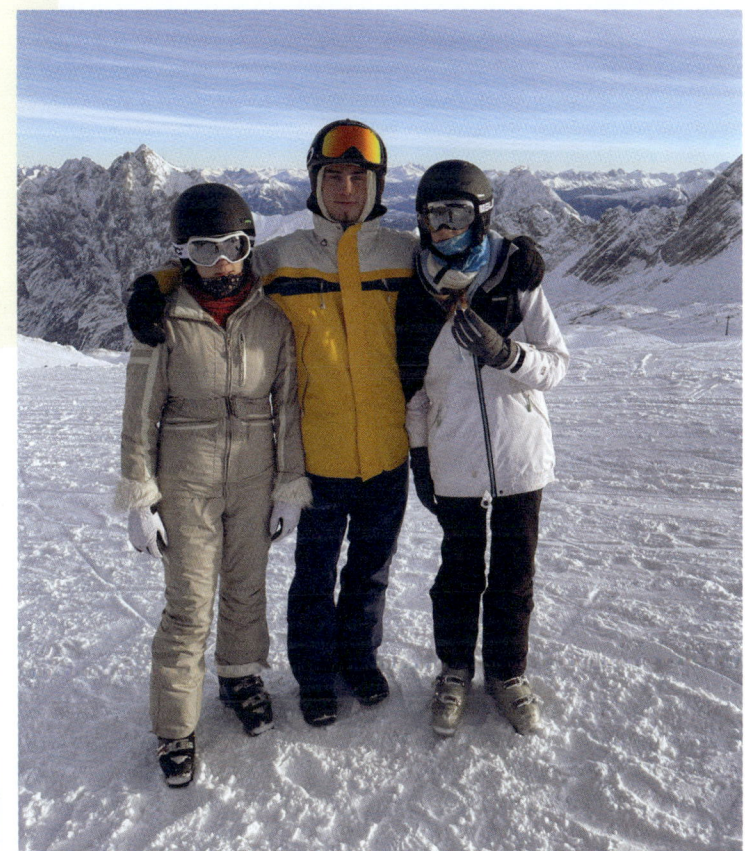

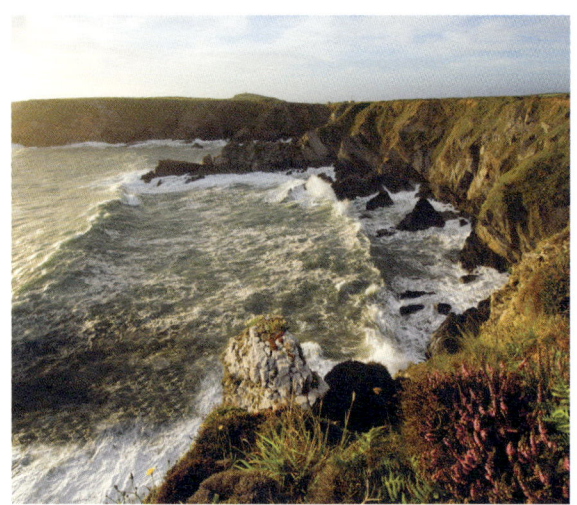
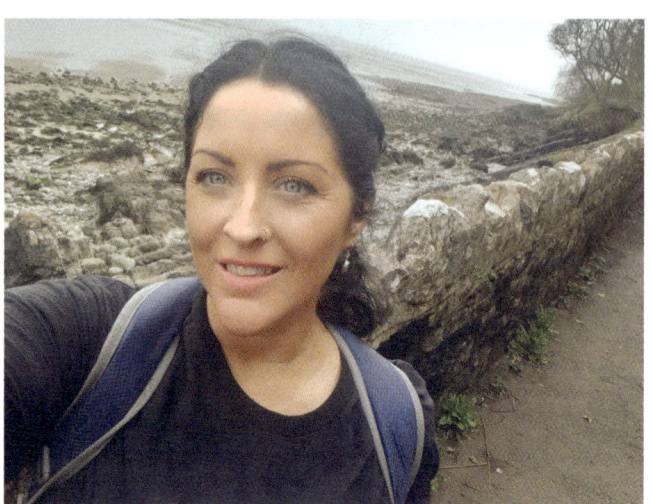
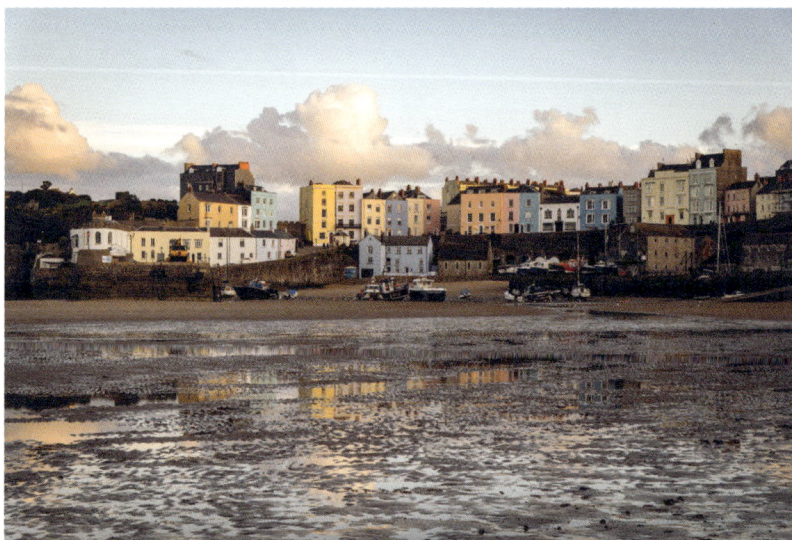
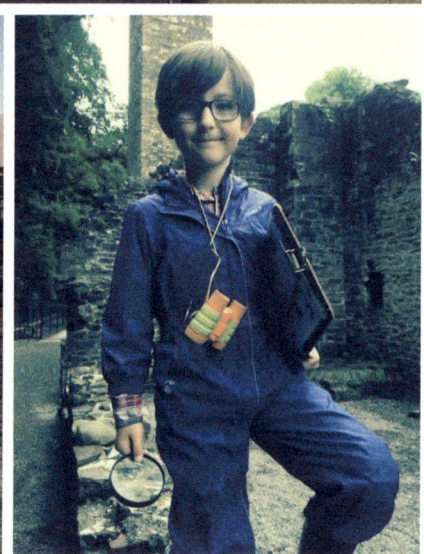
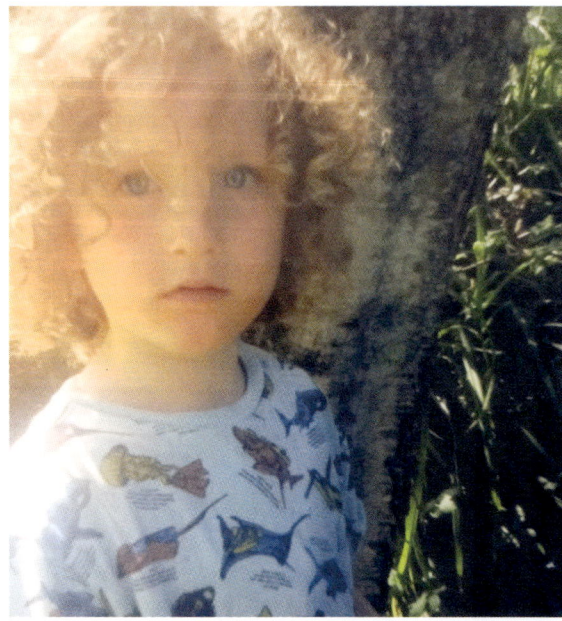
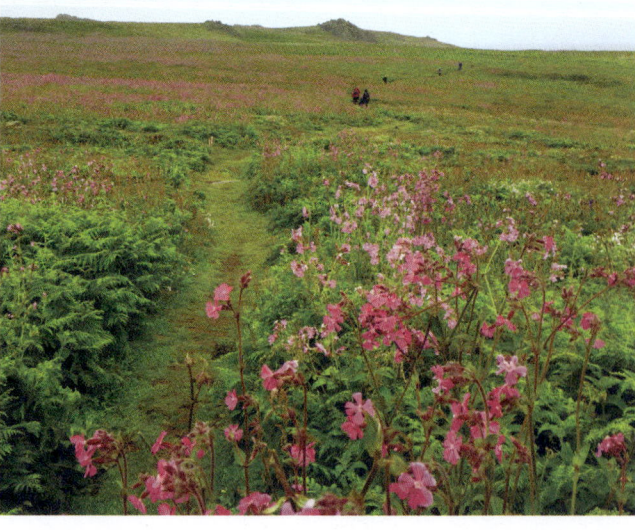

# Wales

## MARIA WOODWARD

**WHERE MARIA LIVES:**
Pontardawe, Wales

**WHERE MARIA IS FROM:**
Cardiff, Wales

Maria was born in Cardiff but moved to the Swansea area after returning from travelling when she was 22. 'All my family was moving there, my brother to university, then my parents to help look after my brother's child – it kind of made sense', she says. 'Having them all fairly close for so long has been brilliant; it has definitely made bringing up three children a bit easier.' She now lives in Pontardawe, a small town in the woodsy hills outside Swansea. She shares custody of her children Laila (17), Oisin (15) and Finley (13) with her ex-husband, but they spend most of their time with her. Maria works as a specialist perinatal mental health nurse. She has worked full-time and studied for her master's degree while raising her family.

**COMMUNICATION:** I always treated the children as friends. We have a great relationship and talk about everything. There were so many taboos for my generation growing up; things we never discussed with our parents like sex and drugs. The children respect me for being open with them and they never have a problem telling me their problems either – or what they want from life.

**PASSION:** I have a zest for life and the children do too. They would always try new food on holiday, and explore nature in different ways. I encourage them to do what they love. I'm really into cooking and Finley is already enthusiastic about it too. Spanish food is his favourite: tapping into our family heritage! Oisin is out mountain-biking with his friends on the trails around South Wales every chance he gets. He has to be good because Pontardawe's trails go through seriously steep woods; they're really challenging. Laila is a folk musician. She has supported big acts like The Shires and sings about growing up in the Welsh Valleys; her lyrics are powerful and poignant. We sometimes think of lyrics together, even though she can write beautiful songs without me! It's true I've always worked hard alongside being a mum, but you have to in order to get what you want – and Laila's got similar values.

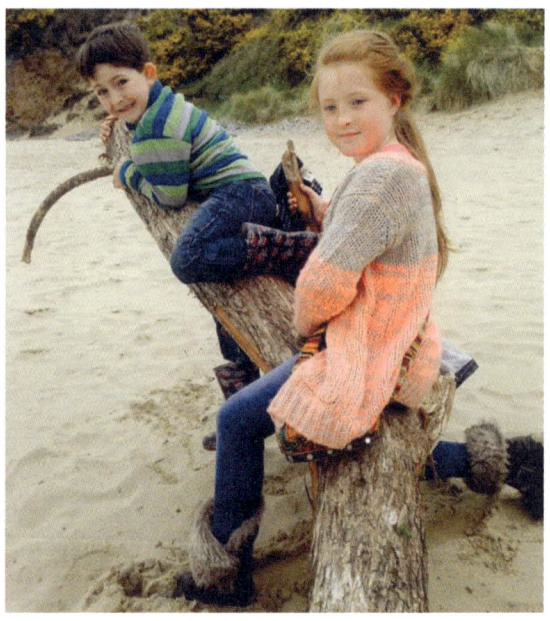

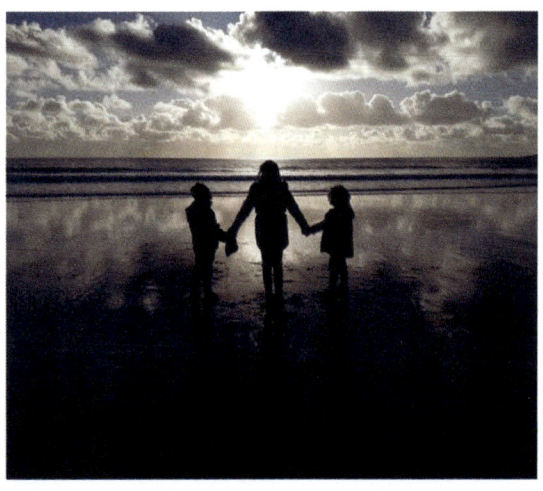

**NATURE:** I've instilled a love of nature and respect for the environment in all of my kids. In Wales you can't wait for a sunny day. You have to be prepared to go out in all weathers, and we always have – walking, swimming, having beach barbecues. We found plenty of ways to make things extra interesting: who could find the bluest shell on the beach, who could make the best seaweed mermaid. Lots of what we did stuck as long-term family traditions, like moon-bathing on the summer solstice at the beach.

**MUSIC:** Some new, weird or wonderful music is always playing in our house. I'm really into it, and I've taken the children to quite a few gigs. Swansea is full of great music venues: the Elysium is our favourite, but there are also gigs in more unusual venues like the Waterfront Museum and the Dylan Thomas Birthplace House. But I also think it helps create a fun, laid-back vibe in the house. We often had a bit of a disco ball going at family get-togethers!

**EATING TOGETHER:** We always eat together, at the table – and nine times out of 10 with some-

> "You have to be prepared to go out in all weathers, and we always have"

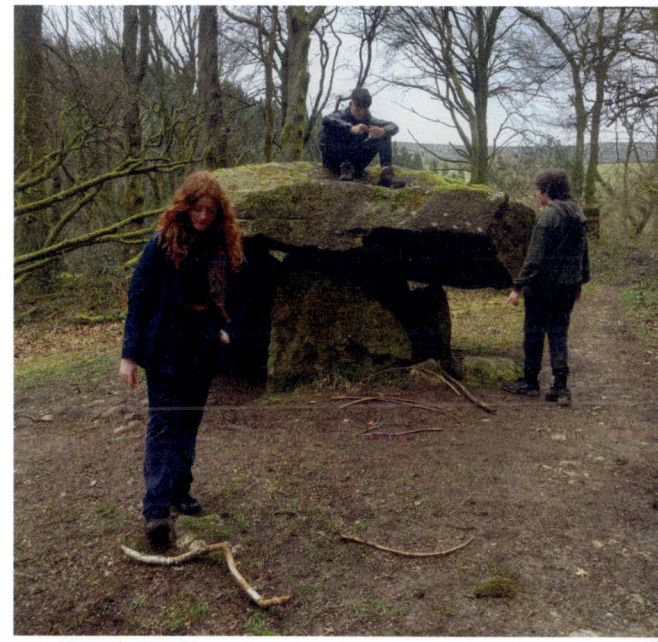

thing I've cooked. It's something everyone in the extended family always did. I think it's made the children quite knowledgeable about good food and has helped them be more communicative.

**CHRISTMAS:** Christmas is way more than a celebration for us; looking back, it kind of shows exactly how our family has always been. We have a very big extended family – there would be well over 20 of us! The highlight was the Boxing Day puppet show in the past. But even though the kids are older now, the build-up to Christmas is the same. The first Saturday in December, the children and I make the decorations. I get things started with duck pancakes, then we make garlands out of shells and pine cones we find on walks. But having home-cooked food and getting creative with the children has always been important to us as a family, year-round: any excuse!

**HOLIDAYS AND DAYS OUT:** I'd always take the kids on adventures – for them and me both. We'd go glamping in Pembrokeshire in southwest Wales, normally at Easter time. We'd have egg hunts, fun things like that. Pembrokeshire's coast has to be some of the best in the UK; there's always a hidden cove to discover. My dad's great-grandmother came from Cartagena in Spain and we went there for holidays a lot. I have hilarious memories of them trying to learn flamenco, or getting all excited about the Roman history there.

*LUKE WATERSON*

## Our favourite traditions

***Bedtime story and song:*** This happened every night without fail when the children were younger. Some songs I made up, I admit!

***Happiness jars:*** We'd decorate old jars with tissue paper and paint until they resembled stained glass. Then I would write down anything that made the children happy and pop it in the jar. When they had down days, we'd pull out what we'd put in; it really did cheer them up!

***Beach bonfires:*** These are what we do at all times of the year. We live near the Gower Peninsula, so there are many beaches to choose from. They have proved so popular, even family friends come now.

***New Year's dip:*** Wales isn't that warm on 1 January, so this is tough but *so* rewarding and invigorating. We go down to a beach on the Gower. Me, Laila and Oisin go in – Finley's less keen! We have learned to pick gently-shelving beaches like Oxwich for easy in-and-outs, and to take hot chocolate to warm up afterwards.

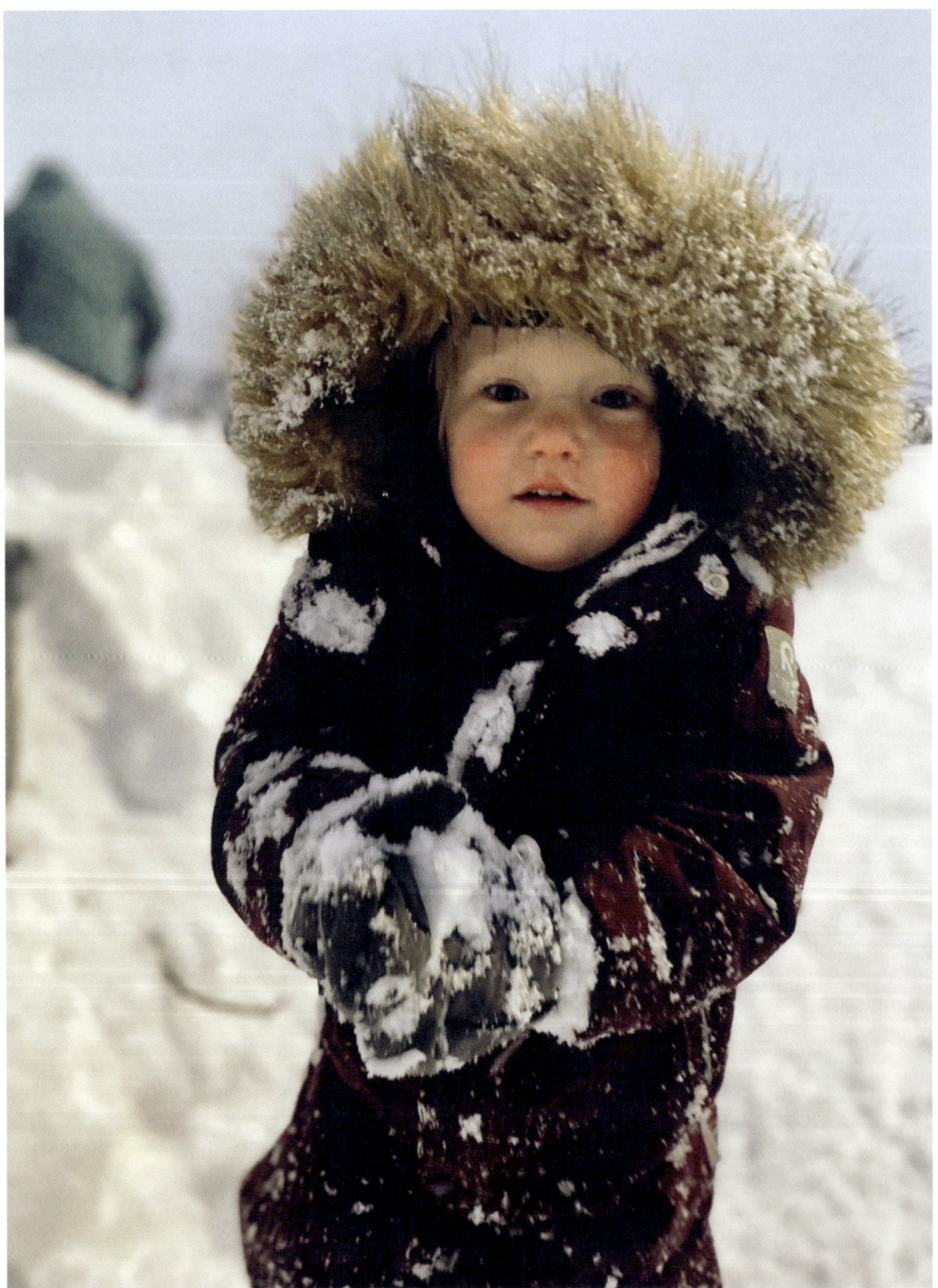

# Norway

## KAJA ANDERSEN

**WHERE KAJA LIVES:**
Horten, Norway

**WHERE KAJA IS FROM:**
Horten, Norway

Always with a keen sense of adventure and a love of the outdoors, Kaja moved from Norway to Australia for her university studies (and to surf those famous Australian beaches). She met Jono on a surf trip. He was bringing up two children of his own as a solo dad. Jono and Kaja got married back in Norway, had two more children back in Australia – Alfie (three) and Mia (six) – then decided to move back to Norway to spend time with grandparents and to immerse their children in Norwegian culture and language. Their mix of Norwegian and Australian approaches to parenting has given Kaja a fresh perspective on her home culture: what works well and what's a bit confounding.

**EVERYONE EATS AT THE SAME TIME:** Our lives are very ritualised in Norway. Everyone seems to hurry to get home and get dinner on the table by 4.30pm – this is almost sacred. After dinner you'll go to after-school activities, play outside in the summer (or enjoy the snow in winter) before having *kveldsmat* (supper) – that's bread with spreads, later in the evening before bed. Why do we eat dinner so early? It might be because it gets dark early, or maybe we think it's better for your health?

**CHILDREN SHOULD BE OUTDOORS:** The focus of early-years learning is on being active, being outdoors and becoming independent from a young age. The children go into the forest for the day, where they explore nature and learn to use knives and saws to cut wood. If they climb a tree, they have to climb down again on their own. For a small accident with a bit of bruising – you won't even hear about it. This is very different from Australia.

**THERE'S NO SUCH THING AS BAD WEATHER:** At the start of the week, we take our children to kindergarten with a big backpack of clothes for every type of weather, especially in spring and autumn. The kids come home covered in sand and dirt and mud from head to toe – and with a bag full of clothes to launder.

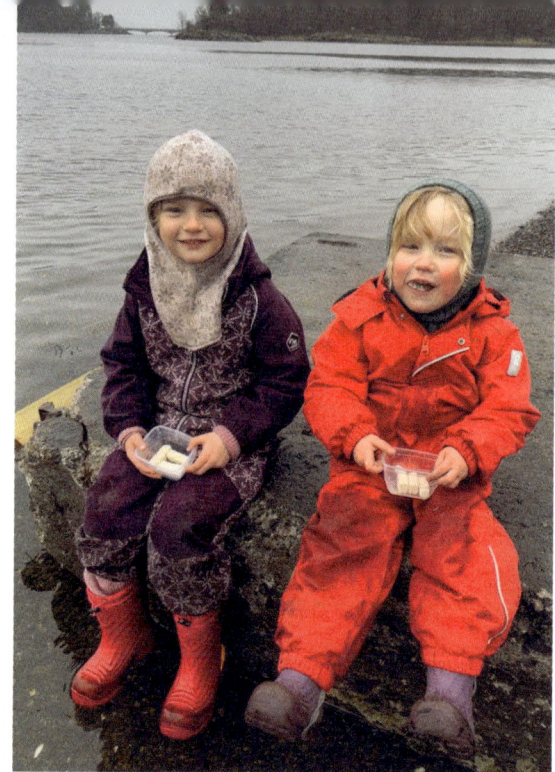

**DON'T BE LATE FOR PICK-UP:** Children go to kindergarten five days a week, from the age of one. Our kids' kindergarten closes at 4.30pm, but if you arrive to pick your child up at 10 minutes past 4pm they will almost be the last child there, because obviously everyone rushes home to get dinner on the table by 4.30pm.

**BABIES NAP OUTSIDE:** A big shock to people arriving in Norway is how we leave our babies and small children sleeping in their prams outside during the day, even in winter. There's no national standard about how cold it can be, but if it's more than -10°C (14°F), maybe you'll consider taking them inside. Nap time is the same time for everyone, so if you walk past a kindergarten in the middle of the day you might see 20 prams in a row in the snow. Even outside a cafe in town, you'll see babies sleeping outside on the street while the parents are inside having a coffee. It's not really feasible to wake up a baby and take off 16 layers of clothes to take them inside (and we live in a very trusting society).

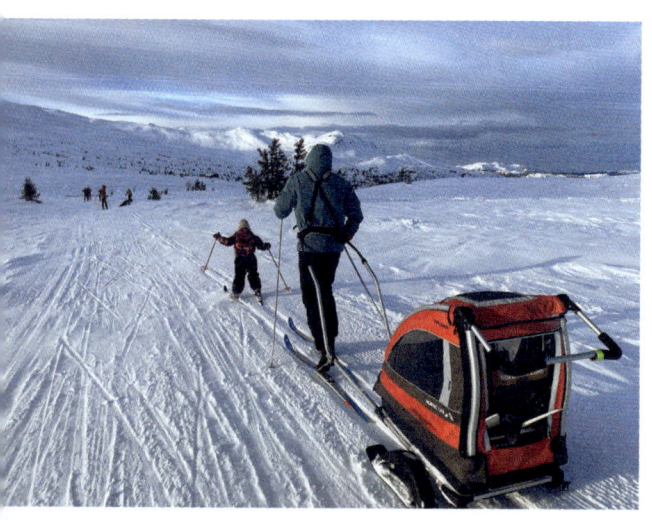

PARENTHOOD AROUND THE WORLD

"Everyone seems to hurry to get home and get dinner on the table by 4.30pm – this is almost sacred."

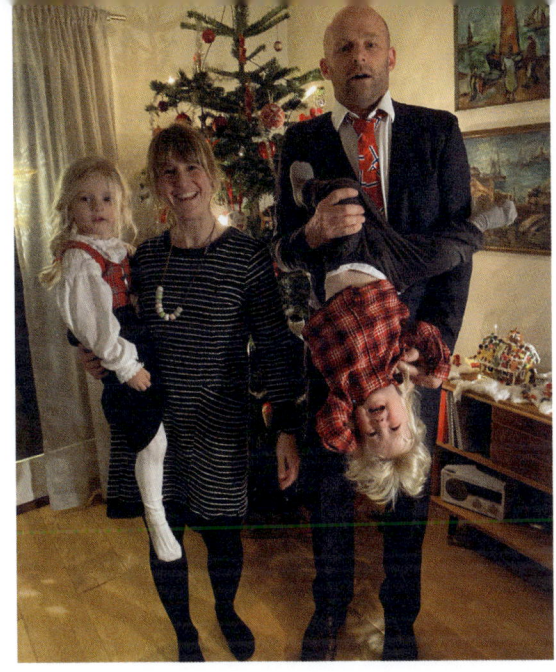

**EQUAL CO-PARENTING IS EXPECTED:** The dynamic between parents is quite equal here – regardless of gender. When you have a baby you get one year's paid parental leave but it has to be shared between both parents. It might be a challenge for some birth mothers: you go back to work just when your baby is getting a bit more fun, and you have to manage breastfeeding with paid work. In Norway you have an hour of 'breastfeeding leave' each day until your child is one, so mums can go home in the middle of the day or leave work early.

**WE LOVE TO CONFORM, BUT ASKING QUESTIONS IS ENCOURAGED:** We all want to be part of the community in Norway, which often means everyone does things the same way...sometimes it might feel like there's not a lot of diversity. We're also not very good at talking about our feelings or struggles, except with the people closest to us, which can be difficult when you're a parent. Maybe this is a result of the climate: we spend half of the year – when it gets dark early – 'hibernating' in our own little bubble at home. That said, children are really encouraged to have their own opinions and ask questions, as long as they do that in a respectful way. We're not a very authoritative society. It's normal to express what you think, even to people in authority.

TASMIN WABY

## Our favourite traditions

***Norwegian flags to mark a birthday:*** Children's birthday parties go for exactly two hours with the same schedule: hot dogs, then cake; play games; distribute the sweets bags; then home. We fly a Norwegian flag outside our houses when it's someone's birthday too – but our relationship with the Norwegian flag is not like it might seem – it is patriotic, but not in a negative 'keep out' way.

***Children's Day:*** 17 May is a big date in the annual diary. Although it's a celebration of Norwegian independence, the day is very focused on kids, with games, toys, balloons, hot dogs and ice creams. Schools organise the children into parades with flag-waving and songs. It's a highlight for our kids.

***Christmas starts on Christmas Eve:*** We begin with a 5pm dinner on 24 December, which is centred around pork belly (a type of salted and dry meat), or fish, then dessert. Next, Santa Claus knocks and comes into the house with a bag of presents for everyone. 'Santa' is usually a family member, or neighbour, in dress-up. As the kids get older they realise it, but they still love it.

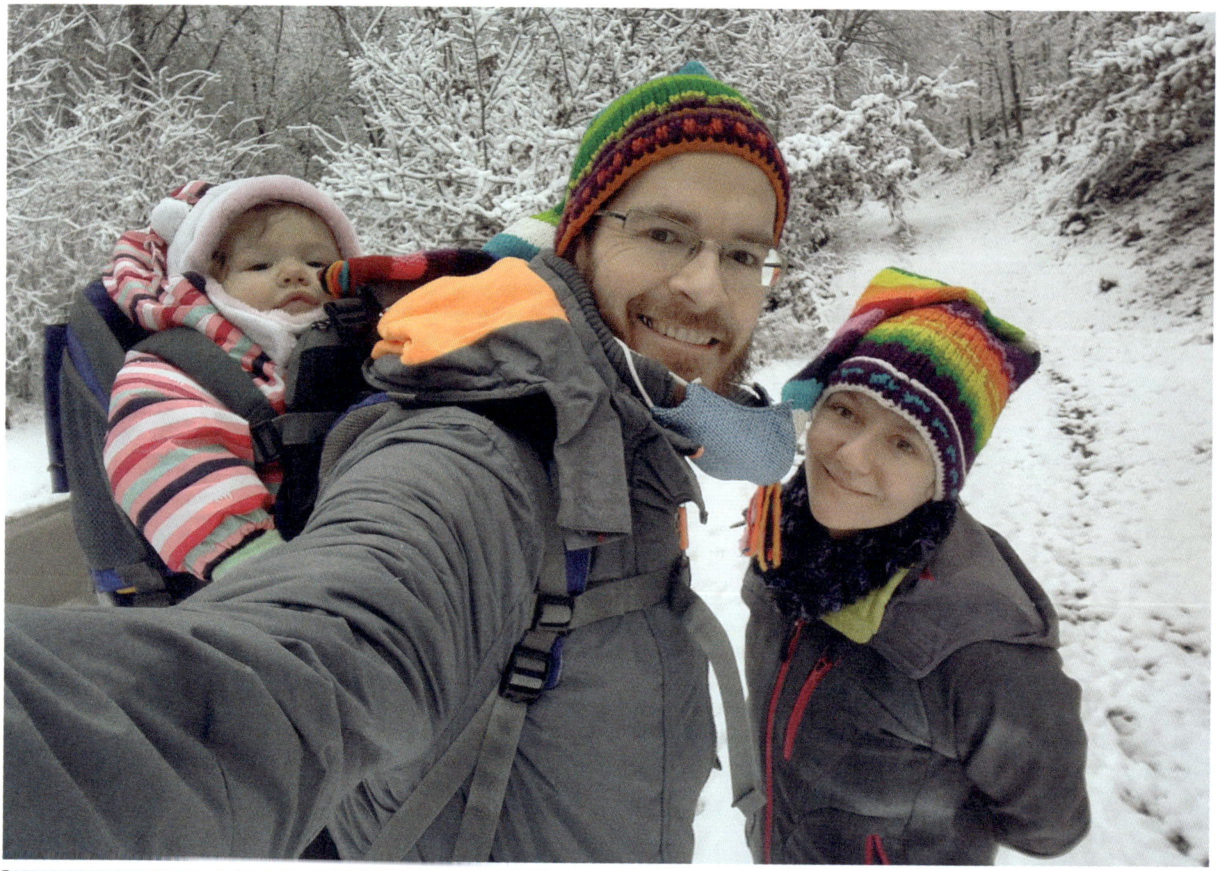

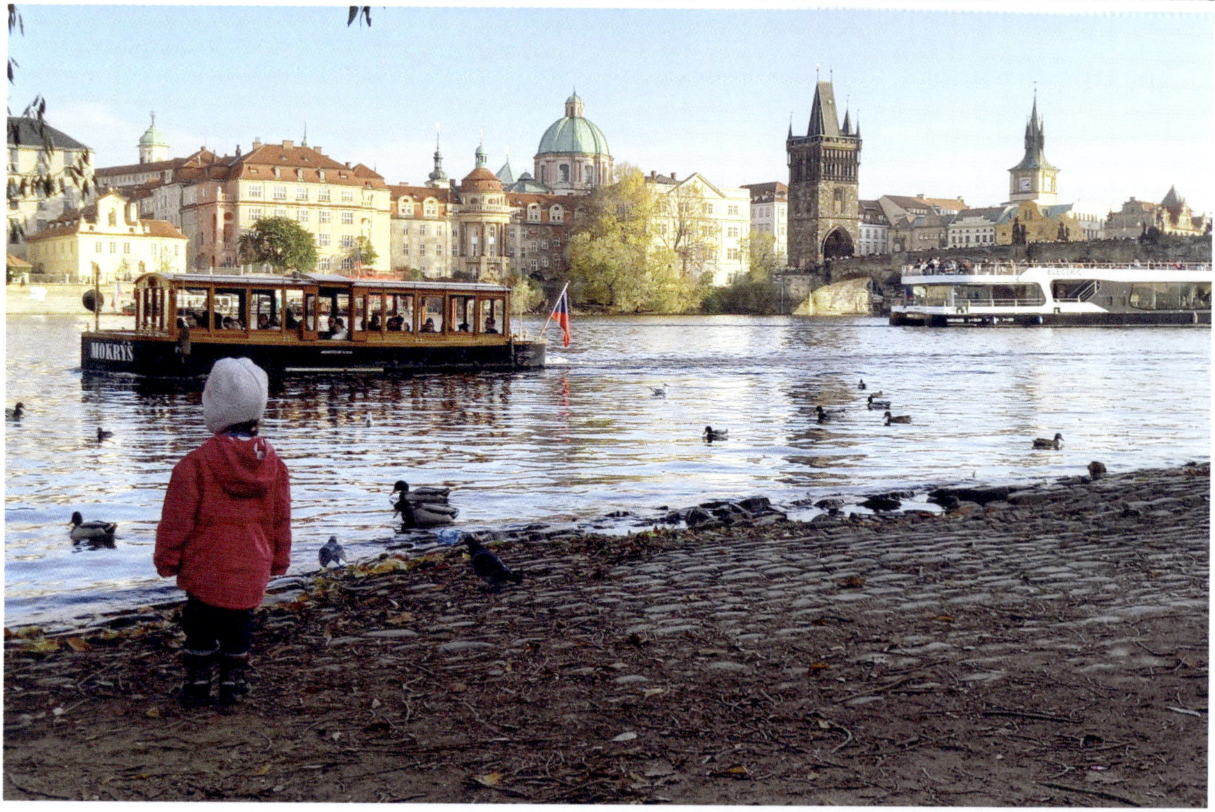

# Czechia

## CÉLINE LECLERC & CALEB HOUSE

**WHERE CÉLINE & CALEB LIVE:**
Prague, Czechia

**WHERE CÉLINE & CALEB ARE FROM:**
France and USA

Céline and Caleb met as exchange students in a Czech language class in 2003. Caleb had stints living in Japan, India and Tanzania before returning to study in Germany and France to be closer to Céline. Though their 2015 wedding was Prague-themed – their rings incorporated sand from Prague's Vltava River – it was to Côte d'Ivoire, Washington, DC and Thailand that their married life would first take them. The couple returned to Prague in 2018, and in 2019 welcomed Maya to the family. They expect to stay at least another five or six years before embarking on another international adventure.

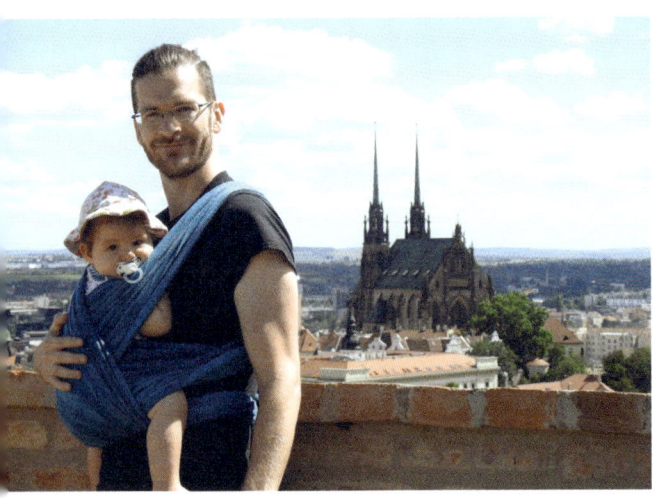

**INTEGRATING INTO PRAGUE:** As Maya was born into a [COVID-19] pandemic-era bubble, the sudden jump into Czech society and schools seems to have moulded her identity as a foreigner living in Czech culture. However, we also integrate our host culture into our daily lives – including local traditions like attending the *Nutcracker* ballet at Christmas time, something our families in the US and France assume is wildly extravagant, based on the ballet culture where we're from! (*Céline*)

**ON CULTURAL WARMTH:** It still feels hard to adapt to the more reserved interpersonal culture of the Czechs compared to our home cultures – it can take years for a connection with an acquaintance or professional relationship to become closer, even with colleagues that we see on a daily basis. But once we get past that barrier, it's a warm and loyal friendship; if a Czech person invites you to their home, you know you're very close friends.

Recently, at the playground, Maya was watching a few Czech kids play on a log and she asked them if she could play. We saw the children turn and ask incredulously: 'Mama, why is she smiling?' So, this is the clash of cultures that, no matter how long she spends here, it's hardwired that she's from a different culture, for sure. (*Caleb*)

**COMBINING HOLIDAY TRADITIONS:** As Maya has grown we've had to pick and choose between our native holiday traditions – do we welcome the Tooth Fairy or the Good Little Mouse, for example? Celebrate Christmas dinner in French formalwear or American pyjamas? Even for Easter, once we get past the choice between Easter Bunny or Flying Bells, Maya is still the only child out in the park hunting for Easter eggs or chocolate – it's not part of Czech culture, and something that we'll have to address in the future once she begins to realise that these holiday characters don't come to visit all of her friends. It's something we've been able to compromise on between ourselves so far, but inevitably will become more difficult as she gets older. (*Céline & Caleb*)

**THIRD-CULTURE, THIRD-LANGUAGE:** When addressing Maya at home, Caleb speaks only English while I speak only French, so that she has a clear delineation between her two native languages. Czech, however, has proven a struggle, as Maya often has the chance to default to English or French in daily life in Prague; even at preschool the teachers speak or understand French and English, as do her close friends. (*Céline*)

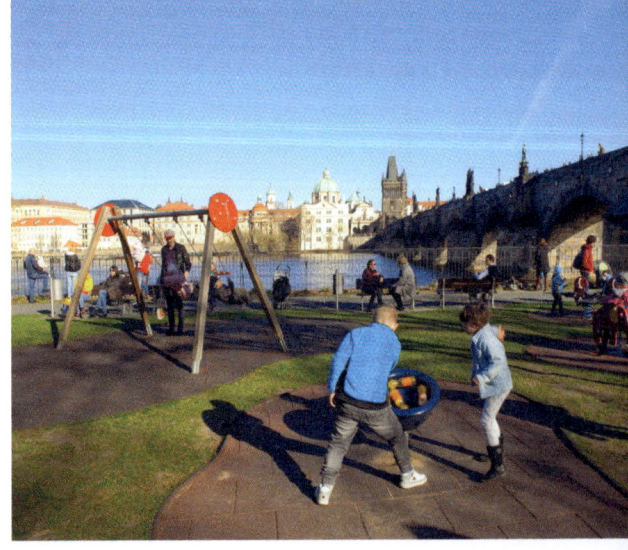

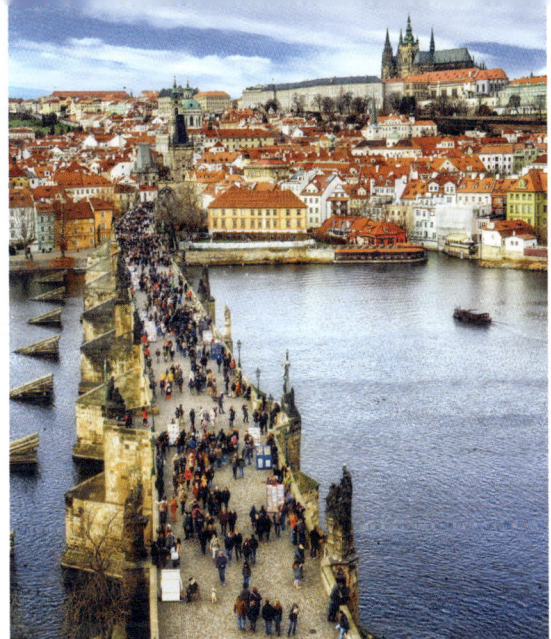

While we're past the point for Czech to be her third native language, and even if it's easier as a four- or five-year-old, we're still gonna have to put more effort into it. (*Caleb*)

Maya does understand basic Czech greetings, instructions and other simple things. But for the moment, she seems content to exist primarily within a world of English and French among her family and close friends, though on rare cases she does manage to come up with a Czech word that neither of us know. (*Céline & Caleb*)

**KID-FRIENDLY FUTURE:** As we've settled here and are both approaching our 40s, there's a lot more consideration of what looks appealing for Maya and whether anywhere else we might go would offer a more kid-friendly environment than Prague. But when we think about safety or friends whose children have chronic pneumonia from the burning season and pollution in Southeast Asia, it's nice that in Czech we're surrounded with parks and it's not uncommon to see children as young as seven or eight on the tram or metro all by themselves. The health system is pretty good, too. (*Céline*)

STEPHEN LIOY

## Our favourite traditions

***Family runs:*** I often go running while pushing Maya in the stroller as a way to spend time together in nature. The three of us have even participated twice in organised races here in Prague, running with a stroller through Hvězda park and Divoká Šárka reserve. (*Céline*)

***Culinary fusion:*** Most weekends Céline makes French crepes at home, topped with American peanut butter and French honey; something like a French Snickers crepe. Similarly, when we've celebrated Christmas at home we've incorporated food traditions from each of our homes and our host culture: Czech fried carp and potato salad, American-style roast ham, and Bûche de Noël cake. (*Céline & Caleb*)

***Travel together:*** Maya was only two years old when she boarded her first flight. Our family's photo album is full of pictures of Maya asleep in someone's arms beneath the battlements of Czech castles, and family trips have slowly grown past the US and France to include Sicily, Slovakia, Germany and Venice; there are even plans for a trip to Kyrgyzstan on the horizon. (*Caleb & Céline*)

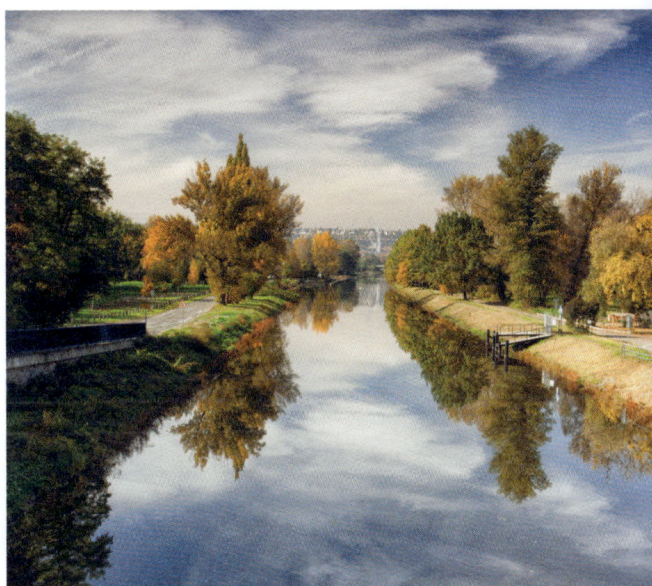

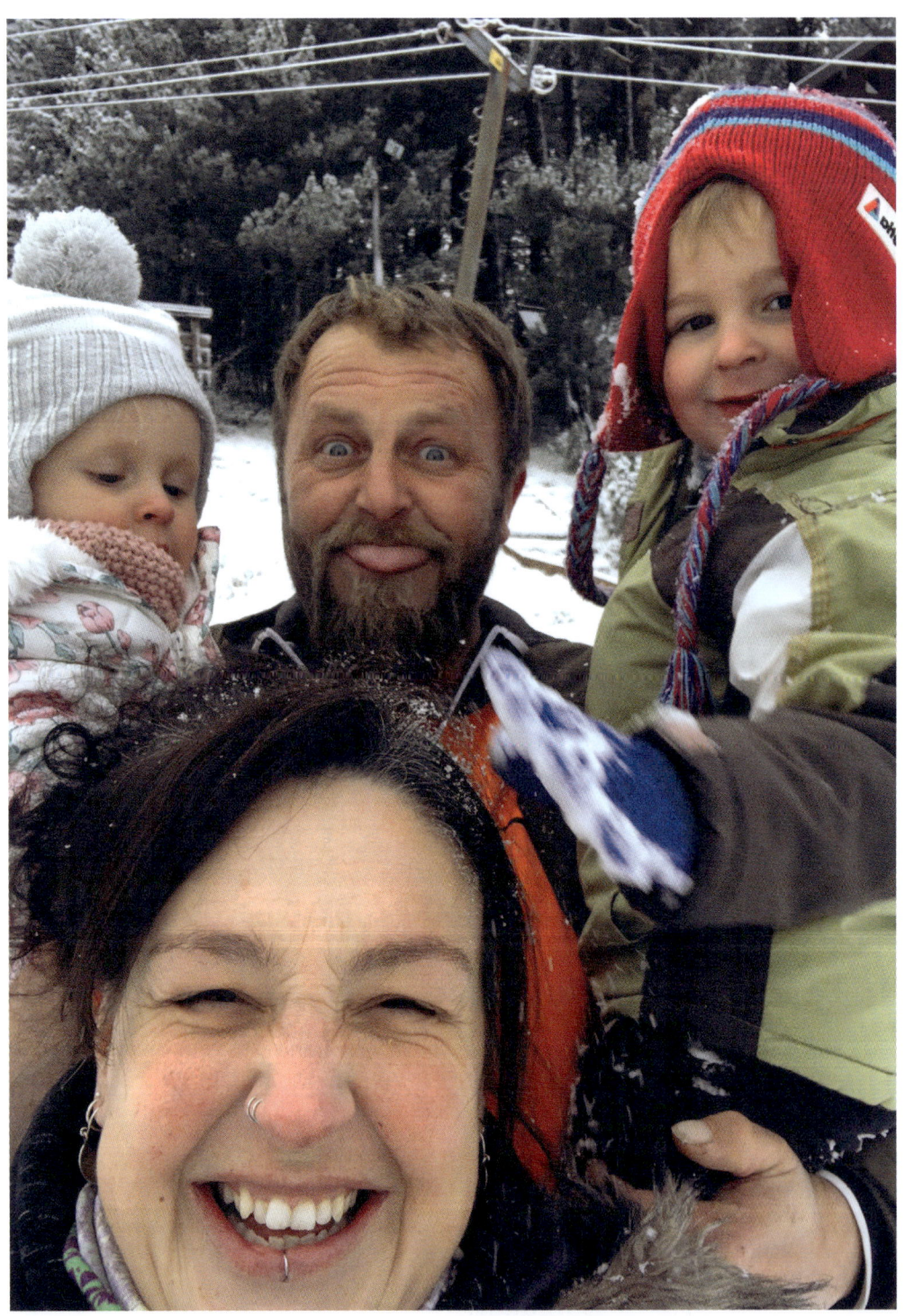

# Bosnia & Hercegovina

## NICOLA MARIĆ

**WHERE NICOLA LIVES:**
Mostar, Bosnia & Hercegovina

**WHERE NICOLA IS FROM:**
Bishop's Castle, England

Nicola's childhood neighbours and friends were a Bosniak family that had emigrated to the UK when war broke out in the Balkans in the 1990s. But never in her wildest dreams did she expect to move to their country of origin one day. After her first marriage ended in a divorce, Nicola went on a holiday to Mostar, one of Hercegovina's most scenic towns. There she met Osman while casually walking down the street; the rest is history. 'When we had to decide which country we'd raise our kids in, I'm happy we ended up choosing Bosnia', Nicola says. Despite the challenges of being a Christian-Muslim household in a country that experienced an ethnic conflict, she says 'it's the best decision we could ever have made for our family.'

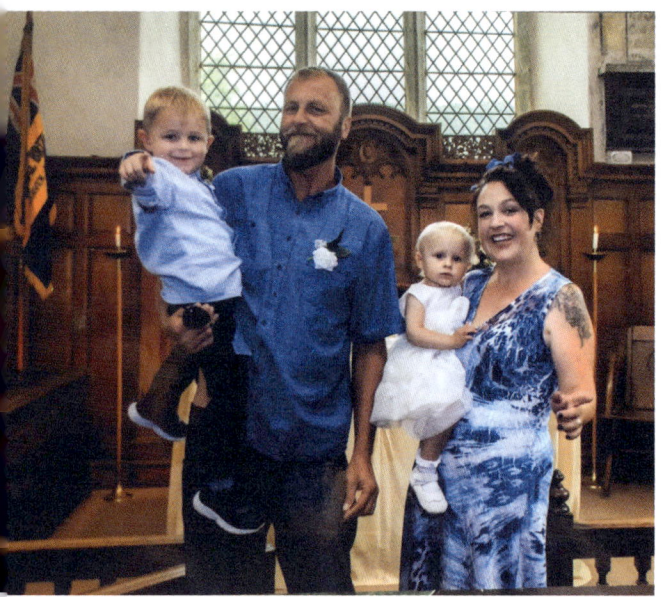

**KNOWING THE PAST:** During the war, Bosnia – an ethnically and religiously diverse country – became more segregated. Muslims and Christians turned from neighbours and friends to enemies quickly, and to keep the peace the two communities live parallel lives. Despite this climate, I've always felt very welcomed by Osman's family, perhaps because I'm a Christian but also a foreigner. But today it is very uncommon to see mixed families. At first I was not completely aware of this, but after having children I noticed other people's gaze. When the children get older, we'll educate them about their country's past, so they can appreciate its peaceful (albeit often unstable) present.

**THE FIRST 40 DAYS:** Raising children from two different cultures is a challenge. The moment I realised that was when, after giving birth, I didn't know about the local Muslim custom of not going outside the house with your newborn for the first 40 days of their life. Everyone was staring at me, mumbling 'How could she bring bad luck to her kid?'. But I kept going out, because I firmly believe that babies need fresh air!

**MIDDLE NAMES:** Here it is not common to register your kids with two names – especially if one is Christian and the other is Muslim – but for me it was really important because it's a family tradition from the UK. So we fought with the registry office until we could register them with both names. As far as we know, we're the first ones in Bosnia to have our children [registered] under two names!

**RELIGIOUS DIVERSITY:** Religious holidays become an opportunity to appreciate Bosnia's diversity and learn how to respect others' cultures. We always celebrate both Christian and Muslim holidays: we love to unwrap presents under a lit-up Christmas tree in our home, and eat goat meat for Bajram, the last day of Ramadan.

**LANGUAGE:** The challenge of raising children in between two cultures is choosing their linguistic upbringing. We decided to let that happen organically, so for now their main language is English. They've learned a few Bosnian words, but refuse to learn it properly or to speak it. But it's important to increase their fluency, so to compensate, we are signing them up for some sports classes, where they'll only communicate in Bosnian.

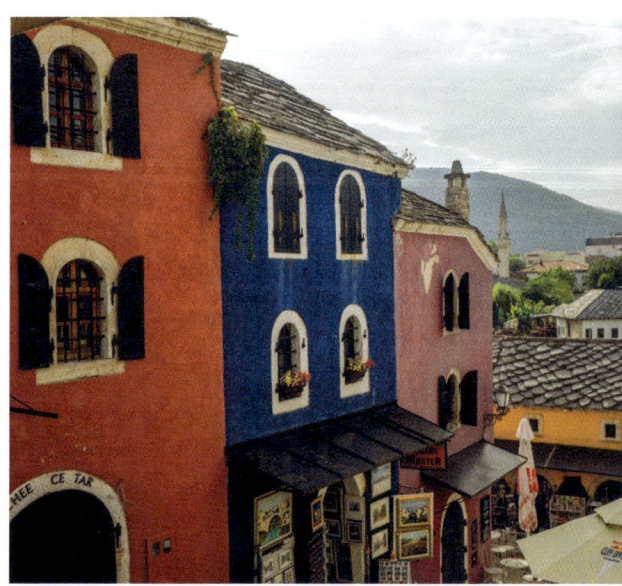

> "Religious holidays become an opportunity to appreciate Bosnia's diversity and learn how to respect others' cultures."

**STAYING UP LATE:** Although our kids are only five and two, their bedtime is past the European average. In England, children are put to bed really early, missing important family moments. But in Bosnia it's normal to see children going around with their parents until 10pm or 11pm, because they're an important part of the family. After dinner we always go for a walk downtown or meet family friends over a cup of traditional Bosnian coffee.

**EDUCATION:** Kids here don't go to school before the age of seven (which I found really odd, since in the UK, David, my youngest, would already be enrolled in primary school). When the time comes, we've decided we'll enrol them in an international school. The Bosnian public curriculum divides children into classes depending on their ethnicity, and we feel that our kids wouldn't fit in anywhere. For now, I'm informally homeschooling them through role-plays, and since Noah, our eldest, loves numbers, we use cards and dice to learn basic maths.

**OUTDOOR LIFE:** Bosnian cities have the highest pollution rates in Europe, but luckily the country is also famous for its lush nature. We want our kids to have an outdoorsy childhood and a healthy lifestyle, instead of letting them spend their time glued to their phones. So, once a month we take them for a hike to Mt Hum, and have a picnic there with a beautiful view over Mostar.

STEFANIA D'IGNOTI

## Our favourite traditions

**Sunday lunch:** Every Sunday we sit as an extended family, which includes aunts, uncles and cousins from Osman's side of the family, and have lunch together. It's a tradition I brought from England, but with a Bosnian twist: we usually have *ćevapi* – Bosnia's most famous dish, made of oval grilled meatballs inside a flatbread with cream cheese.

**Market outing:** On Saturday mornings we visit a local market, where we buy fresh produce for the whole week. It's an important weekly family date, because I try to teach our kids the importance of buying organic products instead of unhealthy junk food.

**Diving competition:** Mostar is famous for its historic bridge, Stari Most. It was destroyed during a bombardment and rebuilt from scratch after the war. Every year there's an international diving competition which has become one of Bosnia's most iconic traditions. We are lucky to live in the town where this important national event takes place, and we go to watch it as a family to let our kids feel part of the culture.

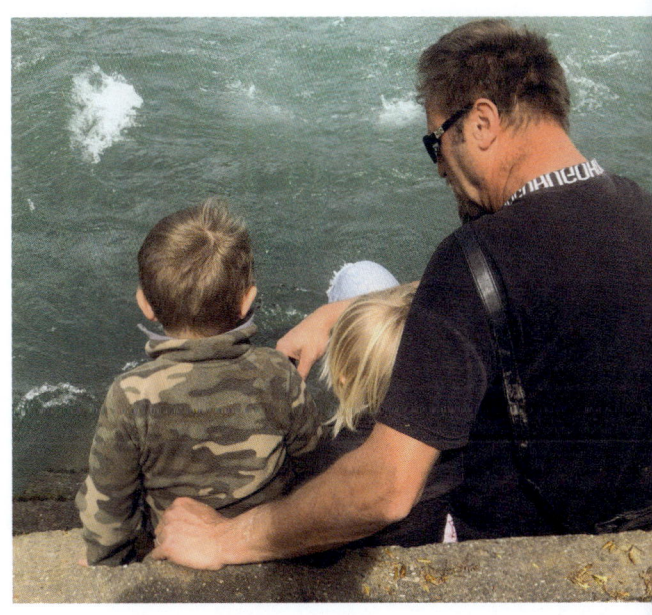

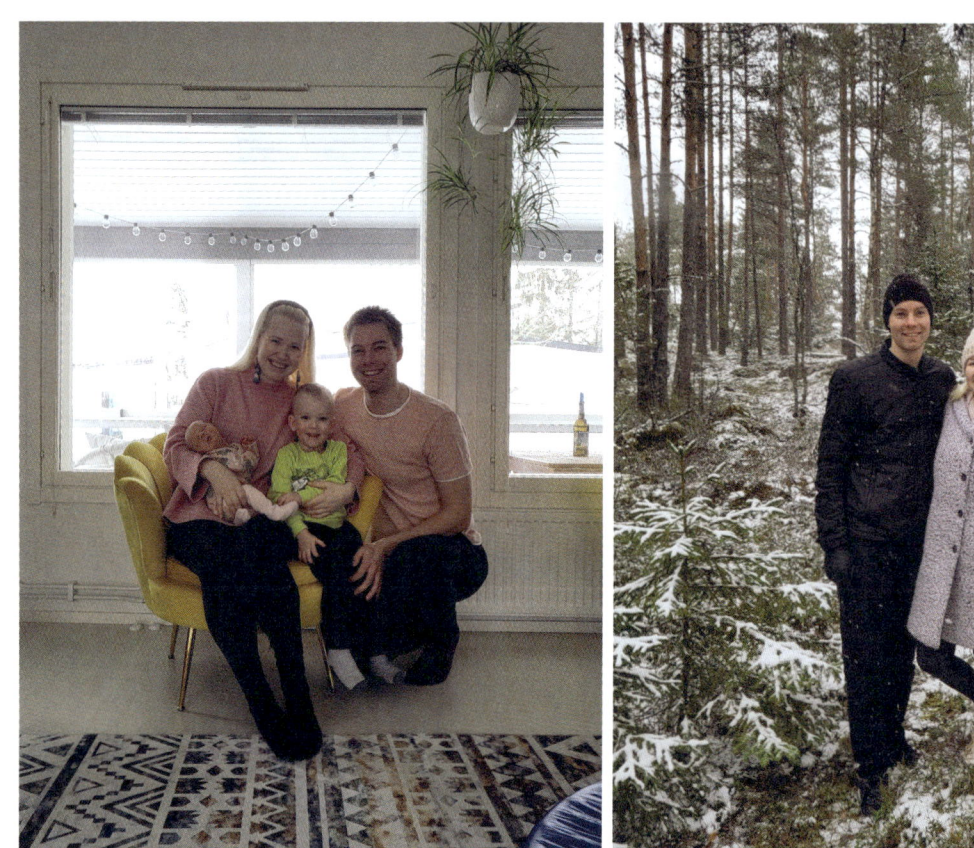

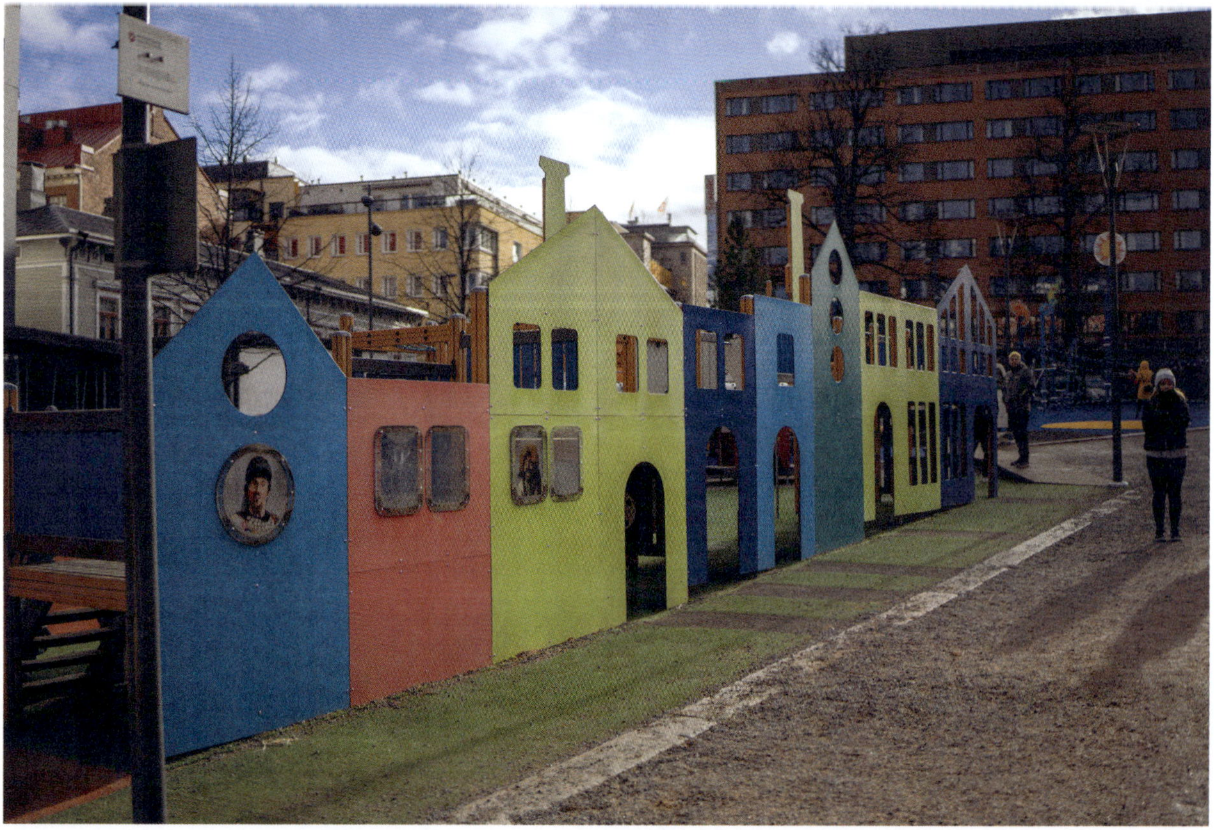

# Finland

## LILLI & IIRO KULTA

**WHERE LILLI & IIRO LIVE:**
Tampere, Finland

**WHERE LILLI & IIRO ARE FROM:**
Kuusjoki (Salo) and Ylöjärvi, Finland

Lilli and Iiro are in their early 30s. Lilli is a sustainability specialist currently on parental leave, and Iiro works as a regional director for a construction company. The couple's last name means 'gold'. You could say that their children – Frans (two) and Stella (three months) – have indeed struck gold being born Finnish; their Nordic homeland has been ranked the world's happiest country for seven years running. In the last decade, Finland has also been selected among the top three places to be a mother and a new parent, and the third-most gender-equal country. 'In Finland families with children are well supported', Lilli says, adding that their family also benefits from having grandparents nearby: 'We didn't realise the importance of a support network before kids.'

**FINANCIAL SUPPORT:** In Finland having a child is not a financial risk. Giving birth cost us around €200. Education is free and daycare is subsidised. We pay €355 per month for Frans' daycare, and adding Stella will raise the price by €185, so the fees are not doubled with each child. We get a monthly child benefit too – a total of €255 for Frans and Stella. Also, public transport is free with a stroller. I use buses every few days. (*Lilli*)

**THE FREE BABY BOX:** The maternity box is a very good starter kit that you can get from the Finnish government after five months of pregnancy. All the basics are covered, like baby nail-clippers, so you can go home from the hospital relying on its contents. The first baby box was kind of ceremonial for us. We went through it and thought, 'Oh, these clothes are so small!' It made it all feel more concrete; soon we will have someone wearing these clothes! (*Lilli*)

**PATERNITY LEAVE:** The new parental-leave system encourages fathers to stay at home for longer. We had Stella under the new system. Among my peers, it seems that now fathers really do take at least three months of paternity leave. Each parent gets about six months and you can donate up to half to the other parent. (*Lilli*)

I have taken just three weeks off so far for Stella, as I have a new job and I am partially an entrepreneur. With Frans I took nearly three months off, which was a fairly long time under the old system. I am very grateful that I was able to do that. I really got to know my child and became very close with him. I also gained appreciation for the time Lilli had spent at home. (*Iiro*)

**GRANDPARENTS NEARBY:** It's worth its weight in gold that Iiro's parents live 10 minutes away by car. If we can't do the daycare pick-up, we can call grandpa. Frans is a huge fan: he always wants to play with grandpa. Sometimes Frans stays overnight with his grandparents. We can also do couples' dancing because Iiro's parents come to babysit during our dance class each week. They are also travelling with us to Italy this September to help out while we attend a wedding. My own parents live two hours away and we visit them once a month. My parents are dear to Frans, too, but my dad doesn't do as much hands-on childcare as Iiro's father, who happily helps with changes and feedings. Iiro's dad is probably closer to his grandchildren than most Finnish grandfathers. (*Lilli*)

I expect the grandparents' role to only grow next year when both of my parents will be retired. They will probably do even more of the daycare pickups or take care of the kids if they get sick, so Lilli and I won't need to miss work. (*Iiro*)

**ENGLISH-LANGUAGE DAYCARE:** Frans goes to an English-language daycare where they speak English four days a week and Finnish one day a week. Otherwise, it's a regular daycare; they spend lots of time outdoors and do baking, singing and arts and crafts. Hopefully Frans will get into the international elementary school in Tampere later. I lived in several countries in my 20s, so moving abroad later might be a possibility. (*Lilli*)

**A LOVE-FILLED LIFE WITH CHILDREN:** Nowadays the little things in life make me the happiest – like when Stella started smiling, my heart melted. When Frans says, 'I love you, Mummy', or runs to give me a hug after daycare, it feels so sweet. There is a lot more love in my life now. Things are more challenging as we are always short on time, but my life has really clear meaning now – taking care of the children and our family. (*Lilli*)

MIRVA LEMPIÄINEN

## Our favourite traditions

**Stroller walks:** We go for stroller walks with the baby in the morning, midday and afternoon. They are a highlight of the day because otherwise with a young baby we are indoors a lot. I like walking on paths in the forest and around Tampere's many lakes, admiring the scenery. If we all walk together, Frans brings his pedal bike and we go to the playground. (*Lilli*)

**Saturday swimming:** Baby swimming is a very popular hobby in Finland. Our swimming hall holds the baby-swimming classes in the morning before opening up to the public. It is very quiet and calm, and the water is heated up to spa temperature. Frans loves water. (*Lilli*)

   Frans started baby-swimming classes at four months at our local swimming hall and we plan to do the same with Stella. (*Iiro*)

**Forest trips:** Frans likes forest walks, though he can't walk long distances yet. In late summer, we pick berries. In the autumn and winter we just walk around and try to spot different animals, trees and plants. (*Lilli*)

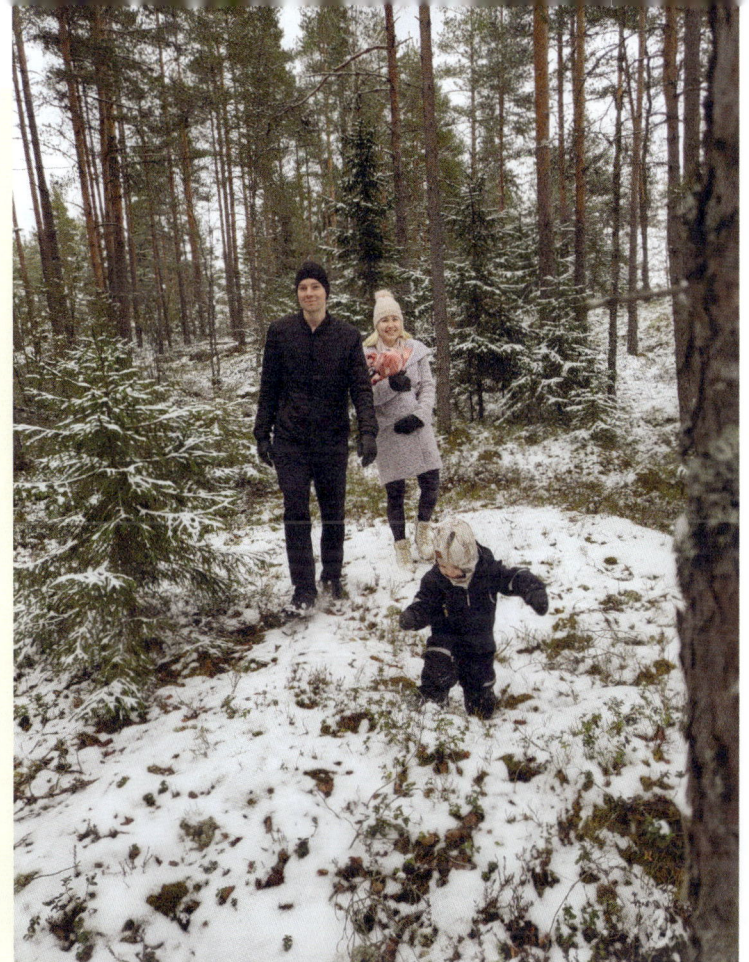

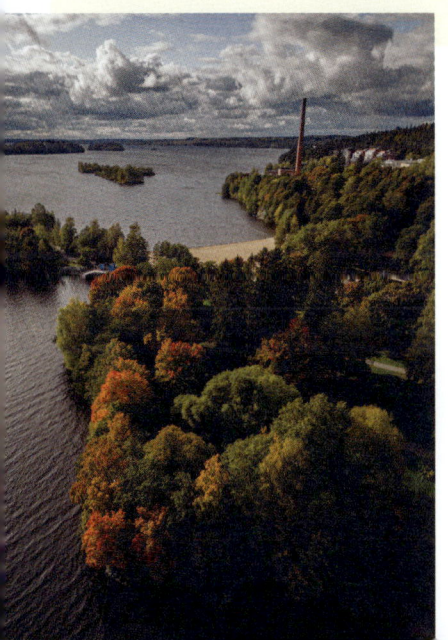

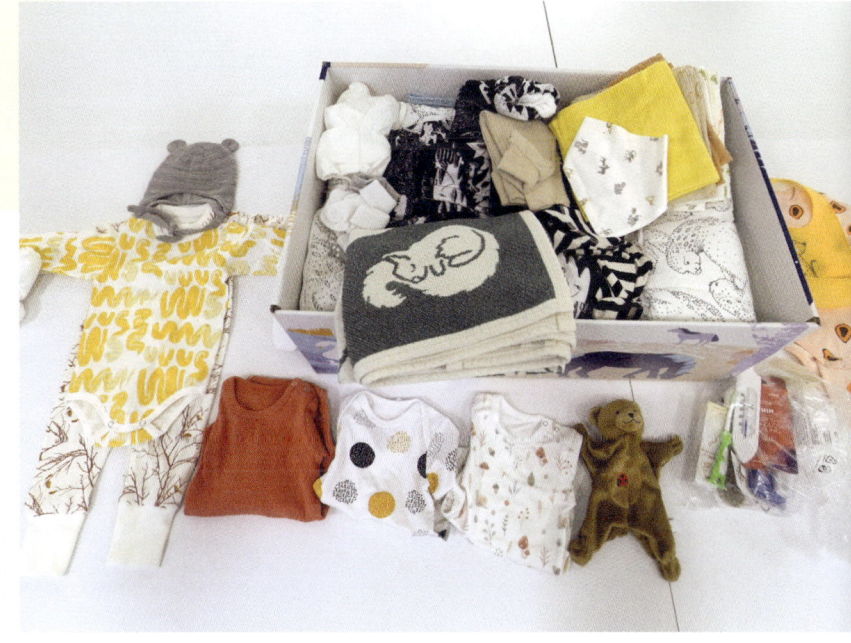

EUROPE

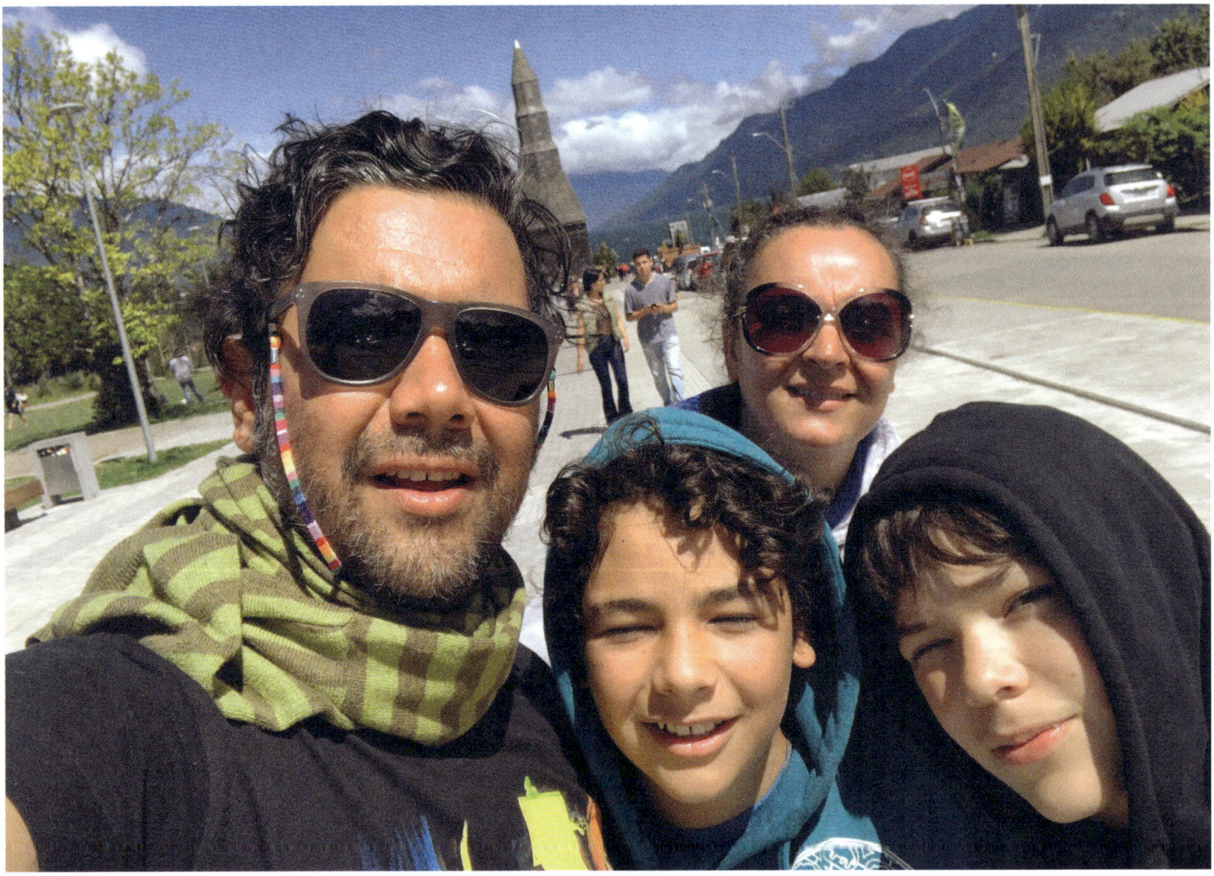

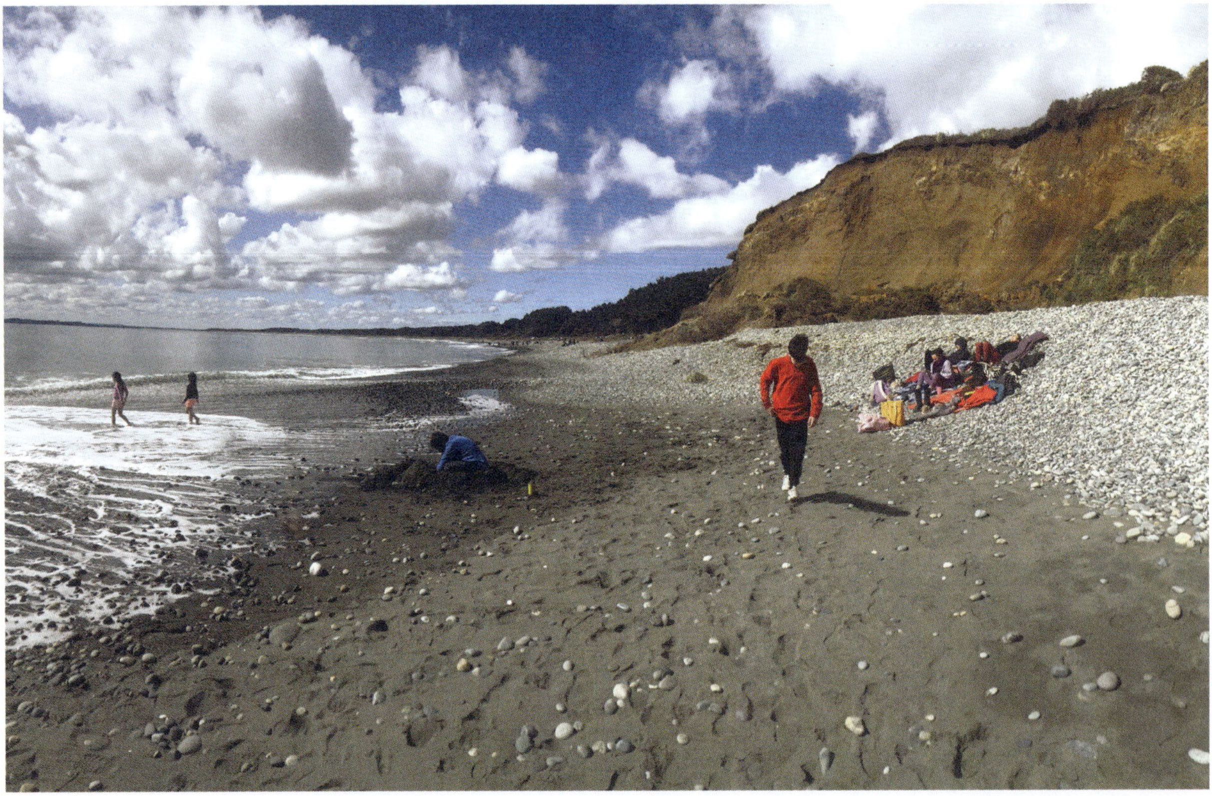

# Chile

## GONZALO BASCUÑÁN & GISELA POSAVAC

**WHERE GONZALO & GISELA LIVE:**
Puerto Varas, Chile

**WHERE GONZALO & GISELA ARE FROM:**
Santiago, Chile

Gonzalo and Gisela both grew up in the Chilean capital Santiago, a sprawling city of seven million people. When the COVID-19 pandemic made Gonzalo's job remote, the pair decided to relocate with their two boys, Mateo (13) and Agustín (15), to the edge of Patagonia. The family now lives in the lakeside resort town of Puerto Varas, in the shadow of two volcanoes. 'We're much closer to nature here', says Gisela, who often goes hiking with the kids on weekends in the rainforests. Mateo and Agustín are obsessed with football, but now have to play under cold rain showers. Despite this, and with the slower pace of life, they've thrived in their new environment. Would the family ever move back to the capital? 'Not a chance', says Gonzalo.

**RHYTHM OF LIFE:** It's been a radical change leaving Santiago and working remotely. Everything has transformed, including our daily rhythm, which is calmer than it was before. Sometimes, when I get off work, and go to the town centre to buy groceries on foot, I'll take a few extra minutes to pass by the lake, where you have the Osorno volcano right in front of you. All of this time that I'm no longer using for my commute, I can use for myself and my family. *(Gonzalo)*

**SELF-SUSTAINABILITY:** Now that I don't have to take the kids to school in the morning (they walk on their own), it gives me more time to build my garden and work toward becoming more self-sustainable. In the city, I didn't have space for a big garden. Now, I have tomatoes, chard, parsley, oregano, chives, avocado, goldenberries, blueberries and blackberries. I love to cook. I also forage for things like rosehip to make marmalades. *(Gisela)*

**SMALL-TOWN CHARM:** Puerto Varas has definitely got a small-town vibe. In school, with the other parents, I feel much more observed. And when you go around town, there are sometimes these folkloric things that happen that you wouldn't see anywhere else. In the summers there are *fiestas costumbristas* (fairs with rodeos and Chilean-style horse racing). Also, local shops will often close for a two-hour lunch break. *(Gisela)*

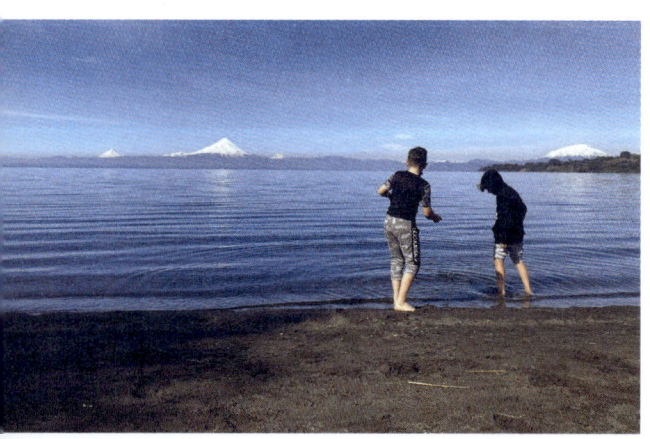

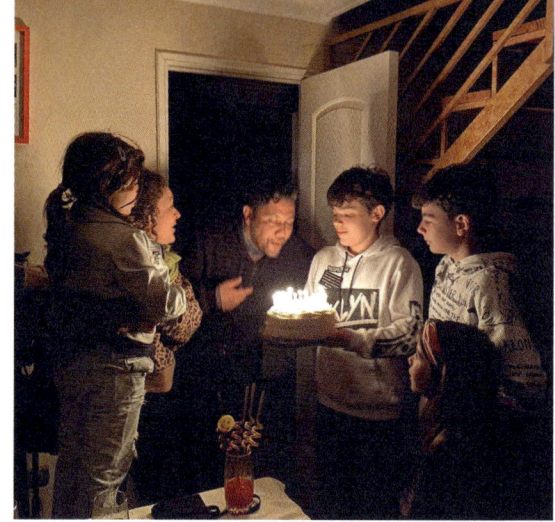

**SAFETY:** The kids feel safer here. They can go off on their bikes, and we're much more relaxed with them now. They're also becoming teenagers, so they're gaining more autonomy and making their own plans with their friends to meet up after school. For us, we're so happy that we're here for this moment in their lives, because it takes away some of the stress. *(Gisela)*

**PARENTING WITH TRUST:** We parent with a view that the children are visible in our discussions. When I was growing up, things were always decided for me by my parents, and I often didn't know the reasons why. So, we've tried to let the kids make responsible decisions for themselves, which helps them mature. They know that when they make mistakes, their decisions have consequences which they can learn from. We give them an education based on love, dialogue and trust, and we also don't lie or hide things from them. If they ask us questions, we tell them the truth…and that has a cost sometimes. That means you have children who are more critical of you, who always question you. *(Gisela)*

**NATURE WALKS:** Living here is like living in a postcard. We're so close to nature, so we try to find new places to visit at the weekends, like hikes in the Valdivian rainforest or secret beaches along the coast. The boys' school also has a strong focus on environmental awareness, and they can choose after-school activities like trekking that help them get in touch with the nature all around us. (*Gonzalo*)

**FAMILY LIFE:** In Santiago, our weekends revolved around visits with our parents and siblings, so we've had to assemble a new 'southern family' with cousins and other relatives who've also moved to the region. They've become our support network. On Sundays, we almost always eat with them. We try to meet up and cook a lunch together. Then, there is a long *sobremesa*, where we sit and chat over the table until late into the afternoon. (*Gonzalo*)

**A PESCATARIAN DIET:** Our family is pescatarian, so we eat mostly vegetables but also seafood. In some ways it's harder here in the south because there is a culture of large barbecues with lots of meat. But in other ways it's easier because we have much more access to fresh seafood. There are big markets along the coast where you can buy salmon, sea bass and shellfish. (*Gonzalo*)

MARK JOHANSON

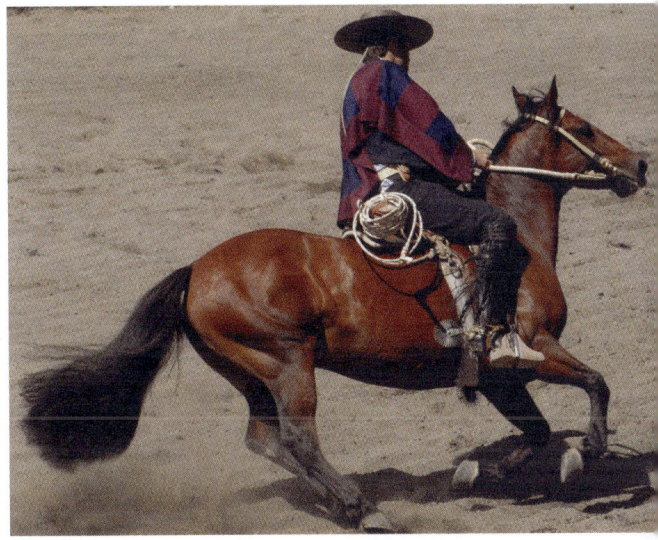

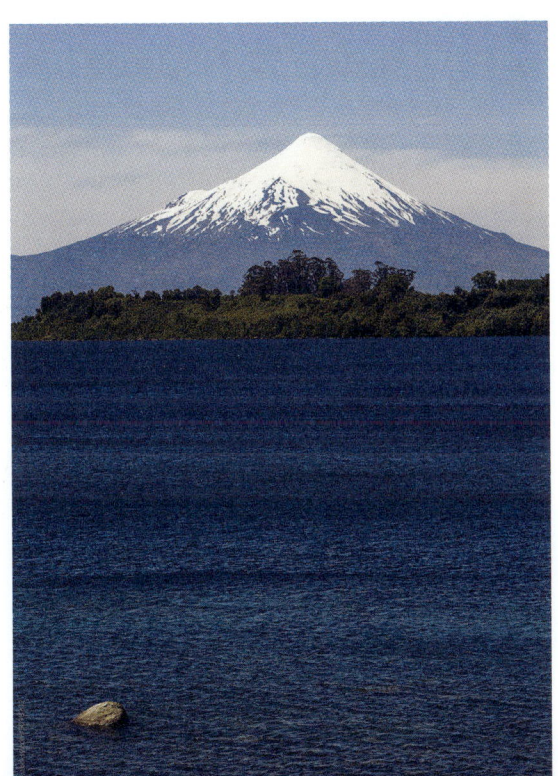

## Our favourite traditions

**Seasonal foods:** In summer, we'll always sit down together and prepare *humitas* (a dish made from corn paste boiled in its husk). Then, during Chile's Independence Day celebrations, the Fiestas Patrias, we make empanadas; and for good luck on New Year's Day, we prepare *porotos granados con mazamorra* (a cranberry bean stew). (*Gisela*)

**Easter-egg wars:** We paint Easter eggs like everyone else, but the big difference is that, in this family, we pair off and have a duel, using the eggs like swords. It's like a little Easter battle, and the winner is the one whose hard-boiled egg doesn't break. (*Gonzalo*)

**BYO kid:** When we meet up with our friends in the evening, we usually bring the boys with us and they hang out among the adults. We've been doing it since they were young. (*Gonzalo*)

**Tea time:** The kids have *once* (tea time, Chile's 'fourth meal') every day around 5pm. As a family, we often do a big *once* at the weekends instead of dinner: there will be bread, cheese and avocados, usually eggs, and maybe some sweets alongside the tea. (*Gisela*)

LATIN AMERICA & THE CARIBBEAN

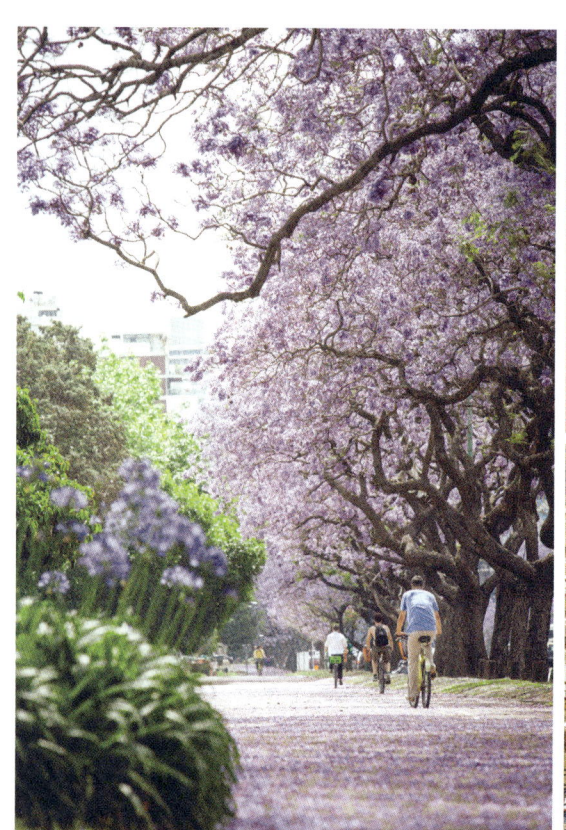
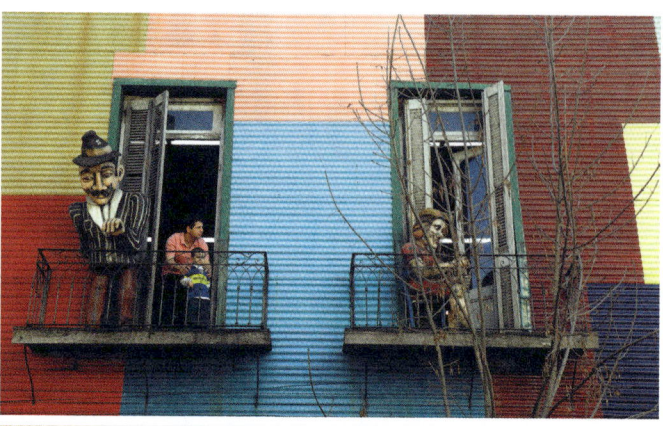
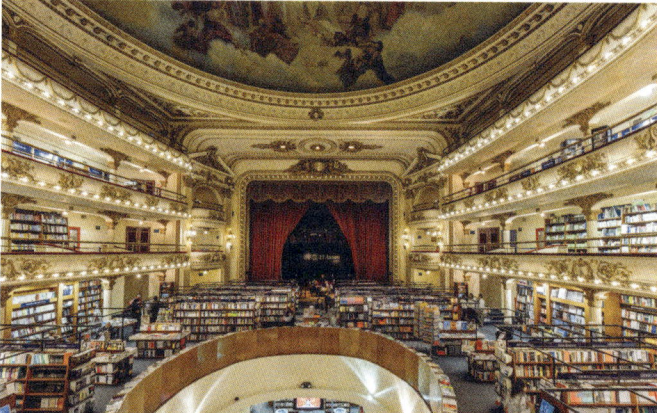
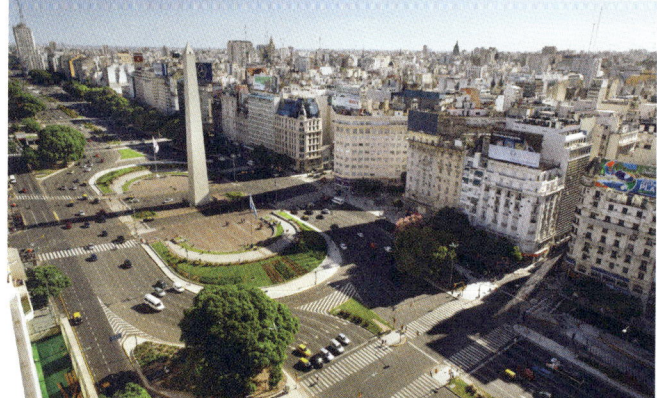
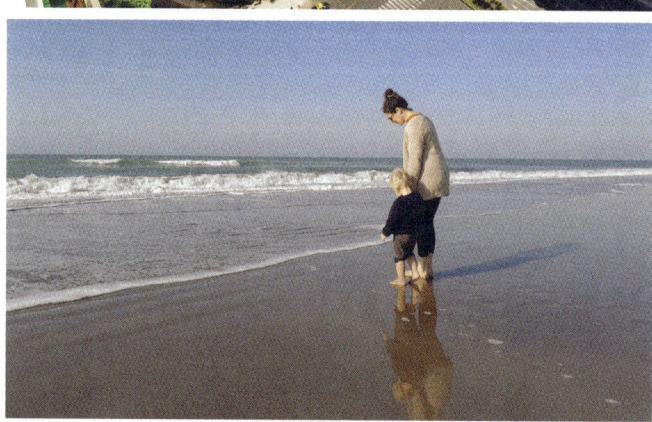
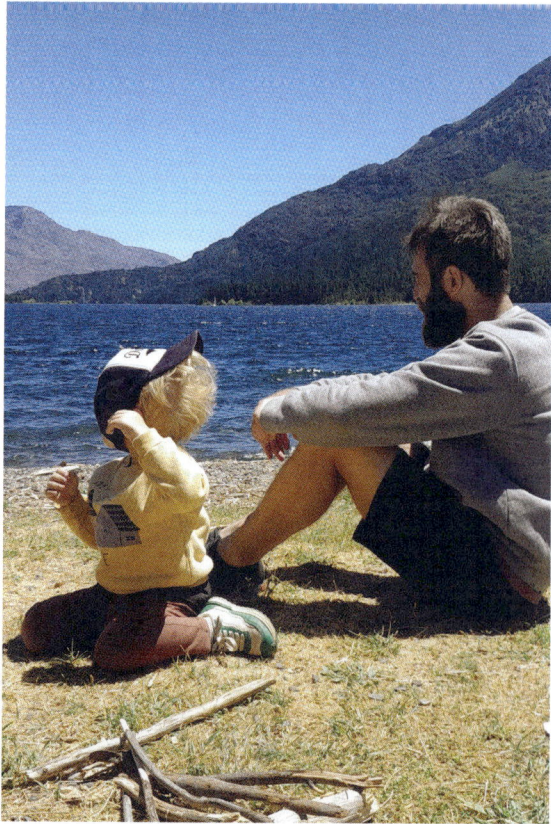

# Argentina

## MARCOS & DANIELA

**WHERE MARCOS & DANIELA LIVE:**
Buenos Aires, Argentina

**WHERE MARCOS & DANIELA ARE FROM:**
Villa Bosch and Avellaneda, Buenos Aires

Daniela and Marcos met in their late 20s – Marcos was close to Daniela's brother, and though they'd known each other beforehand, they only connected at her brother's wedding where, Daniela says laughing, 'everyone was trying to put us together!' Marcos works at Argentina's main international airport, and Daniela teaches high-school English. They named their son, Dimitri, after Marcos' grandfather, and spent months practising saying the name in front of a mirror to make sure it was the right choice. Since Dimi was born in 2020, their work schedules have meant that finding enough time to spend together as a family has been challenging. But, with a little help from Daniela's mum and some creative scheduling, Marcos says that they 'always make time for our family – it's essential.'

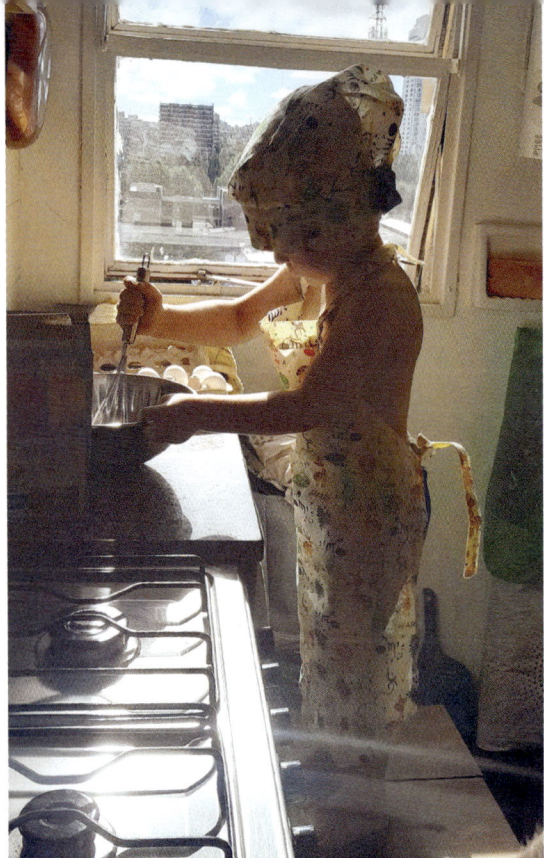

**VISITING GRANDPARENTS:** On the weekends, we try to visit Dimi's grandparents. They obviously love to see him, but we also think it's important that he has them in his life as much as possible. Our grandparents passed on their unique immigrant backgrounds to us – mine Czech, Dani's Italian – including traditions of food and memories of the 'old continent', not to mention that they helped our parents raise us. We want that for Dimi, too.

Our parents still live in the suburbs of Buenos Aires, where we grew up before moving into the city as adults. Buenos Aires doesn't have many green spaces, but my parents have a large property with a yard. In the summer, we break out the *pelopincho* – a plastic temporary pool that is a hallmark of middle-class Argentine life. Dimi also loves their old motorcycle; he always gets on and acts like he's zooming by. At Dani's parents' place he plays outdoors with a box of her old childhood toys. (*Marcos*).

**PUBLIC SCHOOL:** Dimi used to attend a public kindergarten, which we both valued since the public-school system was integral to both of us – Marcos went to public school his whole life, while I taught in high-vulnerability public schools until recently. In Argentina, public schools have been at the centre of a collective vision for the country's growth and identity since the 19th century. We always felt that the diversity public schooling offered was essential. Unfortunately, the system has grown expulsive and less inclusive, not to mention weaker since we were in school, and a series of negative experiences forced us to look elsewhere. Private schooling represents a financial challenge, even though it's quite common and relatively affordable here, but it was the best choice for Dimi. For primary school we'll re-evaluate. (*Daniela*)

**SCHOOL PICK-UP:** We always try to pick Dimi up from school together – we really want him to experience that with us as a family. In the afternoons, he goes to kindergarten very close to home (*Marcos*). We often pass by our neighbours and Dimi will strike up conversations with anyone; *Porteños* (people from Buenos Aires) love to chit

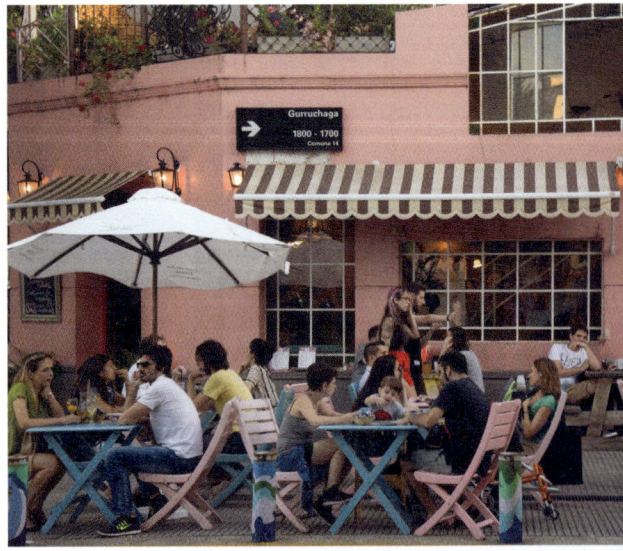

> "It's very common for children to sleep with their parents or in their parents' bed here."

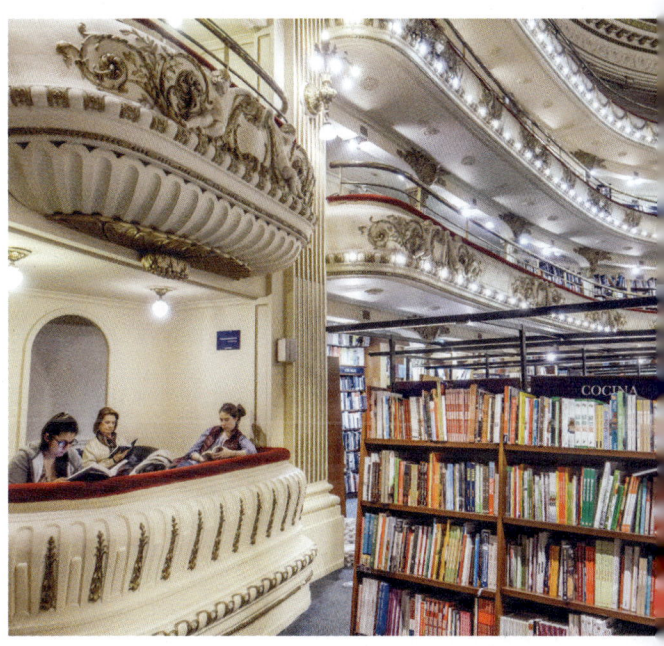

chat. We learn so much about our neighbourhood that way, from people who have lived here longer than us, since we only moved two years ago. We might also stop by a café, a very Buenos Aires thing to do; Dimi loves *magdalenas* (small chocolate muffins) and the little glasses of soda water that come with *cortados* (an espresso-based drink). (*Daniela*)

**SLEEP:** It's very common for children to sleep with their parents or in their parents' bed here. We always heard that babies aren't supposed to sleep with their parents but, honestly, we realised early on that the most important thing was getting rest. And he loves coming up to our bed to sleep with us, so of course we don't mind so long as we can all sleep comfortably. Sometimes, Dani will end up in Dimi's bed, and I'll be on the couch, and Dimi spreads out like a king on our bed! For his first year, we didn't have a second bedroom; now he does have his own space, but even then, he still shows up in the night sometimes. (*Marcos*)

**READING:** Buenos Aires has more bookstores per capita than any other city, and although books have gotten very expensive, we love searching the neighbourhood for something to read. Dimi even has his own library in his room! We've always read to him, and now he reads with us as well – it's a ritual that we all share. (*Daniela*)

FEDERICO PERELMUTER

## Our favourite traditions

**Bath time:** Dimi loves bath time, and we always take our time. We sing María Elena Walsh's songs – a beloved Argentine children's author – and read. A recent favourite book is called *My Body*, which teaches him about bodies, particularly considering Argentina's progressive 'Integral Sexual Education' programme. (*Daniela*)

**Movies:** We love to watch movies, either as a family or just me and Dimi. He loves Pixar and the Argentine children's programme *Pakapaka*. He watches the whole way through, even if it has subtitles. I teach English, and although I don't speak it with him – because English isn't really *my* language, and it's strange for us – he picks it up naturally. (*Daniela*)

**Music making:** I have a guitar, and Dimi makes his drum kit with pillows and we have jam sessions where Dani and I follow his directions, where he becomes our band leader. He also has a piano, and we love rocking out to Argentina's classic rock, La Renga, Taylor Swift and Charly García. (*Marcos*)

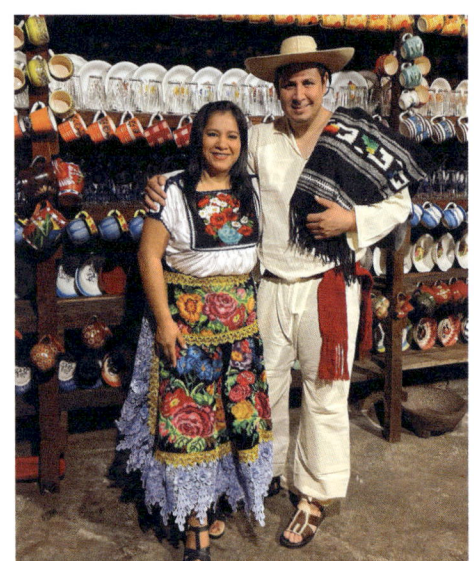
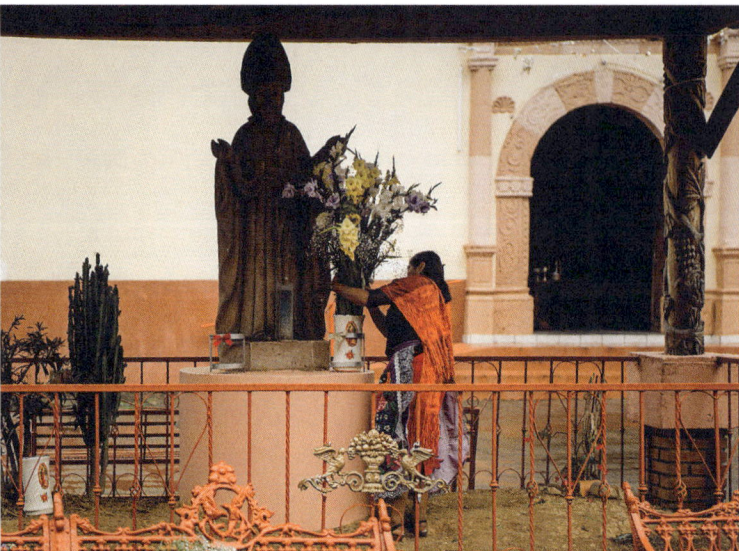
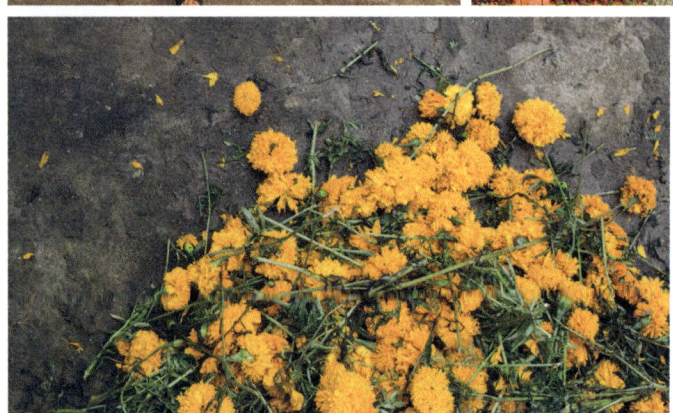
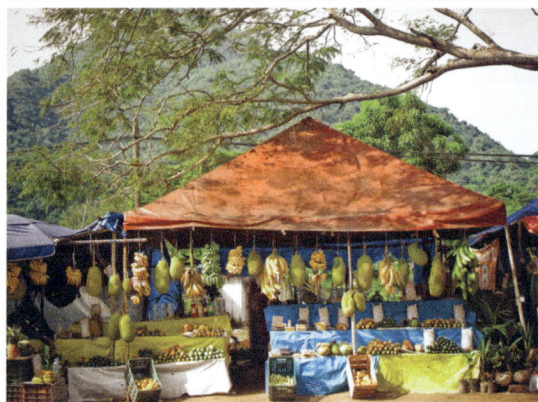

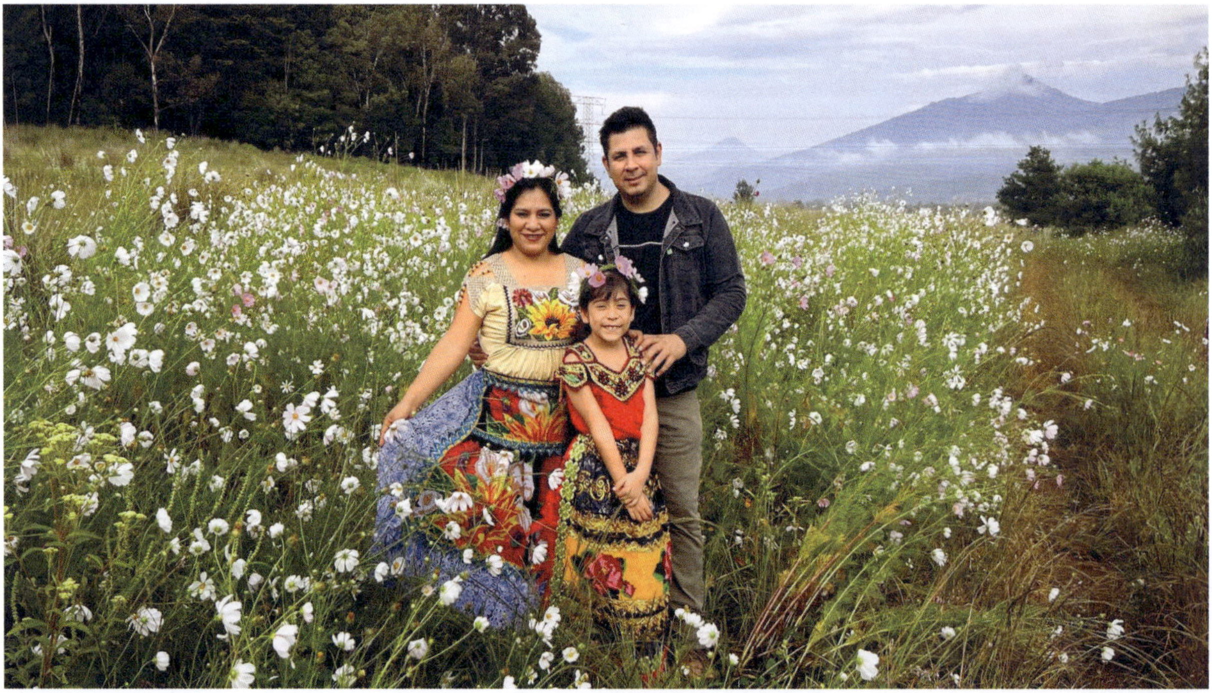

# Mexico

## EDUARDO HERNÁNDEZ & ESTELA RODRÍGUEZ

**WHERE EDUARDO & ESTELA LIVE:**
Colima and Ahuirán, Mexico

**WHERE EDUARDO & ESTELA ARE FROM:**
Colima and Ahuirán, Mexico

On a missionary trip to the tiny Purépecha Indigenous village of Ahuirán, Eduardo 'Hernanditoz' Hernández found both his calling and his love: he met his wife, Estela, and together they launched two YouTube channels (*Hernanditoz* and *Purechíta*) showcasing Purépecha life. More than 400,000 followers later, their videos have become a 'school about our culture' for their daughter Adilene (nine), and a source of pride for Purépechas, a community that today number about 220,000, spread mostly between Michoacán in Mexico and California. The family now lives in the city of Colima, but spends weekends visiting Ahuirán and other pueblos (villages) to document local life. From ancient wedding rituals to mothers carrying babies in artfully woven *rebozo* shawls, 'Adilene is curious about everything we film', says Estela. 'We love seeing her learn.'

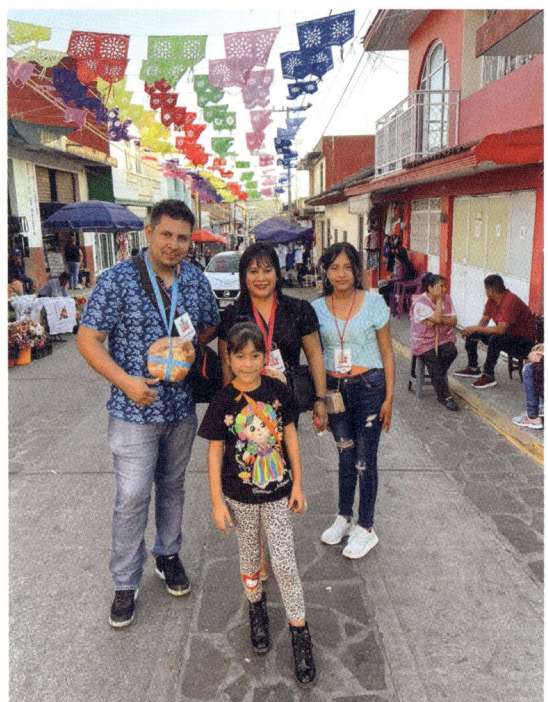

**ROAD TO THE PUEBLO:** It's six hours from tropical Colima to our village in the high plains of Michoacán. As we drive into the mountains, the landscape changes completely, from coconut palms to cold-weather pines and oaks. We pass ranches, little adobe and wood houses, and cornfields. On the way, we talk and laugh, and stop to buy homemade cheese (much better than in the city!). Adilene stretches out across the back seat and sleeps, until we see smoke from cooking fires, and women walking in their colourful traditional clothes – signs we've arrived in Purépecha country. (*Hernanditoz*)

**VILLAGE LIFE:** Visiting the pueblo is pure fun for Adilene. Kids are running everywhere, playing with wooden tops, marbles and dolls. In the city, it's just us three, but here, three generations live together under one roof and they all pamper her. Purépecha grandparents tend to be indulgent. If we scold Adilene, they'll say, 'Oh, she's still little, let her play.' (*Hernanditoz*)

**PARTY CULTURE:** Purépecha families love to celebrate on a big scale, with constant huge parties for school graduations, births, weddings and more (although, traditionally, they ignore birthdays). It's normal to invite up to 250 guests, with a lavish menu of fish, stews, tamales and cakes. The women dress up in embroidered blouses and skirts, and throw brightly-coloured confetti and candies through the streets, announcing, 'Today we celebrate!' (*Hernanditoz*)

**GODMOTHERS OF CAKE:** Luckily, parents never have to cover the giant party costs alone. Guests pin money onto the party child's clothes, and we have a godparent system. For Adilene's kindergarten graduation party, we asked her aunt and uncle to be the godparents of decorations, meaning they donate that one thing. Others could be, say, the godmothers of music, or food. It's a back-and-forth: I know when there's a celebration, I have to give support too. (*Hernanditoz*)

**WORK AS PLAY:** In Ahuirán, children learn adult skills very young. Parents take them along to plant corn, or help build a house. It becomes fun, because everyone's together, and the kids are half-working,

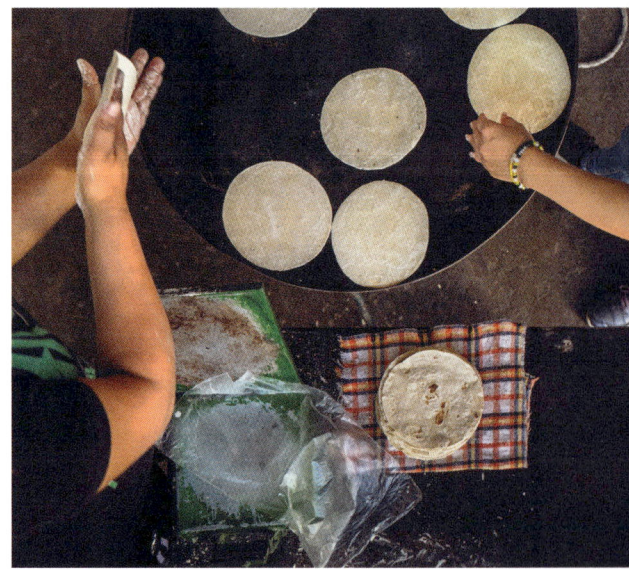

half-playing. Adilene practises making tortillas with her aunt, making all different funny faces, depending if they come out lumpy or round. She learns from our work filming videos too – talking on camera has made her more outgoing. (*Hernanditoz*)

**BECOMING BILINGUAL:** I decided to teach Adilene Spanish first, to help her with school. But recently, I heard her ask my mum in perfect Purépecha, 'What are you doing, Mamá Rosa?' I thought, 'Huh? When did you learn that?' She listens, and absorbs it. That makes me really happy. People used to be ashamed to speak Purépecha in the city, since others would mock them. But Adilene is proud. I have a dream she'll become fluent one day, so our mother tongue is not forgotten. (*Estela*)

**SHOWING OFF:** In Colima, when Adilene's teacher asked who had seen someone Indigenous, she yelled out, 'My mum!' So the teacher invited us to dress up in traditional clothing to show the class. It's a little too hot in Colima for our outfits, with all our hand-embroidered, colourful layers, and a warm *rebozo* on top. But I didn't mind sweating through all the photos the kids wanted to take, because I knew it made my daughter proud. (*Estela*)

**STUDIES FIRST:** One thing I don't want Adilene to learn from our village is marrying young. The village school only reaches ninth grade, so when kids graduate, they're already planning their weddings! If you're not married by age 16, you're considered 'left behind'. When I hear aunts telling Adilene she must learn to cook well to please her future mother-in-law, I tell them, 'Stop! Talk to Adilene about school instead!' I'd prefer that she focus on having a career first. She'd like to use her cooking skills to become a chef. In the pueblo, that makes us different, but I believe it will favour a good life. (*Estela*)

FRANZISKA RENATA BRUNER

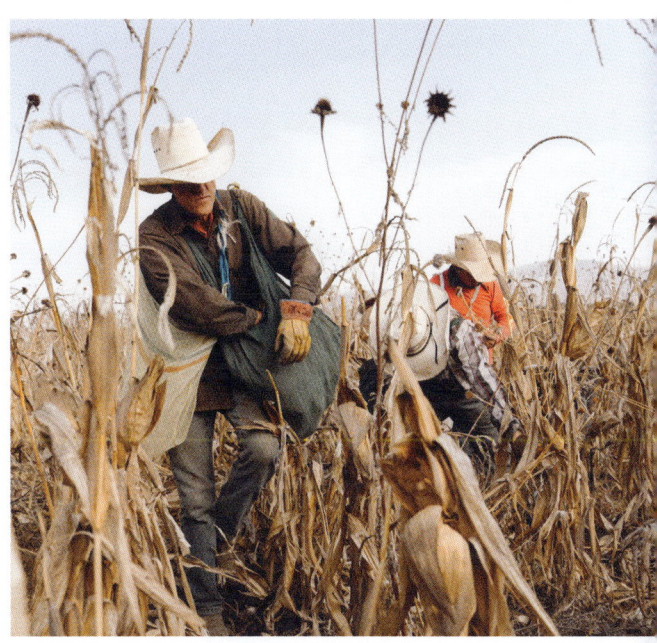

## Our favourite traditions

***Cornfield delivery service:*** When my dad goes to tend our cornfields, my sisters and I round up our kids to bring him lunch. Adeline and her cousins run around the green cornstalks, and we run after them. The air is brisk, and we share *corundas* (triangular tamales) and a tamarind-corn drink with my dad. It's a beautiful time together. (*Estela*)

***Michoacán trips:*** We love filming in other Purépecha villages together. Adeline always jumps right in to play with the local kids. They've seen her say 'Give us a like' at the end of our videos, so they've nicknamed her 'La Niña Like', (The Like Girl). Sometimes, they even prepare little gifts for her, and she feels so welcomed. (*Hernanditoz*)

***Pueblo fashion:*** For Purépecha women and girls, our traditional colourful layers of clothes are our identity and our art. It can take four months to cross-stitch one blouse! The day Adilene got her first Purépecha outfit from my sister, she was so excited. Now she wears it with pride every time she can. (*Estela*)

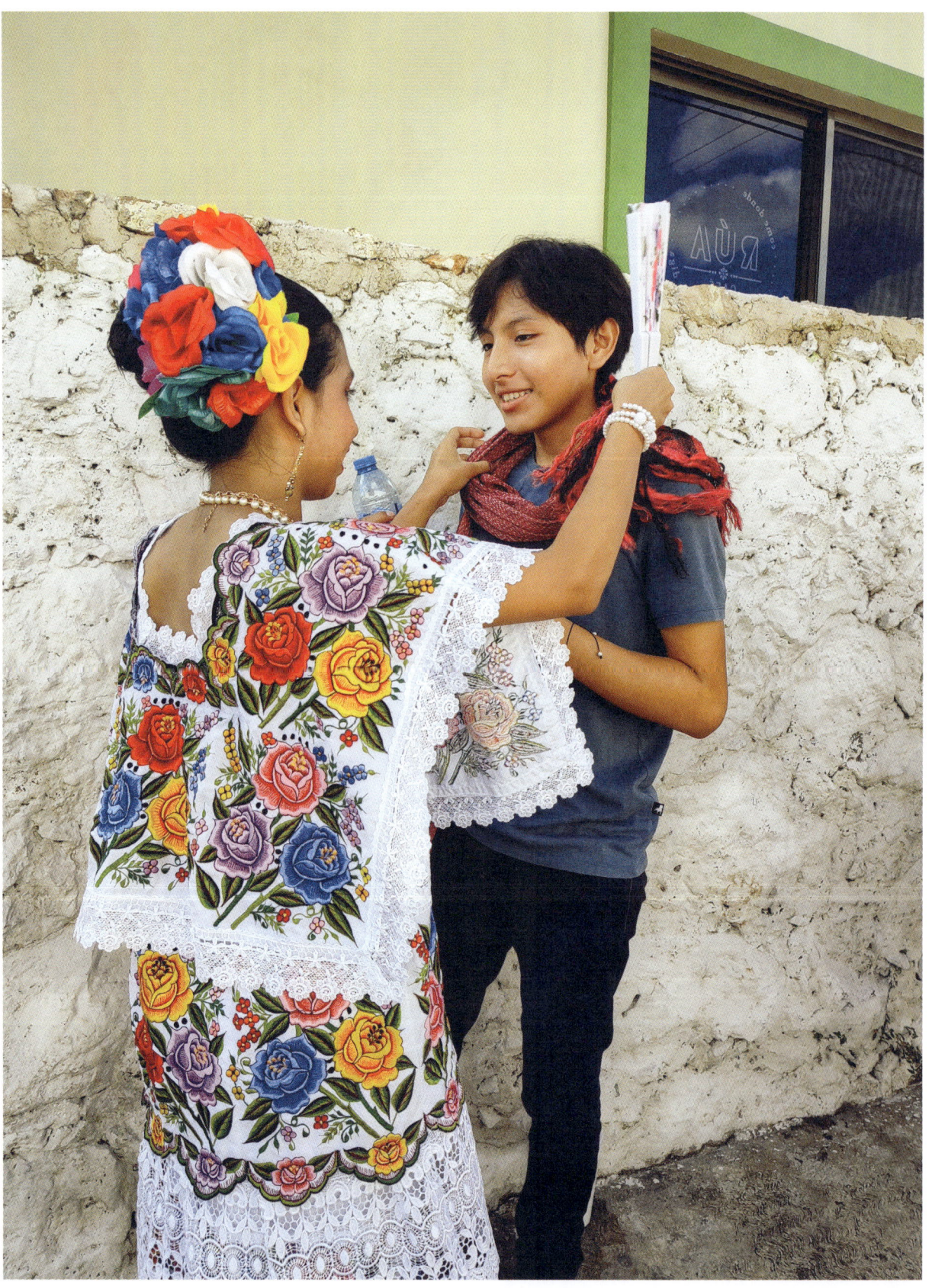

# Mexico

## JENNY CAUICH

**WHERE JENNY LIVES:**
Valladolid, Mexico

**WHERE JENNY IS FROM:**
Valladolid, Mexico

Jenny's family has been living in the Yucatán for as long as anyone can remember; first in small pueblos and, since her grandparents' generation, in Valladolid. She lives with her parents, who help raise her daughter Ayelen (14). 'Valladolid is small and tranquil, everyone knows each other', says Jenny, an environmental engineer. 'I love that our culture's alive here: we hear Maya spoken on the streets, and my grandparents wear their traditional dress every day.' To keep all of this alive, Jenny often asks herself what she will pass on: 'I think for me, it's our ancestral stories about mystical creatures who protect nature. Those stories unite us, and teach us to care for our jungles and water. That's a great legacy to leave Ayelen and her generation.'

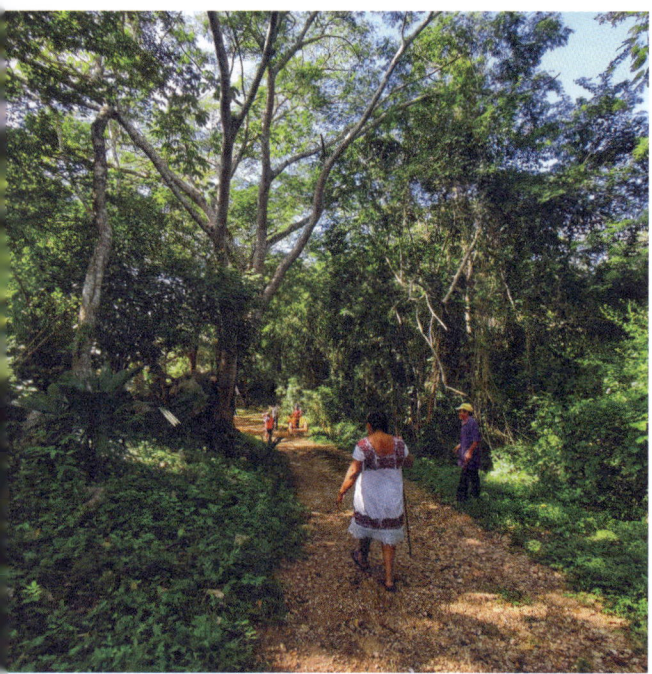

**HELPING HANDS:** Ayelen was born when I was really young, I'd only completed middle school. It could have been a tough situation, but my whole family stepped in to help – even my two little brothers. Thanks to them and a government scholarship for single mothers, I finished high school and university. Now I work 10-hour days at an NGO, Centinelas del Agua, helping rural communities care for their water. The schedule is complicated for a single mum! So, I'm really grateful to my family for raising Ayelen together.

Sometimes, I can sit down and have a great talk with my daughter, and it hits me: I'm able to do this because right now my mum is cooking for us, and my dad picked her up from school. We're united.

**COMFY SLEEP:** Ayelen – like our whole family – has slept in a hammock all her life. When she was a baby, we knotted the sides to create a safe, cosy crib. Now, she still only uses a bed in winter. A well-made hammock is cool and durable; Ayelen's favorite rainbow-striped one is just starting to wear out, after using it for 14 years! Like everyone, she wakes up with her face and arms all marked up by the hammock strings' pattern, and it stays there even after she showers. I guess that's the price we all pay for sleeping exquisitely well.

**SPRING HEAT:** May is our hottest month. In the villages, people wake up at 4am to finish their work by 10am, because the sun is so intense. After that, they stay inside until late afternoon. Our family's routine changes too: Ayelen spends afternoons at home sleeping, reading and painting. In 41°C (106°F), we can't be too active.

**ANCIENT TALES:** I grew up with my grandparents' typical Maya stories about mystical jungle creatures, and now Ayelen loves them too. There are *x´men* (sorcerers) and *aluxes* – tiny mischievous elves who, depending how you treat them, can either watch over your land or give you the famous *mal aire* ('bad air', a feverish illness). Now, as an adult, I've realised these beings are guardians of the jungle and cenotes (freshwater pools), and carry a message from our ancestors. I think Ayelen gets it; she picks up litter and conserves water, without me telling her.

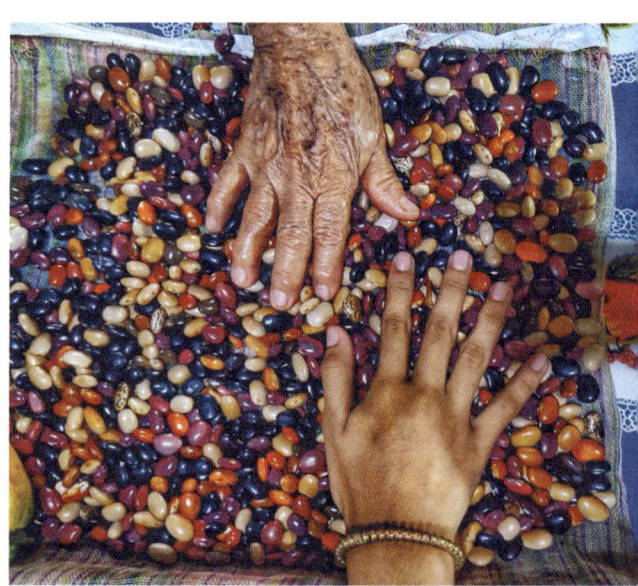

**REMEMBRANCE:** Every October, kids make altars at school for Hanal Pixán, the Maya Day of the Dead. But we never did it at home, because my parents are evangelical Christians. A few years ago I decided: we're Maya, we're going to celebrate this!

Since our beloved little dog died last August, Ayelen and I dedicated this year's altar to her. We go to the municipal market for items; it's bustling, full of sweets, bright colours and the smell of resins like copal, used to call the spirits. Our dog loved bananas and watermelon, so we put that on the altar with kibbles and toys. My dad was annoyed but, for us, it was a loving way to remember her.

**CHANGING TIMES:** There's still machismo here – in some families, women have to ask men's permission for everything. Fathers rest after work, mothers can't. But that's all changing. Now I see dads coming to school meetings – before, never! I like to send Ayelen videos of local women being self-sufficient, like a new village softball team called the Amazonas who play in their *huipiles* (traditional embroidered dresses). She says, 'Mum, I want to be like you, speaking up in public', and we practise giving presentations. I tell her: 'To be a woman, is valuable.'

**FRAGILITY:** During the [COVID-19] pandemic, there was a wave of teen depression and suicides in Yucatán. Being isolated inside, with no school, fearing relatives' deaths; it impacted everyone a lot. I decided to take Ayelen to therapy, and then I went myself. The most important thing, I think, is to ask our teens sincerely, 'How are you, how did things go today?' Not as a script, but from your heart.

FRANZISKA RENATA BRUNER

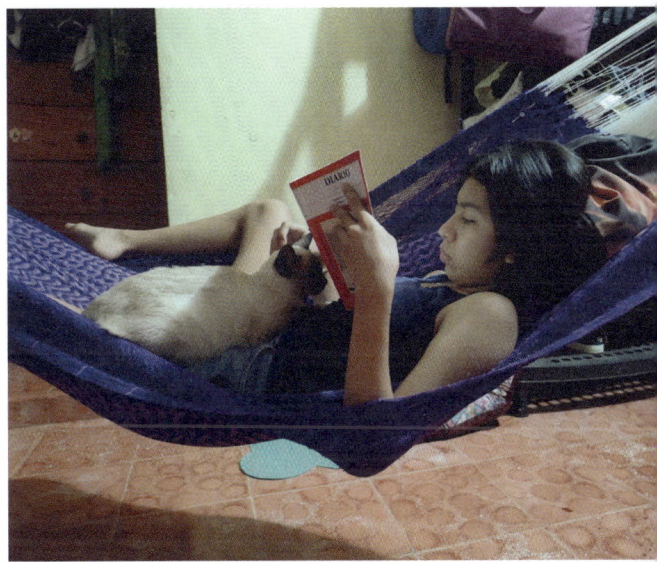

## Our favourite traditions

***Evening outings:*** Ayelen and I love to escape to the city's outskirts on our motorcycle, to feel the wind in our hair and watch the sunset.

***Corn drinks are life:*** In summer, we cool off drinking *pozole* (a cold, sweetcorn-and-coconut drink). At harvest time in October, our family gets together to make *atole nuevo*, a sweet or salty hot drink using freshly picked corn we grind by hand.

***Beating the heat:*** My grandmother's kitchen has a traditional palm-leaf roof – much cooler inside than our concrete city house. In the summer, she cooks outdoors in an underground oven called a *pib*, and Ayelen and I pick mangoes from the backyard trees for ice-cold *aguas frescas* (chilled watery juices).

***New Year:*** Every 1 January we go to my uncle's *rancho* to light a bonfire and break open a piñata. Everyone tells fantastical stories that 'Really did happen in my neighbour's village!'

***Hotcake Sundays:*** We add fruits and vegetables to turn our pancakes bright colours. Ayelen says, 'Mum, I'm not a little kid any more!' but secretly loves it.

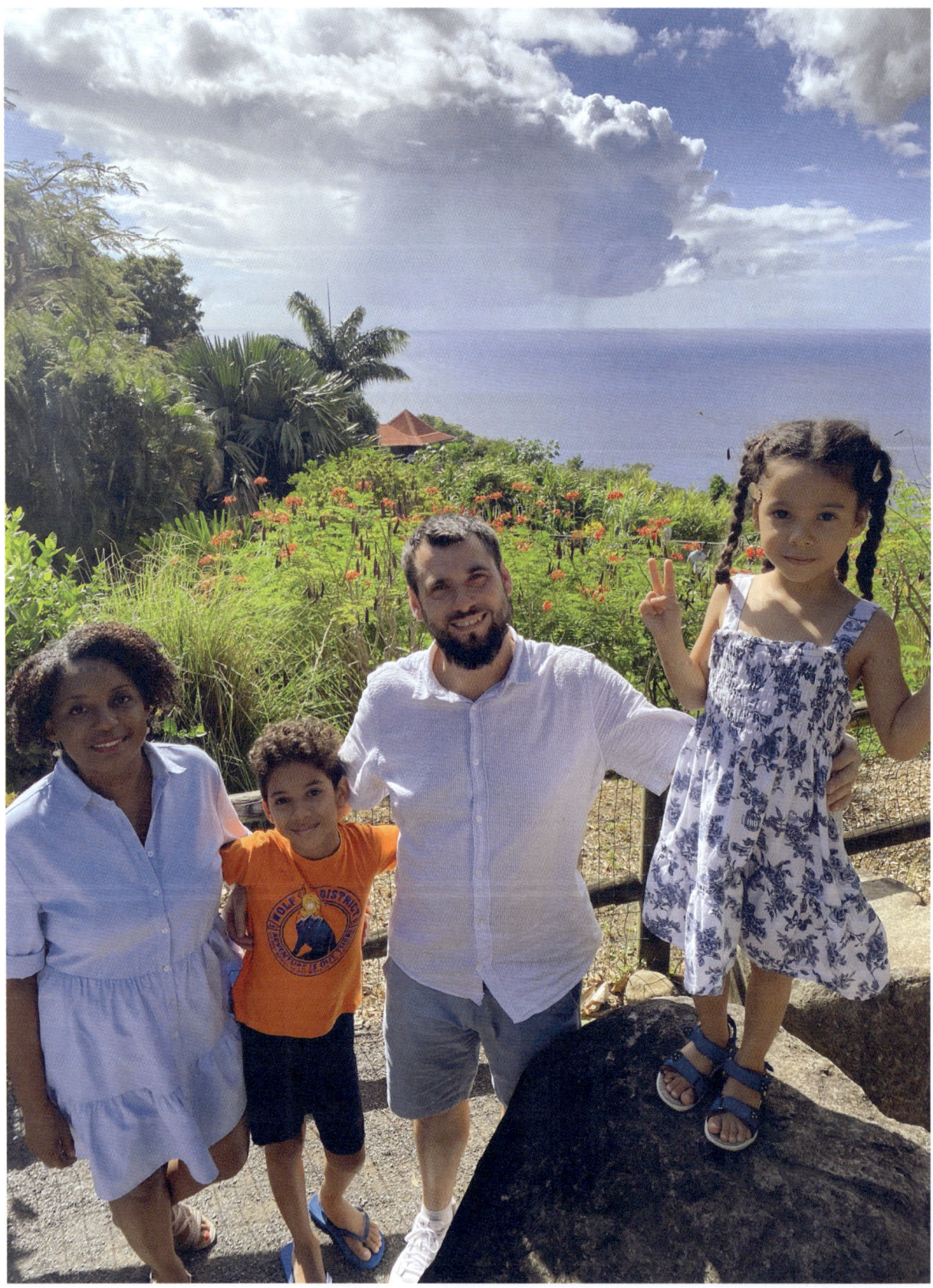

# Guadeloupe

## RAÏSSA & EMMANUEL KERN

**WHERE RAÏSSA & EMMANUEL LIVE:**
Deshaies, Guadeloupe

**WHERE RAÏSSA & EMMANUEL ARE FROM:**
Deshaies, Guadeloupe and Besançon, France

Raïssa, 39, is a native of the butterfly-shaped French-Caribbean island of Guadeloupe. She met her now 43-year-old French husband, Emmanuel, when they both studied business in Rennes, France. Together the two moved to London for four years to further their careers in the field of commerce. 'We really had a good time in London as a young couple without kids', says Emmanuel. Yet, when planning their family, the relaxed life in the Caribbean seemed more appealing. 'We wanted to raise the kids in an environment that was quieter than London, and Raïssa's family was here', says Emmanuel. In 2012, they moved to Guadeloupe's Deshaies, the setting of the popular British-French murder mystery *Death in Paradise*. A few years later, they had their children, Djibril and Malia, now nine and four.

**SMALL-TOWN SAFETY:** Deshaies is a friendly, small village of 4000 residents, where people know who I am and who my parents are – we are all more or less cousins. There is nearly no crime and my children's school is small. I know what it's like to grow up in a place like this and I really wanted that for my kids. (*Raïssa*)

**A TOURISTIC TOWN:** It's an advantage that Deshaies is a touristic town. We have nice restaurants and hotels where you can spend the day at the pool or have a beer at the bar. Sometimes after school we go have crepes at Paradise Kafé right on the beach. We can dip our feet in the sea while the children play in the sand. Even though we live here, we sometimes stay overnight at the Fort Royal Langley Resort. The children are always really happy there. (*Raïssa*)

The kids like to swim in the hotel's pool and go to the beach, and there is a big grassy area to run around. (*Emmanuel*)

**UNSOLICITED ADVICE:** When you have small children, people frequently approach you to give parenting advice. It's the tradition here – especially if you are from the town. As a new parent, it was frustrating as I had not asked for help and the advice was not always good. Honestly, now I think it's a positive thing. I have accepted it. It means you belong to the place and people care about you. (*Raïssa*)

**EXTENDED FAMILY:** The idea of family is extended here. Relatives tend to live closer together. For example, our home was my parents' house before, and my grandmother and my cousin's family live next door. The kids often play together and shout funny things to each other from their balconies. We can see our children creating lasting bonds. When there is a birthday party or a baptism, all the relatives are invited. Our culture is more collective – a bit like 'it takes a village to raise the child'. These family gatherings help keep our traditions alive. (*Raïssa*)

**WEEKDAY ROUTINE:** Since we leave early for work, we drop the kids at my parents' house in the morning so they can take them to school at 8am. My brother picks them up after school so that the kids don't have to stay from 7am to 6pm at the *garderie* (childcare facility). Like in mainland France, there is no school on Wednesdays, so the kids stay with my parents in the morning. I don't work on Wednesday afternoons. (*Raïssa*)

**SPEAKING CREOLE:** I speak Creole, Emmanuel understands it, and our kids understand some. So, at home we speak French. I try from time to time to encourage the children to speak Creole, but it does not come naturally. But usually, the older children get, the more interested in Creole they become, in order to not miss anything! (*Raïssa*)

**BEACH FUN:** Our favorite local beach is Plage de Leroux. The children will play for hours in the waves. (*Emmanuel*)

We often also go to beaches in Ste-Anne or Bois Jolan, even though it's an hour-and-a-half drive. The water is safer for kids, as it is shallow and calm. Plus, we enjoy a change of scenery. (*Raïssa*)

**KIDS' BIRTHDAYS:** Birthdays are a big thing. Djibril gets a lot of invitations and his friends organise parties at the beach, the zoo or in the different parks. Malia is still young, so they celebrate at her preschool. Kids cannot have parties at school once they are in *cours préparatoire* (first grade). (*Raïssa*)

**VISITING EUROPE:** Every year, we visit my parents in Besançon, France, for three weeks. The children get quite excited by the different environment. Djibril saw snow in France once and he keeps asking if we can go back for Christmas. (*Emmanuel*)

MIRVA LEMPIÄINEN

# Our favourite traditions

**Sunday lunch:** We have lunch regularly with my parents and my brother. My mother is a very good cook. It is a nice big Sunday lunch with an appetiser, a traditional Creole meal, and maybe homemade ice cream. We sit around the table and eat together for over an hour. My parents have a swing and a play area where the kids can run and yell afterward. (*Raïssa*)

**Deshaies Botanical Garden:** We visit the garden after school and during weekends. Sometimes I bring my computer and work while the kids are playing at the playground. We may do the full tour or just go to see the birds and fish. (*Emmanuel*)

**River fun:** We go to the river in Deshaies a lot. In the Là-haut area there is a quiet, flat area of the river where you can have a picnic and bathe in the water. We can easily spend the whole day at the river. We bring our pots, barbecue meat and grill, and have river parties with family and friends. (*Raïssa*)

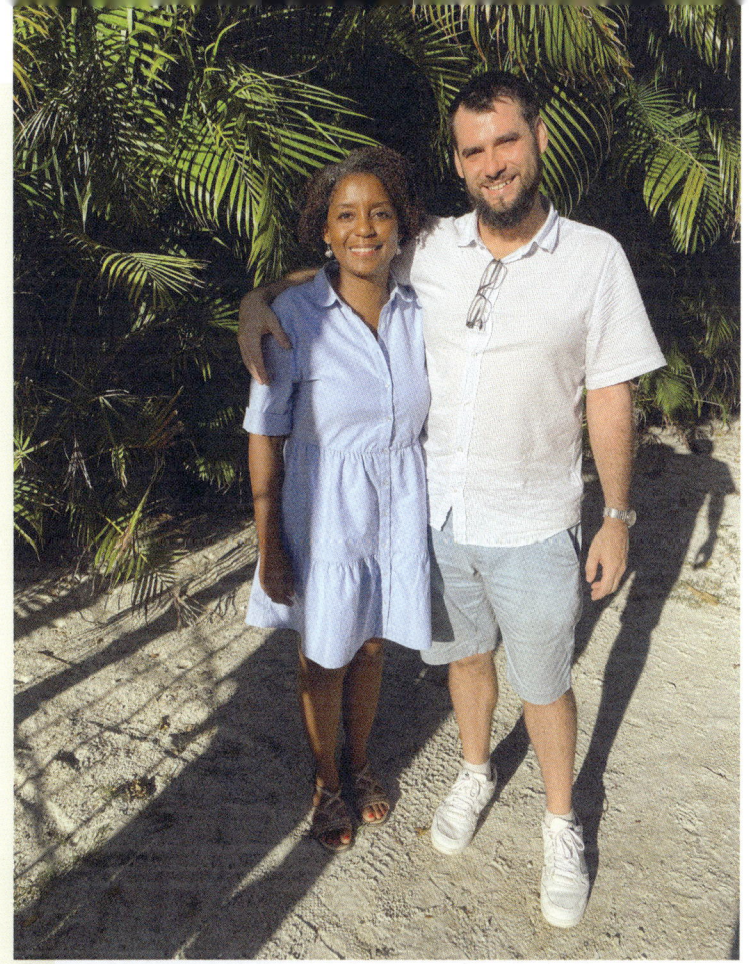

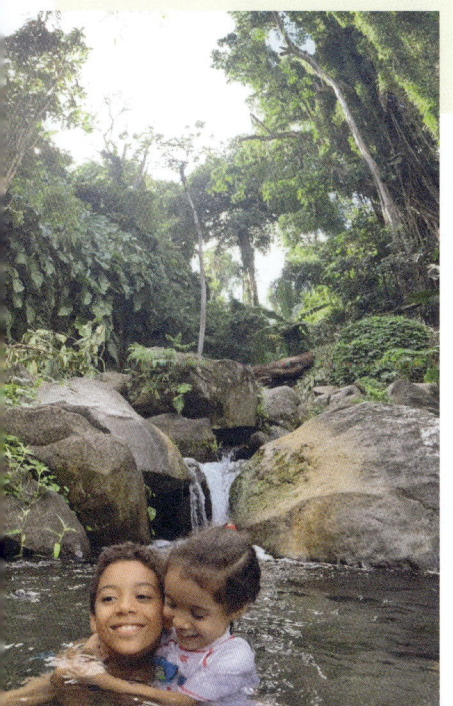

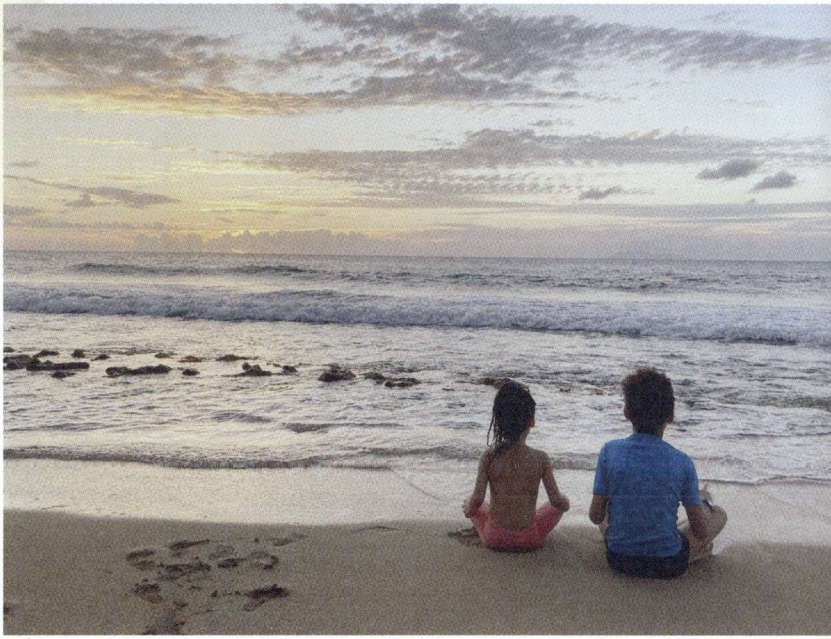

LATIN AMERICA & THE CARIBBEAN

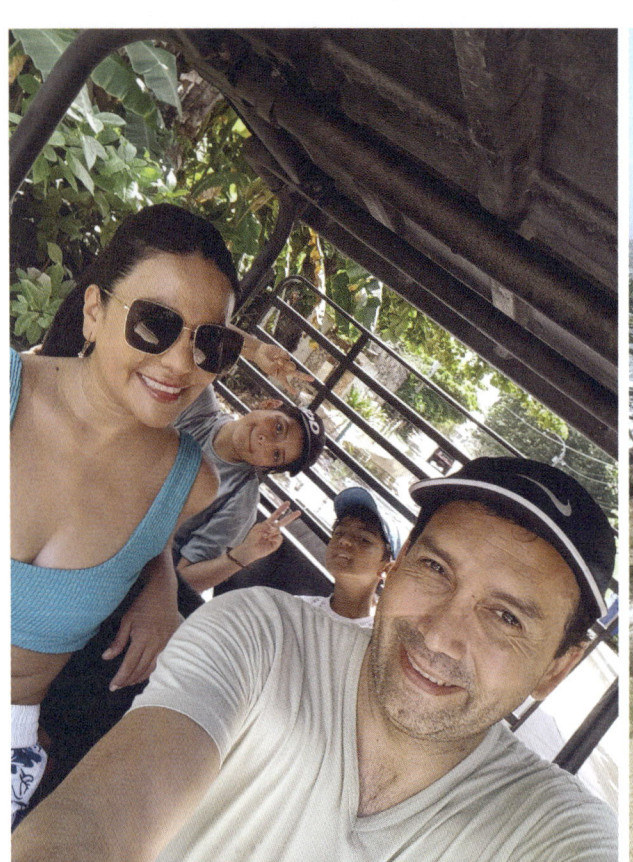
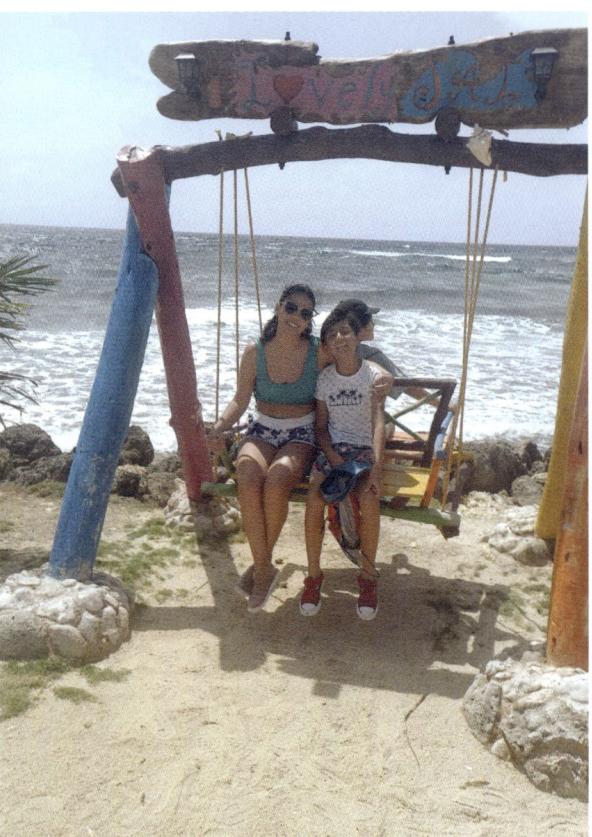

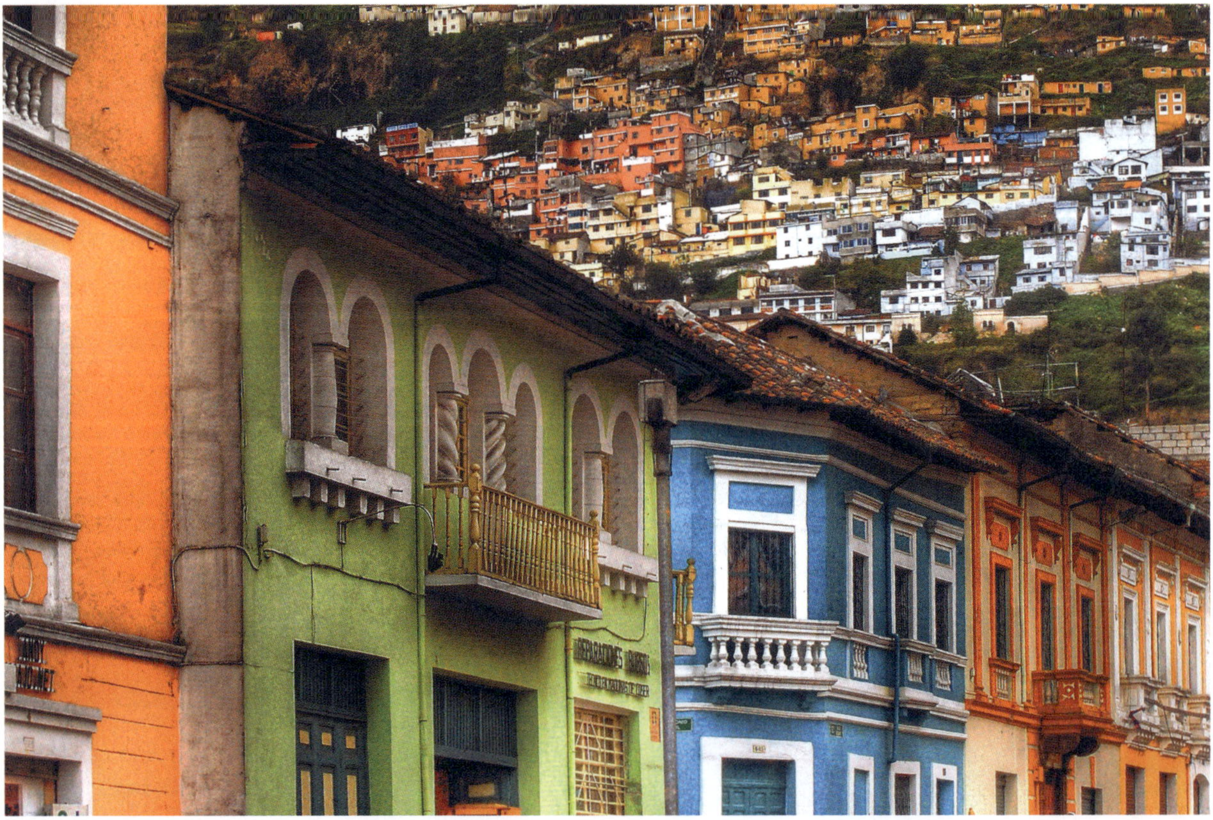

# Ecuador

## FERNANDA ANDRADE & JAIME ACOSTA

**WHERE FERNANDA & JAIME LIVE:**
Quito, Ecuador

**WHERE FERNANDA & JAIME ARE FROM:**
Quito, Ecuador

Much like a medical-drama romance, Fernanda and Jaime first met as resident doctors in one of Quito's largest hospitals. After calling off their engagement and going their separate ways, the couple serendipitously rekindled their relationship years later. Within three months, they married in a civil ceremony with 120 guests. Now both accomplished physicians – Fernanda a dermatologist and Jaime a traumatologist – they juggle their demanding careers while raising two children – Daniel (12) and Luciana (10) – in a Quito townhouse. The couple considers parenthood something akin to a miracle. 'Doctors told us we had a 2% chance of becoming parents', says Fernanda. That's perhaps why the couple has created a lifestyle where their children are their top priority and good communication is non-negotiable.

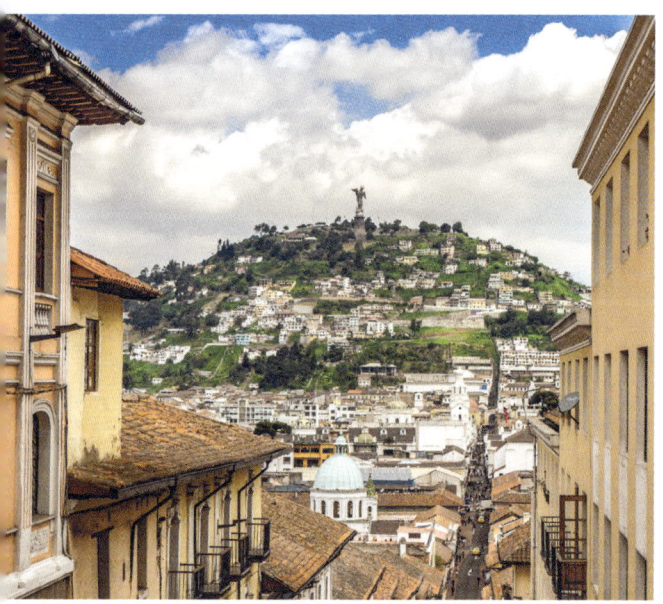

**BALANCING CAREER AND PARENTHOOD:** The way parents traditionally divide their household duties didn't fit our lifestyle. There have been times when I have worked little or not at all and Jaime was the only one providing for the household; then other times when I've worked full-time Jaime has been fully dedicated to taking care of the children. (*Fernanda*)

One of us is always with the children while the other works or studies. We never leave them alone. We take turns and have a good communication system. This has been the key to our success. It is a matter of commitment. (*Jaime*)

**A DAY IN THE LIFE:** A typical day in our household starts at 6am. I prepare breakfast for everybody and send the children to school. There's a school bus but the children sometimes ask me to drop them off. They love that. Then I go to work and usually get home around 2pm and eat with the kids. After doing their homework, depending on the day, Daniel goes to football training and Luciana goes to other activities like dance and box. We always go with them. (*Jaime*)

**FATHER AND SON TIME:** Daniel and I love... ('Eating!' Fernanda chimes in, earning laughs.) No, we both love Greek mythology and spend a lot of time talking about Greek gods and stories. We also love talking about football and, just like many, we enjoy following the Champions League. (*Jaime*)

**FOOD-CENTRED GATHERINGS:** Our traditional food offers a sense of belonging. For example, during Holy Week, a countrywide tradition is to prepare *fanesca* (a creamy squash-and-pumpkin soup) – everybody eats it even if they don't like it. When Carnival arrives, our family travels to the coast and goes to different beaches. It's a time to eat seafood. When the crab-harvest season begins, Shrove Tuesday is the only day we eat crab. There are a lot of food-centred gatherings in our family. (*Jaime*)

**EDUCATION:** There's good-quality education in Ecuador, but sometimes it's complicated to get access. (*Fernanda*) There's also the widespread belief that the amount parents pay for education is proportional to the opportunities their children will have in the future. Most parents encourage their children to keep studying and preparing for life. It's a sort of expectation that each generation continues to improve their family's life conditions. (*Jaime*)

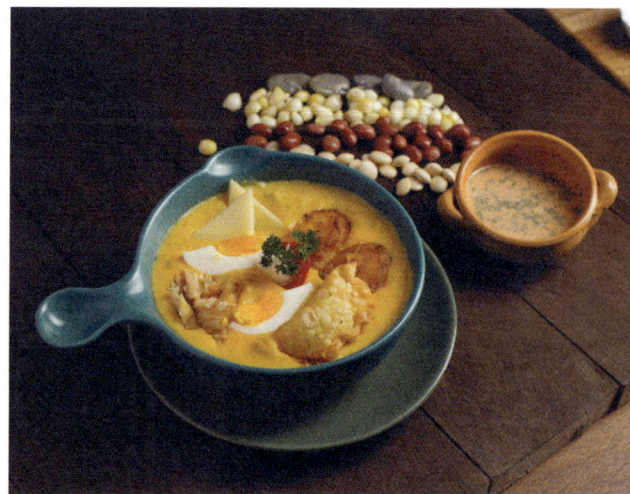

# "Our traditional food offers a sense of belonging."

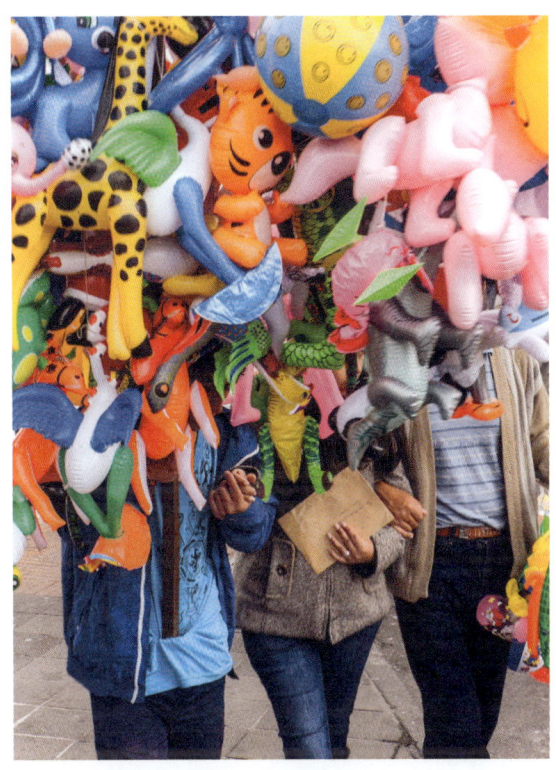

Our children go to a private school. But beyond grades, we want to know that their heart and soul are in a good place and they're trying to be their best version. We don't want perfect children, we want them to have fun, to do the things they like to do; and to be with them. (*Fernanda*)

**ON EXTERNAL HELP:** About 70% or 80% of the time we take charge of absolutely everything, but sometimes things like schedules are out of our hands. The norm in Ecuador is asking for help from family but we don't like to do that because, for starters, we live on opposite sides of the city and then, everybody has their own responsibilities. We also have the support of our housekeeper, Carmita. (*Jaime*)

She has supported us a lot. She has been with us since I was pregnant with my second child Luciana. She feels like a grandmother to the children. (*Fernanda*)

**CHALLENGES AND CONCERNS:** Growing crime and insecurity is a challenging aspect of raising children here. When we were children we used to go out to play in the streets with our friends, but that's not possible for kids now. We live in a private housing complex, so there's a slight advantage for Daniel and Luciana because they can move about freely, but we do understand that this is not the case elsewhere. That's why we always try to be with them. (*Jaime and Fernanda*)

MAYRA PERALTA

## Our favourite traditions

***Wearing costumes on New Year's Eve:*** New Year's Eve is an important day for our family. We go all-out. We put on costumes and try to host a party with the extended family every year: grandparents, uncles, cousins. We dance, the children play with other kids and they eat whatever they want.

***Movie-obsessed:*** Sunday afternoons are our free days. There are no televisions in the children's rooms so all of us, dogs included, go to our room and lie on the bed. For us, watching movies is a lot of fun. Our greatest tradition is watching family-friendly movies together. We make popcorn and comment on the movie non-stop.

***Shaping a new tradition:*** We love cooking together. Recently, we've made it a habit to prepare bread recipes we find on Instagram – sidenote, they work!

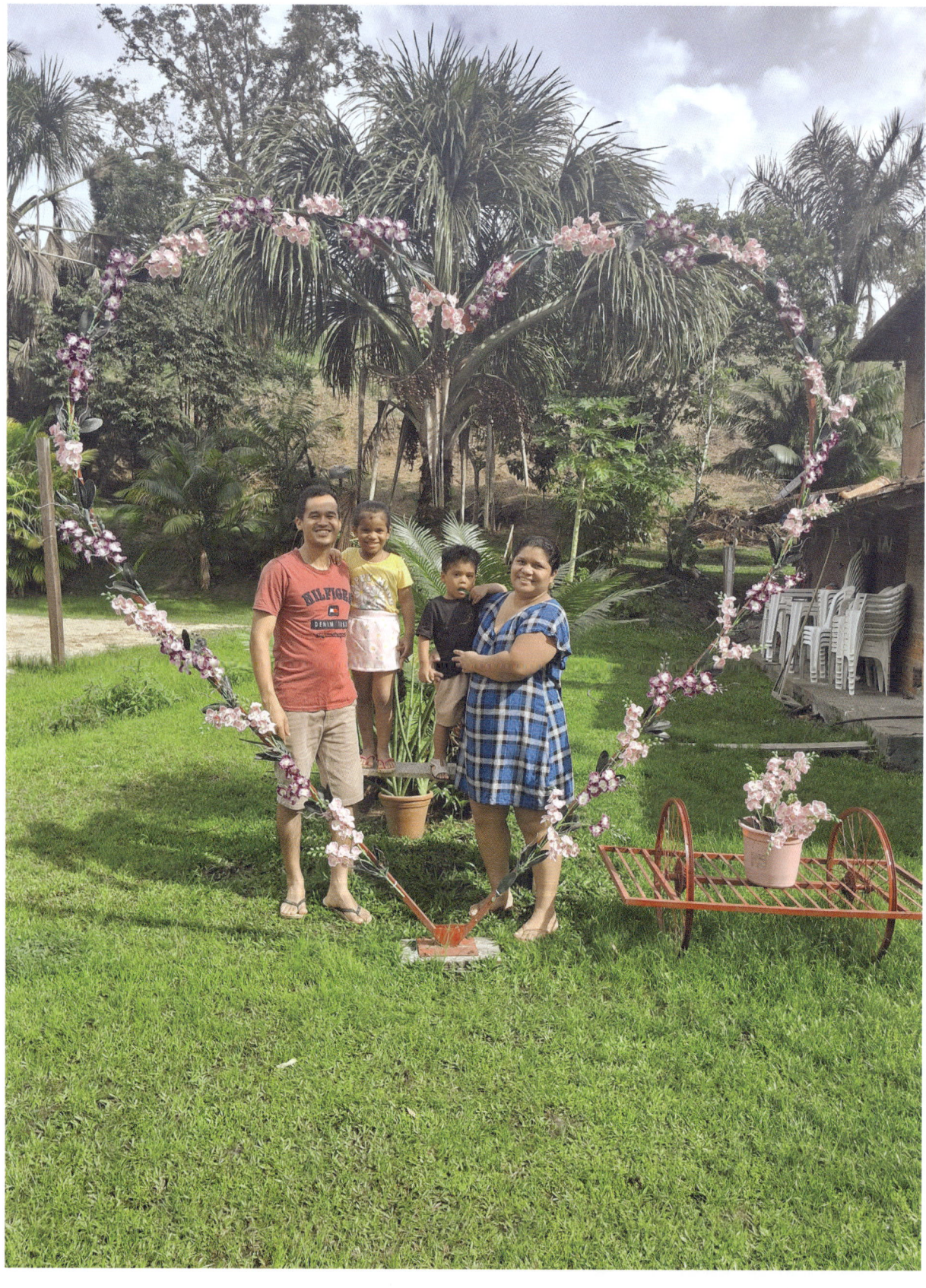

# Brazil

## MARIVANE (MARI) DUQUE & JEFERSON ROCHA

**WHERE MARI & JEFERSON LIVE:**
Manaus, Brazil

**WHERE MARI & JEFERSON ARE FROM:**
Porto Trombetas and Luís Domingues, Brazil

Both Mari and Jeferson were born in northern Brazil's rural interior, and moved to Manaus as teenagers. In the city, Jeferson works as a data analyst, and Mari as a production engineer, while Mari's mum helps take care of their children Sophia (four) and Isaac (two). 'Brazil has changed so much in the last 25 years. I was planting corn as a child; today our kids are born into a world of technology', Jeferson says; 'We like that here in the Amazon, they can still stay in contact with nature.' 'We want them to know the smell of the earth when it rains', says Mari. 'To us, walking barefoot in the mud and eating fruit straight from a tree are important experiences.'

**STAYING COOL:** It's hot and humid here all year long. In August, when temperatures pass 40°C (104°F), memes start circulating showing people casually strolling through Manaus with their clothes on fire! The kids don't complain; they were born here and are used to it. On weekends, we escape to Presidente Figueiredo, a city full of waterfalls called 'baths'. There are shallow parts where small kids can swim surrounded by the rainforest, and the water is ice cold. Sophia usually looks around in awe and says, 'Wow, Dad, so beautiful!' (*Jeferson*)

**FAMILY FARMS:** As a child, I loved going to my family's *sítio*, a plot of land where we grew all our food. It was 12km (7.5 miles) from town, so to go plant our corn, beans and cassava was a long walk, followed by lots of work. Later, things got better and my dad bought us some bicycles! People might think 'What hard work for a child', but I'd love for our kids to experience some of that. Our food was very fresh, we played in the river. My parents gave us little in terms of material stuff, but they gave us so much love. Nowadays, we go to my uncle's *sítio* about 50km (31 miles) from Manaus. The kids collect eggs from my aunt's chickens, run around all day with their cousins, and learn to ride a horse. We eat a big lunch around a gigantic table full of relatives. I like for the kids to see that family unity. (*Jeferson*)

**AMAZONIAN SUPERFOOD:** Kids grow up on açai here – it's a first food for babies, part of school lunches, and a side dish for meat and shrimp. At the *sítio*, we pick the berries, mash them with cassava flour, and the kids all sit in a circle on the floor together to drink it. Of course, it quickly turns into a huge mess of purple faces and stained clothes, but they have so much fun together. (*Jeferson*)

**PUBLIC SAFETY:** I'd love to bring a picnic to a park in Manaus, but we can't – the risk of being assaulted is too high. It's typical Brazilian city life, that our children play inside a gated condominium, next to a checkpoint and security guards. That makes me sad – I had so much more freedom as a child. But we find workarounds, like going to the big playgrounds inside some *sorveterias* (ice cream shops that use Amazonian fruits). It combines our kids' favourites: eating cold treats in a hot city, and climbing jungle gyms. (*Jeferson*)

**HOLIDAY SHOWS:** Like all of Brazil, people in Manaus love giant theatrical spectacles with costumes and dancing. Our favourite is *Christmas Dreams*, put on by the Baptist church, where Sophia attends Sunday School. It's a really well-crafted musical retelling of Jesus' life, with themes like protecting the rainforest. We'd like Sophia and Isaac to understand the story, but at this age, they are more entranced by all the special effects, acrobatics and colourful lights. People from the community spend the whole year rehearsing it, and whether they are rich or poor, everyone can participate. (*Mari*)

**POSTPARTUM TIPS:** When Sophia was born, my mother and grandmother gave me lots of advice. First, to stay in bed for 40 days (while Jeferson and my mum did all the housework, so, not a bad deal!). Second, to avoid sweets and *tambaqui* (my favourite Amazon river fish), because they're *remosos* (inflammatory). 'The doctors don't know this information', was their complaint. Some people think all that's old-fashioned, but we decided to follow it (well, mostly! Jeferson once discovered me sneaking chocolates and we had a good laugh). I figured my mum had three births, and my grandmother [had] 12 with zero complications, so they must know what they're talking about. We feel our parents have all the life experience of raising us, so why not follow their example? (*Mari*)

FRANZISKA RENATA BRUNER

# Our favourite traditions

***Asking for blessings:*** As soon as Sophia and Isaac see their grandparents, they have to say, 'Blessings, grandma/grandpa', and their grandparents answer, 'May God bless you.' With a kiss on the hand, it's a warm family greeting that shows respect. (*Mari*)

***Old-school toys:*** We like sharing outdoor games from our own childhoods, like flying kites, or playing marbles. One is *peteca*, a game from Maranhão where you try to hit other players' marbles on the ground with your own. Any marble you hit, you keep. (*Jeferson*)

***Eating tingly soup:*** An only-in-the-Amazon food we all love is *tacacá*, a shrimp soup usually served in a hollowed-out gourd. It's made with cassava and *jambú* leaves, that make your mouth feel tingly, then numb. These leaves have an anaesthetic supposedly strong enough to stop a toothache! Unusual, but delicious. (*Jeferson*)

***Beach vacations:*** Visiting the ocean 1450km (901 miles) away is a rare treat. I love seeing Sophia and Isaac on a plane – that's something I never even dreamed of as a kid. (*Jeferson*)

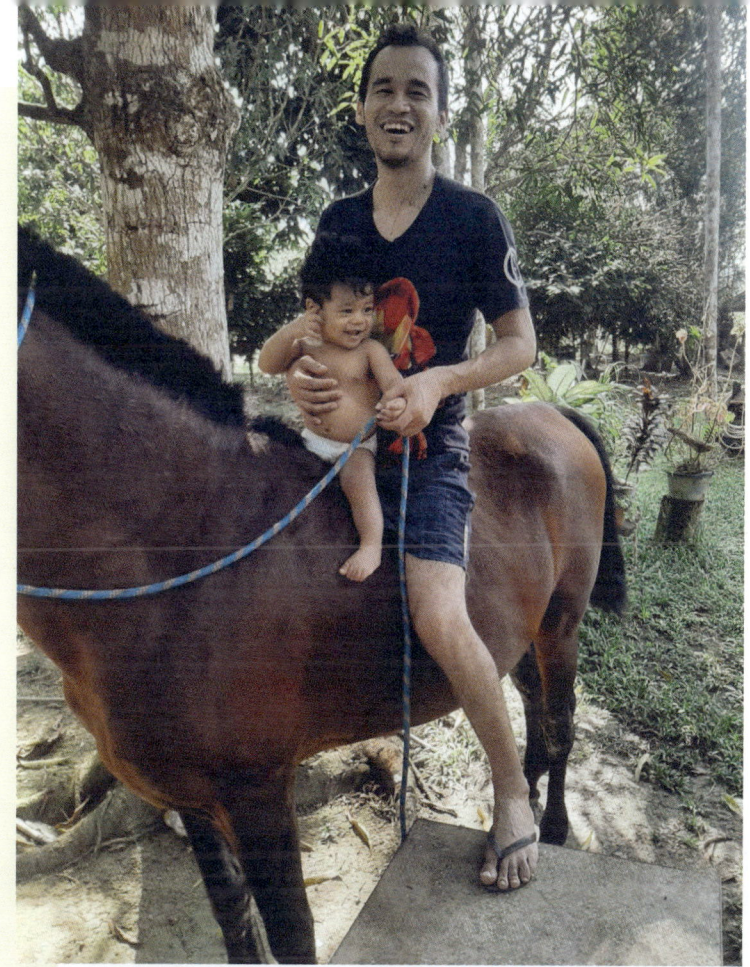

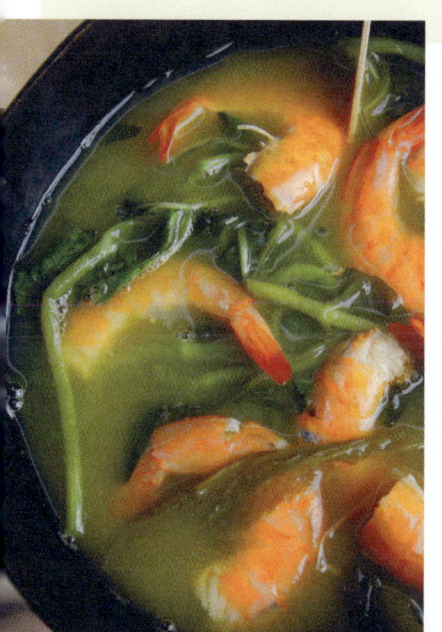

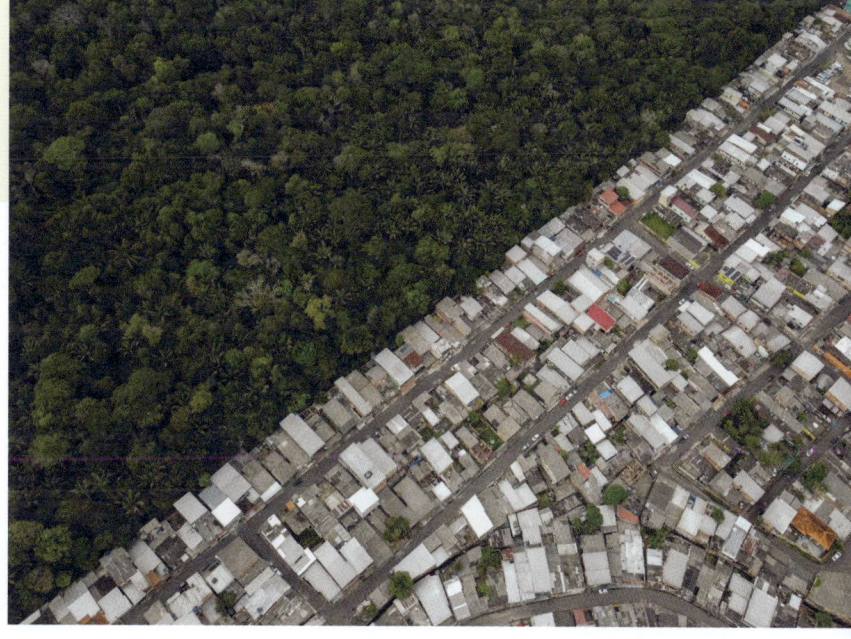

LATIN AMERICA & THE CARIBBEAN

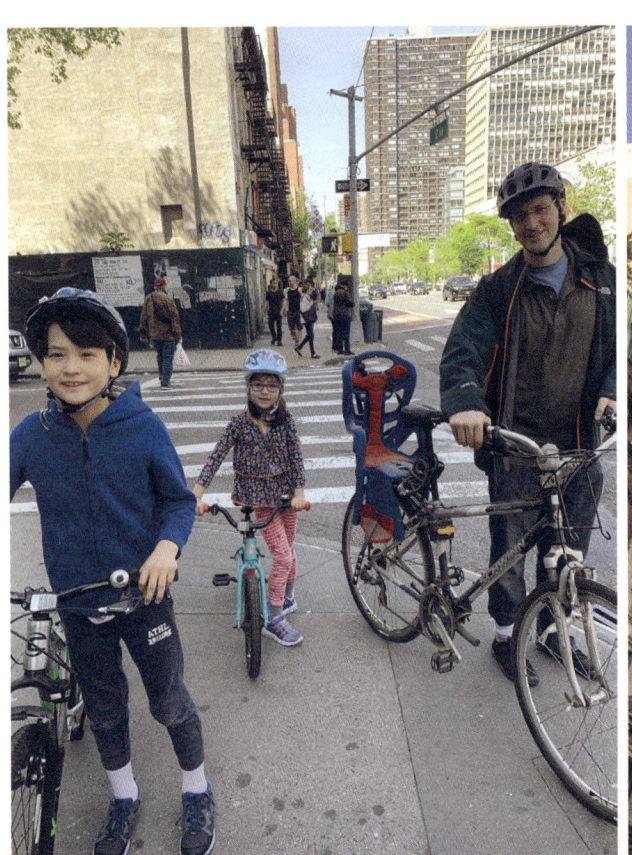
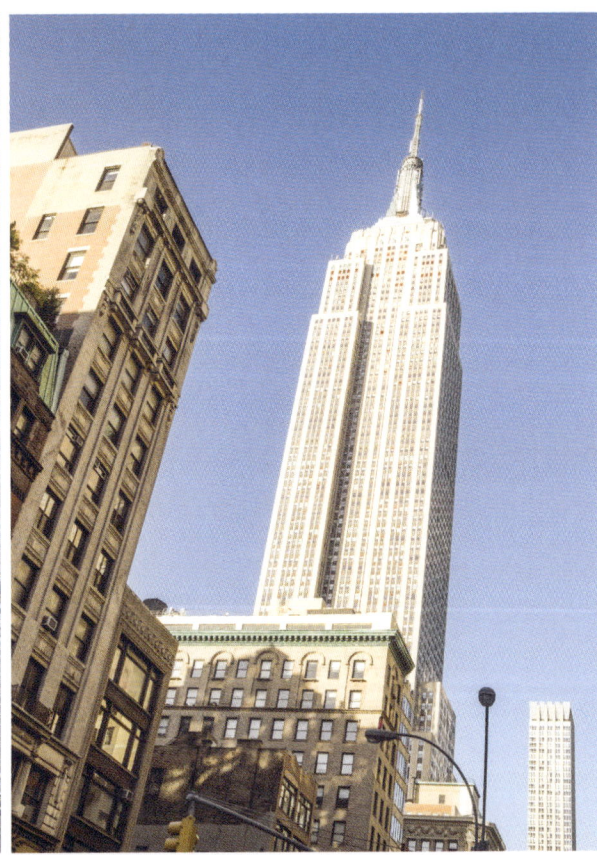

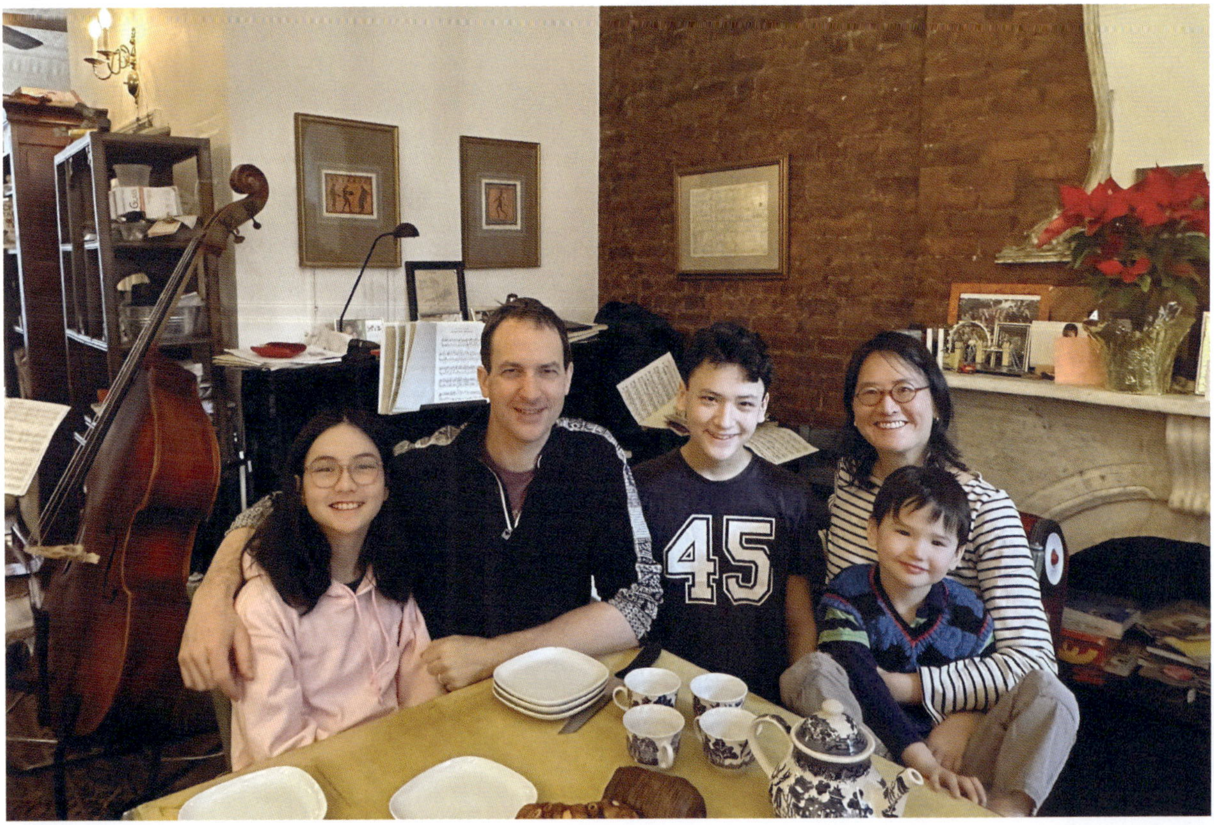

# USA

## DAVID LEFER & YVONNE LUI

**WHERE DAVID & YVONNE LIVE:**
New York City, New York

**WHERE DAVID & YVONNE ARE FROM:**
New York City, New York

David and Yvonne are creating an urban legacy. They raise their three children, Hugo (14), Clara (10) and Luke (four), in New York City's Murray Hill neighbourhood, only a block from Yvonne's childhood home and a short subway ride from where David grew up in Manhattan's Upper East Side. 'We're looking for a quiet place to talk, Hugo is playing the piano loudly and Luke just got back from his grandmother's, so we're actually sitting in bed.' David and Yvonne met each other on their first (and last) blind date. Speaking to them feels delightfully like watching your favourite scene from *When Harry Met Sally*. Both work at New York University, where Yvonne is a doctor specialising in neuroradiology and David is a professor of invention and innovation.

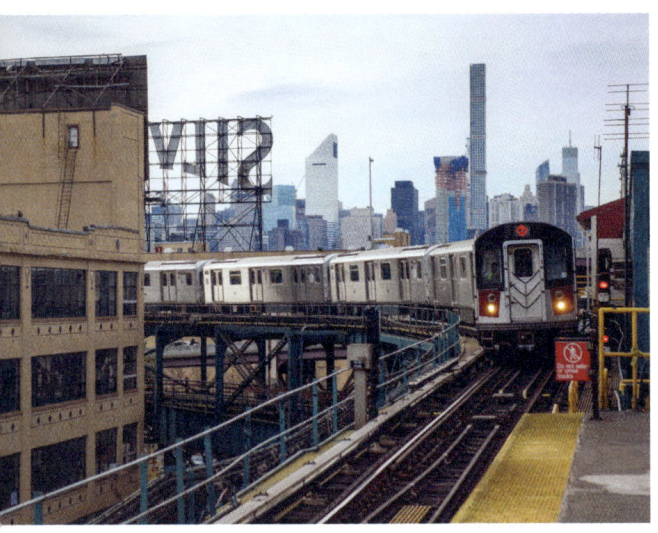

**KEEP FAMILY CLOSE:** Luke loves seeing his grandmother after school. He calls her Popo; they're very close. We suspect she lets him watch her iPad and have popsicles. (*David*) Sometimes… she's gotten better! (*Yvonne*) She's hard of hearing, so it's not that they even speak so much as just really enjoy each other's company. She lives across the street. My mom lives in the Upper East Side, so just a bit further. They call her Mamette. Hugo really enjoyed staying with her recently; they went to a piano concert and spent time with her friends. Popo and Mamette love having Clara as their granddaughter. (*David*)

**FREE-RANGE KIDS:** Suburban parents chauffeur *a lot*; there's almost none of that for us. (*Yvonne*) Hugo heads downtown to see a friend. Many track meets are in the Bronx, so kids come home on the subway together. It's the train to school most days. Clara doesn't ride the subway alone but walks miles. Always motivated by bubble tea! (*David*) She walks to art class or grandma's in the neighbourhood. (*Yvonne*) Or, runs out for a dinner ingredient. (*David*) I'll give her $10 and remind her: 'Get your change!' Sometimes she forgets. (*Yvonne*) Or, she gets change and uses it for bubble tea. (*David*)

**NO AIRTAGS NEEDED:** Hugo didn't have a cellphone until recently, but started taking the subway at [age] 11. He had a flip phone, but you couldn't track him. I could track him now, but honestly, I never click it. I'm comfortable that he's out there and ok. (*Yvonne*)

**THE CITY THAT NEVER SLEEPS:** I appreciate the convenience in NYC. People say 'Aren't you afraid on the subway at midnight?', but it's more packed than rush-hour sometimes. Our kids notice. They attended a chess tournament in Chicago and I panicked about finding dinner because kitchens would close. Clara didn't believe me, then we walked in and they wouldn't seat us at 8.40pm. (*Yvonne*) New York's like: 'It's 2am – let's grab a bite!' (*David*)

**LIFE'S ALSO NORMAL:** We can't do everything – we pick and choose. (*David*) Living here, you don't do all the touristy things; they're expensive, and even if you want to you just never get around to it. (*Yvonne*) Our kids have never been to the top of the Empire State Building, and you can walk past it daily. (*David*)

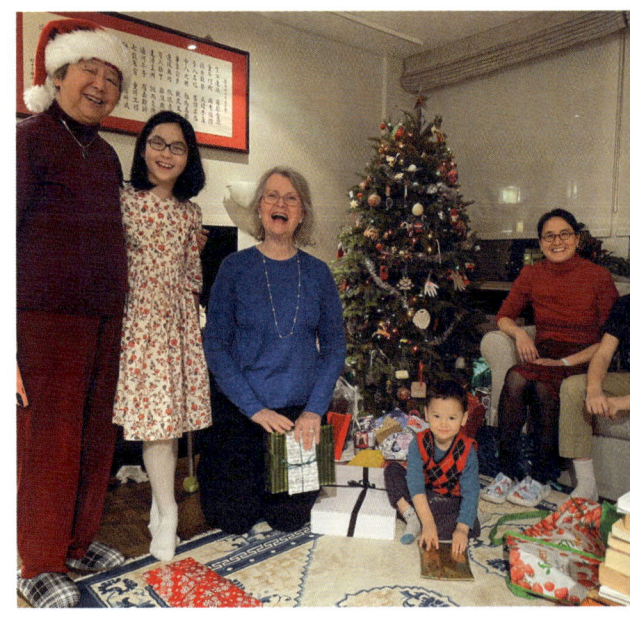

PARENTHOOD AROUND THE WORLD

**A WORLD OF FOOD:** We mainly cook, eating out is pricey. The kids love cooking. Luke shapes meatballs, Clara makes Valentine's Day afternoon tea, and Hugo makes homemade pesto, gnocchi and steaks. Weekends, we'll go out sometimes. (*Yvonne*) Just choose which ethnicity you'd like: there's Chinatown and wonderful Sichuan, we're right next to 'Curry Hill' with fantastic Indian places, there's good pizza nearby, and Clara just loves sushi. (*David*)

**AN EDUCATIONAL MATRIX:** Mine was a fancy private school, Yvonne's a fancy public school – we say we're in a mixed marriage. There's crazy pressure. We know 12-year-olds beefing up applications. (*David*) We just try to maintain our values and not buy into the whole system, yet also not be naive. It's a really complicated lottery. (*Yvonne*) Hugo got the lowest pick possible. Fortunately, he did well enough on his exam, so he'll attend the Bronx High School of Science, a public school. It's a relief – the process was gruelling. (*David*)

**PARENTING GRIT OF CONCRETE:** I think we parent well together because we've many similar family values. We're generally on the same moderately strict wavelength, so the kids tend to listen. We want to make them self-regulating, mindful people. Same with finances; we're not far removed from an immigrant family, so we emphasise being grateful for what you have – who knows what the future will hold. We also share a fundamental personality trait: we can certainly get exasperated at our kids, usually over little things, but over big things, we generally keep our cool. Our daily life is not Zen, but I wouldn't trade it for another. (*David*)

NICOLE HAGG

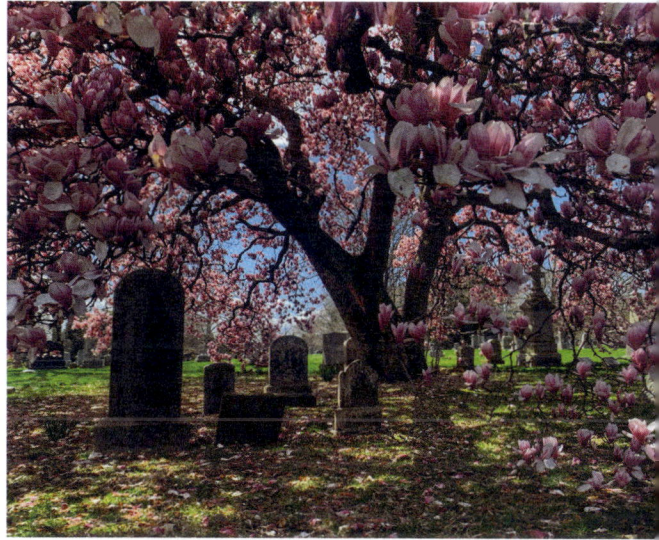

## Our favourite traditions

***Qing Ming* ('grave-sweeping' in Chinese tradition, to honour your ancestors):** We visit Greenwood Cemetery in Brooklyn with my brother's family in April. It sounds solemn but it's joyful. My father's and my grandparents' ashes are there. It's springtime, so it's often lovely. Then we go for Mexican food at a local taqueria. (*Yvonne*)

**Thankful:** NYC Thanksgiving is special with David's family and our moms. We squeeze onto two tables: kids and grown-ups. A Connecticut farmer-friend raises turkeys. Sides are from Eataly and everyone brings tons of pies. The kids love games like Geistertreppe and UNO. (*Yvonne*)

**NYC bagels:** We love getting bagels and lox on weekends, especially when friends visit. Scallion cream cheese, sliced tomatoes and onions. We'll get them fresh, and no toasting the bagels, please (until they are day-olds!). (*Yvonne*)

**Our log cabin:** It's in Connecticut and actually made of logs, we got it 10 years ago to get fresh air and see some trees. We'll just go up and hike. In the summer we go swimming in nearby lakes. (*David*) Sometimes we just go for a holiday or spring break, it's so easy. (*Yvonne*)

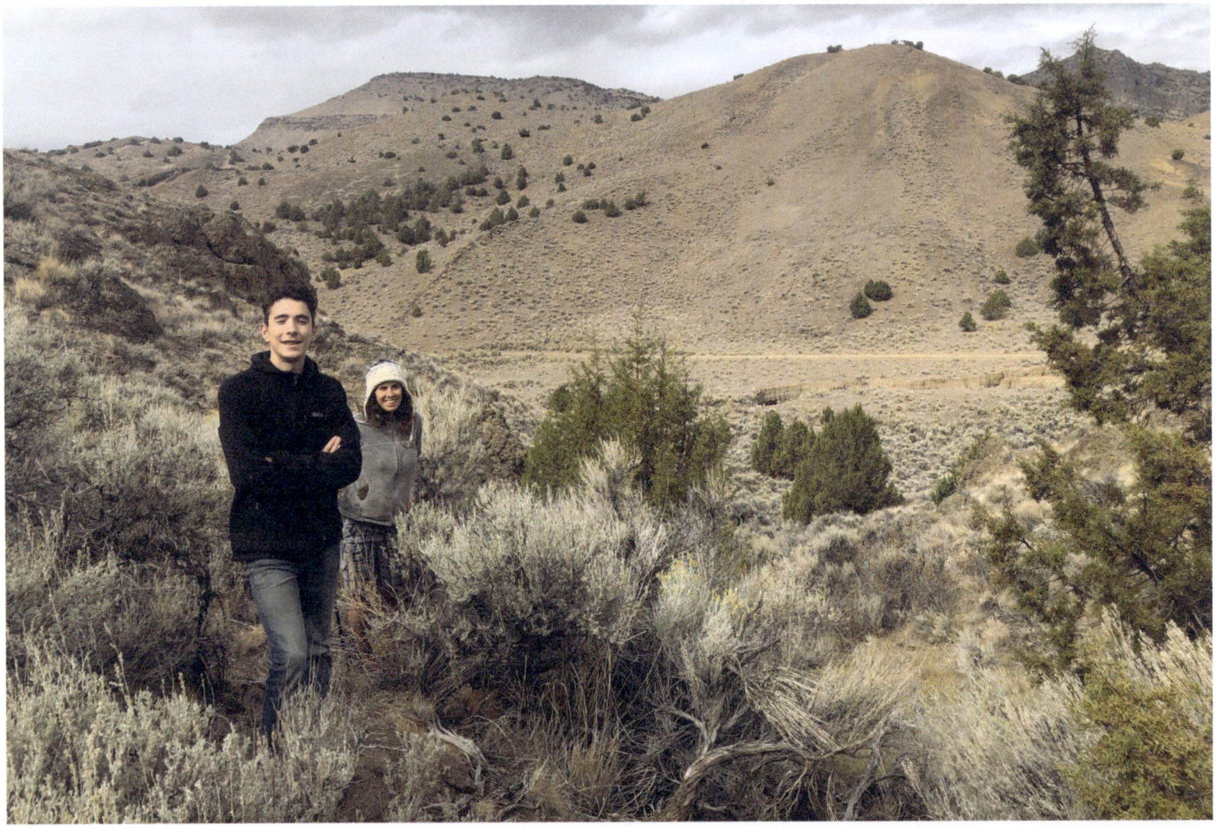

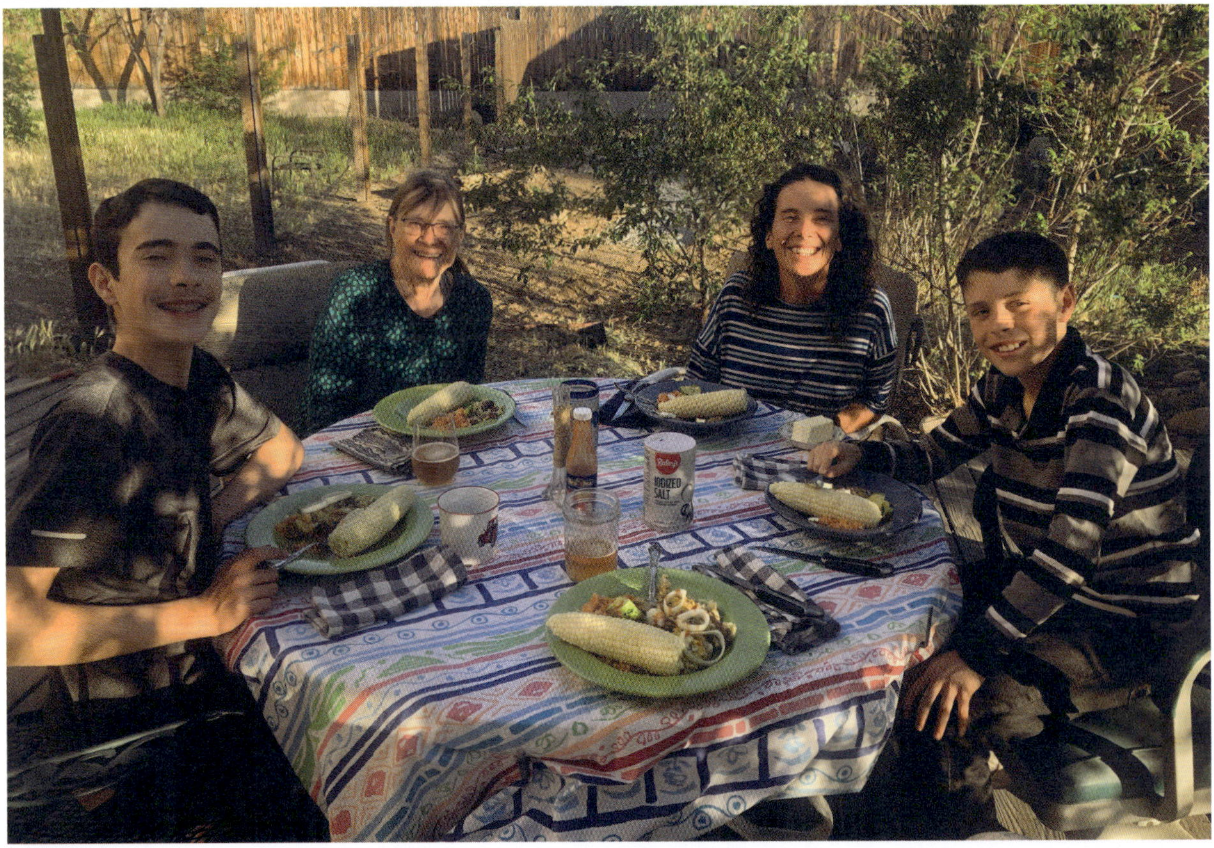

# USA

## KATY CHANDLER-ISACKSEN

**WHERE KATY LIVES:**
Reno, Nevada

**WHERE KATY IS FROM:**
Detroit, Michigan and Kirkwood, California

Katy Chandler-Isacksen has always been purpose-driven – in life and in parenting. She and her husband Kyle have dedicated themselves to a life of community and sustainability. As master gardeners and natural builders, they transformed a foreclosed lot in Reno, Nevada, into a lush oasis, full of trees, vegetables, art, natural-built structures, even farm animals – but no electricity. Katy and Kyle, both also teachers, chose 'unschooling' for their sons. The kids (now 18 and 15) learned through building projects, tending the garden, community volunteering, protest marches and more. Most of all, they learned to be curious, resourceful and empathic, and to live with joy and purpose. Today, Katy and Kyle teach natural-building workshops, locally and across the globe, through their nonprofit Be The Change Project.

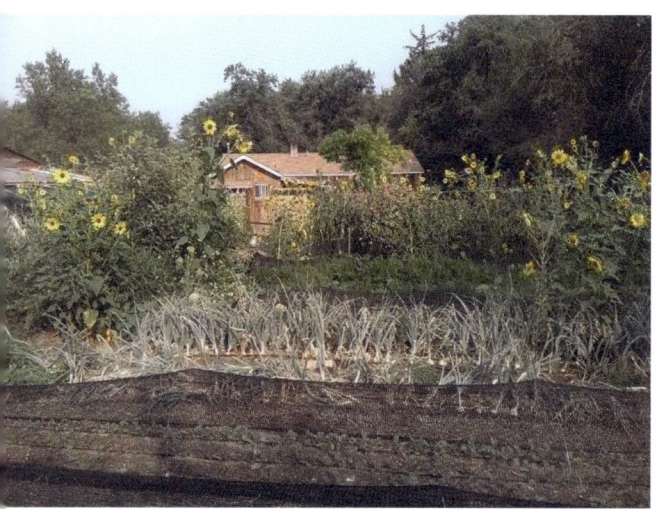

**A FOOD FOREST:** We live a couple of miles from downtown Reno, in an economically and ethnically diverse neighbourhood. We have four small cabins in the back, all made from natural building materials like earth, straw and reclaimed wood. In front we have a food forest: there's a peach tree, apple tree, sour cherry tree, native plum tree, various flowering bushes. There are raised beds for garlic, peas, tomatoes, lettuce, greens. And there's a little pond with pretty little plants called duckweed – wasps will land on them to drink water before flying off.

**MEALTIME:** The kids each cook twice a week. They'll ask, 'What do we have?' I'll say, 'Well, you have carrots in the back, there are tomatoes growing, there are potatoes in the root cellar. There's lettuce and greens in the greenhouse.' Or, when they come home from school and want a snack, if the grapes are in season, they'll devour those. When the cherry tomatoes or the peas are in season, they'll devour those instead.

**UNSCHOOLING:** I have a saying to try to explain unschooling: 'Make your own life sing, so your children can dance.' We're trying to live our lives as richly and dynamically and out-loud as possible, so the kids can see the process and hear the conversations. Kyle and I try to always be learning, whether that's reading, talking to people, or having projects here or in the community. It helps that we're both teachers. We know what it looks like when a kid is learning.

**PURPOSE:** With all the environmental degradation in the world, I get very nervous for the kids. We wanted to create a place where kids could really engage in the living world – the plants, the animals, our neighbours, the community. We wanted to show them that climate change is happening, and why, but also that there are ways you can live and contribute to changing that.

**THE TRUCKEE RIVER:** The Truckee River comes down from Lake Tahoe and runs right through Reno. It used to be trashy, full of broken glass, but people have really cleaned it up. When it gets really hot, we'll go down there almost every day, and just swim or play in the rapids. Sometimes we'll talk about the plants or scouting or do scavenger hunts – more structured stuff. The river eventually flows out to Pyramid Lake, which is amazing – a beautiful blue lake in the middle of stark brown desert, and home to the Paiute Pyramid Lake Reservation.

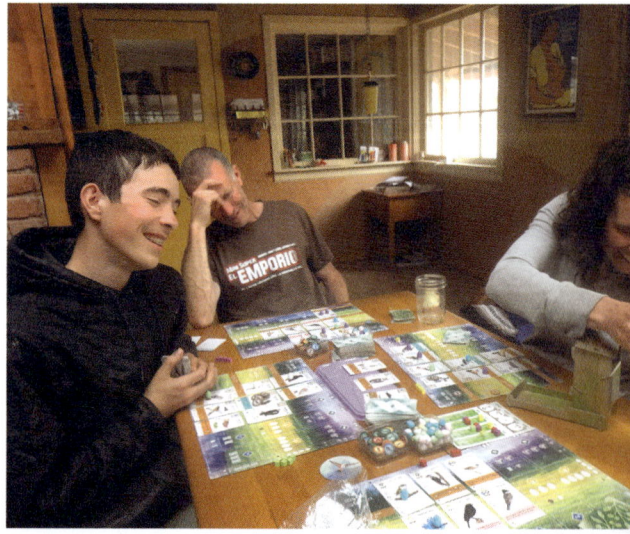

> "I have a saying to try to explain unschooling: 'Make your own life sing, so your children can dance.'"

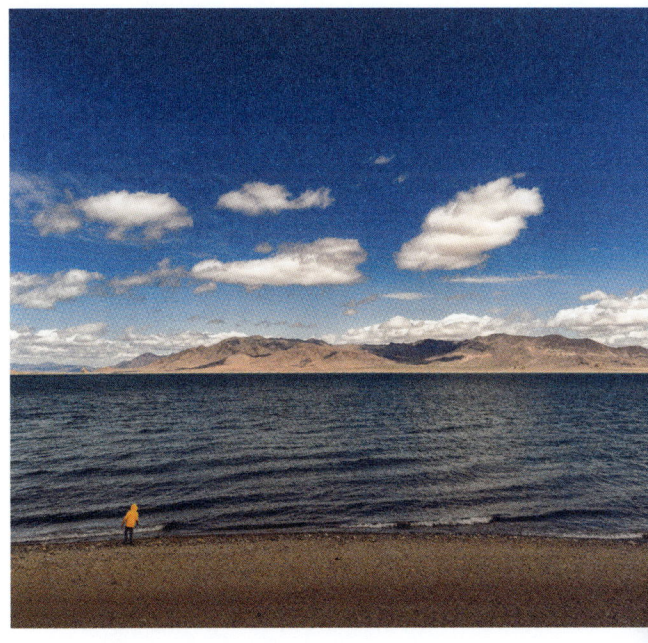

**RHYTHMS:** Kyle and I always wake up half an hour before sunrise. In the summer, that's early. In the winter, it's late. It feels great, we get really good sleep. Wylan used to have a really difficult time falling asleep. But then, when we didn't have lights, it would get dark and he'd actually ask to go to bed. It was very cute. And because they weren't going to school, the kids never woke up to an alarm. Their bodies would wake when they were ready for waking.

**SEASONS:** There are gifts with every season. Winter in the high desert is quiet and reflective, more easy-going. Liam really learned to read in the winter. You're spending more time indoors; it just makes sense to be doing that kind of learning. In the spring, he loves to build, so he'd be out building.

**DOUBTS:** We expected people to think we're crazy. I mean, we can see the casino lights from our yard but we don't have electricity. It's just so different, and people always have a million questions. And it's not like we never had questions: 'Are we doing right by our kids? Are they learning, are they thriving?' But I don't know any parent who doesn't wonder those things. We might have different answers, but it never felt wildly different from what most parents were experiencing.

GARY CHANDLER

## Our favourite traditions

**Board games:** We play a ton of board games together. We didn't have screens in the house when the kids were little – none – so they read a lot of books, told a lot of stories and played a lot of games. Now it's part of how we spend time together.

**Pizza parties:** We have people over semi-regularly; the kids can invite their friends, we all hang out. We built the pizza oven ourselves, and the deck, and the treehouse – the kids play up there and look down on the party.

**Thanksgiving at Lake Tahoe:** We met the director of a beautiful summer camp on Lake Tahoe; anytime they have plant questions, they contact me, and we've become good friends. Spending our Thanksgivings there started because they were travelling and needed help ploughing snow and watching their dog. That's something we could do for them, so we did. And sharing their space is a gift they like to give to us. We do a lot of that with people – we give each other things back and forth.

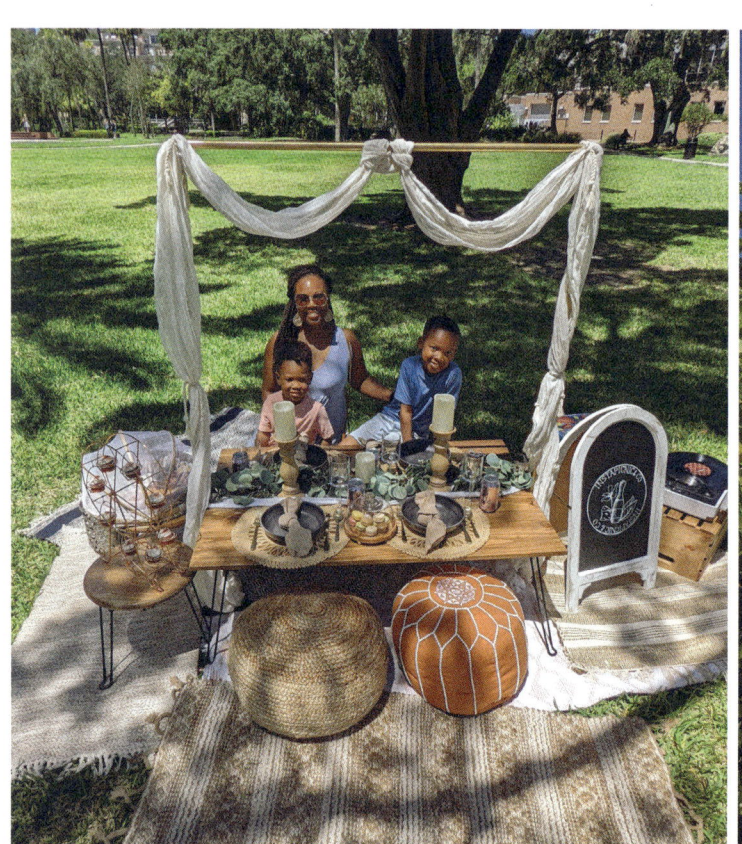
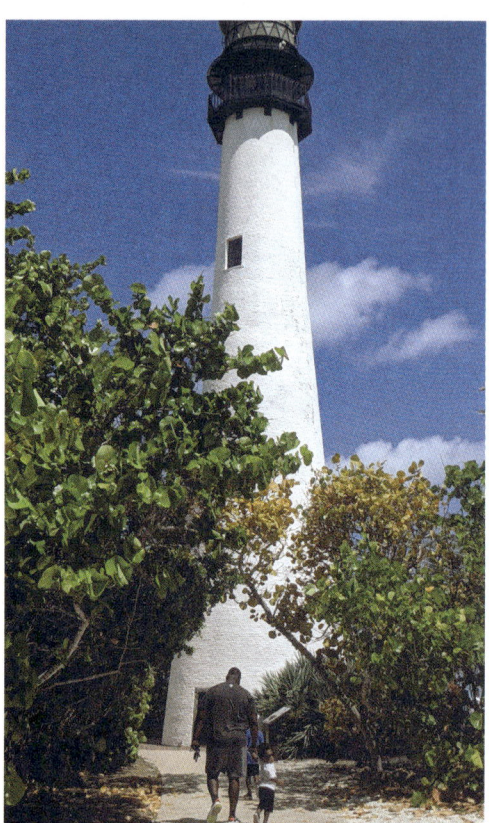

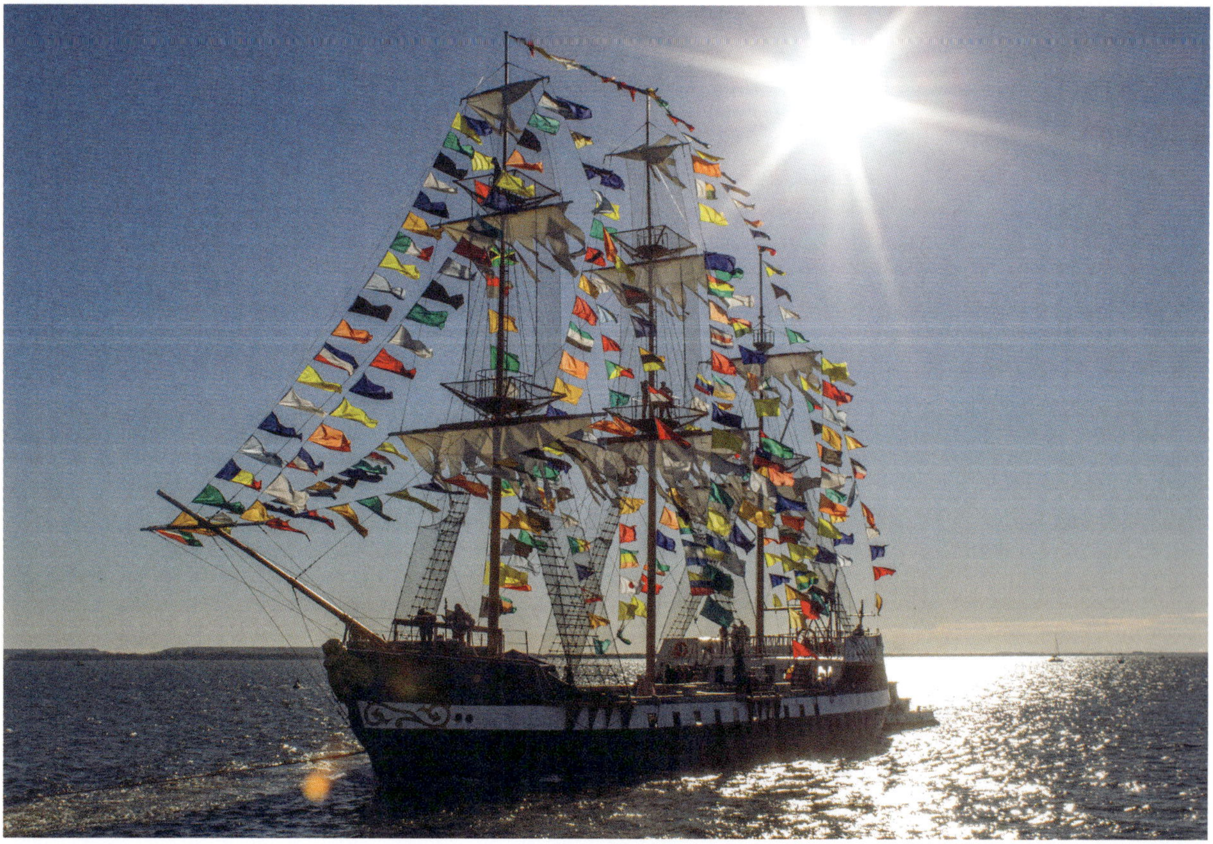

# USA

## KARIMAH HENRY

**WHERE KARIMAH LIVES:**
Tampa, Florida

**WHERE KARIMAH IS FROM:**
New York City, New York and Lakeland, Florida

Karimah was born in New York to Jamaican parents but moved to Florida at the age of four, when she travelled to Lakeland with her family. Her grandmother played a major role in her upbringing, and Karimah's mother later remarried a native Floridian. 'I moved to Tampa in 2002 to go to the University of South Florida and kind of never left', Karimah says. That's where she met her husband, when they were just 20 and 21, at a nightclub during Homecoming festivities. 'He's from the Caribbean, too, and can understand certain things', she says. The couple enjoy taking their two boys (aged nine and five) to football games to cheer on the USF Bulls; and getting back to Lakeland to visit the kids' cousins.

**MORNING RITUALS:** My oldest gets up early, around 6.30am. He'll close our bedroom door, turn on all the lights and watch TV. He wakes me up by 8am and it's time for breakfast – usually cereal, fruits and yogurt with toaster strudel or raisin bread with cream cheese. Sometimes we'll have a big pancake breakfast; they love adding sprinkles to the batter. School starts at 9.40am and we can walk; it's less than a mile away.

**WATER SAFETY:** We live in a neighbourhood with a pool, so it was so important that my kids learn to swim early. We're around the water so much, I want them to be safe when they're not with me. Black kids, especially, are at a higher risk of drowning. Our neighbourhood clubhouse partners with the YMCA to give free swimming lessons to kids in the community for one week every summer. My kids love being in the water, especially when it's hot. It tires them out, too, which I love.

**DISCIPLINE MATTERS:** Growing up in a Jamaican and Southern household, I learned early there was no talking back. Parents were authoritarian. I didn't want that for my kids. If they're upset, they're allowed to show their emotions. They're

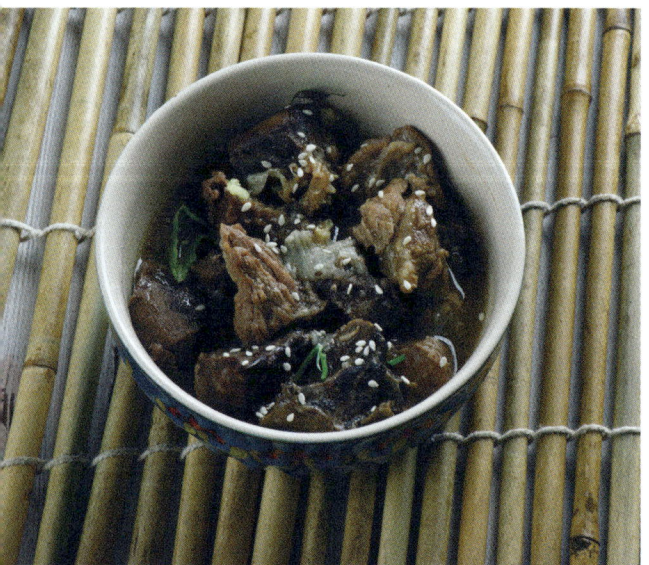

> "My parents were immigrants and we try to hold on to certain traditions while creating new ones."

not allowed to be disrespectful, but if they need time to cool down they can go to their room and we can talk later. If we offend or upset them, they have the option to let us know and we apologise. My husband and I are on the same page. We both grew up in Caribbean households and we know what it's like, so we try to be more understanding with our kids. I say, 'I love you' a lot, we hug a lot.

**BLENDING TRADITIONS:** My roots are Jamaican and my husband is from the US Virgin Islands and has Guyanese and Antiguan parents, so we blend a lot of traditions in our home. During the holidays, it's really a mix. My mother-in-law makes a stew from Guyana called pepperpot and plait bread. And we always have the rum-soaked fruit cake I've started calling 'black cake', because that's the Guyanese name. For oxtail and goat, we go to a great Caribbean market in Orlando. When I was growing up in Lakeland, we used to go to Orlando to buy Caribbean foods, too.

**SIBLING RIVALRY:** As much as our boys love each other, they do argue a lot over simple things. That can be frustrating. I think back to growing up, and [know] it's just a sibling thing. They have such different personalities, so we have to adjust how we discipline them. It might mean taking away electronics for one son and taking more time to talk things through with the other. It can be a lot sometimes. Thankfully, my husband is there.

We may not always see eye-to-eye, but in front of the kids we're a team. Later on, in private, we'll debrief on how things were handled.

**IMMIGRANT BALANCE:** My parents were immigrants and we try to hold on to certain traditions while creating new ones. It's about trying to find that balance and start new traditions with our family, too. The boys know about Carnival and Caribbean food, which they love. They know the holiday traditions – like the salty-sweet Jamaican 'bun and cheese' (a fruit-spice-infused bun filled with a soft yellow cheese) every Easter; and deep-fried turkey, rice and peas, jerk chicken, curry shrimp and lobster at Thanksgiving. But they also know there are sides of Caribbean culture we grew up with that we are letting go of. My grandmother never told my mum that she loved her, so we wore grandma down saying 'I love you' all the time. She started saying it back and my mum was like: 'What?' I think it's because they were in survival mode and that's how they did things. We aren't in survival mode and can do things differently.

TERRY WARD

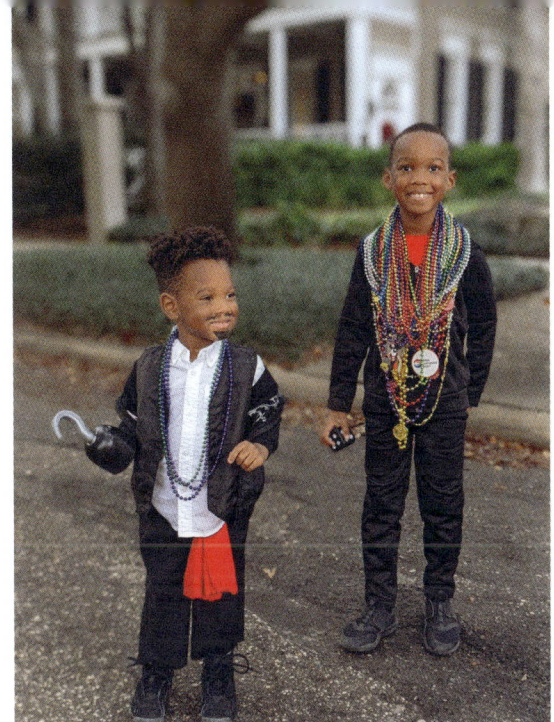

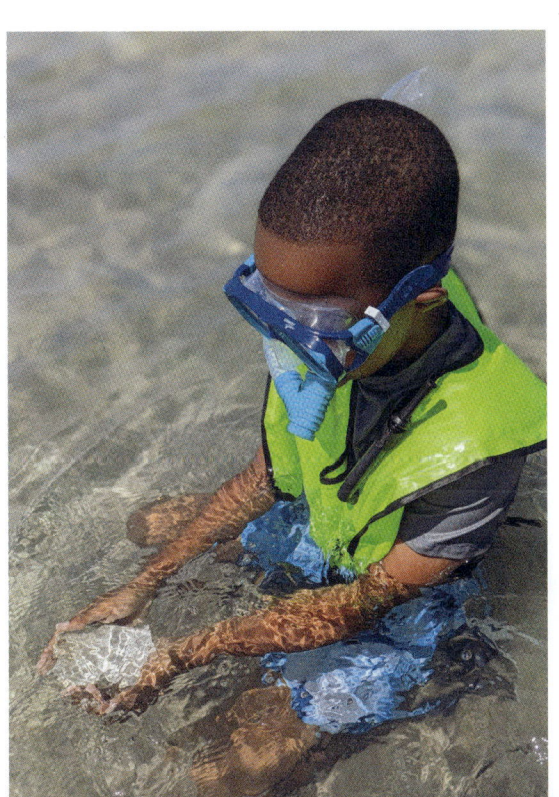

## Our favourite traditions

***Holiday crafts:*** I got into crafting as a preschool teacher in Tampa. And every holiday, we create something different together, whether for Christmas, Juneteenth or Shark Week (Discovery Channel's week-long shark programming extravaganza). Being creative is a huge thing for me and a great outlet for the kids.

***Gasparilla fun:*** Tampa's annual pirate festival in January is a fun time for our family. We decorate a wagon, do the whole pirate look and go watch the parade in downtown Tampa. I put makeup on my youngest, sometimes I'll add chest hair. It just depends on the weather how far I can go with their costumes and mine.

***Bedtime books:*** Since they were little, we've always read to the boys before bed. Now my eldest takes his own shower and my husband will read to him or he'll read to us. After that, it's time for bed for the kids; always by 8.30pm, no later. I have to make sure they get enough sleep! Then my husband and I finally get a chance to hang out together.

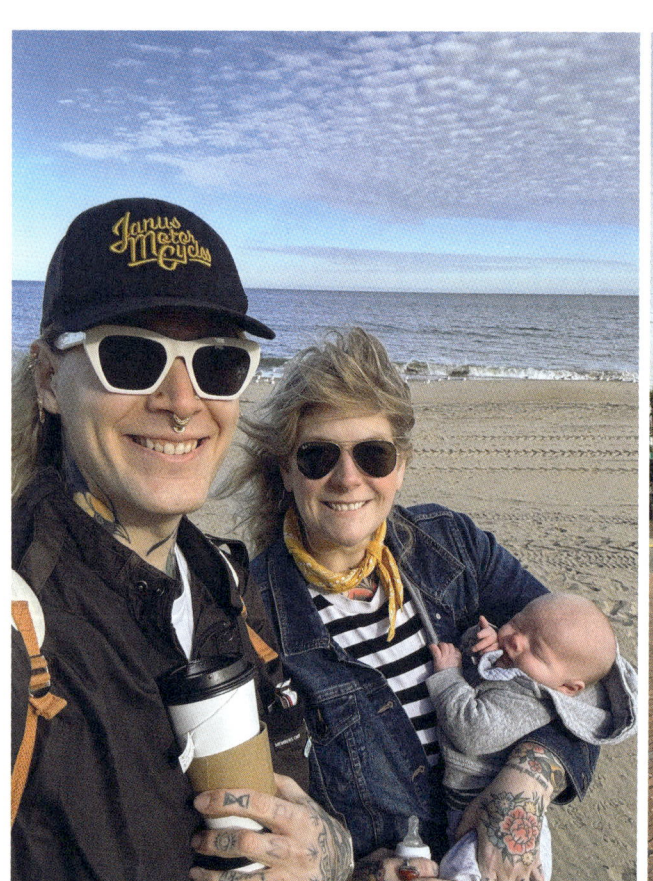
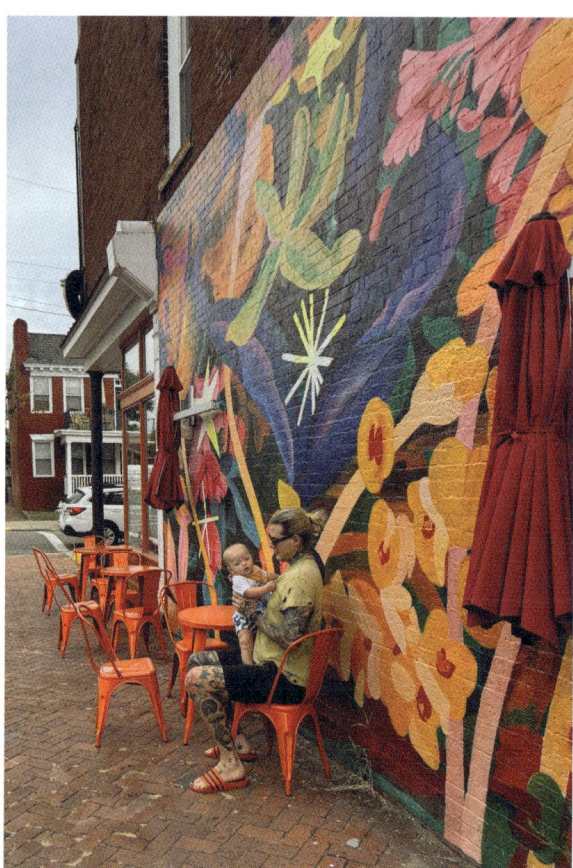

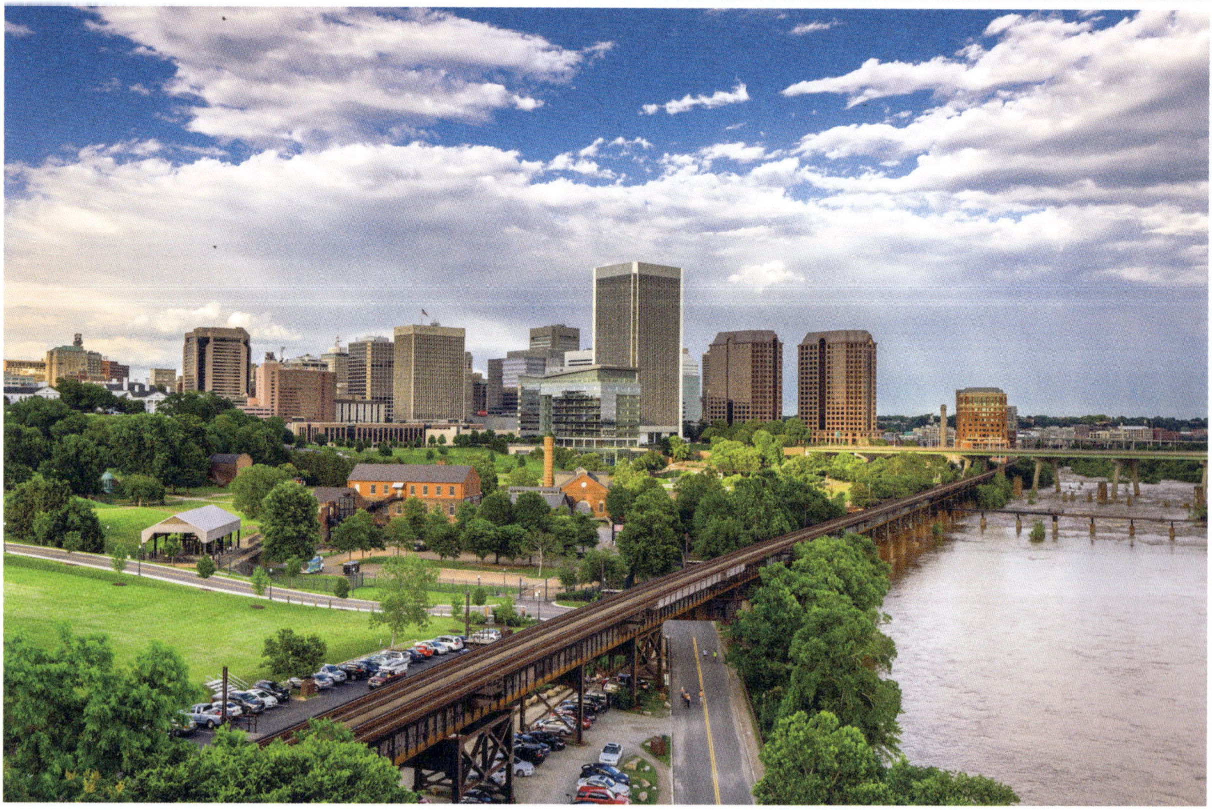

# USA

## HARRISON & CARLY MOENICH

**WHERE HARRISON & CARLY LIVE:**
Richmond, Virginia

**WHERE HARRISON & CARLY ARE FROM:**
Harrison: North Carolina
Carly: South Carolina

When Harrison (they/them) and Carly (she/her) met, they bonded over similar upbringings and interests: both grew up in the rural South (North and South Carolina, respectively), and they share an eclectic taste in music and art, tattoos and dark humour, as well as a deep commitment to social justice. Married in 2016, they focused mainly on their careers; Harrison is a visual artist and arts-college staff member, while Carly is the founder of a hair salon that specialises in safe, affirming styling for clients of all gender identities. When they reached their 30s, Carly and Harrison decided to add to the brood. Marlowe Wren aka Wren was born in December 2023, a happy chubby chap with his parents' penchant for music, disco balls, water, and making others smile.

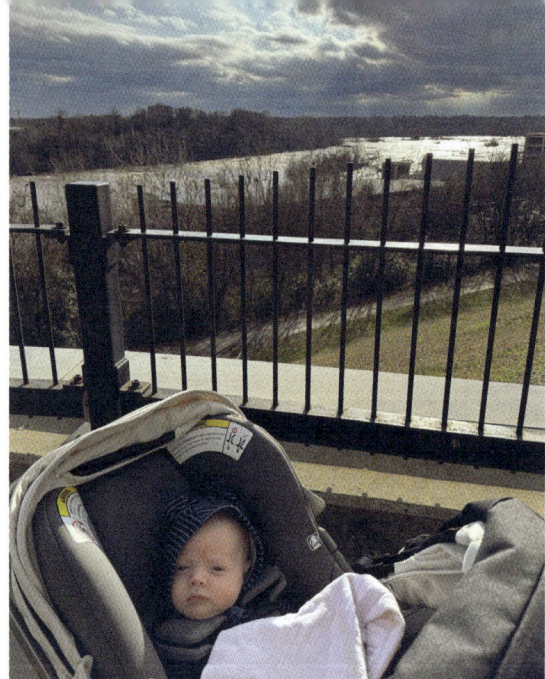

**LABOUR:** No matter how many medical forms we fill out where we indicate Harrison is non-binary, Harrison still gets misgendered. I really didn't want Harrison to feel, at the birth of our child, that they couldn't be authentically them. It's funny, I was in the throes of labour, like 6cm dilated, and someone came in and said, 'Is there anything you need us to know that's not on your chart?' I yelled, 'Harrison is nonbinary and don't circumcise this baby!' They were like, 'Um, OK'. And I said, 'Otherwise, that's it. Let's do this!' (*Carly*)

**MEAL TRAIN:** When Wren was born, we did a meal train and were blown away by people making us food, even people we didn't know that well. One of my hair clients brought me soup. One of Harrison's bike-riding friends brought something. It was a really beautiful outpouring of love. And our tight-knit group of five or six queer and trans friends, none of them have kids, but they still bent over backwards to be involved. (*Carly*)

**ROCKABYE BABY:** Wren loves Abba. The song *Gimme! Gimme! Gimme!* was playing the other night and he was so stoked, he couldn't handle it. It was fun for me, I just kept playing it over and over. (*Carly*) One day Wren was crying and I was trying to get him to go to sleep. For some reason I put on the Blood Brothers, a post-hardcore band that Carly and I both have a love for, and it was like a switch. Now every time I put it on, it lulls him to sleep, which is funny because it's so loud and chaotic. (*Harrison*)

**OBI:** I thought a lot about what I would feel comfortable being called. Some people use 'Mapa', which is a combination of Ma and Pa, but I didn't resonate with that. Then I read some cultures use 'Obi' to refer to a parent or mentor, or else like 'heart' or 'love'. I was really drawn to it, it feels very warm, very loving, and also non-gender-specific. (*Harrison*) A lot of people take it to mean 'Obi-Wan Kenobi', which is funny because we're not really *Star Wars* people. (*Harrison & Carly, laughing*)

**FREE WILL:** We're trying to be really deliberate about decisions we make, and how they'll impact Wren down the line, on issues like social media and religion. We'll give him the resources that we have and tell him what we know, but we want to try to create space for him to make decisions for himself eventually, rather than pushing ourselves on him. Like, we're vegan, and eventually if he decides that he doesn't want to be vegan then we'll respect his choice. (*Carly*)

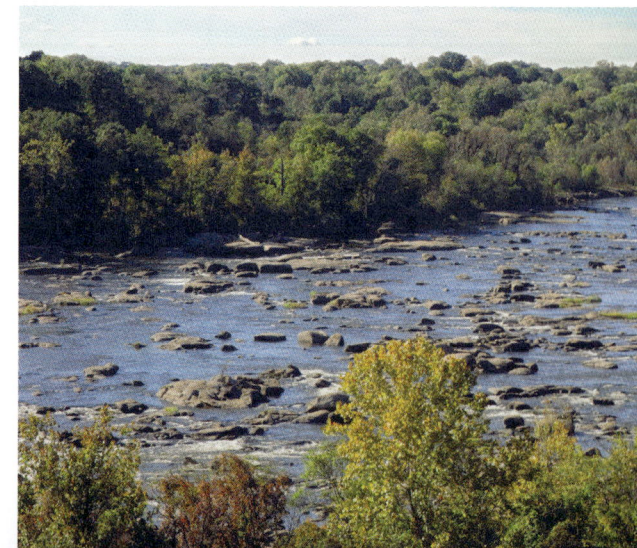

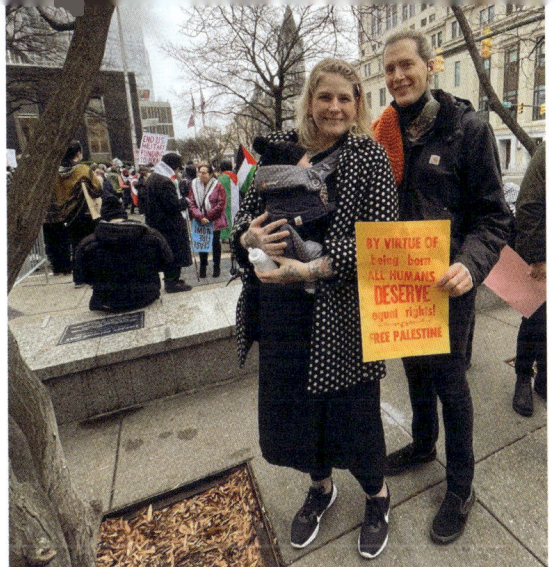

**HOLLYWOOD CEMETERY:** We can walk to Hollywood Cemetery; it borders the James River and kind of overlooks everything. It's filled with trails and these lush, gorgeous trees. We'll walk under the canopy, and Wren will be completely enamoured with the leaves and colours. But of course, there's also the backdrop of thousands of Confederate soldiers' graves and statues, and this really dark history of enslavement in Richmond. There's definitely some cognitive dissonance there. Eventually Wren will ask about all that and we're certainly not going to shelter him from the history of the city. You have to have those conversations. (*Harrison & Carly*)

**SOUTHERN LIVING:** Richmond has such a queer-positive identity, with people coming together as opposed to being divisive. And there's a huge counterculture movement here. Richmond is like the third-most tattooed city in America. There's a real demand for change in the city; we have a lot of marches and rallies, like during Black Lives Matter and for Palestine. We have access to spaces where those conversations are happening, especially with kids. It's very important for Wren to understand the history of this country and for us to do what we can to be involved in positive change. (*Harrison & Carly*)

GARY CHANDLER

## Our favourite traditions

***No-yoga Wednesdays:*** We have a standing date with our friends on Wednesdays. We all meet in Forest Hill Park and everyone brings their kids and blankets. It started with us saying we were going to do yoga, but we didn't really do that. Now we all just sit under a big shady tree with our babies and catch up. (*Carly & Harrison*)

***Art day:*** We love art and take Wren to the Virginia Museum of Fine Arts (VMFA) to admire the works there. The VMFA is kind of like a social gathering area, too, and they have a beautiful sculpture garden. We've taken him to a class called Nature Babies – they do sign-language songs and take you around to look at different nature paintings. He's still too little to really know what's going on, but we have a great time. (*Carly*)

***Farmers market:*** We've always gone to the Birdhouse Farmers Market right up the street. We go to see all the vendors and buy produce – best strawberries ever! Wren loves people-watching, and once he's a little older we'll let him gnaw on strawberries or other fruit. (*Harrison*)

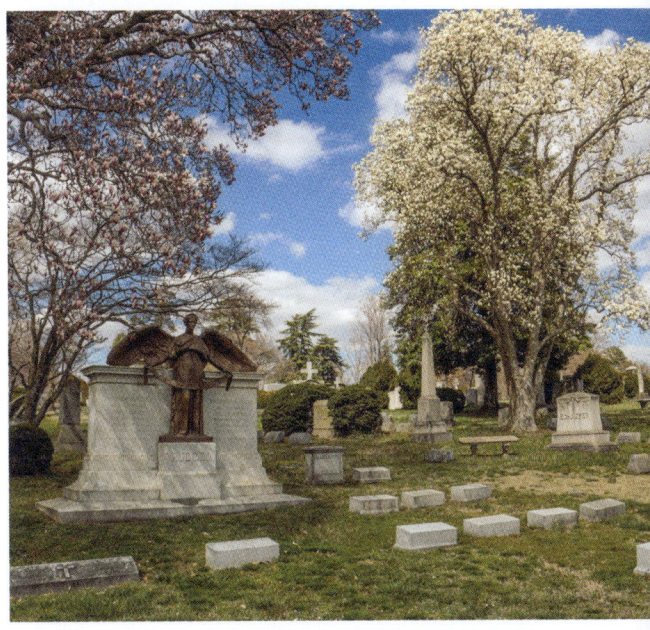

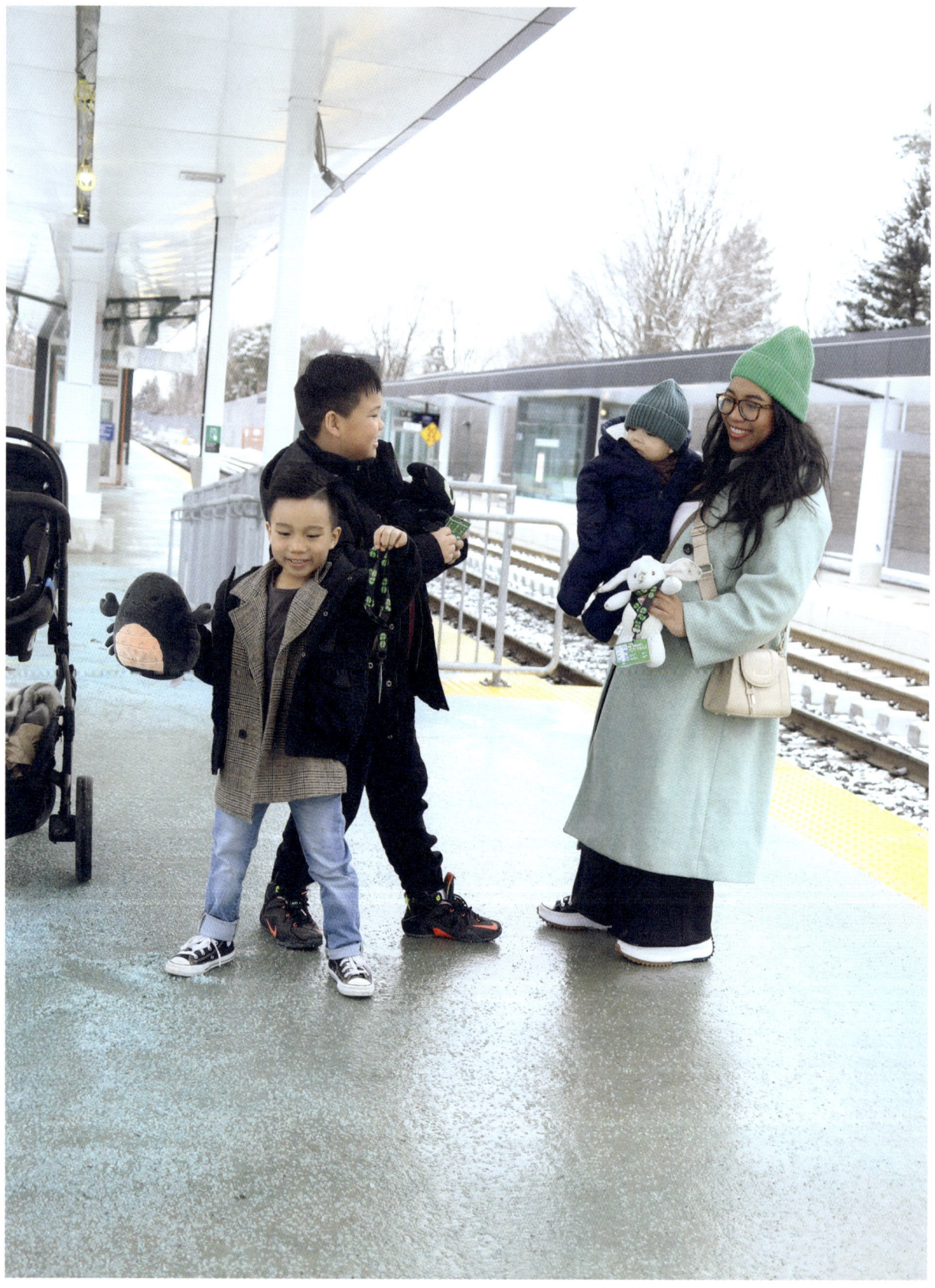

# Canada

## CRISTINA NAVOA

**WHERE CRISTINA LIVES:**
Toronto, Ontario

**WHERE CRISTINA IS FROM:**
Toronto, Ontario

Cristina is a Toronto-based kindergarten teacher and content creator, and she's married to her kindergarten sweetheart, Fergus. 'We've been best friends since we were very young. He had been asking me to be his girlfriend since we were kids', she says with a laugh. 'We finally connected in the first years of college. We got married maybe five years later. I always tease my kindergarteners now – I tell them, "hey, I married my friend from kindergarten, you never know."' Both second-generation immigrants, they hail from Scarborough, a vibrant and multicultural borough in Toronto. Together, they live in a Filipino-Chinese multigenerational home with Cristina's parents and their three young boys: Gabe (10), Theo (seven), and Lucas (two).

**METROPOLITAN LIVING:** We live in a very multicultural community. We have a lot of retired couples, older families, and younger families starting now. I love this community because there's so much going on. We walk to the mall, the library – it's very urban – and we're also right by Thomson Park, so we get a bit of nature. We're also not far from downtown. We love walking the boardwalk at the Harbourfront and going to Jays [baseball] games – we are big fans!

**FAMILY BONDS:** I love that my kids get to experience their grandparents every day. I didn't have that growing up, because my parents emigrated here from the Philippines. Now that we live with my parents, I feel like my kids have an even more special bond with them than I probably do. My parents cook Filipino food for them every night – the kids love *sitaw* (a string-bean dish), *kalabasa* (shrimp and squash cooked in coconut milk), and *lumpia* (meat spring rolls). My parents also speak Bisaya, and my children have picked up a few words.

**WORLD FLAVOURS:** I like that my kids have friends from different parts of the world and they experience all kinds of languages and foods. Honestly, they're really good eaters and they love trying different cuisines. And there are so many options in Scarborough: Filipino, Chinese, Afghani, sushi, shawarma, Portuguese. You get so much culture and learning from food – why you cook with certain spices, how it came to be, what resources are used – and my kids love learning that way, so I love being in this neighbourhood for that reason.

**EMBRACING CULTURE:** My parents had a Filipino takeout place when I was growing up, so my school food was mango juice, *siopao* [steamed buns] and shrimp chips. I didn't get your standard Lunchables or chocolate-chip cookies, like my friends. I kind of raised my kids the same way – they aren't afraid or embarrassed to have different food choices.

We had a Filipino Fiesta for Theo's second birthday – his love of Filipino food inspired the party – and we've continued the tradition every year since. His cake was a giant *halo-halo* (shaved-ice dessert). Now it's his favourite thing to order at Filipino restaurants.

**TIME:** It's busy raising three boys! It's weird when I talk about it, 'cause I sound like I'm talking about puppies. But it's true that boys are physical people; they need a lot of outdoor time to get their energy out! My boys are in lots of sports – we have swimming once a week and both my [older] boys are on baseball teams. My eldest plays rep baseball, which means we're travelling throughout the summer, [with] two practices a week, maybe two games a week. The other one is just starting out in baseball, so we're very busy.

**CHILDCARE:** My first two sons did daycare. But now that my mom lives with us, she happily watches my youngest. She's 77, but very strong and willing and able. And they're very, very close. I have zero worry or trust issues leaving him for work, and he lets me go really happily. It's such a blessing and a comfort to be able to leave him with her. And it's such a help financially as well.

**GRATITUDE:** My favourite thing about raising kids in Toronto is that there's lots to do, and every season presents different things. Like I love that we get the real Christmas feel here in the winter time. And that summers in Toronto are beautiful. We have access to the beaches. Lots of festivals, lots of culture, lots of food. We're right on the subway line and not too far from downtown, so we can get city life. I just love that you get so many experiences in such a little area.

*JESSICA LAM*

## Our favourite traditions

**Schoolyard sentiments:** Our anniversary is 7 July, and my husband always takes me and the kids to the school where we met. It's just down the street, so we'll drive by. My son is named Gabriel, after St Gabriel, the school – so it's kind of like a landmark of where everything started.

**Special place:** St Barnabas church is where my parents started their takeout business, where I got baptised, where my husband got baptised, where my kids got baptised, where we did all our sacraments, where we got married. So, going there as a family is kind of like – we *have* to go to that church.

**Family celebrations:** In Filipino tradition, Christmas is really big. We start right after Halloween – playing Christmas music every morning, watching Christmas movies every weekend, going to Mass. It's a slow build-up to the final few weeks of Christmas, when it becomes a frenzy of family and food. There are family parties, church parties, Filipino Association parties, gift exchanges. It's a loud and fun time, and the kids love it!

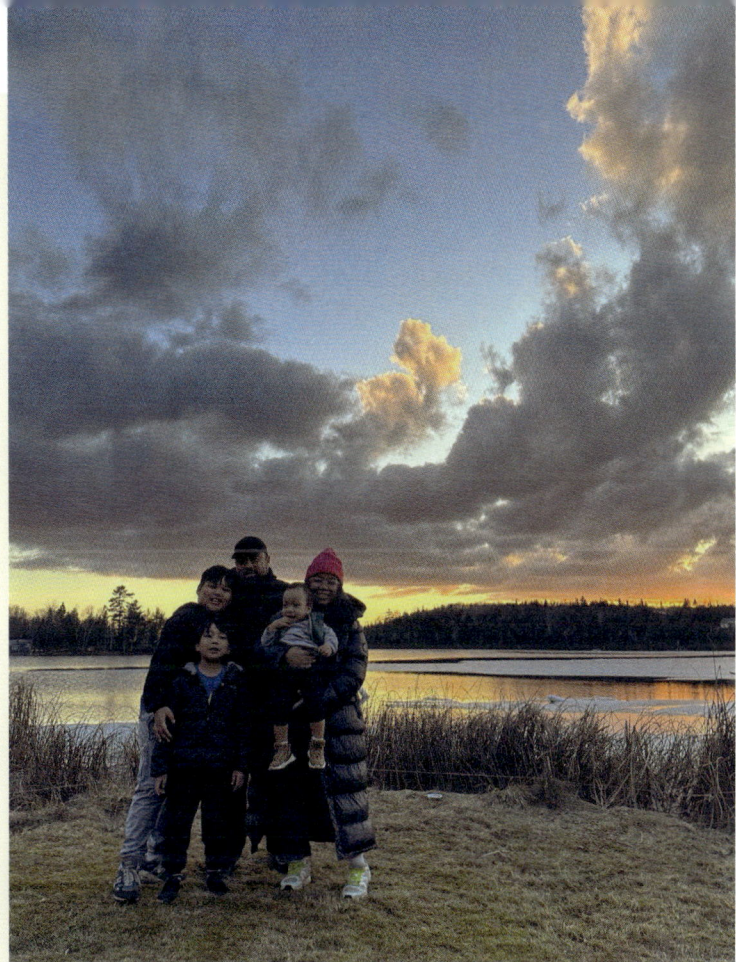

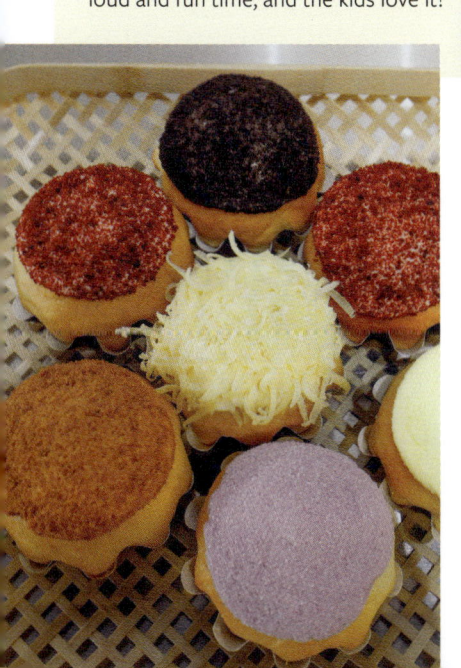

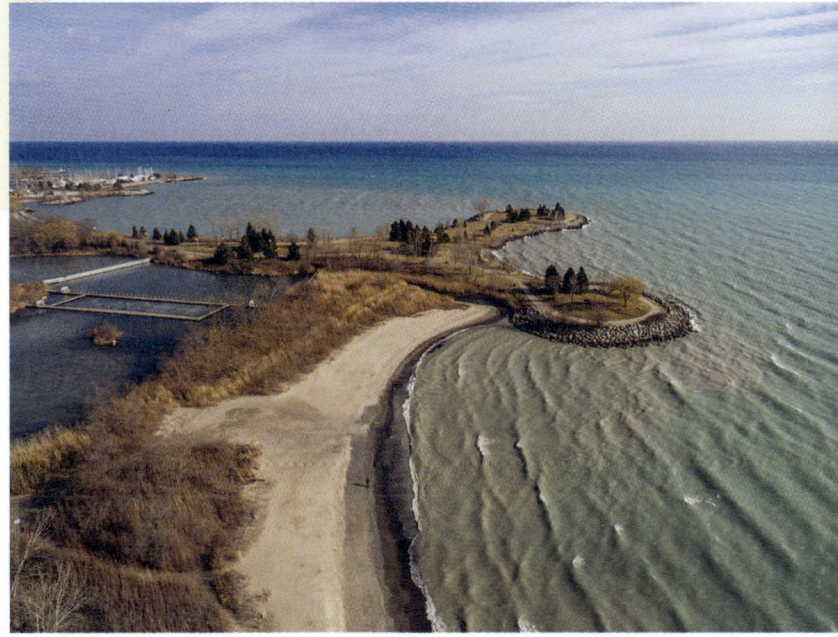

NORTH AMERICA

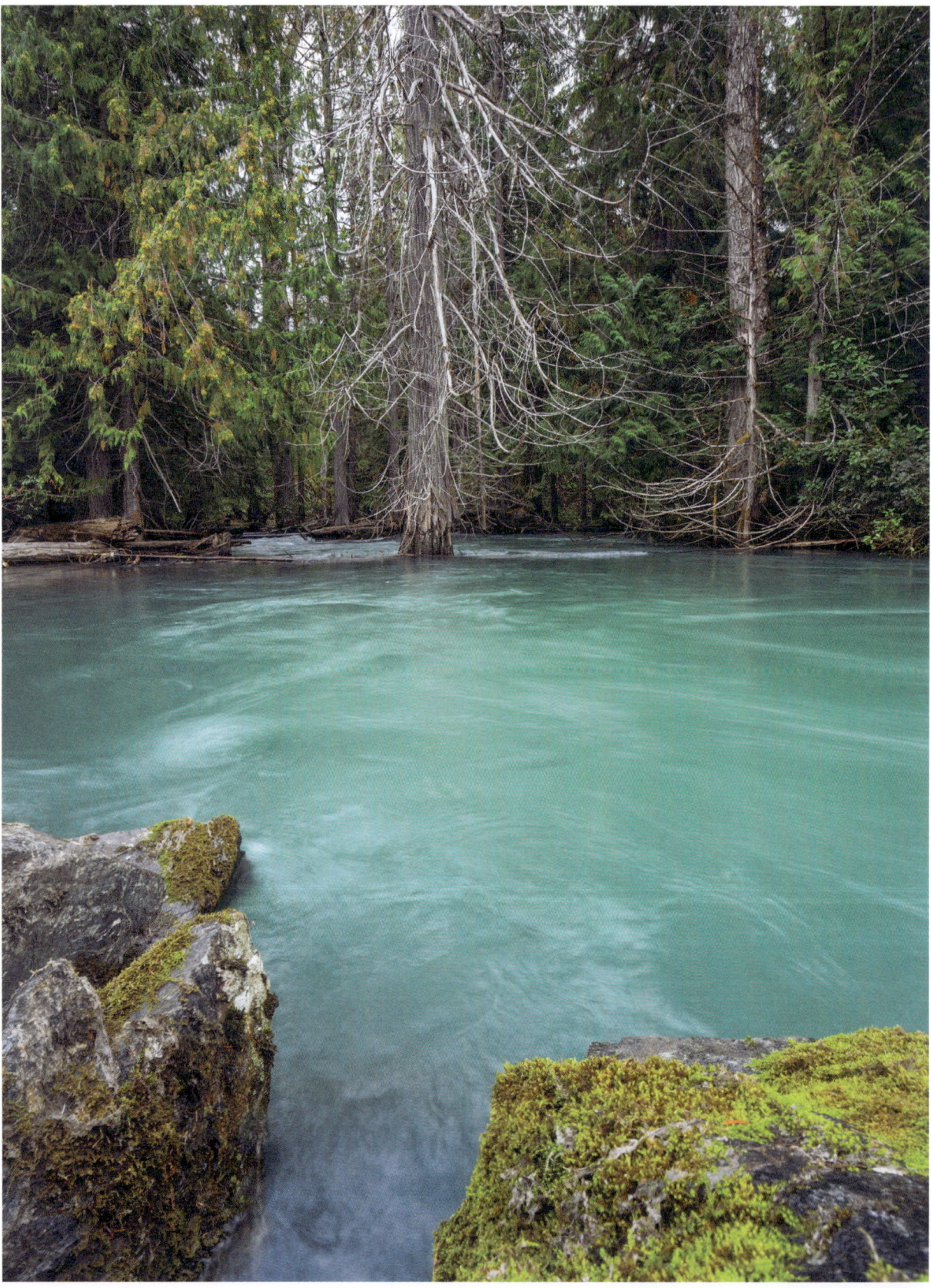

# Canada

## TINA MOORE

**WHERE TINA LIVES:**
Laxgalts'ap, Nisga'a Nation, British Columbia

**WHERE TINA LIVES:**
Prince Rupert and Laxgalts'ap, Nisga'a Nation, British Columbia

The Nisga'a are a nation of about 8000 people, most of whom live in four villages of evergreen trees and lava beds along a winding river in British Columbia's Naas Valley, where Tina and her husband Tyler are raising their children. Tina's crest is the Killer Whale, while Tyler belongs to the Frog crest. 'The Nisga'a are matrilineal, taking the crest, or clan, of their mothers', Tina explains. Their blended family includes Hailey (21) and Erin (19) – Tyler's daughters from a previous relationship – as well as Tina and Tyler's sons Dallas (13) and Craig (three). Tina is the Programs and Education Coordinator at the nearby Nisga'a Museum, while Tyler is employed at a mining camp several hours away, working shifts of two weeks on, two weeks off.

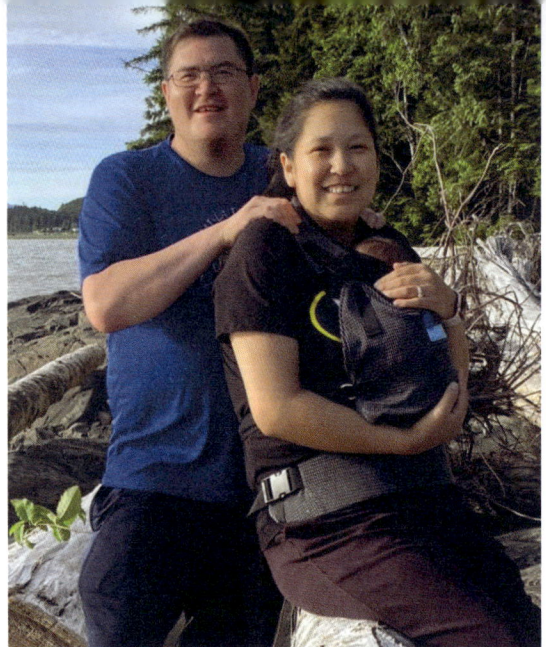

**FAMILY CONNECTIONS:** We live almost smack dab in the centre of our tiny community. We're right across from our firehall, across from our community centre, and a two-minute walk from our elementary school and the church. My oldest paternal uncle lives directly to the right of us. I'm not only related to a bunch of people, but I'm connected to people who have the same crest. We share that connection and support each other.

**LIFE IN LAX̱GALTS'AP:** For my oldest son, Dallas, I wake him up super early. His school bus leaves at 7.45am. The high school for our entire nation is in Gitlax̱t'aamiks, the first community that you pass when you enter the Valley of the Lava Beds, about a 45-minute drive.

I'll drop off my younger son, Craig, at daycare. It takes me about five minutes to get there.

For supper, I'm usually good at having a slow-cooker meal on, but if not, Dallas helps prep our dinners. We taught him at a young age to cook and help around the house.

**PATERNAL RELATIVES' SUPPORT:** The father's family is responsible for a lot of the child rearing: positive reinforcements, correcting behaviors…all of these things start right from birth. When Dallas was born, my *wilksilaks* (paternal relatives) were there in the birthing room and near the hospital to support me and care for him.

Traditionally, the *wilksilaks* would have also presented the baby to the community. They would introduce the baby to signify, 'This child belongs to us. We are taking care of this child for the rest of their lives.' Their support doesn't take away from my responsibilities in a traditional sense. As a mother, I still care for my children. But I lean heavily on my husband's side of the family when I can't do it myself. I'm mirroring what my mother taught me: my paternal aunts and uncles were the ones who helped raise me and my siblings.

When Dallas was born, Tyler missed out quite a bit while he was away at camp rotations. After Craig was born, Tyler took time away from work for about a year and a half. He wanted to be here and develop that connection with our youngest son.

**LIFE CEREMONIES:** The paternal relatives are responsible for the ceremonies marking important milestones, including a child's first ceremonial bath. The bathing ceremony welcomes the

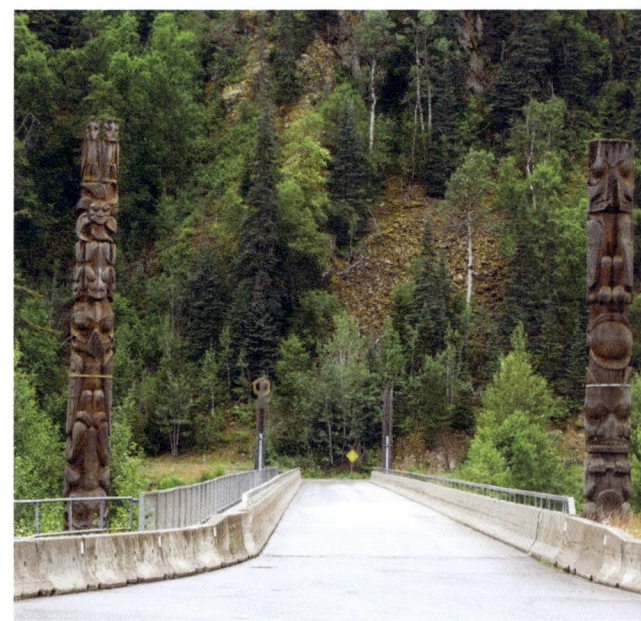

166   PARENTHOOD AROUND THE WORLD

child into their family and takes him into their care. Dallas' *wilksilaks*, my mother-in-law and my two sisters-in-law, gave him his first bath. They purchased his first outfit, and they dressed him, which is ceremonial as well.

When it comes time for my sons to leave this Earth, their *wilksilaks* will be the ones to take care of them. Even though their grandmother and aunts may no longer be here with us, the responsibility still rests on that family.

**EAR PIERCING:** Ear piercing is the same for both genders, traditionally done around seven or eight years old. It helps prepare our children to listen to lessons, because earrings are a symbol of how to take in words. We imagine earrings taking in the positive, the way that a dreamcatcher works, with all negative words trickling down your earrings and falling off.

**LEARNING OUR LANGUAGE:** I am just learning our Nisga'a language (also known as Sim'algax). I'm trying hard to integrate it into our everyday lives. The influence of English is everywhere. Everybody speaks English; it's all over the TV, books. My goal is to have my youngest son, Craig, speak fluent Nisga'a by the time he's 10. He's catching on. I'm teaching my older son and my husband to use Nisga'a words around him, so it reinforces my teachings. I've got my work cut out for me, but it's definitely a big aspiration of mine.

**FISHING AND FORAGING:** Whenever he has time, Tyler is out harvesting. In all the different months, there's some resource available to us. This winter, for example, our family started prepping our *oolichan* sticks (a smelt-like fish): we thread the stick through the *oolichan*'s gills until it comes out of its mouth. It's then smoked for two to four days, burning with alder wood in our smokehouse in the backyard.

CAROLYN B. HELLER

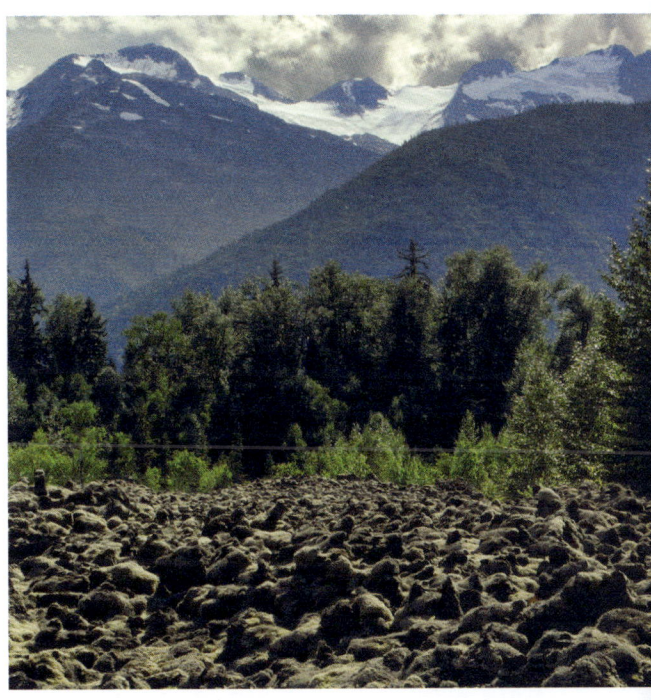

## Our favourite traditions

**Summer fishing:** There's a sweet fishing spot we go to every year, usually in August, on this glacier creek where the fish run; mostly pinks or humpies (salmon). The pinks give you a good fight, but it's something the kids can handle.

**Food for the seasons:** We spend time preparing for the seasons to come. We pick seaweed off the rocks. You can eat it fresh, but we usually bake ours in the sun. We use it as a garnish, on a dish like fish and rice. Or we make a stir-fry with herring eggs and sprinkle seaweed on top. It's delicious.

**Winter 'sacred time':** Winter is our storytelling time. I'll share stories of when I grew up. Or we'll recount stories our grandparents told us. Tyler and I believe it's important for our kids to understand the hardships our people went through just two, three generations ago. We share our stories in hopes that they'll grow up inspired to learn more, and help our people move forward.

# Index

## A

Abu Dhabi, United Arab Emirates 68–71
açai 142
Acosta, Jaime 136–139
advice, unsolicited 50, 82, 134
Agatha, Saint 82
Ahuirán, Mexico 124–127
Altınüzüm, Türkiye 72–75
Amman, Jordan 64–67
ancestral traditions 25, 129, 130, 147;
    see also Multicultural families
Andersen, Kaja 100–103
Andrade, Fernanda 136–139
animals see Farm life; Pets
Antelias, Lebanon 76–79
Argentina 120–123
arranged marriage 29
Artar, Sevim 72–75
Australia 8–15
autonomy see Independence
    and ingenuity

## B

baby swimming 115
Bajram/Bayram 75, 110
balancing career and parenthood 138
Bangkok, Thailand 40–43
Bascuñán, Gonzalo 116–119
bath time 67, 123
bathing ceremony 166–167
Battye, Chris 92–95
Bavaria, Germany 84–87
Bayram/Bajram 75, 110
Be The Change Project 149
bedtime traditions
    Argentina 123
    Bosnia & Hercegovina 111
    Botswana 22
    England 111
    India 47
    Italy 83
    Jordan 66
    Mexico 130
    USA 151, 155
    Wales 99
Benatar, Piers 88–91
Bengaluru, India 56–59
Berkshire, England 92–95
Bhaskar, Dharini 56–59
Bhatt, Neha, interview by 56–59
Bible study 39
biking 50, 58, 59, 115, 118
bilingual families see Multilingual families
Bindloss, Joe, interview by 88–91
birth traditions
    Bosnia & Hercegovina 110
    Brazil 142
    Canada 166
    India 47
    Kenya 38
    Kyrgyzstan 63
    USA 158
birthday celebrations 26, 79, 103, 134, 162
blended families 100–103, 164–167
Bokchari, Kaouther & Mounir 32–35
bonfires/campfires 11, 95, 99, 131
books and reading 51, 55, 58, 123, 151, 155
Bosnia & Hercegovina 108–111
Botswana 20–23
Boxing Day 99
Brazil 140–143
breakfast see Morning routines
'breastfeeding leave' 103
British Columbia, Canada 164–167
Bruner, Franziska Renata, interviews by
    124–131, 140–143
Buenos Aires, Argentina 120–123

## C

Cairo, Egypt 28–31
campfires/bonfires 11, 95, 99, 131
camping 13–15, 19, 22, 94
Canada 160–167
career-life balance 138
Carnival 138, 155
Catania, Italy 80–83
Catholic traditions 82, 83
Cauich, Jenny 128–131
chai 62, 63
Chandler, Gary, interviews by 148–151,
    156–159
Chandler-Isacksen, Katy 148–151
Chekirov, Dastan 60–63
Chen, Piera, interviews by 48–55
childcare 78, 82
Children's Day 103
Chile 116–119
China 52–55
chores and responsibilities 15, 30, 46, 55,
    74
Christian traditions
    Bosnia & Hercegovina 109, 110, 111
    Brazil 142
    Canada 163
    Egypt 30, 31
    England 94
    Ghana 26, 27
    Italy 82, 83
    Kenya 39
    Lebanon 79
    Mexico 131
Christmas
    Brazil 142
    Canada 163
    Czechia 106, 107
    England 94
    expat life 91
    Kenya 39
    Norway 103
    Scotland 91
    Taiwan 51
    Wales 99
Chu, Yvonne 52–55
church attendance 31, 94, 142, 163
circumcision 62, 158
clothing traditions 71, 127
Coburg, Germany 86
Colima, Mexico 124–127
communication
    Chile 118
    Ecuador 137, 138
    England 94
    Norway 103
    USA 154
    Wales 98
cooking see Food traditions
Corne, Lucy, interview by 20–23
COVID-19
    Australia 13–14
    Chile 117
    Czechia 106
    Germany 85
    Italy 83
    Mexico 131
crafts 35, 55, 59, 155
crime see Safety
crops see Farm life
cycling 50, 58, 59, 115, 118
Czechia 104–107

## D

dance 23, 83
Daniela 120–123
'dates' see One-on-one time
dating 78
day of the dead 131
daycare 78, 114, 162, 166
death, mourning, and remembrance 73,
    131, 147, 167
decision-making 118, 158
Deshaies, Guadeloupe 132–135
Dev, Asha 44–47
Dewes, Henare & Ikuko 16–19
D'Ignoti, Stefania, interviews by 24–27,
    32–35, 72–75, 80–83, 108–111
discipline 39, 154
Double-Dutch championships 54
Down's syndrome 53
Dubai, United Arab Emirates 71

Dunee, Evita 24–27
Duque, Marivane (Mari) 140–143
Dussehra Festival of the Mother Goddess 47

**E**
ear piercing 167
earthquakes 47, 73, 74–75
Easter
    Chile 119
    Czechia 106
    Ecuador 138
    Egypt 31
    United Arab Emirates 71
    USA 155
    Wales 99
Ecoexist (NGO) 21, 22
Ecuador 136–139
education
    Argentina 122
    Australia 14–15
    Bosnia & Hercegovina 111
    Botswana 23
    Canada 166
    Chile 118–119
    Ecuador 138–139
    Egypt 30
    England 94, 111
    Germany 86
    Ghana 26
    Guadeloupe 134
    India 46–47, 57, 58
    Jordan 66
    Kyrgyzstan 62–63
    Lebanon 79
    Norway 102
    Scotland 90–91
    Taiwan 50
    Türkiye 74, 75
    USA 147, 149, 150
    while traveling 14–15, 90–91
Egypt 28–31
Eid 35, 71
elderly, respect for 26, 75, 143
electricity outages *see* Infrastructure challenges
elephants 21, 22, 23
England 92–95
expat life 90
extended family
    Bosnia & Hercegovina 111
    Brazil 142
    Canada 166–167
    Chile 119
    Guadeloupe 134, 135
    India 46, 47
    Jordan 66
    Kenya 37–39
    Kyrgyzstan 62, 63

    Mexico 127
    Thailand 43
    United Arab Emirates 70
    Wales 97, 99
    *see also* Grandparents

**F**
farm life
    Australia 10, 11
    Brazil 142
    China 55
    Ghana 27
    India 58
    Kyrgyzstan 61–62
    Mexico 127
    Türkiye 74
farmers markets 159
fasting 31
festivals
    Chile 119
    Ecuador 138
    Ghana 26
    India 47
    Mexico 126
    Tunisia 35
    USA 155
Finland 112–115
fishing 18, 27, 55, 167
food traditions
    Australia 11
    Bosnia & Hercegovina 111
    Brazil 142, 143
    Canada 162
    Chile 119
    China 54, 55
    Czechia 107
    Ecuador 138, 139
    England 95
    expat life 90
    Germany 87
    Ghana 27
    Guadeloupe 135
    Italy 83
    Jordan 66, 67
    Kyrgyzstan 62
    Lebanon 79
    Mexico 127, 131
    New Zealand 18, 19
    Norway 102
    Taiwan 51
    Thailand 42, 43
    Tunisia 34, 35
    USA 147, 150, 151, 154, 158
    Wales 98–99
foraging 87, 167
forest walks *see* Nature; Outdoor time
Fragalà, Valentina 80–83
free-range kids *see* Independence and ingenuity

**G**
games together 79, 143, 151
gardening 87, 118, 149, 150
Germany 84–87
Ghana 24–27
Githere, Neema, interview by 36–39
godparents 126
government assistance 114
grandparents
    Argentina 121, 122
    Brazil 141, 142, 143
    Canada 161, 162
    Egypt 30, 31
    England 94
    expat life 90
    Finland 113, 114
    Guadeloupe 134, 135
    India 46
    Italy 82, 83
    Kenya 37–39
    Lebanon 78
    Mexico 126, 127, 129, 130, 131
    Norway 101
    Scotland 90
    Thailand 42
    United Arab Emirates 70
    USA 145, 146, 153, 155
    *see also* Elderly, respect for; Extended family
Guadeloupe 132–135

**H**
Hagg, Nicole, interviews by 11–15, 144–147
Hanal Pixán (Maya day of the dead) 131
happiness jars 99
healthcare 47, 90
Heller, Carolyn B., interview by 164–167
Henry, Karimah 152–155
Hernández, Eduardo 124–127
Hindu traditions 46, 47
holidays (celebrations)
    Bosnia & Hercegovina 110
    Brazil 142
    Canada 163
    Chile 119
    China 54
    Czechia 106, 107
    Ecuador 138, 139
    Egypt 31
    England 94, 95
    expat life 91
    Ghana 27
    Kenya 39
    Lebanon 79
    Mexico 126, 131
    New Zealand 19
    Norway 103
    Scotland 91
    Taiwan 51

Tunisia 35
Türkiye 74, 75
United Arab Emirates 71
USA 147, 151, 154, 155
Wales 99
see also Festivals
holidays (family trips) 50, 94, 99, 107, 134
homeschooling/unschooling 23, 57, 58, 111, 149, 150
Hong Kong, China 52–55
Horten, Norway 100–103
hospitality 70, 75
House, Caleb 104–107
household chores 15, 30, 46, 55, 74
hunting 18

**I**
Ichke Bulun, Kyrgyzstan 60–63
independence and ingenuity
    Australia 10, 11
    Chile 118
    Germany 87
    Lebanon 78
    Norway 102
    USA 146
India 44–47, 56–59
Indigenous life 125–127
infrastructure challenges 46, 67, 79
Islam see Muslim traditions
Italy 80–83

**J**
Jarukittikun, Mint 40–43
Johanson, Mark, interview by 116–119
Jordan 64–67
journaling 15
jumping rope 116–119

**K**
Kaigwa, Ciru 36–39
Kalybekova, Aizada 60–63
Kenya 36–39, 90, 91
Kern, Raïssa & Emmanuel 132–135
Khan, Imran and Jemima 90
Kikuyu heritage and language 38, 39
Kishan Nagar Village, India 44–47
Kulta, Lilli & Iiro 112–115
Kurds 74
Kyrgyzstan 60–63

**L**
Lam, Jessica, interview by 160–163
languages see Multilingual families
Lax-galts'ap, Nisga'a Nation, British Columbia, Canada 164–167
Lebanon 76–79
Leclerc, Céline 104–107
Lefer, David 144–147
Lempiäinen, Mirva, interviews by 112–115, 132–135
Linden, Australia 8–11
Lioy, Stephen, interview by 104–107
London, England 93
Lui, Yvonne 144–147
Lunar New Year 54

**M**
Majdalani, Nidal, interviews by 28–31, 76–79
Manaus, Brazil 140–143
Mansour, Zeina 76–79
Māori 16–19
map 6–7
Marcos 120–123
Marić, Nicola 108–111
market outings 43, 55, 111, 159
marriage traditions 29, 62, 127
Masarrah (charity organization) 65, 66
matriarchs 38
Maun, Botswana 20–23
Maya heritage and language 129, 130–131
McCulloch, Graham 20–23
McLachlan, Craig, interview by 16–19
mealtimes see Food traditions
medical care 47, 90
Melbourne, Australia 12–15
Meneguzzi, Justin, interview by 11–15
Mexico 124–131
misgendering 158
Miyazaki, Hayao 54
Moenich, Harrison & Carly 156–159
Moffat, Scotland 88–91
Moore, Tina 164–167
morning routines
    Canada 166
    Ecuador 138
    England 95
    India 45, 58, 59
    Mexico 131
    Tunisia 35
    Türkiye 74
    USA 151, 154
Mostar, Bosnia & Hercegovina 108–111
movie-watching 39, 54, 123, 139
multicultural families
    Bosnia & Hercegovina 108–111
    Czechia 104–107
    Guadeloupe 132–135
    New Zealand 16–19
    Norway 100–103
    Taiwan 48–51
    United Arab Emirates 68–71
    USA 154
multigenerational families see Extended family; Grandparents
multilingual families
    Bosnia & Hercegovina 110
    Canada 167

Czechia 106–107
Finland 114
Guadeloupe 134
Jordan 66
Kenya 39
Mexico 127
New Zealand 18
United Arab Emirates 70
museum visits 50, 159
music 30, 83, 98, 123, 158
Muslim traditions
    Bosnia & Hercegovina 109, 110, 111
    Ghana 27
    Jordan 66, 67
    Tunisia 34, 35
    Türkiye 75
    United Arab Emirates 70, 71
Myanmar 90

**N**
Nadia 68–71
Nairobi, Kenya 36–39
naming traditions 62, 82, 110, 158
nap time 83, 102
nature
    Australia 10, 15
    Botswana 21–22, 23
    Brazil 141, 142
    Canada 162
    Chile 117, 118–119
    Finland 115
    Germany 86–87
    India 58
    New Zealand 18
    USA 147, 150, 159
    Wales 98
    see also Outdoor time
Navoa, Cristina 160–163
Nevada 148–151
New Year's traditions
    China 54
    Ecuador 139
    Ghana 27
    Mexico 131
    New Zealand 19
    Wales 99
New York City, New York 144–147
New Zealand 16–19
newborn celebrations see Birth traditions
Ngati Porou 16–19
Nisga'a Nation, British Columbia, Canada 164–167
nonbinary parents 158
Norway 100–103

**O**
Okavango Delta, Botswana 21–23
one-on-one time 58, 95, 138
Ontario, Canada 160–163

outdoor time
    Argentina 122
    Australia 10, 11, 15
    Bosnia & Hercegovina 111
    Botswana 21–22
    Brazil 142
    Canada 162
    Chile 118–119
    Egypt 31
    Finland 115
    Germany 86–87
    Guadeloupe 134, 135
    Jordan 66
    Kyrgyzstan 63
    Lebanon 78–79
    New Zealand 18
    Norway 102
    Taiwan 50
    Tunisia 35
    Türkiye 75
    United Arab Emirates 71
    USA 147, 150, 159
    Wales 98
    see also Nature

**P**
Pakistan 89, 90
parental leave 103, 113, 114
Parsons, Ashley, interview by 60–63
Peralta, Mayra, interview by 136–139
Perelmuter, Federico, interview by 120–123
pets 10, 50, 131, 139
Petzierides, Elia & Nicole 12–15
photography traditions 15, 58, 59, 83
pilgrimages 47, 70
Polsuk, Prin 40–43
Pontardawe, Wales 96–99
Poonagiri Temple, India 47
Posavac, Gisela 116–119
postpartum care see Birth traditions
Pozzan, Olivia, interview by 68–71
Prague, Czechia 104–107
prayer
    Egypt 30
    Ghana 26
    India 46, 47
    Italy 82
    Jordan 67
    Kenya 39
pregnancy ceremonies 38
Prokop, Ambika Anand, interview by 44–47
Puerto Varas, Chile 116–119
Purépecha culture 125–127

**Q**
Queenstown, New Zealand 16–19
Quito, Ecuador 136–139
Quran 66, 67

**R**
Ramadan 27, 35, 71, 75, 110
Ramzy, Sameh 29
reading 51, 55, 58, 123, 151, 155
Rehberger, Alexandra 84–87
religion see specific religions
Reno, Nevada 148–151
respect, fostering in children
    Brazil 143
    Ghana 26
    India 46
    New Zealand 18, 19
    Türkiye 75
    USA 147
Richmond, Virginia, USA 156–159
road trips 13–15, 50, 51, 126
Rocha, Jeferson 140–143
Rodríguez, Estela 124–127
rope skipping 54
running 107

**S**
safety 118, 134, 139, 142, 154
Saint Barbara's Day 79
Samrub Samrub Thai (restaurant), Bangkok, Thailand 41–43
schooling see Education
Scotland 88–91
Scouts 30
Sefein, Christine 28–31
Sham el-Nessim (Egyptian holiday) 31
shrimp harvest 55
sibling rivalry 154–155
siesta see Nap time
Simula, Jessica Wang 48–51
sleeping arrangements see Bedtime traditions
Songhurst, Anna 20–23
Sousse, Tunisia 32–35
spanking 39
stargazing 54
storytelling 167
sundowners 23
Swansea, Wales 98

**T**
Tabbaa, Dina 64–67
Tabbaa, Sanad, interview by 64–67
Taekwondo 67
Taipei, Taiwan 48–51
Taiwan 48–51
Tamale, Ghana 24–27
Tampa, Florida, USA 152–155
Tampere, Finland 112–115
tea traditions 35, 62, 63, 75
teenage years
    Chile 118
    Egypt 30, 31
    England 94

    Mexico 131
    United Arab Emirates 69
Thailand 40–43
Thanksgiving 147, 151
Toronto, Ontario, Canada 160–163
travel abroad 66, 89, 134
Tunisia 32–35
Türkiye 72–75

**U**
United Arab Emirates 68–71
United Kingdom
    England 92–95
    Scotland 88–91
    Wales 96–99
United States see USA
unschooling/homeschooling 23, 57, 58, 111, 149, 150
unsolicited advice 50, 82, 134
USA 144–159

**V**
Valladolid, Mexico 128–131
Virginia, USA 156–159

**W**
Waby, Tasmin, interviews by 92–95, 100–103
Wales 96–99
walks 15, 115, 162
Ward, Terry, interview by 152–155
water supply see Infrastructure challenges
Waterson, Luke, interview by 96–99
weddings 34, 83
weekend rituals
    Bosnia & Hercegovina 111
    Egypt 31
    England 94, 95
    Guadeloupe 135
    Italy 83
    Lebanon 79
    Scotland 91
Whitfield, Jen and Matt 8–11
widowhood 73
Woodward, Maria 96–99
Woolsey, Barbara, interviews by 40–43, 84–87
work-life balance 138

**X**
Xiaoliuqiu Island, Taiwan 50

**Y**
YouTube 46, 47, 125, 127

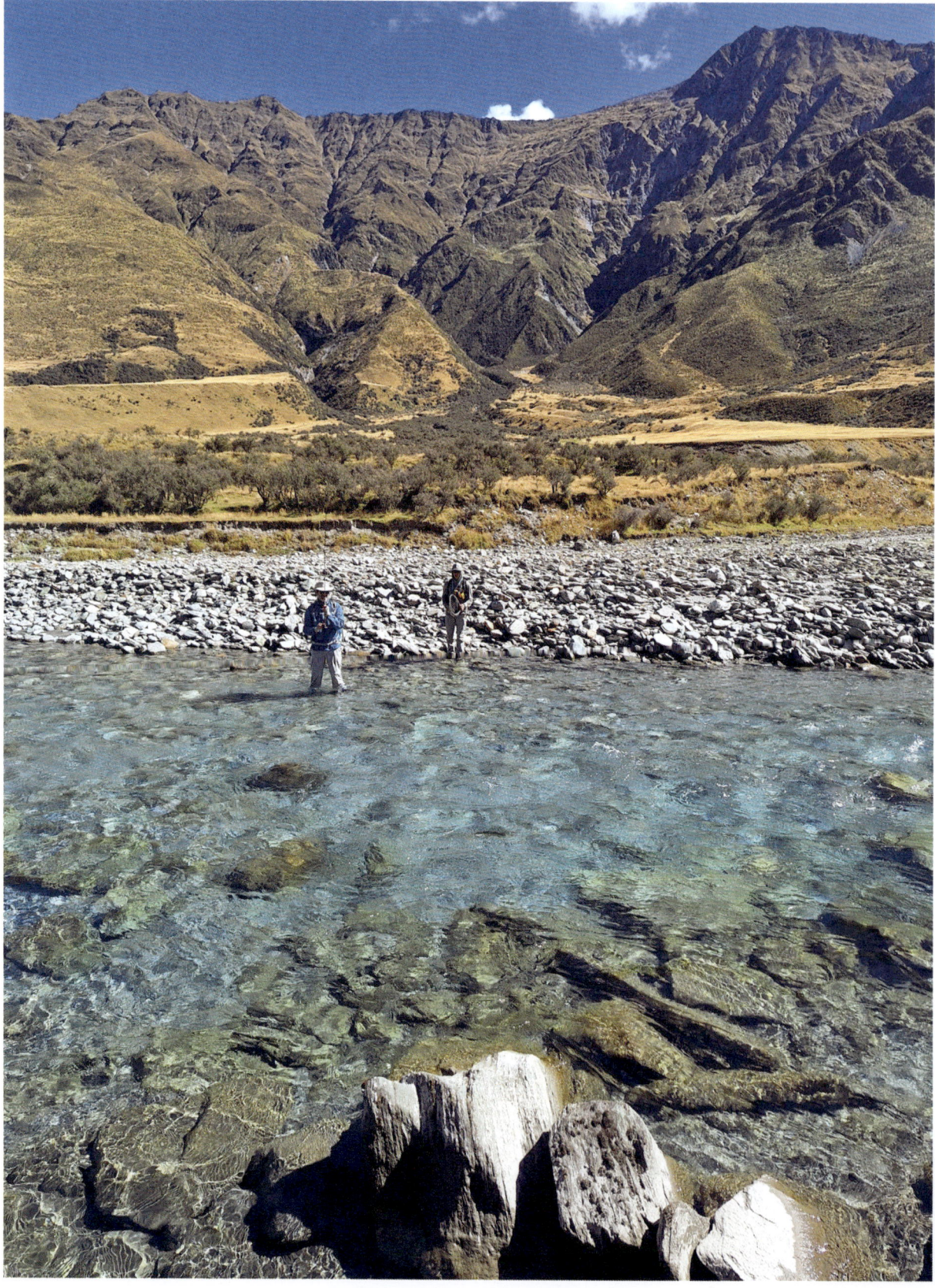

# Photo Credits

Unless noted otherwise, all photos are courtesy of the parents featured in this book.

**11:** Thomas Pickard/Stocksy
**16:** Mark Meredith/Getty Images (Mitre Peak); Keith Levit, Design Pics Editorial/Getty Images (Queenstown)
**19:** Didier Marti/Getty Images
**22:** Mint Images, Art Wolfe/Getty Images
**23:** Gfed/Getty Images
**24:** Image Professionals GmbH/Alamy (Grains); Dave Primov/Shutterstock (city)
**27:** Fanfo/Shutterstock
**28:** Peter Seaward for Lonely Planet (Cairo Souk); Leonid Andronov/Getty Images (citadel); Arsgera/Shutterstock (pool with pyramid)
**31:** Moatassem/Shutterstock
**34:** Juan Carlos Munoz/Shutterstock
**36:** Aleksandar Todorovic/Shutterstock
**38:** James Pearce for Lonely Planet
**42:** Anansing/Shutterstock
**48:** Matt Munro for Lonely Planet (bridge); Chon Kit Leong/Alamy (art installation); Matt Munro for Lonely Planet (Taipei); GlimpseDays/Shutterstock (cows)
**51:** Fanfo/Shutterstock
**54:** Claudine Klodien/Alamy
**62:** Akela/Stocksy
**63:** REDA&CO/Getty Images
**67:** Jordan Pix/Getty Images
**74:** tolga ildun/Alamy
**75:** Turgay Koca, 500px/Getty Images
**76:** diak/Shutterstock
**79:** Ammar Kadhim/500px (sea); HelgaBragina/Shutterstock (meal)
**80:** Matt Munro for Lonely Planet (beach); Prisma by Dukas Presseagentur GmbH/Alamy (procession); Matt Munro for Lonely Planet (sculpture)
**82:** robertharding/Alamy
**83:** ZUMA Press Inc/Alamy
**86:** Ruzhdi Ibrahimi, 500px/Getty Images (bird); teddiviscious/Shutterstock (forest)
**96:** Pete Seaward for Lonely Planet (cliffs); steved_np3/iStock (houses); Kerry Christiani for Lonely Planet (flowers)
**106:** Frank Chmura/Alamy
**107:** Xantana/Getty Images (Prague); Radomir Rezny/Shutterstock (river)
**110:** Wolfgang Kaehler/Alamy
**112:** Henri Elemo/Shutterstock
**115:** Thomas_P/Shutterstock (river); VESA MOILANEN/Getty Images (baby goods)
**119:** Marilar Irastorza/Stocksy (mountain); Ivan Konar/Alamy (cowboy)
**120:** Philip Lee Harvey for Lonely Planet (flowering trees); Terry Carter for Lonely Planet (balconies); Nessa Gnatoush/Shutterstock (book shop); Matt Munro for Lonely Planet (plaza)
**122:** Reed Kaestner/Getty Images
**123:** Jeff Greenberg/Getty Images
**124:** Jorge Fuentes/Stocksy (statue); Gabriela Cardona/Stocksy (flowers); Big Cheese Photo/Alamy (fruit stand)
**126:** Jan Sochor/Alamy
**127:** Mario Martinez/Getty Images
**136:** Mike Matthews Photography/Getty Images
**138:** Eduardo Fonseca Arraes/Getty Images (Quito); williampaulmaster/Shutterstock (meal)
**139:** Gabriel Perez/Getty Images
**143:** Ricardo Lima/Getty Images (soup); MICHAEL DANTAS/Getty Images (city and forest)
**144:** Gary Latham for Lonely Planet
**146:** Tagger Yancey IV/NYC Tourism & Conventions
**147:** girlseeingworld/Shutterstock
**151:** Cavan Images/Getty Images
**152:** Gregg Squeglia/Shutterstock
**154:** Fanfo/Shutterstock
**156:** Sean Pavone/Shutterstock
**158:** Michael Beiriger/Shutterstock
**159:** Atomazul/Shutterstock
**163:** Rick Madonik/Getty Images (treat); Jen Grantham/Stocksy (park)
**164:** davemantel/Getty Images
**166:** Martin Smart/Alamy Stock Photo
**167:** Istvan Hernadi photography, Mountain Visions/Getty Images

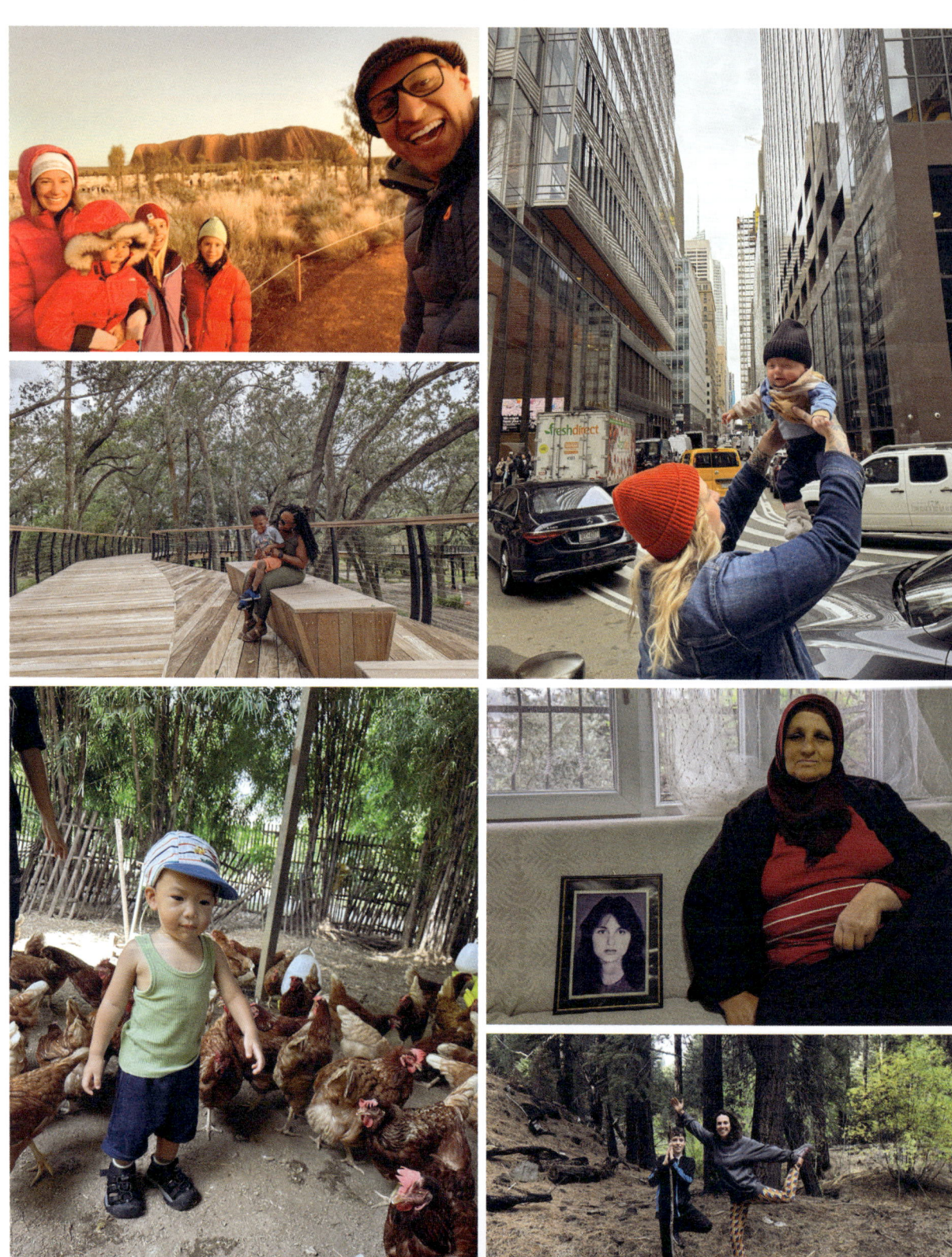

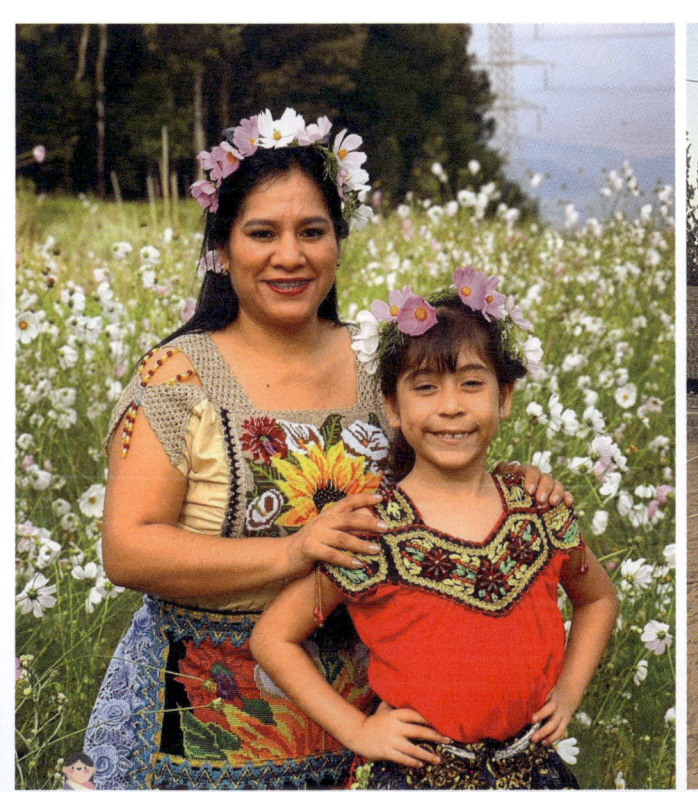
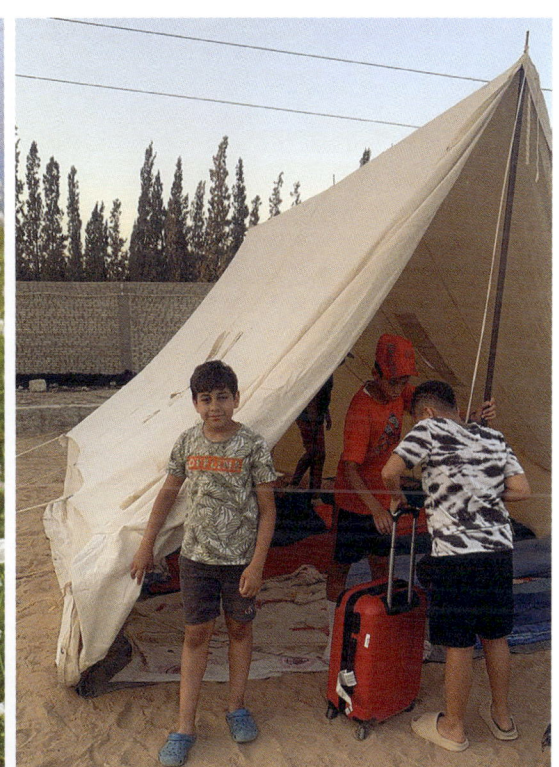
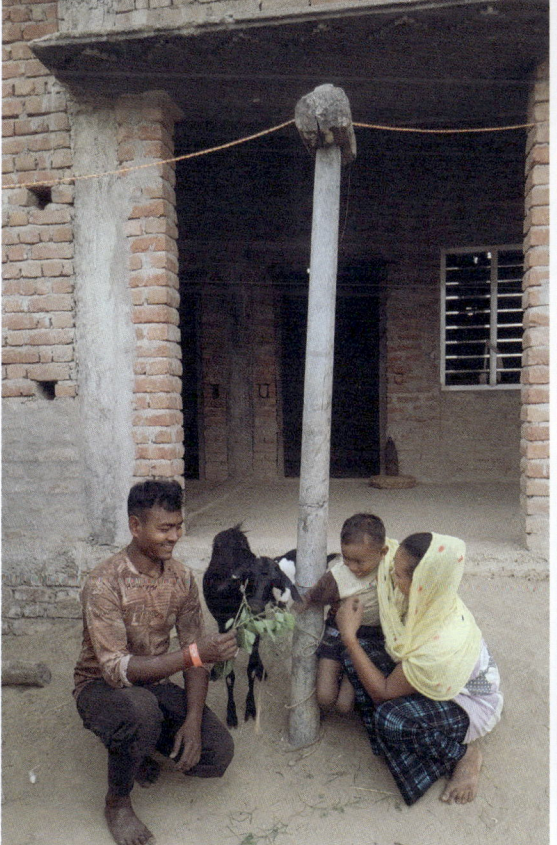
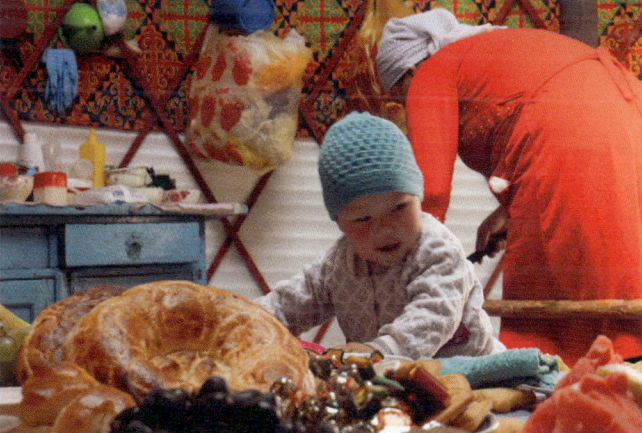
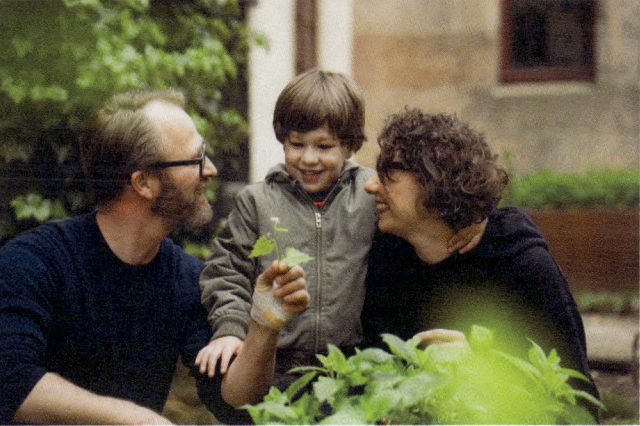

Parenthood Around the World

**Project Editor:** Liza Prado
**Editors:** Karyn Noble, Polly Thomas, Claire Naylor, Anne Mason
**Designer:** Cat Grishaver
**Publishing Director:** Piers Pickard
**Publisher:** Becca Hunt
**Art Director:** Emily Dubin
**Print Production:** Nigel Longuet

March 2025
Published by Lonely Planet Global Limited
CRN: 554153
ISBN: 978 18375 8519 9
© Lonely Planet 2025
10 9 8 7 6 5 4 3 2 1
Printed in Malaysia

All rights reserved. No part of this publication may be reproduced, stored in a retrieval system or transmitted in any form by any means, electronic, mechanical, photocopying, recording or otherwise except brief extracts for the purpose of review, without the written permission of the publisher. Lonely Planet and the Lonely Planet logo are trademarks of Lonely Planet and are registered in the US Patent and Trademark Office and in other countries.

Although the author and Lonely Planet have taken all reasonable care in preparing this book, we make no warranty about the accuracy or completeness of its content and, to the maximum extent permitted, disclaim all liability from its use.

STAY IN TOUCH
lonelyplanet.com/contact

Lonely Planet Office:
IRELAND
Digital Depot, Roe Lane (off Thomas St),
Digital Hub, Dublin 8, D08 TCV4, Ireland

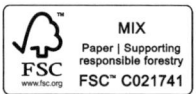 Paper in this book is certified against the Forest Stewardship Council™ standards. FSC™ promotes environmentally responsible, socially beneficial and economically viable management of the world's forests.